P9-CJZ-976

$f\mathbf{P}$

Day of Honey

A Memoir of Food, Love, and War

Annia Ciezadlo

Free Press

New York   London   Toronto   Sydney

Free Press
A Division of Simon & Schuster, Inc.
1230 Avenue of the Americas
New York, NY 10020

Copyright © 2011 by Annia Ciezadlo

All rights reserved, including the right to reproduce this book or
portions thereof in any form whatsoever. For information address
Free Press Subsidiary Rights Department, 1230 Avenue of the Americas,
New York, NY 10020

First Free Press hardcover edition February 2011

FREE PRESS and colophon are trademarks of Simon & Schuster, Inc.

The retellings of the Gilgamesh tales on pages 69–70 and 150–151
draw on both the Standard Version and the Old Babylonian tablets.
Excerpts from *The Epic of Gilgamesh* translated by Maureen Gallery Kovacs.
Copyright © 1985, 1989 by the Board of Trustees of the Leland Stanford Jr.
University. All rights reserved. Used with the permission
of Stanford University Press, www.sup.org.

For information about special discounts for bulk purchases,
please contact Simon & Schuster Special Sales at 1-866-506-1949 or
business@simonandschuster.com.

The Simon & Schuster Speakers Bureau can bring authors to your
live event. For more information or to book an event contact the
Simon & Schuster Speakers Bureau at 1-866-248-3049 or
visit our website at www.simonspeakers.com.

Book design by Ellen R. Sasahara

Manufactured in the United States of America

3   5   7   9   10   8   6   4   2

Library of Congress Cataloging-in-Publication Data

Ciezadlo, Annia.
Day of honey : a memoir of food, love, and war /
Annia Ciezadlo.—1st Free Press hardcover ed.
p.   cm.
Includes bibliographical references and index.
1. Ciezadlo, Annia.   2. Journalists—Iraq—Baghdad.
3. Journalists—Lebanon—Beirut.   4. Journalists—United States—
Biography.   5. Baghdad (Iraq)—Social life and customs.   6. Beirut
(Lebanon)—Social life and customs.   7. Food—Social aspects—Iraq—
Baghdad.   8. Food—Social aspects—Lebanon—Beirut.
9. Iraq War, 2003—Social aspects.   I. Title.
PN4874.C5185A3   2011
070.92—dc22
[B]   2010019739

ISBN 978-1-4165-8393-6
ISBN 978-1-4165-8422-3 (ebook)

For Mohamad

Contents

يوم عسل

يوم بصل

"Day of honey, day of onions."
—Arabic proverb

Much earlier in this century an Austrian journalist, Karl Kraus, pointed out that if you actually perceived the true reality behind the news you would run, screaming, into the streets. I have run screaming into the streets dozens of times but have always managed to return home in time for dinner.

—Jim Harrison, *The Raw and the Cooked: Adventures of
a Roving Gourmand*

PART I

New York

All great change in America begins at the dinner table.

—Ronald Reagan

The Siege

H E WAS ONE of an endangered species: among the few white, native-born cab drivers left in New York. Meaty, middle-aged, face like a potato. A Donegal tweed driving cap. He pulled up beside me, drew down the window, and growled out of the corner of his mouth: "You wanna ride?"

We rode in silence until we reached Atlantic Avenue. "You see this street?" he said, waving a massive hand at the windshield. "They're all Arabs on this street."

He was right, more or less. The conquest began in the late 1800s, as the Ottoman Empire waned and the Mediterranean silk trade collapsed. Between 1899 and 1932, a little over 100,000 "Syrians"—in those days, a catchall term for practically anyone from the Levant, the French name for the eastern Mediterranean—emigrated to the New World. Many of them settled in New York. In 1933, the Arab-American newspaper *Syrian World* described Atlantic Avenue, with gently sarcastic pride, as *"the principal habitat of the species Syrianica."*

By 1998, the Atlantic Avenue strip was such a symbol of Arab-American identity that 20th Century Fox re-created it for a movie called *The Siege.* In the movie, Arab terrorists carry out a series of bombings in New York City, and the government imposes martial law and rounds up all the Arabs, guilty and innocent alike, into detention camps.

"These Arabs, yeah," the cabbie continued. "They come over here, they try to act normal. Try to act like you and me. Like they're fitting in, ya know?"

He barked out a laugh. "Turns out they're al-Qaeda."

It was a relief when people said it openly. I could talk to this guy. He was an ethnic American, and he assumed I was one too. He was right: I'm a Polish-Greek-Scotch-Irish mutt from working-class Chicago. A product of stockyards and steel mills and secretarial schools. I could see where he was coming from. I came from there myself.

But then again: the man I loved was named for Islam's prophet. We had been seeing each other for about five months. I had thought of him as just another ethnic American, but now it was September 13, 2001, and suddenly nobody else seemed to see it that way. On September 11, the landlady had knocked on his door just before midnight. Mrs. Scanlon was an immigrant herself, from Ireland, and no doubt with terrorism-related memories of her own. In a high and quavering voice, she asked, "Mohamad, are you an Arab?"

I had been thinking about *The Siege* quite a bit since then.

When 20th Century Fox started filming *The Siege* in the late 1990s, I had just moved to the heavily Polish Brooklyn neighborhood of Greenpoint. Apparently the real Atlantic Avenue didn't have enough brownstones to look like New York on film, so overnight, Hollywood set designers transformed Greenpoint's Little Warsaw into a cinematic version of the Arab street. Awnings that had once read *Obiady Polski* (Polish Dinners) now surged with Arabic script. Tanks rolled past under klieg lights. Wandering down the imitation Atlantic Avenue, it was easy to imagine that all of our carefully constructed ethnic identities were nothing but Hollywood sets, as specious a notion as *the species Syrianica,* a scaffolding you could put up or tear down in a couple of hours.

The city had papered Greenpoint's streetlights with flyers forbidding people to park because of *Martial Law,* the movie's working title; as it happened, many Greenpointers had fled Poland in the early 1980s, when it was under actual Communist martial law. Middle-aged Polish émigrés would stop and glower at the Hollywood diktats with gloomy satisfaction: *You see? I told you it would happen here too.*

Back in September 2001, red and yellow traffic lights flowed over the dark windshield. The few cars ghosting down the empty avenue ignored them.

Everyone ran red lights during the days after the attacks. Stopping seemed pointless, like everything else.

"No, man, that's not true," I said finally. "A lot of the Arabs here left their countries because they *weren't* al-Qaeda. A lot of them left to get away from those guys."

Al-Qaeda wouldn't have had much use for my Arab: he's a Shiite, at least by birth. But introducing the Sunni-Shiite divide seemed a little ambitious in this case. "They left cause their countries were messed up," I said. "The ones that are here are the ones that *wanted* to come to America."

He looked hard at me in the rearview mirror, his eyes flashing in the little strip of glass.

I sighed. "You know, most of the Arabs here in the U.S. are actually Christians."

A cowardly argument. My own Arab was a Muslim, after all.

"Shyeah!" the cabbie spat. "They act like they're Christians. They *pretend*. But they're really al-Qaeda."

Gray metal shutters hid the store windows, but memory filled in what I couldn't see. Here on my right was Malko Karkanni's shabby storefront, jammed with bins of olives and dusty coffeepots. Mr. Karkanni liked to talk; if you had time, he would pull out a stool, make you tea, and talk about the lack of human rights in Syria, the country he still missed. Ahead on the left was a restaurant named Fountain, with a real fountain inside, like an Ottoman courtyard; once, when I told the waiter where my grandmother was from, he broke into fluent Greek. And here was Sahadi's, the famous deli and supermarket, run by a family that has been part of New York ever since 1895, when Abraham Sahadi opened his import-export company in lower Manhattan, back when my ancestors were still plowing fields in Scotland, Galicia, and the Peloponnese.

"Well, my boyfriend's an Arab," I said suddenly. The words tumbled out, high-pitched and breathless. "And he's not al-Qaeda, and I have a lot of Arab friends, and they're not al-Qaeda either!"

The eyes flashed back at me again, a little more anxiously this time. Was he going to kick me out of his car? Would he call the police, the FBI, and tell them about me and my Arab boyfriend?

Or would he just shake his head and decide that I was a fool—one of a breed of unfortunate women who marry foreign men, put them through flight school, and end up later on talk shows insisting that "he seemed so normal"? Like Annette Bening in *The Siege*, who falls for an educated Arab guy, a Palestinian college professor who acts normal but—*you can't trust them*—turns out to be a terrorist in the end?

He thought about it for a block or two before he spoke. His voice was casual, and unexpectedly gentle, as if we had backed up and rewound the whole conversation to the beginning.

"You know that place Sahadi's?" he said. "Y'ever been in there? They got some *great* food in there, yeah. Hummus, falafel, you know. Boy, that stuff is pretty good. You ever try it?"

There's a saying in Arabic: *Fi khibz wa meleh bainetna*—there is bread and salt between us. It means that once we've eaten together, sharing bread and salt, the ancient symbols of hospitality, we cannot fight. It's a lovely idea, that you can counter conflict with cuisine. And I don't swallow it for a second. Just look at any civil war. Or at our own dinner tables, groaning with evidence to the contrary.

After September 11, liberal New Yorkers flocked to Arabic restaurants, Afghan, even Indian—anything that seemed vaguely Muslim, as if to say, "Hey, we know you're not the bad guys. Look, we trust you, we're eating your food." New York newspapers ran stories about foreigners and their food, most of which followed much the same formula: the warmhearted émigré alludes mournfully to troubles in his homeland; assures the readers that not all Arabs/Afghans/Muslims are bad; and then shares his recipe for something involving eggplants. They were everywhere after September 11, photos of immigrants holding out plates of food, their eyes beseeching, "Don't deport me! Have some hummus!" But a lot of them did get deported, and American soldiers got sent to Afghanistan and Iraq. A decade later, the lesson seems clear: You can eat eggplant until your toes turn purple, and it won't stop governments from going to war.

But then again, there is something about food. Even the most ordinary dinner tells manifold stories of history, economics, and culture. You can experience a country and a people through its food in a way that you can't through, say, its news broadcasts.

Food connects. In biblical times, people sealed contracts with salt, because it preserves, protects, and heals—an idea that goes back to the ancient Assyrians, who called a friend "a man of my salt." Like Persephone's pomegranate seeds, the alchemy of eating binds you to a place and a people. This bond is fragile; people who eat together one day can kill each other the next. All the more reason we should preserve it.

Many books narrate history as a series of wars: who won, who lost, who was to blame (usually the ones who lost). I look at history as a series of meals. War is part of our ongoing struggle to get food—most wars are over resources, after all, even when the parties pretend otherwise.

But food is also part of a deeper conflict, one that we all carry inside us: whether to stay in one place and settle down, or whether to stay on the move. The struggle between these two tendencies, whether it takes the form of war or not, shapes the story of human civilization. And so this is a book about war, but it is also about travel and migration, and how food helps people find or re-create their homes.

One of my old journalism professors, a man with the unforgettable name of Dick Blood, used to roar that if you want to write the story, you have to eat the meal. He was talking about Thanksgiving, when reporters visit homeless shelters, collect a few quotes, and head back to the newsroom to pump out heartwarming little features without ever tasting the turkey. But I've found that this command— *"You have to eat the meal"*—is a good rule for life in general. And so whenever I visit a new place, I pursue a private ritual: I never let myself leave without eating at least one local thing.

We all carry maps of the world in our heads. Mine, if you could see it, would resemble a gigantic dinner table, full of dishes from every place I've been. Spanish Harlem is a *cubano*. Tucson is avocado chicken. Chicago is *yaprakis;* Beirut is *makdous;* and Baghdad—well, Baghdad is another story.

In the fall of 2003, I spent my honeymoon in Baghdad. I'd married the boyfriend, who was also a reporter, and his newspaper had posted him to Iraq.

So I moved to Beirut, with my brand-new husband and a few suitcases, and then to Baghdad.

For the next year, we tried to act like normal newlyweds. We did our laundry, went grocery shopping, and argued about what to have for dinner like any young couple, while reporting on the war. And throughout all of it, I cooked.

Some people construct work spaces when they travel, lining up their papers with care, stacking their books on the table, taping family pictures to the mirror. When I'm in a strange new city and feeling rootless, I cook. No matter how inhospitable the room or the streets outside, I construct a little field kitchen. In Baghdad, it was a hot plate plugged into a dubious electrical socket in the hallway outside the bathroom. I haunt the local markets and cook whatever I find: fresh green almonds, fleshy black figs, just-killed chickens with their heads still on. I cook to comprehend the place I've landed in, to touch and feel and take in the raw materials of my new surroundings. I cook foods that seem familiar and foods that seem strange. I cook because eating has always been my most reliable way of understanding the world. I cook because I am always, always hungry. And I cook for that oldest of reasons: to banish loneliness, homesickness, the persistent feeling that I don't belong in a place. If you can conjure something of substance from the flux of your life—if you can anchor yourself in the earth, like Antaeus, the mythical giant who grew stronger every time his feet touched the ground— you are at home in the world, at least for that meal.

In every war zone, there is another battle, a shadow conflict that rages quietly behind the scenes. You don't see much of it on television or in the movies. This hidden war consists of the slow but relentless destruction of everyday civilian life: The children can't go to school. The pregnant woman can't give birth at a hospital. The farmer can't plow his fields. The musician can't play his guitar. The professor can't teach her class. For civilians, war becomes a relentless accumulation of *can'ts*.

But no matter what else you can't do, you still have to eat. During wartime, people's lives begin to revolve around food: first to stay alive, but also to stay human. Food restores a sense of familiarity. It allows us to reach out to others, because cooking and eating are often communal activities. Food can cut across social barriers, spanning class and sectarian lines (though it can also, of course, reinforce them). Making and sharing food are essential to maintaining the rhythms of everyday life.

I went to the Middle East like most Americans, relatively naive about both Arab culture and American foreign policy. Over the next six years, I saw plenty of war, but I also saw normal, everyday life. I sat through ceremonial dinners with tribal sheikhs in Baghdad; kneeled and ate *kubbet hamudh* on the floor with Iraqi women from Fallujah; drank home-brewed *arak* with Christian militiamen in the mountains of Lebanon; feasted on boiled turkey with a mild-mannered *peshmerga* warlord in Kurdistan; and learned how to make *yakhnet kusa* and many other dishes from my Lebanese mother-in-law, Umm Hassane, who doesn't speak a word of English. Other people saw more, did more, risked more. But I ate more.

If you want to understand war, you have to understand everyday life first. The dominant narrative of the Middle East is perpetual conflict: the bombs and the bullets and the battles are always different, and yet always, somehow, depressingly the same. And so this book is not about the ever-evolving ways in which people kill or die during wars but about how they live before, during, and after those wars. It's about the millions of small ways people cope—the ways they arrange their lives, under sometimes unimaginable stress and hardship, and the ways they survive.

Every society has an immune system, a silent army that tries to bring the body politic back to homeostasis. People find ways to reconstruct their daily lives from the shambles of war; like my friend Leena, who once held a dinner party in her Beirut bomb shelter, they work with what they have. This is the story of that other war, the one that takes place in the moments between bombings: the baker keeps the communal oven going so his neighborhood can have bread; the restaurateur converts his café into a refugee center; the farmer feeds his neighbors from his dwindling stock of preserves; the parents drive all over Baghdad trying to find an open bakery so their daughter can have a birthday cake. They are warriors just as much as those who carry guns. There are many ways to save civilization. One of the simplest is with food.

Chapter 1

The Quiet Assassin

IN A RATIONAL world, Mohamad and I would never last. I talk; he observes. I launch into rambling, circuitous stories whose destinations I sometimes forget before I'm halfway through. He'll listen quietly, then eviscerate with one perfect sentence. I like to drink. He'll take a sip or two of red wine, then sit and watch with a quiet smile. He is calm and rational; I'm proud, opinionated, and easily enraged. I curse like a sailor. He does not. You will never hear Mohamad describe anything as "the biggest in the universe" or "the dumbest thing I ever heard." Without hyperbole I would die.

Nowhere do we disagree so much as over food. I will eat anything, from tongue to tripe to grilled lamb testicles—a delicacy in Lebanon, which is just one of many reasons I like the place. In school I was that kid who sidled up to you and said, "You gonna eat that?" Watching me finish off leftover meatballs, a friend once observed, "You know, Annia, I think you'd eat a roll of paper towels if someone told you it was food."

Mohamad, on the other hand, refuses to consume: asparagus, artichokes, mushrooms, beets; anything cruciferous; pumpkin not in the form of pie; duck; pork; fish of any kind, shellfish, seaweed, and anything else that emerges from water, such as frogs or eels; beef that hasn't been cooked to resemble linoleum; coffee or beer. That is a partial list.

A friend invited us to dinner once and called me first to find out what Mohamad liked.

"How about I tell you what he doesn't like instead?" I said, in case she had any ideas.

There was a long silence as she imagined life with someone who refused to eat all these foods.

"Wow, Annia," she said in a hushed voice. And then: "You must love him a *lot*."

Strange, then, that the whole thing started off with food. And a convoluted, introverted kind of food at that: stuffed grape leaves. If we hadn't eaten the grape leaves, Mohamad wouldn't have asked me about my grandmother; if I hadn't told him about my grandmother, he would never have talked about his mother, and we wouldn't have heard the stories (or was it the stuffed grape leaves themselves?) that made us realize we were falling in love.

In any event, I blame the grape leaves. They got us talking; they instigated our travels—across the Boulevard of Death, to Turkey, on to Afghanistan, and ultimately to Baghdad and Beirut.

But first to Queens.

I watched him for a moment before he saw me. He was waiting for me as I walked down out of the elevated train station, a grave, small figure standing still amid the roaring tide of rush-hour commuters, satiny black hair almost, but not quite, concealing his eyes. They were big and long-lashed, the color of roasted cocoa beans, beneath straight black eyebrows. What saved him from looking too pretty was the long, sardonic nose and the posture of a man whose idea of an exciting evening is poring over city procurement documents. Mohamad covered transportation for *Newsday*, the Long Island–based newspaper. I wrote about urban poverty and politics for a small monthly newsmagazine. It was April 2001.

In those days I believed that transportation, the warp of bridges and buses and subways that wove New York City's eight million souls together, was the most glamorous beat in the world. And so, during our occasional dinners, we spoke of transportation policy. Over Indian food on Sixth Street, we outlined the city's ten-step franchise approval process; at Habib's, a cramped East Village falafel place, where Habib played Ella Fitzgerald and

Louis Armstrong, we spoke of pedestrianization. Over dessert, we discussed the intricate beauties of congestion pricing. Our conversation bristled with acronyms of city, state, and federal agencies: HPD, MTA, HCFA. The stuff of romance, of adventure, it was not.

And yet, every time this new friend called me, I felt a mysterious exhilaration. I saved up anecdotes about obscure city bureaucrats to tell him. Sometimes I laughed out loud for no reason. I told myself these feelings were just the novelty of getting to know a new friend. "A nice guy," I told my friends, "but a little boring. We mostly just talk about work." But the truth was that I would talk about work. He would listen.

Mohamad is a quiet man. He speaks so softly and so seldom that one of his former coworkers christened him "the quiet assassin." That watchfulness made him a formidable investigative reporter. But over dinner it made my palms sweat. If I asked him a question, he would pause before responding, watching me silently, and I would feel that I was the one being interrogated. I avoided looking directly into his eyes; whenever I did, I would forget what I was saying, caught off guard by their expression of amused intelligence. And so I would stare down at his precisely folded hands, or at his mouth, with its occasional crooked hint of a smile, and keep talking. I can talk as much as I can eat, and at the same time too.

He never talked about himself and seldom ventured an opinion. Which was a shame, because something about his voice made my heart beat faster, perhaps because I hardly ever heard it. His eyes hinted at thoughts and stories, hidden away somewhere inside. But maybe I was imagining that. I was about to give up on him when unexpectedly, one sunny spring day, he invited me out to his neighborhood in Queens.

Mohamad pointed out the neighborhood landmarks as we walked: here was Queens Boulevard, so perilous to pedestrians that the *New York Daily News* had christened it the "Boulevard of Death." And here was Sunnyside Gardens, where he lived, the famous Progressive-era experiment in shared urban living. Rows of brick garden apartments all backed onto a massive common garden: a shared backyard for children to play, dogs to gambol, and families to eat picnics together.

"The Gardens is a cool idea because people have to cooperate, and get along with their neighbors, so they can share the space," Mohamad said.

Then he laughed, rolled his eyes. "Of course, what usually ends up happening is they each just take their own piece of the yard and fence it off. But still. It's a nice idea."

Sunnyside was the world in miniature: Irish bars built by migrant contractors; windowless Romanian nightclubs; Mexican women selling tamales out of coolers; Korean barbecue joints. There was even, over across the boulevard, a Turkish restaurant.

"Turkish?"

My grandmother was Greek. She had died a year earlier, and the loss of her was a dull ache that never went away. Eating stuffed grape leaves, one of her signature dishes, relieved it for a while.

"Can we go there?"

He shrugged. Why not? We forded the boulevard at a crosswalk and opened the door.

Inside, the restaurant was quiet and dark. A television flickered soundlessly in the back. A glass case held plates of food in unfamiliar shapes and colors. I ordered grape leaves and *baba ghanouj* and a grainy red substance that looked like it had been shaped inside a clenched fist (which, as it turned out, it had).

The waiter stood over us with our plates. He tilted his head and studied me through narrowed eyes.

"Excuse me," he said, in hesitant, slightly accented English. "But you look Turkish. You are Turkish perhaps?"

"No," I said and smiled. "But you're close. I'm part Greek."

His head flinched back a little, as if I'd gone to slap him. They always do that. The Greco-Turkish War ended in 1922, but people don't forget these things overnight.

"Ah," he said, putting down the plates. Placing one hand on his heart, he swirled the other outward in an expansive semicircle. "Then welcome. My . . . supposed enemy."

* * *

Some recipes are poems. A few scene stealers are novellas. But stuffed grape leaves are short stories—tiny fables of transformation, not of people (though the best recipes can do that too) but of food.

Most of the grape leaves you get in restaurants come from giant industrial cans. But every once in a while you find a place whose owners are stubborn enough to make their own. When they taste right, I am back in Chicagoland, circa 1977. I can hear the asthmatic growl of our old smoke-stained Frigidaire, WGN's theme music crackling out of our black-and-white Zenith; can smell lamb stewing on the stove with tomatoes and zucchini, fogging up the windows; can see my grandmother in the kitchen, smoking Bugler roll-your-owns and wrapping *yaprakis,* which is what our family always called stuffed grape leaves. *Yaprak* is Turkish for "leaf." But it can also mean "layer," like the buttery tulle of baklava; or "page," like the brittle brown pages of *Leaves of Grass,* my grandmother's favorite book.

Yaprakis are the food of people who waste nothing, not even the leathery leaves of the grape. "Waste not, want not" was Grandma's credo: whatever raw ingredient she had, she'd cook it, save it, hoard little scraps of it, and turn them into stock. She composted long before compost was cool. Meat and dairy leftovers she fed to our family's irregular army of half-breed Siamese cats. In her kitchen, nothing was ever wasted: instead, it metamorphosed and came back as something else.

She grew up in the Great Depression, and that was part of it. But it went deeper than just saving money. "I know whatever you take from the earth, you'll have to put back," she told me once, the summer before she died. "You have to give back to the world. That's what they always told me— my parents, my elders—growing up. So I always plant seeds, always plant things, all my life."

Her garden grew bushels of plump green beans, which she added to lamb stew; wine-dark tomatoes, to be salted and tossed with oregano, olive oil, crumbled feta, and onions sliced paper thin (you sopped up the brine with day-old bread); corn and potatoes and zucchini and dill. And along the fence, a grapevine grew glossy dark green leaves, which she stuffed with rice and meat and braised in the lemony egg broth *avgolémono.*

All foods have an invisible ingredient, a kind of culinary dark matter without which the dish will never taste exactly right. Pesto is best pounded by hand with a mortar and pestle; bruised, the cell walls of the basil leaves expel their oils more generously, making a silkier, more emulsified sauce than if they are slit open by the sharp metal blades of a blender or a knife. In this case, the secret ingredient is blunt force: pesto, from the Italian *pestare*, means "pounded."

Sometimes the secret ingredient is time. Make zucchini stew in a pressure cooker and you'll have it on the table in an hour, but it will taste flat and tinfoily. Let the meat and onions get to know each other for a couple of hours, and the flavor will add up to more than what you put in the pot.

Stuffed grape leaves take forever to make. Make them alone and you'll die of boredom, which is why very few people make them these days. You need to be surrounded by relatives, friends, neighbors; you need gossip and stories and talk. Perhaps you have to be a little distracted, so that the leaves come out different sizes and cook in different times. Or maybe the leaves need to be rolled by many different hands: one look at the dark green avalanche that Leena and her nimble-fingered daughters produce in their Beirut kitchen and you can tell whose hands rolled which leaf. Whatever the reason, when they're made communally, stuffed grape leaves create cascading layers of flavor in much the same manner that telling the same story from different points of view adds layers of meaning. Grape leaves are a narrative dish: each ingredient speaks as the package unfolds, containing multitudes, little edible matryoshka dolls.

In some mythical, soft-focus Peloponnesian past, my grandmother might have sat outside, under a leafy arbor of grapevines, rolling *yaprakis* with her sisters. In Chicago, when my grandmother got together with her sisters, they spent more time rolling dice for Yahtzee than grape leaves for *yaprakis*. So my grandmother made the complicated foods that she loved— éclairs, *yaprakis*, foods within food—at home in her kitchen with me. She would swaddle the rice with birdskin hands, as fragile and strong and delicately veined as the *yaprak* themselves. While she rolled each leathery green leaf she would tell me stories that crossed from true to make-believe and back again: stories that contained other stories, though I was too young to understand that then.

In my grandmother's day, the 1930s and '40s, very few of the big supermarkets carried "ethnic" foods like yogurt. "Tahini. Didja ever hear of it?" she asked me once, rolling grape leaves and cigarettes. "It's sesame seeds— food of the gods! When we were children, my mother used to make yogurt. Then when she died, my father used to go to the Greek markets around Halsted and Harrison. He would bring anchovies and the orange fish roe and baklava. We thought that was just the nuts."

She laughed, licked a cigarette paper between her lips. "Yogurt we thought was a treat," she said. "Now you can get that stuff anywhere."

Back in Queens, it began to dawn on me, a little late, that this meal might actually be something like a date. If so, I was committing the cardinal sin of talking endlessly about myself.

"Am I boring you?"

"No, not at all," he said. But he was always exquisitely polite. Unlike me. We stared at each other, then looked quickly down at our plates.

"You know," he said, "my mom used to make grape leaves too."

"Used to?"

"Well, I guess she still does. I meant when I was a kid. She's in Lebanon."

"But I thought you grew up here. Did she move back there?"

"No, she stayed in Lebanon. During the war."

Beirut, circa 1979, a neighborhood called Shiyah: a jumble of crooked concrete buildings. Laundry and electrical wires tangled across the sky. Rebar jutted from the tops and sides of rough cement walls like porcupine quills; many of these buildings would stay just like this, perpetually unfinished, for the next thirty years. People lived in apartments with whole walls blasted open, cross-sectioned dioramas, like ants between glass. The Bazzi family— mother, father, three older brothers, one older sister, and little Mohamad— all stuffed themselves inside one tiny two-room flat.

But behind the building was a courtyard where a kid could play: a tree, a cinderblock wall, a patch of mangy grass. His mother planted gardenias and oregano in rusty powdered milk tins and perched them on the wall where they would get some sun. At night, bullet casings and artillery fragments fell into the yard. In the morning, he collected the pieces of metal in a rattling tin can that used to hold mint candies. Other buildings loomed up and over, protecting the minuscule garden.

This neighborhood belonged to the Shiite Muslim militia Amal. The neighborhood a couple of blocks down the street belonged to a Christian militia. In between was a no-man's-land, a ragged borderline that ran across the entire city. Some parts grew so abandoned, so shaggy with weeds and urban underbrush, that foreigners called it the "Green Line." The Lebanese called it *khatt al-tamaas,* the line of contact. Aside from a few checkpoints where people could go from one side to the other, the snipers on both sides made the line virtually impossible to cross.

The militias did not tolerate neutrality. They called on young men to defend their neighborhoods, their families, their gods. Those who didn't want to fight could be threatened, bullied, or beaten.

Or they joined the biggest militia of all, the army of the disappeared. More than seventeen thousand people, mostly fighting-age men, vanished into the void of the fifteen-year war. They evaporated at checkpoints and into ransomless kidnappings, their fates unknown (and yet a terrible certainty) to this day.

Or, if they were lucky and could get a visa to somewhere, anywhere, they left.

First to leave were Mohamad's three older brothers: Hassan to France, Hassane to Spain, Ahmad and his wife to New York City. His sister Hanan stayed behind, but the brothers faced more danger from the militias that ruled the streets. They planned to return when the war was over.

And in one of those pristine, photographic moments that engineer our fates, his parents decided not to to send their youngest son to Paris, or Barcelona, but to Jackson Heights, Queens. It was 1985. He was ten years old.

The truth is I was never all that interested in the Middle East. I knew the basic story line. But when it came to the endless criminations and recriminations, the bitter arm-wrestling over history, my brain—like those of most Americans—glazed over.

Lebanon was different, though. It was part of my childhood, along with Sesame Street and *Free to Be . . . You And Me* and the war in Vietnam. I would lie underneath my grandmother's piano, stretched out on the burnt-orange polyester shag rug, and watch the war on our blurry old television. Vietnam bled into Beirut with hardly a costume change, or so it seemed to my six-year-old mind. We had won the war in Vietnam, they told us in school, but now there was trouble in a place called *Lebanon*.

This alarmed me, because we went to Lebanon three or four times a year. Lebanon was the sleepy northern Indiana town that we passed through on the five-hour drive from Bloomington, where I grew up, to Chicago, where my grandparents lived. Lebanon had a rest stop where we would stretch our legs. Elderly couples in pastel polyester pantsuits ambled around their Winnebagos. Hoosiers traded fly-fishing tips while waiting in line for the drinking fountain. A family of stray cats lived in a culvert. It seemed harmless enough.

But the nightly news showed a black-and-white Lebanon where cars exploded, buildings fell, and old women screamed and clutched the sides of their heads. Sideburned men in bell-bottomed jeans dashed from building to building, cradling Kalashnikovs, in a life-or-death game of hide-and-go-seek.

The next time the war flashed past on TV, I asked my grandfather if we could skip Lebanon on the drive back to Bloomington.

He roared with laughter. "Hey Dina!" he shouted into the kitchen, where my grandmother was chain-smoking and grinding hamburger, refueling for her own domestic wars. "Listen to this! Putti thinks the war is in *our* Lebanon!"

I was embarrassed; I had said something silly, but I didn't know what.

"No, Putti," he said kindly, once he saw the scowl of confusion on my face. "That's not the same Lebanon. That's a different Lebanon from the one on TV."

Mohamad laughed. Good. He wasn't offended.

I was born in 1970, I told him—smack between Tet and Watergate. To us children of Nixon, Lebanon symbolized all that went wrong between humans, just as Vietnam did for our parents. And so when this man with whom I was maybe on a date told me that he was from Lebanon, I pictured something bigger than a patch of land half the size of New Jersey: a country of myth and symbols, a Lebanon of the imagination. When he spoke of his childhood in Beirut, I nodded and tried to look wise. Afterward I ran home and frantically Googled "civil war lebanon." Who fought whom, and why? How did it start? How did it end?

Google didn't tell me what I know now: that we are still fighting over the answers to these questions—still fighting, to this day, over the questions themselves.

Queens had its green lines too, but they were invisible. South Asians on one block; Irish on another. A shift in continents, from South Asia to South America. There were no checkpoints, no snipers—the boundaries only existed inside your head.

Ahmad lived with his wife and their baby daughter in a two-bedroom apartment in a massive red-brick building. The skinny, brooding ten-year-old from Beirut slept on the living room couch. Ahmad's wife was unhappy in the new country, and food was one of the few things that she could control: if she had a treat—candy, cake—she would hide it from Mohamad and feed it to her daughter. In pictures from that time he looks ravenous, temporary, a skinny scowling kid hovering in the frame as if he were trying to disappear.

He learned English immediately and with no accent. His seventh-grade English teacher, Mrs. Hertz, convinced him to write stories for the school newspaper. By eighth grade he was covering local news—a church concert, a library exhibit—for the *Western Queens Gazette*. People laughed at the quiet, serious thirteen-year-old sitting in the back of the room with his notebook. But he didn't care: in Lebanon, surrounded by older brothers and sister and cousins, he had always been the youngest person in the room. When he wrote stories, he missed Lebanon, and his mother and father, a little bit less.

* * *

In 1994, nine years after he left Beirut, Mohamad finally sat down to dinner with his entire family again. The war had been over for four years, but none of the brothers had returned to live in Lebanon. They were scattered, funneled into separate lives, with jobs and wives and children in different countries. They spoke English, French, and Spanish as well as Arabic. They gathered at Hassane's house in Barcelona. Nobody said it, but they didn't have to: there wouldn't be any going back now.

That night, his mother made stuffed zucchini and grape leaves, one of her most spectacular meals. Holding each plump, stubby zucchini in one hand, she bored out the inside with a long metal file. She kept the *boub al-kusa,* the pale green curlicues of interior flesh, and braised it with onions and seven spices to serve as a side dish. She kneaded rice and ground meat, flavored with cinnamon and allspice, and stuffed the delicate hollowed-out shells of zucchini, then the grape leaves one by one, holding each leaf in the palm of one hand while rolling it up with the other. She lined the bottom of a 12-quart pot with flat grape leaves to protect the vegetables from burning. She laid down a layer of stuffed grape leaves, then a layer of stuffed zucchini shells, packing them tightly together like masonry, alternating all the way up to the top, pressing them down with a plate, as if by making the most complicated food possible, nesting food within food, a Shahrazad of the stove, she could trick time and keep her family together forever.

When the meal was done, her children got up from the table and prepared to leave her once again. She began to cry.

"She said something I've never forgotten," Mohamad told me, so quietly I had to lean forward to hear him. "She said, 'What did I do, that God has cursed me this way, so that all my children have to live in different corners of the world?' "

In Bloomington, Indiana, where I grew up, we had a farmer's market in the town square outside the courthouse. Every Saturday, farmers would drive in from the countryside before dawn, setting up stands heaped with whatever was in season: spring meant strawberry-and-rhubarb pie, wild chives, and ramps. Summer brought peach pie, succotash, gooseberries, and corn. In fall we would drive out into the countryside and buy apple cider straight from the orchard. Giant lumpy green pumpkins right from the patch. Purple, white, and yellow Indian corn candy-striped with red. And in winter, when there was no harvest, we still had stone-milled cornmeal and Amish cheeses. The market was where my mother taught me to eat what was in season instead of the hard bright strawberries I always begged for at the grocery store. On Saturday mornings my mother would run into people she knew buying homemade pies, dried sassafras bark, or green bell peppers (such exotic items in the southern Indiana of the early 1970s, before globalization folded the ends of the earth together, that people referred to them as "mangoes").

But when I was thirteen, my mother married the wrong man, at least according to my grandfather. Driven by demons that no one understood, least of all himself, my grandfather declared us "disowned." His anachronistic gesture meant we were no longer welcome to visit the house I had always thought of as home—the piano, the burnt orange carpet, and my grandmother's kitchen. My grandmother wasn't happy about this, but what could she do? Her power stopped at the kitchen walls.

My mother and I packed all our possessions into the backseat of a beat-up old Honda and drove to her new husband's place in Arizona. I didn't know it then, but it would be years before we would settle down.

Our first stop was Ganado, a tiny northern Arizona town in the Navajo Indian Reservation. Ganado was my first high school, a series of double-wide trailers in the desert. Ganado was fry bread and posole and Navajo tacos, a giant flap of fried bread layered with beef, beans, cheese, onions, lettuce, tomatoes, and as much hot sauce as you could stand. My mother got divorced, and soon Ganado was just a tiny desert outpost disappearing in the rearview mirror.

In the mid-1980s (jelly bracelets, Wham! on the radio, Latin American death squads), we moved to San Francisco. Jobs were scarce, apartments even scarcer: landlords had their pick of tenants, and none of them wanted a single mother with a teenager. After looking at some terrifying transient hotels and running out of other options, we ended up in a homeless shelter called Raphael House. An obscure Christian sect ran the place for families who needed to get back on their feet.

On the first night, my mother and I filed into a dining room full of long communal tables. The brothers and sisters passed out plates containing livid, gelatinous little squares of something called "tofu."

I stared at the stuff. It stared back at me, quivering wetly. *You're a long way from home, and California is a foreign land*, it seemed to say. *Eat me, my pretty, and you will never find your way back home again.*

Tofu was a phenomenon I had vaguely heard of, but naively imagined I would never encounter, like homelessness. A good midwestern girl, raised on corn and chicken and food you could grab ahold of, must have done something unforgivable to deserve this slippery thing.

I looked at my mother: she looked as appalled as I was, which did not seem like a good sign. Clearly, we were in the grips of some California cult.

One of the brothers saw me staring at the tofu—they ate communally with the shelter residents—and sensed my distress. "We don't usually eat this stuff," he said, a little apologetically, and we all laughed.

It turned out the brothers and sisters were godly folk, despite their taste for Satan's flesh, and most of the time they made real food. They ran Raphael House off the proceeds from a restaurant; once they invited us to a picnic with more than a dozen different kinds of bread. I remember thick brown boules with nuts and cheese baked inside; fluffy white loaves flecked with dill; and my first taste of Irish soda bread. I didn't even know bread came in such permutations, all of them like opening up a new book, and it more than made up for the tofu.

We stayed at Raphael House for three and a half weeks. It was difficult to register a homeless child for high school back then, but after some fast and elegant talking my mother managed to get me into a San Francisco magnet school, which I attended for one week before we pulled up stakes and left again.

Overland Park, Kansas, was my third high school; but I remember it most for something the natives called "pizza" but which bore no resemblance to the pizza I knew—this was a kind of giant cracker enameled with Day-Glo orange Velveeta and cut into squares.

St. Louis, Missouri, was a real city: it had the Sting Burger, the glory of the Delmar Loop, a hamburger blazing with spices and barbecue sauce and "not recommended for the faint of palate." But the suburbs had a better tax base. My mother researched the public schools and moved us into the cheapest neighborhood of the best school district. This was high school number four, and by now my math skills were too shot to get into a good college, never mind the tuition. I didn't care by that point anyway. I just wanted to keep moving. You might say I was looking for something; a psychiatrist might have described it as a desire to return to the Chicago house with the piano and my grandmother's kitchen. That wasn't it though—my grandfather had relented by then, and we had gone back to visit, but it wasn't home anymore.

There were days when we didn't know where we'd be sleeping that night; months when I longed to go to school like a normal kid. But one thing I never questioned: dinner. Somehow my mother saw to it that we sat down to a proper meal every evening. A glass or two of wine and a Crock-Pot turned cheap cuts of meat into *daube Provençal* while she was at work; bacon, leeks, and cream (you only need a touch of each) transformed the proletarian potato into a queen. No matter where we found ourselves—a homeless shelter, a friend's couch, our car—we would sit down to eat, and we would be home.

Toward the end of my senior year, a friend with a car gave me a ride home. I didn't usually let my classmates see our one-bedroom railroad apartment, where my mother slept on a foldout sofa in the living room so I could have my own bedroom. But Wendy was all right, so I brought her in, and my mother invited her to stay for dinner.

That night we were having Suleiman's Pilaf, a lamb and onion stew topped with parsley and chopped almonds and sultanas, served with rice and yogurt. It was one of my mother's standbys, adapted from the British cookbook writer Elizabeth David, the woman who introduced postwar England to the warm sunlight of Mediterranean cooking—a nomad by choice, a vagabond aristocrat who learned how to make sumptuous meals from nothing.

Wendy lived in what I thought of as a mansion, with multiple bedrooms and an actual dining room. I always imagined people in houses like that eating duck in aspic off matching plates under crystal chandeliers. But when we all sat down at our small kitchen table, which was also where I did my homework, Wendy looked stunned. In her house, she told us, everyone just foraged in the fridge or got pizza somewhere. Nobody cared what or when the kids ate.

"Do you eat like this *every* night?" she asked, with something that sounded like awe, and when my mother said yes, I saw that home could be something you made instead of the place where you lived.

I continued to wander throughout college and beyond: Chicago, Portland, Minneapolis, Oakland. Back to Bloomington for a while (Hinkle's Hamburgers, where they would always ask, in one breath: ketchupmustard? picklesonions?). After college I shuffled off to Buffalo, where I waited tables in a series of greasy spoons and waited for the recession to end. Buffalo was icy sidewalks and urban blight, $1.99 steak and eggs, and a bottomless cup of coffee at the old Pano's diner at three in the morning.

After four years on America's frozen rim, I migrated south to the big city. Aside from a handful of native New Yorkers, most of the people I knew there were transplants like me, which is probably why it was the first place I felt at home.

And then I met Mohamad. Another reluctant nomad.

Chapter 2

Afghanistanism

A FTER THE DAY of the grape leaves, Mohamad and I started calling each other every day. A few weeks later he took me to his favorite restaurant, Afghan Kebab House. The restaurant's name blazed in crimson neon in the window, surrounded by the green neon outline of Afghanistan's borders. Underneath, lavender neon spelled out: HALAL MEAT.

Inside, the ceiling was draped in canvas, making the restaurant feel like a tent. Small tables lined the walls. Waiters hustled through with sizzling trays of kebab that filled the room with the fragrance of allspice, cinnamon, and roast lamb. As soon as we sat down, Mohamad got up again and went to say hello to the owner. He knew him from a story he had done about the Afghan community in Queens. They gripped each other's hands, talking quietly, and for a moment I felt the world billow about us like a sail.

The waiter brought us *bolani kashalu,* crisp oily little turnovers packed with soft potatoes and herbs and blistered brown on the outside. Next came *banjan burani,* charred, buttery eggplant slices buried under yogurt sprinkled with dried mint. Finally the kebab arrived, tender and smoky, flanked by light brown basmati rice, grilled Afghan flatbread, and salad drowned in creamy white dressing flecked with herbs.

Mohamad always had chicken kebab. He loved the way it all came on one big plate, the rice and meat and salad each staking out its own semi-autonomous zone. It reminded him of his mother—how she'd used to arrange the food on his plate in exactly the right proportions, the proper configuration of meat, salad, pickles; how she would smother everything in yogurt sauce. I was the one who tried the fish kebab, the *bolani* stuffed with scallions, and the *narinj palau,* rice pilaf studded green and orange with pistachios and orange rind.

A poster hung on one of the rough brown walls of a young girl, glaring out from deep red folds of wool. Her name was Sharbat Gula, though nobody knew that back then. In 1985, the year she had appeared on the cover of *National Geographic,* the frozen stare of her sea-green eyes fixed the world's attention on the flood of Afghan refugees fleeing the Soviet occupation.

Then the Cold War ended, Soviet troops left Afghanistan, and aside from military historians and feminists, most Americans forgot about Central Asia. There was even a word for this willful oblivion: Afghanistanism. People used it to criticize newspapers for wasting space on faraway, irrelevant topics like Afghanistan.

But the orphans of this forgotten war grew up to join the Taliban, and they were growing bolder and more extreme. In February 2001, the bearded militants publicly executed two women accused of being "prostitutes" by hanging them in a soccer stadium while hundreds watched. Three weeks later, the Taliban dynamited two sixth-century statues of Buddha. The Taliban's leaders had declared them idols, forbidden by Islamic law. The giant Buddhas were historic enough to make the front page of *The New York Times.*

"Why is it that people are more upset about the statues than the fact that a month ago they publicly executed two women?" I asked Mohamad.

"Or that they just massacred three hundred people a couple of months ago," he agreed, a whiplash of anger in his voice that I didn't recognize. I hadn't heard about that.

The Taliban, it turned out, weren't as far away as they seemed: they had opened an office in Queens. Mohamad had interviewed the genial, richly bearded Taliban ambassador to the United Nations, who served him sugared almonds and green tea, and had written a story about the Taliban's New York outpost. The small Afghan community in Queens was divided, Mohamad told me; some were pro-Taliban, others were anti. Only a few managed not to get reeled back into the politics of home.

The owners of this Afghan Kebab House were Hazaras, Shiite Muslims, like most of the people the Taliban had killed that January. Mohamad was a

Shiite too, or so I was vaguely aware; at the time it seemed like the kind of detail only the Taliban would care about.

Our courtship continued through spring and summer. We called it our "cross-border romance," because Greenpoint, in Brooklyn, was just over the border from Queens. I would ride my bicycle across the Newtown Creek, past the sewage treatment plant and the cemetery, then take Queens Boulevard to Sunnyside, and more often than not we would end up at Afghan Kebab House.

One warm evening in early fall, I rode to Sunnyside after work. We went to dinner as usual, then went back to his apartment. By that point I was slowly colonizing all the empty space in his kitchen. I had clothes piled up on his floor, and I was rooting through them looking for a clean shirt to wear to work the next day.

"Maybe we should think about living together," he said slowly. "Not now," he added hastily when he saw my expression. "But maybe sometime next year, like in the spring."

I was in love with him. But I liked my ritual of riding my bicycle back and forth, the feeling of freedom it brought me; on some inarticulate level, I thought maybe we could just keep doing that forever.

"Let's think about it," I said. "We've only been going out for five months."

We agreed to sleep on it. We both had a long day ahead: the next day was the mayoral primary election, the culmination of a long and bitter campaign, and we would both be writing about it until after the polls closed.

I woke up late, as usual, and wandered into the living room. He already had the television turned on. But there was no news of the election, no lines of New York voters streaming to the polls. Just a tall black-and-white building flat against a light blue sky with smoke coming out of its side.

Six days later, he was on a one-way flight to Pakistan.

In the months that followed, New Yorkers discovered a world that most of us had not known was there. We snapped at our friends for no reason. We forgot simple names and numbers. We lay awake at night, unable to sleep, and sleepwalked through our days. We coughed and wheezed our way through fall and winter. We swayed silently on the subway, a city of zombies, and stared at each other with baleful understanding.

I worked on Wall Street, about eight blocks from Ground Zero. After work I would head out into the smoky night, past National Guardsmen and dump trucks full of twisted metal, through the militarized construction site that lower Manhattan had become. Mohamad called me every evening, no matter where he was. Islamabad, Quetta, Peshawar. Jalalabad when it fell from Taliban control. And every time the phone rang, my stomach would contract, fearing bad news.

One winter evening, while waiting for him to call, I walked past a square where we had almost kissed on one of our first dates. Normally the little courtyard was bathed in the comforting orange glow of sulfur lights. Now it was dark and heaving with the hard gray bodies of rats. There were rats all over lower Manhattan those days, and the thought of why they had suddenly proliferated sent me home sobbing stupidly.

That night, when Mohamad finally called, I tried to explain to him. It wasn't the rats, but something else, something I couldn't express: the dark streets, the checkpoints everywhere. The fire that burned underground for three months, insinuating the smell of rotting wet ashes into everything. Uniformed men with guns in the subway. The ruin that continued to loom over us long after the concrete and metal itself had been trucked away. This city had been our home, a living thing; now it was a militarized zone surrounding a mass grave.

He sighed. A group of Pakistani militants had offered to let him interview a wounded al-Qaeda member. He was trying to figure out if it was safe. (A few weeks later, after the *Wall Street Journal* reporter Daniel Pearl disappeared, they would break off contact with Mohamad.) But I didn't know any of this until long afterward.

"Look, I have to go," he said. His voice was tight. "I just wanted to let you know I'm okay."

"Can't we talk a little longer? I just want to hear your voice." We had been separated, at that point, for almost as long as we had been together.

"Annia, there are wild dogs here," he said. "I'm standing out in the open to get a satellite signal and they're starting to circle around me. I have to go."

During that long, dark winter, I dragged all my friends to one Afghan Kebab House or another. I would inflict on them detailed reminiscences: Mohamad won't eat fish kebab, but only chicken; Mohamad likes *firni*, the milky white pudding scented with rosewater and cardamom and sprinkled with crushed pistachios; Mohamad says it reminds him of Lebanese *mhalabieh*.

Every time I was there, I would remember the last time Mohamad and I had dinner there together. It was a couple of days before he flew to Pakistan. I was struggling to hold back tears, to be tough and cool and not think about where he was going.

"Look, I don't want you to worry about me," he said as we sat down to eat.

"That's ridiculous. How am I not going to worry about you?"

He was silent. He was working long hours, spending most of his days writing about Osama bin Laden and the Taliban, and then coming home late at night to pack. I was concentrating on drinking and crying. I'm not usually a weeper, but I bawled like an infant in the six days before Mohamad left, when I wasn't drinking heavily, and also when I was. Doing anything else felt completely useless.

"Did I ever tell you the story about the window in our old place in Beirut?" he asked finally.

I shook my head.

In Beirut, in those days, there was always shelling. You didn't know where it came from; it could have been one side, could have been the other. The courtyard in Shiyah was too dangerous to play in. But the Bazzi family's apartment had bars on the living room window, just the right size for a kid to climb on. He would scamper up them and hang there like a little spider monkey. He called them his monkey bars.

One day he was playing on the monkey bars while his mother and father made a yogurt salad in the kitchen with Hassane. Everybody else was in the living room: Hanan, Hassan, Ahmad, and their neighbor Amal.

Three Lebanese in one room, goes the saying, and you'll have four opinions. This applies to food as well as other forms of politics. As Hassane and his father watched his mother crush the garlic and slice the cucumber, everyone thought they knew the best, the *only* way to make the salad: *Two cloves of garlic! No, that's too much—only one clove of garlic! No, two cloves of garlic, but more cucumber! Less mint! What it really needs is more time to let the flavor soak in!*

Finally their mother called Ahmad into the kitchen to see if the salad had enough garlic. Mohamad leapt off the monkey bars and followed his big brother into the kitchen—whatever it was, he wanted a taste of it too.

Just then a giant invisible fist punched all the breath out of the room. An artillery shell had hit the house next door. The window exploded into flying knives. Metal blades cut deep into the walls—shrapnel, fragments of bomb casing. Glass daggers tore all the way through the sofa; the family found them later sticking out the other side. One of them bit into Amal's thigh. She didn't even feel it at first, didn't notice she was bleeding until Hanan saw the blood and started to scream. Suddenly everybody was screaming. The house filled with smoke. If Mohamad hadn't joined his family in the kitchen—if he had still been playing in the window, on his monkey bars— he would have been killed.

He sat back, folded his arms, and smiled at me with benevolent expectation.

I stared at him, dumbfounded.

"Is this story," I said, "supposed to make me feel *better?*"

"Well, yes," he said, with a mystified shrug. Obviously I had missed the point: "The way I see it, if I was going to die, I would have died then."

The gambler's fallacy. I laughed. This man prized reason more than anyone I knew. But men are superstitious creatures.

"You realize that's completely irrational, right?"

He laughed. "Well, okay, maybe it is. But it always makes me feel better."

Yet somehow later, sitting in Afghan Kebab House without him, I found the story inexplicably comforting. Perhaps I'd picked up some of his faith in the invisible, in the web of circumstance that he believed could keep him safe. Or perhaps it was because he almost never talked about Beirut, yet he had handed me a story, a fragment of his past experience with war, in the hope that it would make the world seem like a safer place.

And in the end there was simply the story itself. My family made yogurt and cucumber salad too (Greeks call it *tzatziki*) and I knew the flavor: the dried mint and cucumber, the coppery bite of garlic embedded in the creamy yogurt. I could see him now, in the kitchen with his family gathered around, as the deadly metal shell hurtled toward them through the sky, tasting the salad that saved his life.

Chapter 3

Bride of the World

Cities choose their people, not the other way around.

—Vassilis Vassilikos, *The Few Things I Know*
About Glafkos Thrassakis

I N JULY 2002, Mohamad and I moved into an apartment in Brooklyn. But he spent most of his time abroad: Pakistan, Syria, Lebanon, the West Bank. In January 2003, *Newsday* appointed him its Middle East bureau chief. He would have to live somewhere in the region. Jerusalem and Cairo were the traditional choices for most American newspapers. But he wanted to move to Beirut, and he had asked me to move there with him. So that May, I went to Beirut for two weeks to see what it was like.

By day, cars owned Beirut. The city stewed in angry coils of traffic. Automobiles bullied through the streets and over sidewalks. The air throbbed with diesel. But at night people crept out into the streets. They sat and smoked water pipes, played music, drank coffee. They walked up and down by the seaside eating lupins, the little legumes that Mediterraneans serve with salt as appetizers or cheap street food. Men streaked past on mopeds, delivering embers for water pipes, and spangled the darkness with comets of orange sparks. If you want to see Beirut, the best place to begin is at night.

We started out at Regusto, where we collected Mohamad's sister Hanan, their cousin Huda, and her husband Ibrahim. We proceeded to the back of a shopping arcade, to a bathroom-sized bar called Chez André, where the bartender snipped off the ties of anyone foolish enough to show up wearing one and hung them up over the pornographic cartoons, varnished in smoke-stain yellow, and the sign that commanded: "No Politics!" We drank Lebanese beer beneath a fringe of decapitated neckties, and somehow accumulated a mustachioed writer who looked exactly like the brooding old 1950s Hemingway. I never did catch his name.

And ended up at Baromètre, lurking behind thick curtains in the back of another shopping center. The girls were beautiful, the boys were studiously unkempt, and everyone seemed to know one another. The menu was written in Arabic on a green chalkboard that was barely visible through the haze of cigarette smoke and music. Ziad Rahbani, the brilliant composer, presided from a photograph hanging in the corner; in the picture he hunkered over a table and smoked intensely with his button-down shirt half open, which was what everyone in Baromètre was doing too. We drank a lot of *arak*, the milky, anisette-flavored spirit, while long-haired girls prowled from table to table like lions and Rahbani's Arabic-inflected jazz jangled through the smoky dark. Shouting to be heard, everybody asked me the same question:

How do you like Beirut?

Berytus, Biruta, Beyrouth. The city goes back to the third millennium before Christ at least, and ever since then visitors have tended to fall in love with it. It's a city of migrants, of people perpetually coming or going, where exiles and opportunists of all nations make themselves at home. "No, but Lebanon, we're a special case," as my friend Munir put it once, laughing. "We've been invaded by all of them: the Canaanites, the Phoenicians, the Turks, the Greeks, the Arabs. We have the blood of all these invaders in our veins!"

When Lebanon was under French control, people used to call Beirut "the Paris of the Middle East." (Some called it the Switzerland, a more accurate moniker, in light of all the money laundering that went on there.) But this borrowed finery didn't do the place justice. Old Beirut was *Medinat al-Alam,* "City of the World," where people spoke Greek in the port, Turkish in the *souq,* and French in the cafés.

In the years after World War II, Beirut became the cosmopolitan cultural capital of the Middle East—an Arab city, a Mediterranean city, but also a city that spanned the entire world. Poets, partisans, and soldiers of fortune all poured into Beirut. Some of those émigrés weren't what they seemed—like Kim Philby, the mild-mannered Beirut-based correspondent for *The Economist,* who turned out to be one of the Cold War's most notorious double agents. Dissidents fleeing tyrants came to Beirut to hide. Books fleeing censorship came there to be printed, like *Awlad Haratina* (published in English as *Children of the Alley*), Naguib Mahfouz's epic allegorical masterpiece about the Abrahamic prophets: unpublishable in Cairo but welcome in Beirut. Exiled authors came to plot their next novels; exiled tyrants came to plot their next coups (including, for a very brief period, an up-and-coming young Iraqi named Saddam Hussein). Empires, real and imagined, rose and fell over *arak* and Arabic coffee in the cafés and bars of Beirut. By 1951, an estimated 30 percent of the world's gold trade passed through the merchant houses of Beirut. Downtown Beirut had about twenty-five movie theaters at midcentury, making it one of the most moviegoing countries per capita in the world. The capital alone had fifty newspapers; by 1975, the government had issued licenses to more than four hundred—an empire of words. *"Babel des accents Arabes,"* wrote the Lebanese journalist Samir Kassir (son of a Palestinian and a Syrian, making him a quintessential Beiruti). A refugee city, a city of plots and pluralities, a city so packed with ideas they overflowed into the sea.

It was during that cosmopolitan moment, old-timers told me, that Beirut acquired another alias: *Sitt al-Dunya,* "Lady of the World," and sometimes *Arous al-Dunya,* "Bride of the World." And Beirut was in cahoots with Mohamad there too, that warm summer evening, because he hadn't asked outright, but he had hinted that he wanted to get married.

I didn't want to get married. I hated the idea, for complicated reasons that had nothing to do with Mohamad and everything to do with my own history. Marriage was the boot that had kicked me out of my peaceful midwestern childhood and halfway across the continent to California. Marriage meant exile, catastrophe, and homelessness. Marriage was a mistake other people made and then tried to lure you into: a colossal, cross-generational human Ponzi scheme.

More philosophically, it seemed to me that marriage was part of an identity imposed by others—families, churches, governments—rather than one
you chose yourself. But Mohamad wanted me to move to Beirut with him,
so it seemed like a good time to meet his parents. The marriage question
could wait, preferably forever.

I had already met Mohamad's brother Ahmad in New York. Ahmad's
wife had waited for a lull in the conversation. Then she pounced, and demanded, with a truculence I only later realized was defensive, "So, Annia.
What do you think of Arabs?"

I would have thought the answer was obvious—I was living with one,
after all. But she watched me through narrowed eyes, as though I might
crack under interrogation and start calling them all terrorists.

Meeting the parents had all the makings of an equally awkward encounter. They didn't speak any English (perhaps luckily, considering the sister-
in-law), and I didn't speak much Arabic. And they were Muslims. I was
Catholic—a bad Catholic, in many ways, but I doubted that would improve
my case.

A friend of ours had paraded several prospective brides before his parents. His Iraqi father had delivered a series of arbitrary verdicts: one was too
old, another was too short. But one of them, I remembered, had been just
right. *She's nice,* our friend's father had decided, *she smiles.* I resolved that
I would smile a lot.

Mohamad rang the doorbell. The heavy maroon metal door creaked open,
and I faced the enemy: a tiny old lady about five feet tall, wearing a faded
blue cotton housedress. Black eyes gleamed under thin arched eyebrows, the
same as her son's. Her mouth drew down into a frown, but her eyes laughed;
the combination suggested she was trying to look severe while struggling
not to smile. Umm Hassane was seventy-one years old. Her skin was hardly
wrinkled, but her face was beginning to collapse toward the middle, nose
and chin clamping together on her mouth, creasing into an expression of
permanent grudging amusement.

I smiled. She smiled back, an almost imperceptible crinkling of the
mouth.

I smiled harder. "Hello!" I bellowed, using up one of my hard-earned Arabic words, and jacked up my smile like a Miss America contestant.

"Welcome," she said, "welcome," and she reached out and gripped my shoulder fiercely, pulling me down and kissing me on the cheek three times. I smelled garlic, lemon, and something green and grassy—cilantro. She looked at me, knowing and humorous, as if she had a good joke and planned on keeping it to herself but wanted me to know she had it anyway.

Abu Hassane, Mohamad's father, peered anxiously over his wife's shoulder. "Welcome, welcome," he repeated, shuffling forward in his slippers. I smiled at him. He smiled back, a broad and intermittently toothy grin. We went inside.

Umm Hassane had cooked zucchini stew. Her method involved grinding garlic and cilantro together in a mortar and pestle into a fragrant pesto, which she then sautéed to bring out the flavor even more. She had also made *fattoush*, the Levantine bread salad. She dressed it by mashing lemon juice, salt, and garlic together in the same worn wooden mortar, then letting them sit so the garlic could macerate into the lemon juice. The whole place smelled like garlic, beef stock, simmering vegetables, and lemons; to me, it smelled like home.

But before we could eat, we would have to talk. In Arabic.

Back in New York, I had learned a slew of useful Levantine Arabic idioms, from the general "How are you? What's the news?" to more telling phrases like "The border is closed today, but I don't know why." And then there were the ones I called the Untranslatables: words or phrases that had no real English equivalent, but in my opinion should have, especially *sahtain*. It means "to your health" (literally, "double health"), and like *bon appétit* or *buen provecho*, *sahtain* is used for the highly civilized purpose of congratulating someone who is either eating or about to begin eating.

Almost all of these words abandoned me the minute we walked in the door. I clung to "Hello," and stoked my smile. We trooped into the living room and sat on matching brown sofas.

"You got fat!" Abu Hassane said to Mohamad as soon as he sat down. He wheezed with laughter like an old accordion.

Mohamad had gained a little weight, but this seemed awfully direct. I was not yet accustomed to the Lebanese way of welcoming wandering sons and daughters home. Over the next six years, I would learn many things; one of them would be the unfortunate habit of greeting people by pointing out minor fluctuations in their weight.

"Do you speak Arabic?" asked Abu Hassane, planting a hand on each knee, leaning forward, and squinting across the room toward me with good-natured curiosity.

"A little," I replied, and added ungrammatically, "I am going class New York one time each week."

He responded with a happy garble of Arabic, a rapid unintelligible stream from which I could snatch only isolated words: "Beirut . . . learn Arabic . . . good . . . New York . . . welcome."

"She only speaks a little bit," said Mohamad, laughing.

"Oh." We went back to smiling.

It is strange to study a new language as an adult. Your comprehension leapfrogs ahead of your ability to articulate, and because you can't converse at their level, people think you don't understand them. The result is that you spend a lot of time listening to people talk about you in the third person.

"She's pretty," said Abu Hassane.

"Yes, she is," replied Mohamad, who had an inkling I might be following some of the conversation.

"Does she have a job?"

"Yes, she works very hard. She's an editor at a magazine."

"At a magazine!" Abu Hassane exulted.

"Not like Ahmad's wife! She doesn't work!" Umm Hassane tilted her chin up, a typically Levantine gesture of negation, and flapped a dismissive hand.

Of Mohamad's three brothers, only Ahmad had married a Lebanese woman. But Umm Hassane's belief in work, as I would learn, trumped any feelings of national solidarity.

"How much money does she make?" asked Abu Hassane.

"Oh, well, not quite as much as me."

Mohamad avoided meeting my eye. We didn't explain to them that I was thinking of quitting my job and moving to Beirut with him. All that could wait until we'd passed the initial interview.

"Still, she works, she doesn't just sit around," said Umm Hassane. "That's good."

Abu Hassane beamed at me. I smiled as if I'd been lobotomized. Umm Hassane regarded all of us with her usual expression of secretly amused tolerance. And then she made up her mind. I had a job; I spoke some Arabic; I smiled. There was only one possible response.

"She's very nice; we like her," she said, nodding her head with finality. "She's trying to learn Arabic, and she's not lazy, like some women."

She scowled momentarily, possibly thinking of her daughter-in-law, then continued:

"I'll arrange everything. We'll call Hajj Naji, and he'll make an appointment with the *Sayyid*"—a *Sayyid* is any descendant of the Prophet Muhammad, but in this case she was talking about a local Shiite cleric—"and you'll get married."

There are two main verbs for getting married in colloquial Lebanese Arabic. But only one of them, *tazawaja,* means simply "to get married." The other, *katab al-kitaab* (literally, "writing the book"), is more commonly used for an Islamic marriage contract. In my Arabic classes, I had learned only *tazawaja.* Umm Hassane, devout Muslim that she was, used *katab al-kitaab.* So fortunately I didn't understand the matrimonial portion of the conversation, which Mohamad didn't translate until much later, in the safety of our hotel room. To me, it simply sounded as if I had gotten Umm Hassane's stamp of approval. And so I sat there, still smiling extravagantly, oblivious to our impending marriage.

Umm Hassane had it all planned out: she and the relatives would marry us off before we could get away. But first, we would celebrate my visit, and my acceptance into Mohamad's family, in the simplest manner possible: we would eat. We trooped over to the dinner table, which was spread with placemats made of yesterday's newspapers, and sat down.

After the meal comes the tea: that's the rule in Umm Hassane's house. After the tea, relatives must be visited, especially when the family has a new acquisition to display. Abu Hassane wasn't feeling well, so he stayed at home.

Umm Hassane put on her long black robe and the headscarf she wore when going out of the house, and we went to Hajj Naji's apartment building.

"This is the bride!" proclaimed Umm Hassane, sweeping inside and producing me with a triumphant little one-handed flourish, like a game show host.

A roomful of faces turned and stared. A roomful of eyes looked me up and down and then back up again. A bulky, square-shouldered woman with severe eyebrows and deep furrows of discontent bracketing her mouth, heaved herself out of an armchair. She put one hand on my shoulder, as if to pin me in place, and surveyed me with mercenary appraisal. Her gaze traveled from my face all the way down to my feet, taking it all in—the wrinkled green cotton shirt, the dusty black leather shoes, the probably insufficiently modest skirt—before heading back up to my now-rickety smile.

"Congratulations!" she declared, hoisting her eyebrows in theatrical surprise. "She's pretty!"

She kissed me on the cheek three times. Umm Hassane retired to a chair in triumph, tucking her chin up under her nose and looking pleased with herself.

This was Batoul. Mohamad and I ended up inventing secret nicknames for most of his relatives: Khadija, with her husky laugh and fashionable headscarves, was Cool Aunt; and Hajj Naji became Stern Uncle. But Batoul was always just Batoul, unadorned. The room was plain, even stark: no pictures on the cracked plaster walls, no carpet on the tile floor. Just hospitality stripped down to its barest essentials, chairs and sofas arranged around a coffee table. But it was a marble-topped coffee table, and at its center blazed an exuberant spray of lipstick-red fake roses. An ornate gold-metal Kleenex dispenser huddled underneath. In a house without much frivolity, these little luxuries marked off the living room as public space, a special zone for guests.

We sat down. A headscarved daughter of about fifteen or sixteen circled around proffering a tray of little glasses of pineapple juice to everyone, starting with me. She darted furtive, fascinated glances in my direction as she served the others.

"She looks Lebanese," said Batoul, still eyeing me with an air of assessment.

"She's *faqirah*!" Umm Hassane declared with pride.

Faqirah: literally, it means poor. But it belongs among the Untranslatables. *Faqir* (male) or *faqirah* (female) can mean that you are downtrodden or impoverished. But like so many words born as insults, *faqirah* grew into a source of pride. In Lebanon, and especially among country people, it means down-to-earth, not stuck up. "She's *faqirah*," translated into midwesternese, would be something like "she's good people" or "she's just folks." Umm Hassane had once told Mohamad she didn't care who he married, as long as she was *faqirah*.

"Ah!" Batoul nodded, raising her eyebrows in appreciation. "That's good!"

My brideworthiness was established. Now it was Mohamad's turn. Batoul and Hajj Naji hadn't seen him in years; you can probably guess what came next.

"You've gained weight," said Batoul. "She must be feeding you well!" Everybody laughed and looked slyly at me.

Hajj Naji did not laugh. Eating together implied other kinds of communion—like living together in sin.

"When are you going to get married?" he said, laying his index finger thoughtfully next to his nose.

In traditional Lebanese families, whether Muslim or Christian, the father's older brother or paternal uncle is often a guardian of the family's collective morals. As Abu Hassane's paternal uncle, Hajj Naji was the family patriarch. It was his job to ensure that family members did not stray from the path of righteousness. Hajj Naji took this role very seriously.

"I'll call the *Sayyid*," he said, getting up from his chair. "I'll take you. We'll go get Abu Hassane, and we'll go to see the *Sayyid* right now."

Even if I wanted to get married, this meant trouble. Like Israel, Lebanon had no civil marriage: you could be wed only by religious authorities. Young Lebanese had been pushing for civil marriage for decades, but the men of God—Muslim and Christian alike—had defeated them every time. Neither mosque nor church was willing to surrender the power, or the revenue, that came from controlling the most intimate decisions in people's lives. If two Lebanese from different religious backgrounds wanted to tie the knot, they had a couple of options: they could take a twenty-minute flight to Cyprus, on an airplane packed with young Lebanese in love, and get a civil marriage. Or one of them could convert.

Some liberal clerics would marry a Christian and a Muslim without requiring the Christian to convert. But Hajj Naji would not choose this kind of cleric, and Mohamad knew it. An uncivil marriage, like the one we were being hustled into, was the last thing either of us wanted. Unless he acted fast, we would end up married, and I would end up Muslim; or he'd have to tell Hajj Naji why we couldn't. Either way he'd have a lot of explaining to do.

Somehow Mohamad didn't think Hajj Naji would understand my existential bohemian angst over marriage. I could barely articulate it myself. So he thought of a better excuse. "Well, we can't really get married right now," he said, with a regret that was at least partly sincere. "You see, I haven't spoken to Annia's family yet. If we got married without her family's consent, they would be insulted."

Offending the family of the bride: Hajj Naji, with his bevy of daughters, could scarcely suggest it.

The relatives murmured assent, impressed at Mohamad's prudence. A marriage would happen, there was no doubt. But it would be negotiated in the correct manner, as an agreement between families and in this case also between nations. Mohamad would make the pilgrimage to Chicago, as I had made mine to Beirut. I would present him to my family, as he had presented me to his, and an alliance would be arranged.

Reluctantly, Hajj Naji sat back down. We had escaped for now, and he knew it.

"You have reason," he said, nodding. "Reason is with you."

"We're going to get married when we go back to America," said Mohamad, improvising wildly. "In New York, a civil marriage."

This would have been news to me if I had understood it. But luckily for him I had completely lost the conversation's thread by then.

"That is good," said Hajj Naji, holding up a forefinger. A civil marriage, after all, was better than no marriage whatsoever. "But you still have to do a *katab al-kitaab* for it to be valid."

As we left, he reminded us: "Don't forget to do a *katab al-kitaab*. I'll call the *Sayyid* whenever you're ready."

As we walked down the dark hallway of Hajj Naji's building, Mohamad turned to me with a relief I only partly understood. "No more relatives," he said. "I promise."

Luckily this promise only lasted a few hours. Later that evening, we met up with Mohamad's older sister, Hanan. The three of us went to visit Huda, who was Hanan's best friend, and Ibrahim, who greeted us by shouting "Welcome!," and throwing open the door as though we were visiting royalty. Ibrahim was tall and courtly, a little stooped, with sad, wise eyes and a haze of curly hair around his ears. Huda was wearing pink lipstick and her tiny cherry-painted toes poked out of glamorous strappy sandals.

Inside Huda's apartment, which was full of Japanese prints and art books with colorful reproductions of paintings, we sat and drank mango juice and talked. Hanan spoke a little English, but she was shy about her grammar, so mostly she just sat and stared at me with those big oil-black Bazzi eyes. She made Mohamad look like a talker. Huda made up for both of them: chain-smoking Huda only stopped talking to smoke and only stopped smoking to talk, and sometimes collapsed into coughing laughter.

Both Ibrahim and Huda worked for the Ministry of Labor (unemployment was about 20 percent, said Ibrahim), so I asked Huda what she did at work.

"Do? What do I do?" she scoffed in French, frowning and rearing back her head at the idea. "Why, I write poetry!"

Everybody was a poet. Later that night, when we got to Baromètre, Ibrahim got very drunk and began reciting Arabic poetry to the guy who looked like Hemingway. I got very drunk and confided to Huda that I wasn't so sure about this marriage thing.

"I am bigger than Mohamad five year," I said in my Arabic baby talk.

Huda shrugged; she was bigger than Ibrahim, too, so what's the fuss? *"C'est mieux comme ça."* She stared at me, goggling her eyes with exaggerated innocence. She sucked the last drag out of her cigarette and lit one more.

"*Nous sommes Chiites,*" she explained, pronouncing "Shiites" the French way: *she-eats.* "*Et nous avons une forme de mariage—*"

"*Mutah!*" I shouted.

"*—qui est le meilleur du monde!*" she agreed, wheezing into a spasm of husky laughter.

Mutah is a form of temporary marriage, mainly practiced by Shiites, between a man and an unmarried woman. The marriage contract expires after a mutually agreed-upon period of time—anywhere from a few hours or days to decades—and the couple can get married without a cleric. I knew that *mutah* sounded better on paper than it was in practice—that women who did *mutah* were stigmatized, while men were not, and that Iranian clerics popularized it after the Iran-Iraq War partly to get out of paying pensions to war widows. But I still thought that if applied properly it was the most civilized form of marriage I'd ever heard of.

Huda agreed: you can be married just as long as you want to and no longer, she said, tossing a flirtatious glance toward Ibrahim. He expounded on how *mutah* is better for the woman, and better for the man, too; it can be renewed ad infinitum; you can convert it into the regular kind of marriage, if you like, but why would you want to?

We drank more wine. An old man hauled out an *oud* and started singing Arabic folk songs and everybody sang along: "*Al-Hilwa di Cou Cou.*" I asked Huda what the words meant and she turned and batted her kohl-ringed eyes at me and started to sing it (everybody did that if you mentioned a song): the pretty girl gets up at dawn to bake bread; the rooster crows, cou cou, and the workers get ready to work. "Oh you who have the wealth, the poor man has a generous God . . ."

A terra-cotta bowl of chicken livers bathed in lemon juice and garlic taxied down onto the table. The others started ordering *meze* in combinations I'd never imagined, Jabberwocky food, portmanteau creatures from a parallel world: slices of sausage, thick like pepperoni but spicy like chorizo, stewed in sweet pomegranate syrup. Little saucers of hummus with tender spoonfuls of sautéed lamb and pine nuts nestled in their belly buttons. Tiny glasses of crystal-clear *arak* that clouded into milky iridescence when you added ice. A pickled baby eggplant stuffed with chopped walnuts and hot red peppers and slicked with olive oil.

"What is this?" I asked, when the eggplant appeared.

"This is *makdous*," said Hanan. "It is good to eat with wine or *arak*."

Who thinks of such things? What god leant down and whispered in what mortal ear to put walnuts inside an eggplant? And then to eat it with wine? I wanted to cry. I ate all four *makdouses* and ordered four more. The aquamarine smell of anise fogged upward from the *arak*.

"Should we order *kibbeh nayeh*?" someone asked.

Sudden quiet. Everyone looked at each other. Some shook their heads sorrowfully: *don't say we didn't warn you*. But others nodded and elbowed each other with shining, conspiratorial eyes.

A few minutes later, it appeared: raw lamb ground with spices and cracked wheat and patted into a mound the size of a large man's hand. Scored with a fork and topped with roasted pine nuts. Hedged with raw onion slices and sprigs of mint. Hanan anointed it, pouring dark green olive oil over the small mountain until it pooled on the plate. Hands descended from all directions, one of them mine, ripping off rags of bread and tearing into the raw meat like lions. The *kibbeh* slid into my mouth, smooth and almost buttery, until the kick of the spices unfolded. Watching the others, I took a bite of mint and one of raw onion, and the two sharp blades of flavor tore open the bloody taste of raw lamb.

Drunker now. Hanan leaned over the table toward me. She was shouting something and smiling; I couldn't hear. She said it again: "How do you like Beirut?"

I opened my mouth to answer. The lights went off. An ear-splintering screech, then an industrial-strength grinding noise that I realized, when I saw the cake with the giant sparkler stuck in it, was a scratchy old cassette recording of "Happy Birthday" in Arabic. The girls at the next table leaped up and started swaying their hips, tossing their arms in the air and snapping their wrists; at the break, they threw back their heads like old women at a wedding and ululated.

Chapter 4

Mjadara

MOHAMAD RETURNED TO Baghdad, and I went back to New York. But something had changed. A few months after we fended off Hajj Naji, I was talking to Mohamad over the phone when he mentioned that he would get more vacation time if we were married.

"So why don't we?" I said.

I hadn't planned to say it, but the minute it came out of my mouth I knew I meant it. And not just for the vacation time.

There was a long pause. "Really?" he said finally.

That was the romantic part. To this day I'm not sure who proposed to whom.

Umm Hassane sent my mother a green embroidered robe and some prayer beads. My mother sent Umm Hassane dried mint from the garden of our house in Chicago, where she lived with my grandfather, who was now in his nineties and mellowed considerably. I conquered my fears and we were wed—not by a cleric, as Hajj Naji envisioned, but in a New York City apartment, in an extremely civil ceremony presided over by a family court judge I had interviewed for an article about domestic violence. The judge spoke so movingly about marriage that I wondered why I had ever been afraid of it. Marriage is a journey, she pointed out, not a destination; for a lapsed Catholic and an accidental Muslim, getting married by a Jewish lesbian judge, and about to leave for Baghdad, this seemed like the best possible map.

In September 2003 we packed our lives into a hundred boxes marked

NEW YORK: STORAGE and BEIRUT: SHIPPING. In October we followed our boxes over the sea to Beirut.

In Beirut, late-summer sun glinted off the Mediterranean. The rains had not really begun yet, and the sea still held the summer's warmth. Green-grocers lined the sidewalks with the last of the *jabalieh* tomatoes, big meaty pink and green fruits whose rippling flesh puckered into circles like little baboon butts mooning you all in a row.

Because we hadn't found an apartment yet, we were staying with Mohamad's parents. They wanted us to do one more wedding, an Islamic one. Then I would be family under the laws of God as well as man. But Aunt Khadija ("Cool Aunt") told them it didn't matter, and there was no time anyway—we were based in Beirut, but Mohamad had to go back to Baghdad. And so, in lieu of a honeymoon, I decided to go with him and try to freelance.

It was not bravery that took me to Baghdad but fear. When I thought about how it would feel to sit by the phone waiting to hear from Mohamad every day, wondering whether he was all right, my heart pounded in panic. It had been bad enough in New York, where I'd had my own life. What would it be like in Beirut, a strange city where I had no friends, no home, no ten-hour workdays to keep me exhausted enough to dull the fear? And so I decided that instead of sitting at home, waiting for the fear to find me, I would go out and find it first.

Abu Hassane wasn't sure about this plan of taking the new bride to Baghdad. But Umm Hassane clucked with approval. The way she saw it, Mohamad would have someone to take care of him—to cook for both of us and to see that he ate properly. That I intended to work (not like some other wives!) was the best part.

"It's good—she'll be working, not just sitting around," she would say, and nod. "And she can cook for Mohamad. He needs someone to take care of him."

Secretly, I think Umm Hassane believed Mohamad would be more careful if I was there in Baghdad with him. I would be her emissary, a spy in the masculine house of war. We didn't tell her that he'd probably be taking care of me more than the other way around. But there was a lot we didn't tell her.

Mohamad's parents grew more and more worried as our departure approached. Saddam Hussein was gone, and that was good; but Iraq was still no place for a nice Shiite boy, let alone his brand-new American wife. On August 19, a truck bomb outside the United Nations headquarters in Baghdad had killed twenty-three people, including the U.N.'s chief envoy to Iraq. Ten days later, a massive car bomb in Najaf had killed the Shiite Ayatollah Muhammad Baqir al-Hakim and more than a hundred other people. They watched this and other catastrophes unfold on Al-Jazeera with growing dismay.

"We sent you to America so you could get away from all this war," Umm Hassane would grumble, pointing at the television as if Iraq were just the latest chapter in the Lebanese civil war. Abu Hassane would nod. "And now you chose this job where you're going straight back into a war!"

Most reporters would sell their own mothers to land a war zone assignment. That meant nothing to Umm Hassane. To her, "bureau chief" sounded like a *mudir kabir,* a big boss. In Lebanon, a big boss sits in an office with shiny drapes. He waves his arm: coffee is fetched. He yells into his telephone: an army of underlings is dispatched. If her son was such a *mudir kabir,* why should he have to go to Iraq in person? He should ship some unlucky minion there while he stayed in Beirut. They didn't understand that covering Iraq made it possible for him to be in Beirut—that for their son, the road home led through Baghdad.

"What is this job?" she would demand suspiciously, as if the newspaper were trying to put one over on us. "How much do they pay you? Why can't they send someone else?"

They were proud of Mohamad's career: he had gone to America and returned a success. When he covered the Arab League summit in 2002, his Lebanese press card had translated "Bureau Chief" as *Kabir al-Murasileen*—literally, "Biggest of Correspondents," which made him sound like a king among correspondents. He won a silver journalism award shaped like a round medal; Umm Hassane thought it was the Nobel Prize, which it resembled, and when he handed it to her she held it at arm's length and harrumphed a little, to show what she thought of the Nobel people for not giving it to him sooner.

A few days before our departure, Mohamad's father came to us with a last-ditch conspiracy. "Don't go to Iraq," he begged. "I'll go to Dr. Nabil and get him to write a report saying you're sick. Then the newspaper will have to send somebody else!" Abu Hassane blinked his watery eyes, looking bewildered and frail, as Mohamad gently explained that he couldn't weasel out of a foreign assignment with a note from the family doctor.

Torn between pride and worry, Umm Hassane responded like mothers the world over: with food. She stuffed us as if layers of fat could cushion us against car bombs and RPGs; as if she might keep us in Beirut by making us too fat to heave our bodies away from the dinner table.

She made all of Mohamad's most beloved foods: *yakhnes,* the hearty vegetable stews with zucchini, okra, peas and carrots, fat green beans, or whatever else was in season. Glistening mounds of oily Lebanese rice cooked with toasted vermicelli. *Fattoush* with chopped scallions and cucumbers and mint bathed in garlicky lemon dressing. Salty hand-cut French fries that we dipped in fresh yogurt instead of ketchup. And for me she made *mlukhieh* and *freekeh,* the green leafy stew and the roasted wheat with chicken that were rapidly becoming my new obsessions. And of course, she made Mohamad's favorite, *mjadara hamra.*

Mjadara is classic peasant food, an ancient dish whose name means "the pockmarked one," for the dark lentils embedded in grain. But people also call it "the favorite of Esau," because they believe it was the biblical "mess of pottage," the famous red lentil stew that the hunter Esau traded for his birthright.

Most of the *mjadara* that you see these days is made with rice. But in Lebanon, especially in the villages, people still make it with bulgur, cracked parboiled wheat. And in some villages, people flavor it with onions caramelized so deeply they are almost charred. These blackened onions turn the whole dish a deep, dark reddish black that never fails to make me think of Esau telling his brother Jacob, "Quick, give me some of that red, red stuff." That's how they make it in the southern village where Umm Hassane grew up.

The first time I tasted *mjadara,* I couldn't understand why Mohamad rhapsodized over it so. It was just lentils and grain. But the red-black onion flavor lingered on my tongue: the burnt onions gave the *mjadara* a bacony depth. The bulgur was chewy, almost meaty, and had a lot more to say than rice, and I found myself craving that red, red stuff.

Very few restaurants know how to make *mjadara hamra.* Caramelizing the onions to this color without burning them is like making the roux for a Cajun gumbo—look away for just a moment, and it will burn, and even the most experienced cook will have to throw it out and start all over again. Umm Hassane stirred the onions for almost forty minutes, brought them just to the point of charcoal, and then there was always a moment where she looked worried, muttered that maybe she had burnt the onions after all, and if I had been sitting down instead of hovering over her shoulder I would have been on the edge of my seat. But she never burned them.

As she set down the dish, she never failed to remind us, flipping a reproachful hand toward the table: "You're not going to get *this* in Iraq!"

Mohamad was happy that I had decided to go to Baghdad with him. But as our departure date approached, we found ourselves erupting into little fights. This was not necessarily a bad thing: we were learning how to fight constructively, the way kittens learn how to hunt by play-fighting with each other. But it took a lot of practice. We fought over food, and over taxis, and over my halting attempts to speak Arabic. We fought over little questions like what we were going to pack and big questions like why we had decided to move to Beirut. We fought over French fries. But every time we fought over these very small things, we were really fighting over the larger question of what it would be like to be together in Baghdad.

A few days before our departure, we were walking down Hamra Street when I saw a rusty metal button on the sidewalk. Without thinking, I did what my mother had showed me as a child: I bent down, picked it up, and slipped it into my left shoe for luck. *Find a button, pick it up, all the day, you'll have good luck.*

"You can't do that kind of thing when we get to Baghdad," said Mohamad, frowning. He was not amused by my quaint midwestern superstitions.

He warned me that in Iraq I'd have to stop picking up coins and buttons and interesting hunks of metal. And I couldn't go wandering off to poke through piles of debris or break into abandoned buildings, other habits of mine that he failed to find endearing.

"Look, I'm not an idiot," I told him, starting to get angry. "I'm not going to walk around picking up strange objects in Baghdad."

"I'm not talking about picking up strange objects," he snapped, his voice suddenly taut. "I'm talking about objects that look familiar."

"Oh," I said.

During the invasion, American and British forces had fired cluster bombs loaded with submunitions that looked like batteries or pieces of scrap metal. Aside from these mass-produced munitions, insurgents were already planting diabolical little devices disguised as harmless everyday detritus—a tin can, a tire. These were improvised explosive devices, first introduced to the Middle East by T. E. Lawrence and others during the Arab Revolt against the Ottomans, when they trained their Bedouin cadres in the art of disrupting rail traffic by placing explosives along the tracks. Iraq's British-installed monarchy did not survive, but Lawrence of Arabia's tactics endured; now Iraqi insurgents were using them against the British and the Americans and whatever civilians got in the way.

There was an entire world of things I had never thought of. While I had been watching *Sesame Street*, Mohamad had been listening to a battery-powered radio announce which streets had snipers. While I had been digging trilobites out of the creek behind our house or building up my interesting-hunks-of-metal collection, he had been collecting artillery shells. I had visited this world for a few months in New York after September 11. Mohamad had grown up there. He knew its shifting, unwritten rules. Now I would have to learn them too.

The day approached when we would fly to Amman, the Jordanian capital, and drive across the border into Baghdad. The day before our flight, Umm Hassane made *mjadara hamra*. We were in the bedroom having one of our fights when she came to tell us it was ready.

Two child-sized white wooden beds dominated the room, side by side, divided by a nightstand. They were the beds Mohamad had slept in as a kid, and we had reverted to childhood ourselves: we each sat planted on a bed, arms folded, glaring into opposite corners of the room.

Umm Hassane stood in the doorway of the bedroom. She looked from one of us to the other, then back again. She narrowed her eyes in my direction and muttered a few gruff sentences in Arabic. Then she stalked off toward the kitchen, nursing her usual expression of strenuously withheld opinion.

Beautiful, I thought. I barely know her, and now she hates me. My ex-boyfriend's mother had blamed me for his drinking. Now this one blames me for her son's job. And I can't even communicate with her to explain that it's not my fault.

"What did she say?" I asked Mohamad. I looked toward his general direction from the corner of my eye, but without turning toward him, to show that I was still mad.

He sighed. He hates translating. He did it slowly, grudgingly; I could tell by the distance of his voice that he wasn't looking at me either.

"She said, 'What is he doing this time? Do you want me to beat him up for you?' "

Without moving my body, so he wouldn't think it was a truce, I inched my head around to the side. He was looking at me sidewise the same way. Our eyes met. We burst out laughing.

"We shouldn't fight," he said.

"Especially not over stupid things," I said.

We stood up and walked down the hall, into the kitchen, where Umm Hassane was waiting to serve us *mjadara*.

PART II

Honeymoon in Baghdad

Of all the countries that we know there is none which is so fruitful in grain. It makes no pretension indeed of growing the fig, the olive, the vine, or any other tree of the kind; but in grain it is so fruitful as to yield commonly two-hundred-fold. . . . As for the millet and the sesame, I shall not say to what height they grow, though within my own knowledge; for I am not ignorant that what I have already written concerning the fruitfulness of Babylonia must seem incredible to those who have never visited the country.

—Herodotus, *Histories, Book One*

Chapter 5

The Benefits of Civilization

I N OCTOBER 1929, a thirty-six-year-old Englishwoman named Freya Stark set out for Baghdad from the port of Beirut. She was disappointed to find the Iraqi desert crowded with cars, trucks, and six-wheeled tour buses, and signs in English imploring picnickers not to litter the desert with bags. At Rutba Wells, in the heart of Anbar Province, she found to her distress that the British military garrison served "salmon mayonnaise and other refinements," including custard and jelly. "Even now," she sighed, in a book she wrote to preserve the memory of the old Iraq before it disappeared, "the crossing of the desert is an everyday affair."

She was too late. Iraq was Westernizing rapidly. The British had installed a constitutional monarchy in 1921 (the same year, not coincidentally, that they had backed a coup in neighboring Iran). They had imported enough colonial officials from India to establish a mini-Raj, complete with English memsahibs who sipped tea, nibbled crumpets, and lamented The Servant Problem. In 1927, they had discovered oil in Kirkuk. Soon the Simplon-Orient-Express and Taurus-Express railways threatened to link London and Baghdad in a journey of just eight days.

For Stark, who had devoured *The One Thousand and One Nights* as a child, this was a catastrophe. In a few years, she predicted, the old Iraq would be gone—drowned in a tide of custard and crumpets and other unwelcome "benefits of civilization."

And yet, through her cynicism, she sensed the weight of some great power in that ride across the desert. So she added a hedge-betting line, one that time and history have polished up to a high reflective gloss: "Whether these Western floods, to which all her sluices are open, come to the East for baptism or drowning," she concluded, almost as an afterthought, "is hard to say."

Seventy-four years later, in the dark hours after midnight, Mohamad and I set out across the same desert road. We left Amman early to avoid the dangers of the road: militants and robbers—Iraqis called them Ali Babas—and the overwhelming heat.

Our driver was a lanky middle-aged man from Ramadi. He had a dark angelic face, weathered by years of desert driving, and a voice so soft we had to strain to hear him. He looked away shyly whenever addressing me and even when talking about me to Mohamad. His belt buckle announced its bootleg pedigree in massive, misspelled silver letters: *Calven Klein*. The supersized buckle pinned his red polyester shirt into stiff blue jeans and made him resemble an Iraqi cowboy. Silently, I christened him The Ramadi Kid.

His car was a "Jimse," the Kid assured us with soft-spoken pride as we loaded bags and boxes into the back. We would be safe inside it; we were his guests, under his protection. He invited us to lunch with his family, in Ramadi, on our way into Baghdad.

I was excited: already invited to lunch, and we weren't even in Iraq yet.

"We'll see," said Mohamad, in a tone that said, unmistakably: no. It was a generous offer, the famous desert hospitality in action, and I was eager to try Iraqi food. But Ramadi was the buckle in Anbar's banditry belt. Bringing a carful of foreigners to lunch was a good way to attract the Ali Babas.

After 1990, when the United Nations Security Council had imposed sanctions, few goods could enter or leave Iraq legally without United Nations approval. Many Iraqis relied on U.N. food rations—rice, flour, cooking oil, sugar, and other basics (including tea)—for survival. After the 2003 invasion, U.S. occupation authorities opened the borders and abolished import duties, and suddenly the benefits of civilization were flooding into Iraq once again: Food, stereos, satellite dishes. Opels, Renaults, Mercedes. Right-hand drives, left-hand drives, it didn't matter. Car-starved Iraqis christened the black Mercedes-Benzes "Lailas," after the Egyptian actress Laila Elwi. The huge white Toyota Land Rovers were "Monicas," after the former White House intern Monica Lewinsky. Towering tractor-trailers roared and surged past us as they made their way toward Iraq, loaded with cars, cattle, television sets, refrigerators.

The postwar traffic in goods flowed out of Iraq too. Upon his return from Iraq, an American scholar got caught at John F. Kennedy International Airport with three four-thousand-year-old cylindrical seals from the Iraqi National Museum. The sculpted limestone head of King Sanatruq I of Hatra, from the second century B.C., ended up gracing the mantelpiece of a Lebanese interior decorator. Three Lebanese nationals working for Iraq's American-appointed Interior Ministry were detained at the Beirut airport for trying to bring almost $20 million worth of Iraqi dinars into the money-laundering mecca of Lebanon. An entire country was for sale, everyone either buying or selling, our little Jimse a tiny speck bobbing on a river of loot that rushed between East and West.

All this wealth attracted the Ali Babas. There were no banks functioning in Iraq—no traveler's checks, no wire transfers, no cash machines. Foreigners came bearing currency, computers, satellite phones. Bandits and smugglers posted lookouts on the highways and in the rest stops. The grocer who sold you gas or served you tea might also be selling information on the side. A short while later, the Ali Babas would pull up behind you, outracing your bulky Jimse in swift, sleek BMWs. One car ahead, one car behind, and you were trapped: the Kid kept a hand grenade in his glove compartment for just this contingency. Surely Freya Stark, with her longing for the unexpected, would have approved.

After Amman, the landscape flattened, stretched itself out, and gradually slunk off into the night. I lay down, at Mohamad's suggestion. "It's safer if nobody sees you," he said. I didn't argue. I hadn't been able to sleep for days.

The Kid had fitted out his Jimse with dark curtains, like a Bedouin caravan, so his customers could travel invisibly. I drew the curtains and lay down with my head on my backpack. The two of them stayed up and talked softly in Arabic by the firefly glow of the dashboard light. "Road," I heard dimly. "Baghdad." And "Jimse," which rhymed with limps.

Most Arabic words are constructed from a root, usually three consonants, called a *jazr*. Vowels and other consonants weave in and out among the root letters, changing the form, pronunciation, and the meaning: with other letters, the root KTB becomes book, books, write, wrote, writer, library, bookstore. *Jimse,* I realized as I was drifting off to sleep, was an Arabized version of an American *jazr:* GMC.

I woke periodically and pulled back the curtains to look out into the darkness. I could see sand, sky, stars. No telephone poles or mile signs or truck stops. Occasional murmurs of orange light in the distance signaled that there were people out there guarding sheep or fixing cars or baking bread.

A truck flickered up ahead. It was pulled over by the side of the road, its headlights illuminating the driver prostrate in the sand on a small prayer carpet. He prayed toward the east, the direction in which we were driving; kneeling in the flood of light, a tiny, private flame in the cavernous dark, he looked like the only other human in the world.

I woke again as the Jimse pulled into a patch of dusty road off the side of the highway. It was a tiny store, not much more than a shack in the desert. We stumbled in half asleep, going in seconds from the velvety black-on-black of the road to a rainbow of packaging: Turkish candy bars with iridescent lavender wrappers. Posters advertising Gauloises cigarettes with a streak of French blue. Oily pink scented tissues that reeked of gasoline and roses.

We stood squinting at the excess, the highway still buzzing inside us. A thin, dark-faced boy rushed up to us, his windbreaker zipped up against the predawn desert cold. With an urgent expression, he thrust two little plastic cups at us. "Drink," he said.

What makes us civilized? Writers and scholars from the eighteenth-century biographer James Boswell to the French anthropologist Claude Lévi-

Strauss have suggested that cooking makes us human. But there is a more basic distinction between us and the millions of other species on this planet: We are the only creatures who share food with strangers, people not from our family or tribe, points out Cambridge University archaeologist Martin Jones in *Feast: Why Humans Share Food.*

If we can claim that civilization began anywhere, a good candidate might be Jerf el-Ahmar, a tiny village along the Euphrates about four hundred miles and eleven thousand years away from the road Mohamad and I were driving down. Jerf el-Ahmar and a handful of other sites mark a turning point in human history that the historian and archaeologist Gordon Childe christened the Neolithic Revolution. Anthropologists are still arguing about where and when it began—somewhere between eight and ten thousand years before Christ in the fertile crescent, but at different times in different places—and whether it was a sudden upheaval or a long slow evolution. But we do know that before that point, people lived nomadically, following herds of gazelles and fields of wild edible grasses whose location shifted with changes in season and climate.

And then (again, scholars still argue over why) people began to breed the wild wheat and barley they gathered for food. They settled down and began to live in one place. At Jerf el-Ahmar, archaeologists found some of the earliest evidence of permanent human habitation: grindstones, a storage pit, and, in a room that Jones points out may be the world's "oldest known 'kitchen,' " seeds of barley, mustard, and wheat. The barley had been cracked exactly like the bulgur we use in tabbouleh and *mjadara* to this day, and most likely for the same reason—to make it last longer in storage.

But the villagers of Jerf el-Ahmar also had fragments of obsidian from Anatolia in what is now modern-day Turkey, many days' travel away by foot. The earliest permanent habitation, then, contained some of the earliest evidence of travel. And therein lies one of humanity's most profound paradoxes: that we cannot travel, in the sense of leaving home and coming back, until we have a home to leave. Enter Cain and Abel, Jacob and Esau, farmer and rancher—those who stay, and those who roam.

Ibn Khaldun, the fourteenth-century Andalusian scholar, divided society into two categories, nomadic and sedentary. Most civilizations, he believed, begin like Bedouins—strong, proud warriors who survive on little beyond their basic needs. It is their nature to plunder. "Their sustenance," he wrote, "lies wherever the shadow of their lances falls."

Ibn Khaldun admired the Bedouin *asabiyah*, solidarity or cohesion, an attitude summed up by an old proverb still common in Iraq: "Me and my brother against our cousin; me and my cousin against the outsider." Travelers not under a tribe's protection were outsiders, and therefore rightful prey.

But inevitably, according to Ibn Khaldun, nomadic people succumb to the temptations of sedentary life. They settle down and start producing culture—law, art, architecture, cuisine. They erect great buildings, write books, and soon grow lazy and weak from eating too much rich food, especially food made with animal fats (an evil that Ibn Khaldun warns against on several occasions). They lose their *asabiyah*. A new crop of nomads comes, hardened by desert life and fat-free food, and destroys the decadent urban settlements. They tear down great buildings and use the stones to build campfires for cooking their simple nomadic food. They bring civilization back to its beginnings, and the cycle begins all over again.

But that is only one part of the story.

Crossing the desert is always a gamble. Will the people you meet kill you and rob your caravan? Or will they slaughter a camel or sheep, a symbolic sacrifice, and feed you with it instead? The outcome depends on a language (and I am not talking just about Arabic) that most of us do not fully understand. We cannot go on journeys unless we have a place to stop, food to eat and water to drink, somewhere to sleep in safety and people to give us these things.

And so the desert code of hospitality was born. Hospitality evolved as a way to ensure survival, not just of individuals but of a social network—a fragile web that supports human life in the vastness of the desert. This ideal of hospitality is beautifully articulated in the Old Testament story of Lot, which teaches us to protect guests because they might be angels in disguise. (It also teaches us to value the lives of male strangers more than those of our own daughters, a less beautiful ideal.)

The Arabic language retains in its DNA a history of water and survival in the desert. Before Islam, the word *shariah*, the path to God, meant the path to a watering hole. The word for spring, *ain,* is the same as the word for eye—both are essential; both produce water. Arabic folklore and literature abounds with stories of Bedouins who die nobly giving their share of water to another. To this day it is a desert tradition to greet outsiders with a liquid: a glass of water in the heat, a cup of tea against the frigid desert night.

I thanked the boy sleepily and drank the tea. It was sugary hot and tannic. Light and heat shot through my limbs, calming the highway buzz and anchoring me in place, at least for a moment.

I was already internalizing the tyranny of tea, the millions of gallons of minuscule glasses hospitality forces you to consume in the Middle East. In Beirut, tea was a sign that your meal was over; you drank your tea, shook the cup, set it down, and said, *"Daymeh, inshallah"*—may it always be, God willing. Here it was something more basic: a welcome.

Hospitality, whether offered by an emperor or an illiterate goatherd, is what makes us civilized. Without it, the junk that we think of as "civilization"—cars, crumpets, salmon mayonnaise in the desert—can disappear overnight. Any traffic in goods can be disrupted, by sanctions or Ali Babas or the looters of the so-called civilized world. But the old custom of hospitality to strangers, of entertaining angels, still survived.

Mohamad bought a package of Turkish cookies, puffy biscuits mortared together with a sugary pink paste. We ate them together, the chemical sweetness of the cookies dissolving into the ferric tea.

I looked at my husband. He looked at me and smiled.

This is why I'm here, I thought. We have drunk oceans of tea, and we will drink oceans more—*daymeh, inshallah.* But this one we are drinking right now, right here, together.

And so our honeymoon began here, with this elemental act of kindness: a small, anonymous offering in the bottomless desert night.

Chapter 6

"Iraq Has No Cuisine"

FTERWARD, WHENEVER ANYONE asked me what Baghdad was like, I would tell them about the topiary.

Like a lot of Americans, I had a particular mental image of Baghdad, made up of a montage of Gulf War footage and old Douglas Fairbanks movies: palm trees, minarets, tanks, lots of sand. When we rolled into Baghdad under the strong October sun, I expected to see certain things. Topiary was not among them. But there it was, dark green hedges neatly trimmed into rippling, abstract carnival shapes, like Joan Miró paintings come to life. I looked out the window and thought there was another Baghdad, just like the other Lebanon, that was different from the one on TV.

The topiary lined the wealthier neighborhoods, like Mansour and Jadriyah, setting off the façades of mansions. The mansions of Baghdad! They were the real clash of civilizations, a frantic pastiche of international kitsch. Some had high vaulted entranceways, like old-fashioned banks. Some looked like toy crusader castles, with cylindrical turrets and half-moon windows. A few were built to resemble Roman ruins. Others echoed the Alhambra, but with modern accents: a massive diamond-shaped window, glazed silver-blue, or an enormous inverted pyramid resting on its point. The most ornately Orientalist houses, with arched windows and latticed balconies, flaunted the most enthusiastically Western touches. A miniature Taj Mahal with a baroque wrought-iron gate. An Ottoman villa guarded by a tall Victorian lantern. Most of them were in good repair: their owners had prospered under Saddam.

To enter Baghdad in those days was like walking into a time capsule. Whole neighborhoods looked like the set of an early James Bond movie: Soviet cars, curved white plastic chairs, abstract expressionist art. The country had spent the past several decades cut off from the rest of the world, conducting a dialogue with the past. The result was a cargo-cult fascination with idols the rest of the world had replaced long ago. After a few months in Baghdad, I was no longer surprised when people stopped in the middle of a conversation and broke into songs by The Doors or Bryan Adams.

Centuries collided. A bent-backed little donkey pulled a wooden cart past the giant gray metal elephant of an armored personnel carrier. Contractors in shiny white four-by-fours muscled farmers riding tractors to the side of the street. The poor lined up and waited a day and a half for subsidized gasoline; those who could afford the extra few dollars bought jerry cans of black-market fuel at the side of the road. Barefoot children hawked gasoline, Kleenex (or the Middle Eastern knockoff, Khaleenex), straw hats, Marlboros, and red plastic roses to people trapped in traffic.

Low-slung buildings squatted and baked under the sun, surrounded by walls, scrubby trees, the ever-present dust of a city constantly trying to keep out the desert. If Los Angeles had experienced a brief burst of oil wealth, then been sealed off from the rest of the world for several decades, it would have looked a lot like Baghdad: long highways, swollen with more cars than they had been designed for, squeezing the city like pythons. A vindictive oily smog. A city of roughly five million people, sprawling and complicated, bisected by a river; a few of its major bridges shut down; main traffic arteries closed off with tanks and checkpoints whenever there was an attack or the threat of an attack, which was several times daily, or whenever an official traveled from one military zone to another in a massive armored convoy; big bullying white Jimses full of contractors who might open fire on anyone, at any time, for any reason; and no cell phones to communicate with wives, husbands, or children waiting anxiously. All of these frustrations, which were the general conditions on a good day in Baghdad in late 2003, made for the mother of all traffic jams.

And then we came to the Tigris, where everything changed. The river threads through the heart of Iraq and splits the capital city in half, a long, supple line of water fringed by trees. The unrelenting squareness would have been oppressive without the river and the date palms: tall, generous towers that soared upward until they exploded, arcing green in every direction. Trees that mimicked the graceful spray of a fountain.

I spent seven and a half months in Iraq, stretched out over fifteen months, most of them with Mohamad. A short period in a long war; a honeymoon of sorts. A time in which many things were possible, until they weren't.

The big newspapers rented mansions. Freelancers and smaller papers like *Newsday* set up shop in hotels, a cavalcade of them, ranging from the shabby to the terrifying. All of them were in the Red Zone, which was anything outside the fortified U.S. military compound called the Green Zone. We drove directly to the Hamra Hotel in Jadriyah, a quiet residential neighborhood.

The Hamra consisted of two big, blocky Bauhaus-inspired buildings with a courtyard in between. A man sold carpets and jewelry in the vestibule of the main entrance. A sign on the door said: PLEASE NOTES: ALL GUNS MUST BE LEFT AT SECURITY DESK.

Mohamad and I dumped our dusty bags on the bed and headed downstairs to the restaurant. Through the lobby, past the café with its orange chairs, we came to the courtyard between the buildings. There was a swimming pool—the famous Hamra pool, a shimmering blue—and around it a galaxy of white plastic tables and chairs. We hadn't eaten anything since Jordan but cookies and tea, and we were ravenous. I ordered *fattoush*, the salad I had loved in Beirut; hummus; and chicken tikka, the local name for what they called *shish taouk* in Beirut.

With *fattoush*, the secret ingredient is the assembly, the tightly choreographed contrast of opposing elements. You have to keep the ingredients separate until the last possible minute, so the bread doesn't soak up too much liquid; it should provide a crisp, crunchy counterpoint to the soft lettuce and the juicy tomatoes. The tangy dressing binds the different elements together. Sometimes the souring agent is lemon juice or pomegranate molasses or both. Sometimes it's sumac, the maroon powder that tastes like a thousand lemons bursting open in your mouth. In Lebanon, *fattoush* usually comes with a light dusting of sumac—enough to "open your appetite," as people say in Lebanon, but not enough to make your taste buds run screaming.

This *fattoush* was different. Someone had strafed it with so much sumac that eating it was like sucking on a bottle of citric acid. The bread was heavy and soul-crushingly soggy. It wanted to dissolve into waterlogged slime, but it was impregnated with rancid frying oil that kept it stiff. The iceberg lettuce had gone transparent from its long bath in the dressing, whitish and shriveled, the way your fingers get when you soak in the tub for too long. It recoiled limply, chewy and stringy as a bowl of rubber bands. The tomatoes were grainy, staring resentfully up from their sumac bath at the bottom of the plate as if to say: eat me if you dare.

Defeated by the *fattoush,* I turned to the hummus. It looked like hummus always does: a round plate of beige paste, dimpled in the middle, dusted with more of the inescapable sumac. It was paler than any hummus I'd known, a little stiffer than usual and weirdly translucent, like edible beige Noxzema. But hummus is hummus—what could go wrong? Tearing off a piece of bread, I dug in.

In Buffalo I had briefly worked on a house-painting crew, and although I had never actually tasted the various pastes I had smeared into walls, this hummus reminded me of grout. Somehow it managed to be slimy and chalky at the same time. It was nothing but canned chickpea paste with water—a lot of water—blended in. (Adding one ice cube to hummus gives it a light, creamy texture; adding more than one is a trick some restaurants pull to save money.) No tahini, no garlic, no lemon juice. No olive oil. And it had been sitting in the kitchen for a long, long time.

I looked at Mohamad.

"I should have warned you," he said, smiling a tight, rueful little smile. "The food here's pretty bad."

I was embarrassed. I had read an armful of books about sanctions and Saddam. But still, this was something I had not expected. The Middle East was not a region I had ever associated with inferior food.

"Is it all this bad? Or just here?"

Of all the foreigners in Baghdad, Mohamad was one of the few who didn't disparage Iraqi food. He pulled off a piece of the football-shaped baguette, troweled up some of the joint compound, and put it into his mouth. He chewed on the stuff and considered the question.

"Iraqis," he said, "have really good bread."

War destroys supply lines. It disrupts the natural order of ingredients and labor. It forces people to concentrate more on sustenance than on taste. It seemed crazy, even criminal, to come to a war-torn country, to a people crushed between occupation and insurgency, and expect a decent meal.

But I knew from Mohamad and other Lebanese that food was one of the few things that had kept people going during their grim and endless war; that eating good meals, in the company of people they loved, helped them endure what was happening. How did Iraqis manage without that?

It wasn't just the Hamra. At the Hunting Club, the playground of the country's petro-elite, they served wads of gristly meat buzzing with a nimbus of lethargic flies. Other upscale restaurants weren't much better. The menu never varied: meat. Meat kebabs, fried meat, boiled meat. Meat with rice, meat with bread, meat with meat. All of it larded with the dripping white globs of fat that Iraqis adored but everyone else loathed.

It wasn't the war. Iraqi food, everyone said, was just plain awful, even before the invasion. Some speculated it was genetic; others cultural. Most assumed it was endemic to the place. An American journalist who spent years in Baghdad described Iraqi food as "a war on your taste buds."

As the war dragged on, Iraqi cuisine became a standing joke among the contractors, aid workers, war correspondents, and other outsiders flocking to Baghdad. People laughed about going on the "Iraqi Atkins." Vegetarians nibbled piously on pasta and hummus. A few converted back to carnivorism out of sheer desperation. Iraqi food, everyone joked, was the real weapon of mass destruction.

The harshest critics were other Middle Easterners: Syrians, Iranians, Lebanese. In Iran, when people want a derogatory term for Arabs, they reach for the ancient epithet "lizard-eaters"—a Persian slur, centuries old, against the traditional Bedouin diet. "The Iraqis have *never* had good food," maintained Rebecca, a Lebanese friend of ours who was working as a translator in Baghdad. "My father used to travel here on business before the first Gulf War, and it was the same way then. Their restaurants were terrible. All the Lebanese would bring their own food!" She added something I would hear a lot in Lebanon: "We've *always* had the best food."

Much later, another journalist I knew summed up the prevailing opinion. After years in Baghdad, she had a rare sensitivity and compassion for Iraqis. But she had no sympathy for their food. "How can you write about Iraqi cuisine?" she asked, with an incredulous laugh, when I told her I was writing this book. "Iraq *has* no cuisine!"

I wondered. In New York I often heard people expound with serene authority on the blandness of midwestern food. According to these urban sophisticates (many of them transplants from the hinterlands themselves), we Hoosiers subsisted on potato-chip casserole. Our cuisine consisted of opening cans; our spices were salt and pepper. We had souls of Wonder Bread.

Yet I'd grown up eating persimmon pudding, a traditional southern Indiana recipe perfumed with cinnamon, ginger, nutmeg, and cloves. My mother cooked morels from the mossy flanks of the dark wet woods. She took me to the Porthole Inn for peppery fried catfish, served with hush puppies, crisp little balls of cornmeal with melting soft insides. Chicken trucked in before dawn to Hays Market by farmers from the countryside—birds that tasted more like bluegrass and wild chicory and wet earth, more like *chicken,* than the shrink-wrapped little cadavers from Perdue. Cornbread so sweet it could make you swoon. Apple butter so rich it should have been sued. Real midwestern food tasted like foxfire and sassafras, primeval forests, and wild spicy meadows of black-eyed Susans and Queen Anne's lace.

So when East Coasters held forth on our bland midwestern cuisine, I would just nod and keep my mouth shut. *You go right ahead and say that,* I'd think to myself. *More persimmon pudding for me.*

What if Iraq was the same way?

The food foreigners were eating in Iraq—which was not necessarily the same thing as Iraqi food—tasted bad. But was it bad because Iraqis were uncivilized, lizard-eating Bedouins who had never mastered the culinary arts? Or was there something else going on?

Once you asked that question, the whole equation changed. It might be arrogant to expect good food from people beaten down by decades of war, sanctions, and dictatorship. But it was also arrogant not to. Saying a country had no cuisine seemed like saying it had no culture, no civil society. That hideous meal at the Hamra was a challenge, a riddle. This was the Fertile Crescent, where civilization and agriculture began. It had to have a cuisine, and I suspected that cuisine would be good. I decided to go out and find it.

Chapter 7

Becoming Human

A LONG TIME AGO, in a country far away, there is a king named Gilgamesh. He's brave and handsome. He's two-thirds god and one-third human. He builds the metropolis of Uruk, with its great wall, the biggest city the world has ever seen. When a terrible flood destroys the city, he builds it back again.

But gradually Gilgamesh starts to go bad. He takes the young men from their fathers and destroys them. He demands to sleep with brides on their wedding night. "He struts his power over us like a wild bull," people start to grumble. The people of Uruk appeal to the gods for help.

The gods go to Aruru, the goddess who started all the trouble by creating Gilgamesh and the entire human race. "You have do something about this guy," they tell her. "Make us a man who can kick his ass."

Aruru sighs, closes her eyes, wonders why she didn't take up archery instead. Then she washes her hands, pinches off a piece of clay, and molds it into a guy who can kick the mighty ass of Gilgamesh.

Enkidu is shaggy, long-haired, and twice as tall as a normal man. He lives in the wilderness outside the city walls. He strides around naked, drinking at the watering hole with the animals and eating grass with the gazelles.

One day a hunter sees Enkidu crouched at the watering hole. The wild man looks up. Their eyes meet. Suddenly the hunter realizes this hairy savage is the animal rights activist who has been wrenching his traps out of their holes, filling in his pits, and untying wild animals from his snares. The hunter is so terrified that he runs all the way back to the city, straight to Gilgamesh, and pants, "You gotta do something about this guy."

The mighty Gilgamesh, just like the gods before him, immediately runs to a woman. And what a woman! Shamhat—part priestess, part prostitute. She works the temple of Inanna, the goddess of love and war. Shamhat knows exactly how to handle this wild man: she goes straight to the watering hole and takes off all her clothes. When Enkidu sees that, he immediately forgets about his animal friends.

Shamhat brings him out of his state of nature with the world's two oldest and most effective civilizing influences: first she sleeps with him until he is "sated with her charms." This takes exactly six days and seven nights.

And then (they must be pretty hungry by this point) she takes him to get some food and beer. He stares at it and squints: What is this stuff?

> Enkidu knew nothing about eating bread for food,
> and of drinking beer he had not been taught.
> The harlot spoke to Enkidu, saying:
> "Eat the food, Enkidu, it is the way one lives.
> Drink the beer, as is the custom of the land."
> Enkidu ate the food until he was sated,
> he drank the beer—seven jugs!—and became expansive
>   and sang with joy!
> He was elated and his face glowed.
> He splashed his shaggy body with water,
> and rubbed himself with oil, and turned into a human.

* * *

If you're anything like me, the first thing you think after hearing this ancient Mesopotamian epic of food and sex and civilization is: So what did they *eat?*

In the beginning was the word. With the word came the ability to say *I'm hungry.* So not long after the word came the recipe.

Until the 1980s, scholars believed the oldest cookbook in the world was *De re coquinaria* ("On the Subject of Cooking"), a collection of Roman recipes believed to be compiled in the late fourth or early fifth centuries but attributed to the first-century Roman gourmand Apicius.

Then a French historian named Jean Bottéro began to painstakingly translate three cracked clay tablets, originally from southern Mesopotamia, at Yale University's Babylonian Collection. Most historians believed that the tablets contained pharmaceutical formulas. But when Bottéro started translating the wedge-shaped cuneiform writing, he discovered that the tablets held a collection of about 40 recipes dating back to around 1600 B.C.—making them not just the first Iraqi recipes or the first Middle Eastern recipes, but the first recipes, that we know of, in the history of the world.

Bottéro, ever the academic, did not consider the tablets "cooking manuals" in the modern sense of the word—they were more like records of the palace cuisine and its rituals. But in the essential ways, the tablets are as unmistakably a cookbook as my mother's dog-eared, butter-stained old copy of *Fannie Farmer*. The recipes (which were probably dictated to scribes by different cooks) contain instructions for a series of stews and sophisticated, tantalizing arrangements of meat and grain. Some are terse professional lists of ingredients (like those of Elizabeth David, who gives no measurements for ingredients or cooking times). Others deliver meticulous instructions broken down by individual tasks (like those of the talkative, generous Julia Child). The basic actions are the same ones we carry out in our kitchens today: split open the chicken, take out its gizzards, sear the flesh, add water. Our anonymous cooks (who were probably men) even trussed the bird's legs with string, exactly as we do today. And they gave credit for borrowed recipes: they attributed one recipe to "the Elamites," who lived in what is now southeastern Iran, and labeled another "Assyrian style." The most appealing, complex recipe is for an elaborate poultry dish seasoned with onions and herbs and served in a two-part bread crust with a top and a bottom: 3,600-year-old chicken pot pie.

But what did they eat? The tablets don't tell us exactly, because they were written about a thousand years after the Gilgamesh era (the period when the character the epic is based on supposedly lived), which scholars believe was around 2600 or 2700 B.C. But thanks to Bottéro and other translators of ancient texts, we have a better idea than ever before, and what's most surprising about these ancient recipes is not how strange they are but how little some things have changed.

We know that the Mesopotamians liked stew, and as the Iraqi cookbook author Nawal Nasrallah points out in *Delights from the Garden of Eden*, her definitive guide to Iraqi cuisine, their vegetable and meat stews evolved into the *margas* that are a staple dish in Iraq to this day. We know that the ancient Mesopotamians drank a lot of beer. (They even had a beer flavored with pomegranates, which is something I wouldn't mind trying.) They also liked cracked, parboiled, and roasted grains very similar to modern-day bulgur and *freekeh*. They made bread from barley, wheat, and emmer, the ancient strain of wheat better known today as farro. And we know they liked strong flavors: along with herbs and spices such as coriander and cumin, a lot of the stew recipes in Bottéro's tablets end with some variant of "add crushed garlic, onions, and leeks"—an instruction I would remember later, when Mohamad's mother showed me how to make her zucchini stew.

About 3,600 years after Bottéro's cooks dictated their recipes, give or take, I was cooking chicken stew with an Iraqi refugee named Ali Shamkhi. He was living with two Iraqi friends, also refugees, in a neighborhood on the outskirts of Beirut. The three men fed themselves and fought off homesickness by making traditional Iraqi food, occasionally calling their mothers in Iraq to get advice on recipes. Ali cooked the bird in a way I had never seen before: first he washed it under running water in his kitchen sink, whispering "*Bismillah,*" "in the name of God," in respect for the meat we were about to eat. He boiled it for about five minutes in just enough water to cover the meat. Then he strained off the chicken stock from this initial boil, and—much to my distress—poured it down the drain.

"We pour off the water from the chicken when we first boil it to take away the gamy smell," he explained. "The chicken tastes better this way."

I noticed this again and again when Iraqis cooked. They would boil meat, rice, fish—even vegetables like okra—for a few minutes first. Then they would pour off the water and add a new round, sometimes even switching to a new pot, for a second cooking. Something about this practice nagged at me. I had heard of it, but where? Then I remembered: that was how the Sumerian cooks instructed their readers to prepare poultry. (Bottéro called it their "mania for washing meat after each cooking stage.") Iraqis have been making stews this way for the past three and a half thousand years.

After the Neolithic Revolution, but before Gilgamesh—historians don't know exactly when, but probably well before 3,000 B.C.—people figured out that the land between the Tigris and the Euphrates would be a lot greener if they could control the mighty waters of the two rivers. They dug canals between the rivers, invented irrigation, and settled down as farmers. Suddenly they needed to keep track of things like seasons, surpluses, and seeds. And so writing followed not long after—which is probably why the goddess of grain, in ancient Mesopotamia, was also the goddess of writing and book-keeping. (The Mesopotamians also had a goddess of beer.)

Bread was the heart of this agrarian revolution. In Akkadian cuneiform, the Semitic language of Bottéro's tablets, bread was synonymous with food: the word for eating, *akâlu,* was the symbol for bread going into the symbol for mouth. Babylonian clay tablets from around 2,000 B.C. list at least three hundred kinds of bread, all with different ingredients, flavors, and cooking methods. They made loaves shaped like human hands and even women's breasts—a sly reference to bread as the essential, original food.

The Mesopotamians baked a lot of their bread in a *tinuru,* a cylindrical clay oven with an open top and diabolically hot radiant heat inside. They rolled the dough into little round pats and left them for the gluten to relax. Then they flattened them into pancakes and slapped them onto the oven's scorching inside walls, where they bubbled into chewy flatbreads.

Thousands of years later, Iraqis still make bread exactly this way at neighborhood bakeries. The Akkadian word for eating, that little bread-in-mouth ideogram, survives to this day as the Arabic verb *akala,* "to eat," and the closely related noun *akil,* "food." (The three-letter root AKL becomes food, eat, dish.) The Akkadian *tinuru* lives on as the Arabic *tanoor,* the Iranian *tanura,* and the South Asian *tandoor.* Next time you order chicken tandoori at an Indian restaurant, chew on this: you are speaking a word that human mouths have been pronouncing, in one form or another, for at least four thousand years.

Chapter 8

The Movement of Democratic Lovers

OUR ROOM AT the Hamra had a real kitchen, so on our second day in Baghdad, I went looking for groceries. I ended up in *souq al-ajanib*, the "foreigners' market," in which the only foreigner I ever saw was myself. It became one of my favorite places in Baghdad and I went there often, especially when I needed the consolation of produce. Romaine avalanched off the backs of trucks. Handwoven baskets overflowed with dark purple figs, wrinkled and soft as a baby's balls. Eggplants gleamed like giant obsidian teardrops. In dark storefronts, bananas dangled from the ceiling on hairy strings like bait from some giant jungle spider. And the tomatoes: deep, wet, and red, piled in bloody pyramids like the heads of Hulagu's victims. On that first visit I bought tomatoes and oily black olives imported from Turkey, and that night, instead of eating downstairs in the restaurant, Mohamad and I dined on pasta puttanesca.

Puttanesca is my favorite pasta sauce. Like a good friend, it is flexible and forgiving; reliable, constant, yet also willing to evolve. And like a good friend, it can be there for you in about twenty minutes when you really need it. And then there is the name: "the pasta of prostitutes." Legend has it puttanesca was invented by working girls who needed a sauce they could whip up and wolf down between clients. These food origin myths are almost always apocryphal, but they flavor the dish. The name gives puttanesca a residual taste of sex—this, it says, is a sauce for working women.

There were a few desperate moments when I was pitting the olives with a blunt paring knife. I cursed myself for leaving the Leatherman in Beirut and wondered if I had come all the way to Iraq only to become some kind of demented housewife. But then I remembered the spackle they were serving downstairs and suddenly making puttanesca in Baghdad didn't seem so irrational.

We pushed our computers and sheaves of printouts and Iraqi newspapers to one side of the table. We opened a bottle of Massaya, an excellent Lebanese wine that you could get in Baghdad, and sat down to eat.

"I'm glad you're here," said Mohamad.

A few days later, Mohamad and I went to visit the Institute for War & Peace Reporting, a nonprofit group that trains independent reporters in post-conflict zones—which Iraq, at that point, was supposed to be.

I sat in on a class taught by Maggy and Hiwa, journalists that Mohamad knew from his previous stints in Baghdad. The students bombarded them with questions. They were all eager to write real stories, not the propaganda they had been raised on, and tell the world what was happening in Iraq. Most of the students were in their twenties, but there were also a couple of retired military officers, older men who had wasted their youth fighting wars they did not believe in and wanted to begin a new life. What they wanted was so much, but it seemed possible at the time—to cross decades in the space of one summer, to vault over the past thirty-five years in a single, exuberant leap.

"Before, we couldn't say anything," said a thin, passionate young Communist named Salaam. "So now we are trying to say everything at once—just talking about food, or anything." Salaam was the first Communist I had ever met who praised George W. Bush, but he would not be the last.

After class, I sat outside at a picnic table talking to the students for a long time. There was a muscular twenty-one-year-old named Ali with a slow, crook-toothed smile. He was driving from Babylon and back every day—a four-hour commute—just to take the classes.

"He's a warrior!" said a girl with pale, delicate features and sandy blond hair. She sat on the picnic table and tipped her tiny round chin in the air looking from Ali to me with a fierce expression.

For a split second I was angry at being interrupted. But then I decided

I liked her fearlessness: how she planted herself on the table and presented her opinion as though I should have asked for it.

Her name was Roaa. I hired her as my translator. But like most translators, she ended up being much more.

In 1951, an Iraqi sociologist named Ali al-Wardi delivered a famous speech at Baghdad University. Revisiting Ibn Khaldun, the fourteenth-century philosopher who divided civilization into nomads and urbanites, Wardi outlined two coexisting tendencies in Iraqi society: *badawah,* or bedouinism, and *hadarah,* or settled civilization, which he equated with urbanism and modernity. "The traditional Ibn Khaldun view is that there are two kinds of people: the city dwellers and the nomads, always in conflict," Faleh Jabar, a prominent Iraqi sociologist and author, told me. "Ali al-Wardi reverses this: he puts both sides in the same person, the same character. He transforms it into a kind of psychological struggle—a schizophrenia, if you like." This struggle, Wardi argued, defined the history and character of Iraq—and, by extension, the entire Middle East.

By the mid-twentieth century, Iraq was one of the most modern countries in the region. Despite the religious and ethnic divisions in Iraqi society, Baghdad had a thriving civic life: a museum of ancient art, a museum of modern art, a symphony orchestra. Its hospitals and universities attracted students from all over the Middle East. The Bauhaus architect Walter Gropius designed a library for Baghdad University whose towering arches, Iraqis told me decades later, symbolized an open mind. In 1948, Iraq became the first Arab country to grant women the right to vote. Eleven years later, the government appointed the Arab world's first female cabinet minister. That same year, a personal status law prohibited child marriage and strengthened Iraqi women's rights to divorce, inheritance, and child custody. The literacy rate soared: "Cairo writes, Beirut publishes, and Baghdad reads," went the well-known saying. If Beirut was the Paris of the Middle East, then Baghdad could claim to be its London or its Berlin.

But there were still deep divisions among Iraqis, which the Baath Party exploited when it seized power in 1963 and again in 1968. A secular movement that emphasized pan-Arab identity, the Baath channeled the revolutionary fervor sweeping through the region. The party conducted bloody purges of writers, intellectuals, artists, and professors, and even among its own ranks. The few remaining Iraqi Jews were "Zionist agents." Iraqi Shiites were Persian infiltrators. Iraqi Communists were Russian spies. Show trials, followed by public executions, reinforced the old proverb: me and my cousin against the outsider—or else.

The main power broker in this new regime was Saddam Hussein. He was a man of the rural tribes, from a class the urban elites dismissed as "those who eat with five," meaning the five fingers of their hands, the Bedouin way. But the Bedouin way won in the end. (Ibn Khaldun, who always did like to side with winners, would probably have blamed the bourgeois silverware.)

By the mid-1970s, the Iraqi president was mostly a figurehead: his cousin Saddam, who headed an elaborate web of intelligence networks, was effectively running the country. Saddam supervised the nationalization of Iraq's oil assets, seizing them from foreign companies just as prices began to rise during the oil crisis; oil revenues went from $1 billion to $8 billion in just over two years. Much of this new revenue went toward weapons and the military. But there was enough left over to build highways, hospitals, and water filtration plants, and to fund agricultural and industrial projects. In the 1970s, Iraq's economic and social development, as measured by the World Bank, ranked with European countries like Czechoslovakia and Greece.

But Saddam had already begun to wall off Iraq from the outside world. "Teach the child to beware of the foreigner," he instructed in a speech, published in 1977, to employees of the Ministry of Education, "for the latter is a pair of eyes for his country and some of them are saboteurs of the revolution." Giving your business or even your child a foreign name was suspect. Meeting a "foreigner" was enough to get you interrogated. When Saddam finally became president in 1979, he purged the Baath Party once again and filled top government posts with loyal tribesmen, his cousins and uncles and brothers-in-law.

That same year, an Islamic revolution ousted the tyrannical shah of Iran and brought the Shiite Ayatollah Ruhollah Khomeini to power. In 1980, alarmed by the ripples among Iraq's Shiite majority, Saddam invaded neighboring Iran. Western countries, including the United States, and their Arab allies lavished him with aid, weapons, and intelligence support throughout the Iran-Iraq War.

The eight-year war killed at least a million people in total, drained Iraq's oil wealth, and left it billions of dollars in debt to other countries, including its neighbor Kuwait. The tiny desert kingdom refused to forgive Iraq's debt. Saddam invaded in August 1990, and the oil-rich American ally Saudi Arabia worried that it would be next. The United Nations Security Council isolated Iraq and imposed sanctions that prevented Saddam from exporting his oil.

In January 1991, a large U.S.-led force drove Iraqi troops out of Kuwait and rolled into southern Iraq. President George H. W. Bush urged Iraqis to rise up against Saddam, and they did: rebellions flared in the southern Shiite heartland and the mostly Kurdish north. But Bush and his advisers feared that if Saddam's Sunni-led regime fell, the Shiite majority would take power—and align itself with Iran. The U.S. military allowed Saddam to crush the rebels using helicopter gunships. Once the regime put down the uprisings, it executed tens of thousands of Iraqis, mostly Kurdish and Shiite rebels. By the end of Saddam's reign, his regime had executed at least several hundred thousand of its own citizens.

U.N. sanctions remained in place until the U.S. invasion in 2003. Throughout the 1990s, up to half a million pounds of raw sewage poured into the Tigris every day, because Iraq was banned from importing the chemicals and equipment needed for water filtration plants. With no oil exports and little economic activity, Iraq's currency collapsed. Food prices shot up: by August 1995, wheat flour cost 400 times the prewar price. Peoples' salaries became almost worthless. Middle-class families had a hard time affording basic food staples like eggs and milk. Meat became a luxury. In 1988, 7 percent of Baghdad's children had shown signs of childhood obesity; by the mid-1990s, hundreds of thousands of Iraqi children were dying from a lethal combination of malnutrition, tainted water, and infectious disease.

By the mid-1990s, researchers for the United Nations Food and Agriculture Organization estimated that 567,000 children under the age of five had died as a result of sanctions. (Later estimates put the number closer to a quarter million—still very high.) In a 1996 television interview on *60 Min-*

utes, CBS correspondent Lesley Stahl asked Madeleine Albright, then the American ambassador to the United Nations, if isolating Saddam's regime was worth so many deaths. "I think this is a very hard choice," said Albright, in a comment that she later came to regret, "but the price—we think the price is worth it." By 2003, most Americans had forgotten Albright's remark. Many Iraqis had not.

Sanctions did little to hurt Saddam and his cronies: his inner circle managed to get whatever they needed, thanks to oil smuggling and hoards of cash. He turned the U.N.'s oil-for-food program, meant to feed impoverished Iraqis, into a lucrative kickback scheme. But by plunging average Iraqis into poverty, sanctions had made them even more dependent on the regime: a schoolteacher earning $10 a month was not going to imperil her food rations by criticizing Saddam. Iraq had become, as the Iraqi writer Kanan Makiya described it in his 1993 book *Cruelty and Silence,* a giant prison. During that era, Iraq's educated middle class began to sell its books—one more link with the outside world—in order to buy food. In Wardi's historic struggle, there was no doubt which side had won.

Roaa was born in Baghdad in 1980, the year the Iran-Iraq War began. Like other young Iraqis, she learned how to fire a Kalashnikov in grade school. The teachers instructed the children to call their president "Uncle Saddam," and at the beginning of every class, she shouted with all the other students, "Long live the great Saddam!"

In 1988, as the war waned, Saddam's troops sprayed poison gas on the Kurdish town of Halabja. About five thousand people died—some within minutes, their bodies frozen in agony where they fell, and thousands more later as the poison attacked their nervous systems. Roaa and her family are Kurdish, and several of her aunts and uncles died at Halabja. She was eight years old.

Roaa's father worked for Iraqi Airways as a flight engineer, a good job that put them comfortably in the ranks of the Iraqi middle class. Her parents traveled to Turkey, Greece, Lebanon—even to China and Japan. When she was a child, they took her to Canada for two months and France for a month. Those early trips made her eager to learn foreign languages and see the world. But after the first Gulf War, when sanctions banned flights into and out of Iraq in 1990, her father lost his airline job, and they joined the rest of the disappearing Iraqi middle class.

Roaa and her brothers belonged to a generation of young Iraqis whose intellects were going to waste, and they knew it. Anyone born after 1968 had grown up never knowing a world without Saddam. Girls like Roaa dreamed of the things their miniskirted mothers had reveled in—travel, parties, advanced degrees. "When my mother talks about her life, and the fun that she had in the sixties and seventies, it makes me feel that I have missed my life," Roaa told me once. "It's not just me. All of us feel this way."

One of their few connections to the outside world was Shabab TV, "Youth TV," a television channel owned by Saddam's son Uday. Shabab TV would occasionally play bootleg versions of American movies, and one of them became an icon for young Iraqis: *The Truman Show*, the 1998 film whose hero is the unwitting star of an elaborately constructed reality TV show. "For Iraqis my age, it is exactly how we lived under Saddam," she told me. "You were always being watched—you were never alone, not even at night, in bed."

Roaa and her family lived near one of Saddam's many palaces. In early 2003, as the invasion loomed, they were afraid their small house would be bombed. In case they had to leave suddenly, they each had a suitcase packed. They had to decide what they would need if they never saw their home again.

Looking over her room, Roaa realized that her most important possessions were the stuffed animals her schoolmates had given her. She took a teddy bear from her best friend, yellow with gray ears, that she had named Champagne, "because he was exactly the same color as champagne."

A year later, telling me about her bear, her eyes filled with tears. "It might not be very important to other people, but it is for us, because it is our memories," she said, a little defensively. "I don't like to throw things away. I like to keep every small detail of myself. It's important, because that's all what is left to us from the past."

The past had not left her much: a few pictures and a teddy bear named for a drink she had only tasted once, years ago. At the age of twenty-three, she was preparing to die without ever having lived.

* * *

When the war came and their house was not bombed, Roaa found herself thinking for the first time about a future. Before, she had dreamed of being a diplomat and visiting foreign lands. But for her generation, weaned on myth and propaganda, Iraq itself was terra incognita: even within the country, the regime had kept close tabs on where people went and who they talked to. Now her journalism classes gave her a chance to explore her own country and communicate with the rest of the world.

For average Iraqis, travel still wasn't easy—they needed new passports, which required bribe money, and countries willing to issue visas to Iraqis. But in the summer and fall of 2003, foreigners began to converge on Baghdad: Nepalese Gurkhas, American contractors, Lebanese civil war militiamen, Chinese restaurateurs, British travel writers, and Iraqi exiles who had fled to London, Paris, and Beirut decades earlier. By the time I got to Baghdad in late 2003, half the world was already there.

The city was changing. In the months after the invasion, marriage rates went up; rents went up; newlyweds moved in with their parents, and divorces went up. On commercial drags like Arasat, Photoshopped vinyl banners shouted the names of brands that were flooding in over the country's newly porous borders: Samsung. Davidoff. Gauloises. In the public squares, hand-lettered signs in Arabic and English announced proud new political parties and groups whose very names thrilled with optimism: The National Front of Iraqi Intellectuals. The Movement of Democratic Lovers of Iraq. The Iraq Humanity and the Aggrieved Families Society. The Nexus of Retarded Civilians. The Organization Defenders with Outzoom from Iraqi People.

It was the first time I had been in a foreign country for longer than two weeks. Everything seemed new and strange to me too. Customs were different: Iraqi men walked down the street arm in arm, nuzzling each other's necks like lovers, but Mohamad and I couldn't hold hands in public without attracting attention. Iraqis talked about Hammurabi and Ashurbanipal as if they were relatives who just stopped in for tea last week. People had a wild, cockeyed sense of humor. The guys at the Internet café across from the Hamra decorated the walls with printouts of homemade jokes, one of which said: "Dont worry if your computer crashes it is only a matter of BOMBS!"—punctuated by a smiley face and the clip art icon for a computer bomb.

I started spending time with a crowd of artists, poets, and playwrights—hanger-outers at cafés and bookstores, chain-smoking intellectuals who held long, passionate conversations about art and literature and Jim Morrison. They called themselves *Al-Najeen*, "The Survivors." Most of them were young men in their twenties: Basim Hamed, the sculptor who had replaced the famous statue of Saddam in Firdous Square, that Iraqis and American soldiers had pulled down the day Baghdad fell, with a modernist sculpture of an Iraqi family against a sun and crescent moon; Basim al-Hajar, the playwright who debuted a play in the ruins of the Al-Rasheed Theater less than a month after the regime fell; and Oday Rasheed, a thirty-one-year-old filmmaker who was shooting Iraq's first postwar feature film. After many rejections (most editors wanted stories about insurgents) I had managed to convince a newspaper to take an article about Oday's film. Roaa and I made an appointment to meet him and his friends at their apartment.

Roaa liked the *Najeen* boys; we both considered them friends. But as we walked through the busy streets trying to locate their apartment, she started to look around uneasily. When we got to the dark, narrow alley outside their building, she stopped and looked up at the sooty windows with an expression of uncertainty and fear. She didn't want to go in.

"You don't understand," she said. "In our culture, it is this sort of thing—going to the house of some men . . ." she trailed off. "If anybody were to see me going into this house, they would say I was doing wrong things."

The phrase "wrong things" came up frequently in my conversations with Iraqi women. Its very vagueness was corrosive: you could imagine anything, and people did. It had the power to keep women like Roaa from visiting a group of gentle, intelligent men her age. It kept women out of public life; out of any life except the kitchen.

"Look, you don't have to come in," I said, probably less patiently than

I should have. "The guys speak enough English, I can talk to them. You can go home."

She took a deep breath. "No," she said, and set her little chin.

"This is one of the old ways of things, one of the things we have to leave behind," she said. "I still respect my culture. I would never do something that would harm Islamic culture. Never. But everything is changing—the world is changing. And if we stay in the same mind as a hundred years ago, we will never change anything."

And with that, she walked across the alley and into the building.

Chapter 9

The Sumer Land

A FEW WEEKS AFTER we arrived, our Lebanese friend Rebecca took us to dinner at the hotel where she was staying, which was called the Sumer Land. "Wait until you taste their *shish taouk*!" she told us, and then gave it her highest compliment: *"It's almost Lebanese!"*

Nationality aside, it was real *shish taouk:* chunks of chicken breast stained orange with spices, marinated in yogurt until it was tender and juicy, nothing like the hard brown pellets at the Hamra. We resolved to move into the Sumer Land as soon as we could. This required a triangular onslaught of meetings: first between Rebecca and Muhammad, the hotel's manager, to convince him to give us a room at her special rate ("Don't be a fool—they're ready to move in, but you have to give them a good price!"); then between Mohamad and Muhammad; and finally among Muhammad, Mohamad, and me, to consummate the deal by drinking coffee out of little china cups in his office.

Muhammad the manager was a tall, stooped man with a sagging mustache. He seemed like a dour fellow at first, as he shuffled around the dark, echoey marble-tiled lobby. Everything about him sloped and sagged, like an empty suit hanging from a hook. But he warmed up to us once we moved in and even showed a slouching sense of humor. Muhammad and his employees had a cynical camaraderie, and we formed friendships in the lobby, the restaurant, the Internet café. We settled in and started to feel at home.

Our room even had a little kitchen, with a real stove and a sink and a small refrigerator. We started going to the markets more, and eating more

Iraqi food: near the hotel there was a bakery where you could buy falafel and another where you could get *tanoor* bread. The falafel place made its sandwiches on *samoun,* a baguette-like bread that Nawal Nasrallah refers to as a "domesticated version" of French and Italian bread, and slathered them with mayonnaise. We started buying just the falafels themselves, then wrapping them in *tanoor* bread with fresh vegetables from the market. At home, we would eat them with hummus that I made myself, with imported Lebanese olive oil and a pinch of Iraqi *bharaat,* a spice mixture heavy on black pepper, cumin, coriander, and cinnamon.

Mohamad missed the food in Lebanon, and I loved finding food in Iraq, so we made our own fusion creations with Iraqi ingredients made Lebanese style. We developed a ritual: after reporting all day, we would stop at the markets for a bag of bread and whatever fruit or vegetables were in season—tomatoes, okra, figs, and the legendary Iraqi dates. I got hooked on *tamur rutab,* the fresh dates picked early in the season. They were unlike any other dates I'd ever eaten—juicy and featherlight on the inside, with a skin so sheer it crackled when you bit into them.

But on days when we were too tired to cut tomatoes or traffic was too heavy to get to the markets or the bakery was out of bread—or all of the above—there was always the Sumer Land's restaurant. It was another world: the 1950s orange-and-brown décor; the chunky brick walls; the rustic summer-camp tables carved out of thick slabs of wood. I would go into the kitchen sometimes, just for a look, and the portly cook would laugh. He always wore a clean white chef's vest. I eventually convinced him to make me an entrée of the vegetables the restaurant normally served only on the side: zucchini, carrots, and cauliflower perfectly sautéed in butter. It got to the point that whenever the restaurant staff saw me coming, they would chant: *"Shajar, jazar, wa qarnabeet?"*—"Zucchini, carrots, and cauliflower?" Hussein, the tall, talkative young waiter, would try to tempt me with new dishes: "Today we have shrimp, direct from Basra," he would say, leaning over our table, whispering conspiratorially, "and they came in a *refrigerated truck!*"

The Sumer Land served a brilliant appetizer, a cross between the modern Middle Eastern staple of *kibbeh* and a deviled egg, with roots that went back to medieval Iraq: the Egg Basket. It resembled the fried ball of meat and grain called *kibbeh qras* in the Levant. Shaped like an egg but varying in size, the classic *kibbeh qras* consisted of two layers: a thin, crisp layer of cracked wheat and meat blended together forms the shell of the "egg." Spiced ground meat, sometimes mixed with pine nuts, made the yolk. Most places left it at that. But the chef at the Sumer Land would cut out two quadrants from one side of the *kibbeh*, leaving a strip in the middle like the handle of an Easter basket. Then he hollowed out the inside and slid in half a hard-boiled egg, sliced lengthwise. He topped this concoction with gooey orange Russian dressing, so that it resembled the stuffing in a deviled egg. The Egg Basket was like an Easternized Scotch egg or a Westernized *kibbeh*, depending on where you came from; a cross-cultural pun par excellence, a play on the form and function of *kibbeh* and egg. In fact, it was a culinary echo of medieval Iraqi cooks, who concealed hard-boiled eggs in their meatballs to surprise and delight the guests. It filled you up and made you happy and cost about two dollars.

An Iraqi friend told us that before the war the Sumer Land had been famous for its parties—wild, Beirut-style bacchanals where Iraq's prewar elite would end the night by dancing on the tables. The image of the lugubrious Muhammad presiding over such debauchery seemed unlikely. But when Mohamad asked him about it, the manager's gloomy face drooped into a nostalgic smile. "Yes, our parties were the best," he sniffed, squinting down his pendulous nose. "People used to come from Mansour, from all over. The Hamra was *nothing*."

Late one night, at around 10:30, I was sitting in the Sumer Land's Internet café when a tall woman walked in. Something about her commanded attention. Maybe it was the baby-pink sweatsuit, which seemed unusual for Baghdad. Or it could have been the long, honey-gold hair tumbling over her shoulders in careless waves; her slender waxed arms; the birdwing arches of her nose. Whatever the reason, the men in the room sat up straighter, the women tried to ignore her, and one by one, all the male hotel staffers found an excuse to drop by the café.

I noticed her a few more times after that. She would always come in late at night, and although she seemed to know the hotel staff very well, she didn't speak to anybody else.

The next time this mystery woman came in I said hello in Arabic. She looked back at me, her tawny eyes calmly assessing, and without much preamble she demanded in English, "Did you make love with your husband before you were married?"

I knew the hotel staff had probably told her who Mohamad and I were. But I didn't know who she was, or anything about her, and in Iraq you didn't discuss your sex life with strangers.

"What do you think?" I said finally.

She laughed, and then smiled sleepily. We were friends now, or at least accomplices. She reached out and rubbed the fuzzy golden hairs on my forearm. "This!" she scolded. "Why you don't take care of this? Your husband will like you better."

"Oh, I don't think he really cares about that kind of stuff," I said.

"Ha," she barked. With satisfaction she added, "He will leave you."

The first time I visited Layla's room, she was sitting in a chair crammed close to the television. There was barely enough room for the sofa and a couple of armchairs in the claustrophobic living room of her suite. Grubby handprints greased the walls. Her two daughters, six and seven years old, both as beautiful as their mother, were playing video games on a computer. The screensaver was a picture of Saddam after one of his famous swims across the Tigris, a reenactment of his watery escape after failing to assassinate Iraq's prime minister in 1959. The dictator was dripping wet and wearing nothing above the waist but a dazzling white smile. Layla was watching *Friends*.

"I love Ross," she sighed, closing her eyes dreamily and draping an exquisitely manicured hand over her heart.

I visited Layla often over the next year. We would sit in her living room and share coffee, tea, cigarettes, and Arabic sweets. Layla was around my age, in her early thirties. She had studied art and classical poetry at Baghdad University, but quit her studies when she got married at twenty-three. She had divorced her philandering husband a few years before the war. "He was very tender, very romantic," she said. "But he didn't really care about me and our girls. He just wanted my money."

When Layla found out Mohamad and I were on our honeymoon, she was appalled: a newlywed, and I was already letting myself go—no pedicures, no waxing, and hair that had never known chemicals. "Eastern women, we like to look beautiful for our husbands," she said.

She looked at me accusingly, as if I were part of some American imperialist uglification campaign.

"They like us to be beautiful," explained her niece, Shirin, who was visiting her that day. "Soft."

"Also, they like us to have big breasts," said Layla. Lifting her T-shirt, she exhibited a shiny padded beige bra. "Iraqi women, we have bigger breasts than American women," she said, and tucked her T-shirt back in.

After we'd known each other for a few months, Layla decided to save my marriage by giving me a full Iraqi makeover: legs, arms, eyebrows, manicure, and pedicure. "I will call a woman, a friend, and she will come to the hotel," she said, looking happy to have a project. "She can do everything except hair. For coloring you must go to the salon." I didn't tell her that the only time I'd had my hair done at a salon was the day I married Mohamad, or that I hated it so much I ran home before the wedding and scrubbed off the hairspray encrusted to my scalp.

Before the war, Layla went to mixed-sex parties where she could wear the fashionable clothes she liked, and "talk, dance, laugh—things that girls do." She went to concerts by Lebanese pop stars at the Alwiya Club, where Uday Hussein was said to have held his birthday party. Tickets were $50—a fortune for most people in Iraq, especially after sanctions. She didn't miss a single show. She traveled abroad without a *mahram*, the male chaperone required when women left the country. The rules did not apply to people like her.

"I did everything I wanted," she said. "That's why I'm not happy now. Because before the fall of the regime, I had more freedom."

Layla was a Baathist in spirit, if not a party member. Ethnically, she was Kurdish; but above a certain tree line of wealth and privilege, ethnicity or sect didn't matter as much as it did for others down below. There were plenty of Shiite and Kurdish Baathists. Her friends were Christians, Kurds, Shiites, Sunnis; it didn't matter. What mattered was money, and she had plenty. Layla owned a mansion along the Tigris. But after the invasion, she couldn't live in it; she was too kidnappable. Fortunately, the owner of the Sumer Land was a family friend, so she moved into the hotel with her daughters.

Despite her fanatical devotion to beauty, hardly anyone ever saw Layla: she rarely left the Sumer Land. She reminded me of a British colonial official, dressing for dinner every night so as not to let civilization go to the dogs. She seemed to pass most of her days sitting alone in the cramped living room, drinking coffee with perfectly manicured hands, watching Rachel and Ross and the gang prance around their fairy-tale apartments in sinful coed luxury and dreaming of herself among them.

A beautiful woman yearning for David Schwimmer and Saddam Hussein. It surprised me at first. But it made sense: to her, they both meant freedom.

Chapter 10

The Flavor of Freedom

If you go into any town, eat of its vegetables and onions,
for they drive away the sickness special to that town.

—*The Medicine of the Prophet,* Mahmud bin
Mohamed al-Chaghhayni

A FTER A FEW weeks in Baghdad, Mohamad hired a driver named
Abu Zeinab, a cheerful giant who drove the tiniest red car in Baghdad. (Abu Zeinab is a *kunyah,* a nickname derived from the name
of the firstborn—in this case, "father of Zeinab," his four-year-old daughter. In much of the Arab world, parents usually name themselves after firstborn sons, but among Iraqi Shiites it is not uncommon to take the name of a
firstborn daughter.)

One day Abu Zeinab was driving us along the Tigris when we passed a
grove of date palms the size of a football field. Tall, graceful trunks marched
off in stately rows. The tops wove together into a green canopy. Grass grew
underneath them so Granny Smith green I thought at first it was AstroTurf.
Looking out over this oasis from Abu Zeinab's hot little car, wedged in acres
of diesel-fumed traffic, I realized it had been months since I had touched
grass. And just like that, the homesickness got me.

Back in Chicago, my mother wrote me e-mails describing fall in the Midwest: the magnolia tree was shedding its leaves. The crab apples glowed
like bright red cherries. The deer invaded the backyard every evening and

looked up, startled, when they heard the screen door slam. The air smelled like wood smoke and cinnamon.

Homesickness was exactly that—a sickness. A misalignment of the limbs. A chemical imbalance in the blood. Body and soul out of balance from trying to straddle two different places at once. My skin remembered the precise level of moisture in the air; it rebelled against the heat, the dust. My feet recalled the exact surface tension of New York City pavement, northern Illinois soil, hardwood floors. My eyes needed green.

If you couldn't bring the body back to the place it remembered, you did the next best thing: you brought a bit of the place to where the body was. You could fool your metabolism, at least temporarily, with music. You could numb it with drink. But the best way to trick homesickness, as every traveler knows, is with food.

After that first, disastrous meal at the Hamra, I asked every Iraqi I met about food. Even then, people were growing tired of politics. But everyone loves to talk about food. And food was one of the few things I could talk about in Arabic.

In the beginning, I simply wandered around Baghdad, speaking to people in the little Levantine dialect I knew. Pickles in Beirut are *kabees*, "pressed." In Baghdad they're *mkhallal*, "the vinegared," or *turshi*, a Farsi word for pickle. In Lebanon zucchini was *kusa* or *courgette;* in Iraq, it was *shajar*, which in Lebanon meant "tree."

But even when I knew the words, I couldn't understand the guttural Iraqi accent. Their words were heavier; they clanked with consonants the Lebanese would simply swallow or spit out. If Iraqis didn't understand me, it might be because I'd gotten a word wrong; it might also be that I was using a Levantine word they'd never heard before. The times I actually communicated seemed like small miracles, and I would whisper the words to myself like a blissful incantation: *Dajaj:* chicken. *Mai:* water. *Rumman:* pomegranate. *Masquf: masquf.*

I started asking everyone to recommend a favorite dish. Everybody said the same thing: *masquf.* You have to try *masquf.* The best place for *masquf* used to be on Abu Nuwas, along the Tigris . . .

Here they would sigh, and a montage of expressions—pleasure, pride, and regret—would pass across their faces.

Nowadays, they would resume, the best place to get *masquf* is a restaurant in Karada, next to the leather factory. Here, I'll write it down for you . . .

The search for food led me to the places where Baghdad was at its best. Karada was my favorite neighborhood, especially the long and bustling market street of Inner Karada. American magazines described Iraqi women as cowering in their homes, kidnapped and raped if they set foot outdoors. The streets of Baghdad, according to these accounts, were empty of the fairer sex. But Karada swarmed with women: working-class Iraqi women didn't have servants to do their shopping. They had to work, get groceries, and pick up their kids. They wore short-sleeved T-shirts, long black *abayas*, and everything in between. The women wearing *abayas* billowed along the sidewalks like black jellyfish. Every so often, a hand shot out to snare small children, point out tomatoes, or clutch the surging black cloth underneath a rounded chin.

At Mahar *masquf* shop, the man led me to a bathtub where fat gray carp circled sluggishly. He asked me to choose my victim. I pointed to the liveliest one. The cook reached in and grabbed the fish, laid it on a worn wooden plank, and smashed its head with a mallet. The fish lay stunned, but not quite dead—I had chosen that one, after all, for its fierce attachment to life.

Starting at the back of the fish's head, he slit it down the spine with a knife, then grabbed each side of the incision and turned the fish inside out. The two halves of its own face gazed inward at each other in a macabre kiss. Pressing it open with quick, strong hands, he flattened the fish, now thoroughly deconstructed, into a large round O. He folded it between the metal jaws of a hinged barbecue rack (later, I visited more traditional places that propped their fish up on little wooden sticks). He splayed it out over a large open vat of smoldering wood.

"Come back in one hour," he told me, "and your *masquf* will be ready to eat."

* * *

There was a phrase Iraqis were always using: the flavor of freedom. For a lot of Baghdadis, that flavor was *masquf*. It was more than just a fish, or a way of preparing it; the ritual of *masquf* embodied a vanished place and time and way of life.

Masquf can be made anywhere—they make it in Basra, or even, these days, in Beirut. But it is meant to be savored in the open-air restaurants on Abu Nuwas, the corniche along the Tigris where Iraqis used to stroll at sunset.

Traditionally, the best *masquf* was made from barbel, a carp-like fish that Iraqis have been eating since the ancient Mesopotamian days. But *masquf*'s flavor also came from the hour of anticipation while you waited for your fish. During that hour, people would eat, drink, gamble, and talk. Girls and boys would stroll up and down the corniche laughing and making eyes at one another. Mothers and fathers would rent boats and float up and down the moonlit river, drinking in the sound of music and laughter over water, the flickering fires, the smell of roasting fish from the riverbank. "The important thing on Abu Nuwas was drinking *arak*," explained Salaam, the young Communist I had met at Maggy's journalism class, who had become a good friend, "and eating *meze* like *jajik* while you waited for your fish to be done."

Abu Nuwas had its heyday in the 1950s and '60s, when the city rented out small plots along the riverfront every summer. Families would take them for the season and set up temporary wooden ramadas with roofs woven out of river reeds. On hot summer nights, everybody would head for the riverfront to talk, play the oud, take boat rides, and eat *masquf*.

Some people said *masquf* was imported by the Ottomans. Others maintained it was a Babylonian tradition, thousands of years old. Muslims claimed it was a Christian dish (the Christian taste for fish being well known). Christians whispered that it was a specialty from the old Jewish quarter along the river (the Jewish affinity for fish being well known). Some believed it had come from the Mandeans (the Mandean love for the river and its waters being well known).

I found this frustrating. I wanted facts, dates, scholarly references, not a vague mash of exoticized nostalgia. Everybody talked about *masquf*, but nobody knew where it came from. Etymology was no help: as with many

Arabic dishes, its name describes the form of the dish more than its contents. *Masquf* means "the ceilinged," from *saqf,* "ceiling"—a poet's description of the fish spread out over the fire like the roof of a little open ramada.

Ancient Sumerian tablets mention fish "touched by fire," an ambiguous phrase. Herodotus wrote that three Babylonian tribes lived on fish alone, but according to his detailed description, they dried their catch in the sun, pounded it in mortars, and made it into cakes or "a kind of bread." (An Iraqi from the marshland tribes told me they still make fish this way.) Pedro Teixeira, a Portuguese merchant-adventurer who traveled through Baghdad in 1604, noted that "Fish are plentiful and good, and the Moors use them." But the usually thorough Teixeira does not say *how* the Moors used the fish. And so it was with all the sources I could find: the more I read, the more people I asked, the more *masquf* and its origins receded into mystery.

In Iraq, as everywhere, food was an instant geographic indicator. There was the famous black pickle of Najaf, made with date syrup; the tiny, delicate okra of Hillah; the tender and juicy kebabs of Fallujah. There was a kind of oven-roasted lamb that is a specialty not just of Basra but of one particular family in Basra. This culinary GPS system often overlapped with sect. "I can enter an Iraqi house, and from the food I can tell if they are Sunni or Shiite," an Iraqi man once boasted to me. "I'm not saying that Sunnis don't make Shiite dishes, or vice versa. But you do have certain foods that are associated with certain places."

Masquf was one such dish. It might be made in other cities, but its soul was still in Baghdad. It got its flavor from the Tigris, even when the fish never touched its waters, and from Abu Nuwas Street.

Abu Nuwas Street was named after an eighth-century poet. He was a companion of the Caliph al-Amin, son of Haroun al-Rashid, the storied caliph of the Arabian Nights. Nicknamed the "Father of Locks" for his luxuriant hair, Abu Nuwas was a bisexual bon vivant famous for his *khamriyaat,* "wine songs"—hymns in praise of wine and the nights he spent drinking it with beautiful girls and boys. He was the patron poet of bars and drinking and unrepentant freedom. "Accumulate as many sins as you can," he wrote once, because when Judgment Day arrives, and you see how forgiving and gracious God is, you'll gnaw your fingers with regret at all the fun you didn't have. "[So] drink the wine, though forbidden / For God forgives even grave sins."

The nomadic bards of pre-Islamic Arabia padded their poems with grandiose invocations like the famous *qifa nabki*, "halt, and let us weep." They wept over the abandoned campsite, the spot in the desert where the caravan of their lovers had once stopped, and the romance of endless travel. The formula persisted long after poetry moved to the cities; in medieval Baghdad, citified poets who wouldn't know a camel if it bit them in the behind were still invoking the cold campfire, the traces in the sand, the lost ladylove. Abu Nuwas mastered the old nomadic form first. And then he updated it with a parody more suited to modern urban life: "This loser stopped to talk to an abandoned campsite," he wrote (the paraphrase is mine), "while I paused to ask what happened to the neighborhood bar."

In the 1960s and '70s, a generation of Iraqi intellectuals discovered a world of ideas, debate, and friendship on Abu Nuwas Street. The Iraqi journalist and memoirist Zuhair al-Jezairy described how Baghdad's relationship to the river changed as the street and its restaurants had evolved: "The river became a kind of lung by which the city breathed—a boon for the eye and the spirit."

Faleh Jabar grew up in Baghdad during the golden age of Abu Nuwas Street. Today he is a well-known sociologist and author. But back then he was a penniless young student, eking out a living with occasional writing and translation work, "producing horrible sentences" out of his precious *Webster's Collegiate* dictionary. Every evening, Jabar and his circle of friends would gather at Abu Nuwas and spend long summer nights drinking, talking, exchanging books and arguments and ideas.

One night, a friend of Jabar's brought his wife to the café. Some of the *masquf* restaurants had introduced "family sections," where families could eat together. But for young men and women who weren't blood relatives to mingle at cafés and bars—to sit and drink together in places where alcohol was served—was still shocking. Nobody had seen anything like it. The place was in an uproar.

The owner came to their table. "We don't have a private section for families," he said, meaning no women allowed.

"It's none of your business," replied the lady, her green eyes flashing. "I'm drinking tea. Is there anything in the Quran, in the *shariah*, or in the law, that forbids drinking tea in a café with my husband? With my cousins, with all my brothers?"

Such a thing could happen only on Abu Nuwas, Jabar told me—lowering his voice and looking back over his shoulder as if, thirty years later, the café owner might still hear him.

After the Prophet Muhammad's death in 632, the leadership of Islam passed to a succession of caliphs. The caliph was the "commander of the faithful," the political and military leader of the worldwide community of Muslims, and the city where he lived was the caliphate—the capital of the Muslim world. In 762, the Caliph al-Mansur moved the caliphate from Syria to Iraq. He built the round city of Baghdad in a small but strategic site on the banks of the Tigris. He christened his new capital *Medinat al-Salam,* the City of Peace, and immediately set about constructing an enormous palace.

Then as now, Baghdad was a city of *souqs.* Every profession had its market: the silversmiths, the booksellers, the perfumers. And right in the middle of the bustling marketplace, surrounded by soap makers, butchers, and cooks, stood the caliph's new palace. Just as the palace was finished, an ambassador from the Byzantine Empire came to visit.

Scribes and scholars tell different versions of what happened next—*kan ya ma kan,* as the storytellers say; literally, "it was and it was not," or "once upon a time." But here's more or less what took place:

"How do you like my city?" the caliph asked his Byzantine visitor, expecting lavish praise.

"Indeed, you have built a palace like no one before you," said the ambassador. "Yet it has one flaw: the markets. Because they are open to all, your enemy can enter, and the merchants can pass on information about you. The leader who lives close to his subjects can have no secrets."

The caliph frowned, went stiff, and considered flying into a rage.

"I have no secrets from my subjects," he said coldly.

But as soon as the Byzantine ambassador left, the caliph ordered his servants to bring a wide garment. He unfurled it across the table and drafted a new plan for the city on its fabric. He banished all markets from the city center, leaving only a few *baqqals,* greengrocers whom he barred from selling anything but vinegar and greens. He moved the markets across the river, putting each merchant in a specific place, with the butchers at the very end because "their knives are sharp and their wits are dull." With a stroke of his pen, he rewrote the city.

Saddam Hussein fancied himself among the great caliphs. He too built a palace along the Tigris; he too rearranged the city. In 1968, after its second coup, the Baath Party had banned the renting of small plots along the river. In the mid-1980s, Saddam began his assault upon Abu Nuwas Street and its culture of cosmopolitan freedom. He diverted water from the river to feed his palace's fountains and swimming pools. He fenced off its banks with barbed wire. He posted guards along Abu Nuwas who watched pedestrians with hard eyes. He tore down blocks of old Baghdadi houses, with their graceful cantilevered balconies, and replaced them with a row of identical brown brick townhouses. Ugly as they were, these brownish barracks were prime real estate, rewards for loyal party henchmen; Saddam filled them with his Republican Guards, "and with that," wrote Jezairy, "the river became their prize." The street of the drunken bisexual poet, of *masquf* and beer and summer nights, turned into a district of drugs and prostitutes and wild dogs. Some restaurants still sold *masquf* along the river. But with the eyes and ears of the regime all around, it had a different flavor.

During sanctions, the sewage pouring into the Tigris made it too polluted for fishing, and the *masquf* trade shifted to Karada. Now the fish were farmed in giant hatcheries, trucked into the city, and sold out of bathtubs on Karada's sidewalks or at restaurants like White Palace. The fishermen who had once made their living catching *shabout* and *bunni* from the Tigris went elsewhere or died out.

In June of 2003, Jabar returned to Baghdad for the first time in almost twenty-five years. He headed straight for Abu Nuwas. Near the Jumhuriyah Bridge, he looked down at the Tigris; once a silver ribbon, it had become a poisonous chemical green. A metal fence blocked off the water from anyone foolish enough to approach. Whorls of concertina wire grew along the riverbank like a mutant metallic weed. *Qifa Nabki*—halt, and let us weep.

But then, looking closer, Jabar saw a gap in the fence. Somebody had cut a ragged hole with wire clippers. A toothless, wrinkled face peered up at him from the riverbank: an ancient fisherman, a remnant of the old Abu Nuwas.

"What's this fence, who put up the fence?" Jabar asked him.

"It's been there for twenty years," said the old man.

"And who cut this hole?"

"We did it," he said, triumphant. "We took back our river for the first time in twenty years."

The old fisherman told Jabar he would wake at dawn every day, go to the fish market in Karada to buy *bunni,* and bring them all the way to the river, where he would put them in a pool to keep them alive—just to grill *masquf* by the side of a river too polluted to fish from. Economically, it made no sense: the money the old man spent on gas was probably more than the little he made from the handful of fish that he sold. But that wasn't the point; the point was to be there by the river, making *masquf.* "He couldn't leave that place," said Jabar. "The river was his home."

Back at Mahar, in Inner Karada, my *masquf* was finally ready. Each part of its surface had been licked by radiant heat until it was roasted golden brown and fragrant, like a giant, edible fishy halo. They had wrapped it in *tanoor* bread and packed it with a plate of chopped onions and tomatoes and parsley.

The flavor of *masquf* comes from the wood over which the fish is grilled. Applewood is prized, but other fruit trees—pomegranate, orange, and apricot—are good too. The surface that faced the flames directly had a leathery outer layer that was charred in a few spots. But underneath that was tender white flesh with a delicate wood smoke flavor. I have never eaten trout right after it has been smoked, but I imagine it might taste something like *masquf.* Using scraps of *tanoor* bread, I pulled off pieces of the white flesh. I folded them into tiny sandwiches, alternating smoky mouthfuls of fish with an acidic burst of tomato and onions and parsley. At the time, Mahar served only takeout, so I'd intended to take my *masquf* somewhere and eat it sitting at a table. But I was so hungry by the time I got it, and its firewood flavor was so irresistible, that I devoured the entire fish in the car with Abu Zeinab in the middle of a Karada traffic jam.

Chapter 11

Iftar Alone

IN LATE OCTOBER Mohamad and I were walking down the street in Baghdad when we heard a husky, teasing voice exclaim, in Lebanese Arabic: "Mohamad Ali! Do you remember me?"

We turned around and saw a lanky, wicked-looking fellow with dark brown eyes and curly black hair. This was Maher, whose brother was Hanan's ex-husband, and it taught me something about the interconnected nature of the Middle East, not to mention diasporan family relations, that Mohamad didn't seem particularly surprised to run into his sister's ex-brother-in-law strolling down the sidewalk of a foreign capital with a population of five million.

Maher was an independent filmmaker, a freelancer like me—or as he put it, throwing his arms wide and flashing a double-edged smile: *"Je suis libre—comme Irak!"* He was staying with Hazem, a reporter Mohamad knew from Beirut, who worked for the Arabic newspaper *Al-Hayat* ("Life"). They were at the Cedars Hotel, but it was too bombable, so Mohamad got them a room at the Sumer Land. They lounged around their hotel room in baggy white T-shirts chain-smoking, telling stories, and drinking whisky with the television blasting. Neither of them spoke much English, so our conversations veered wildly from Arabic to English to French. They were both ex-Communists, both as crazy as bandicoots, and I adored them.

In addition to being our honeymoon, the fall of 2003 was the first time Mohamad and I had been in the same country for our birthdays, which are eleven days apart. That fall Mohamad's birthday also coincided with

the beginning of Ramadan. When Hazem and Maher heard about this align-
ment of special occasions—honeymoon, Ramadan, two birthdays—they
decided to celebrate with an impromptu hotel-room *iftar*.

Iftar is the dinner that breaks the daylight fast during the month of Ramadan. But ours was thoroughly secular; an infidel *iftar*. Maher had brought
a bottle of *arak* all the way from Beirut. It smelled like my first night at
Baromètre, back in May—by this point, that felt like years ago. But on that
October evening, with the Lebanese diva Fairouz playing in the background,
three languages colliding, and the cold astringent fire of *arak*, Beirut's liberal intellectual life didn't seem so far away. I made hummus with olive oil
and Iraqi spices. Hazem and Maher made scrambled eggs with *sujuk*, and we
ate *makdous*. I could feel my Arabic fluency rising miraculously as the level
of *arak* in the bottle sank lower and lower. I would forget it all the next day,
and the hangover wouldn't help, but for one night, I felt like I was exactly
where I belonged.

Ramadan is the ninth month in the Muslim lunar calendar. It commemorates
the period when the angel Gabriel first began to reveal the Quran to the
Prophet Muhammad, commanding him to "Read!" During Ramadan, Muslims believe that the gates of Heaven are open, the gates of Hell are closed,
and angels come down to walk among us. It's a month to reflect and re-
evaluate your life, to get closer to God, and to be forgiven for all the sins
you committed in the previous year. People fast all day, and refrain from
smoking, sex, or drinking water. At sundown, as the evening call to prayer
echoes from the mosque, they break the fast with dates and yogurt, just as
the Prophet and his companions once did. A good Muslim spends Ramadan
fasting, contemplating hunger and the suffering of others, giving alms and
food to the poor, and going to the mosque at night for special readings of the
Quran.

That's the idea, anyway. The reality of Ramadan, in much of the Muslim
world, is different. For the food business, Ramadan is one long Black Friday.
Restaurants are booked. Charities and companies and political parties throw
lavish *iftars* for dozens or hundreds of guests. Families spend all day cooking
enormous *iftars* featuring every dish in their repertoire, including elaborate

dishes and sweets that they don't usually make the rest of the year. Everybody goes to *iftars;* it's common to invite non-Muslim friends to dinner. At its best *iftar* gives everybody, even infidels and godless ex-Communists, a chance to celebrate together.

After *iftar,* people socialize. Stores stay open late into the night, lights blazing, and happy shoppers walk up and down until the wee hours. (The later you stay up, the later you sleep in and the less of the next day you'll have to spend fasting.) Some people even stay up until *suhoor,* the predawn meal that prepares people to fast for an entire day. The Arabic satellite channels premier blockbuster monthlong soap operas, which people gather to watch. Theaters put on plays. In Beirut, it's not uncommon for sweet shops to make more money in the month of Ramadan than during the entire rest of the year. People consume so much bread during Ramadan that bakeries often run out of flour, and sometimes revert to the age-old practice of making bread out of ground barley flour. It's a time of fasting and deprivation, but the entire month of Ramadan revolves around food.

For a generation of Iraqis, 2003 was the first Ramadan without sanctions or Saddam. For the first time in decades, people would be able to gather freely and have political discussions they could never have dreamed of before. Roaa planned to see friends she hadn't seen since before the war. Everyone had high hopes. They had been fasting for more than thirty years.

On Monday, October 27, the first full day of Ramadan, simultaneous bombings at the Red Cross headquarters and three police stations killed thirty-five people and wounded more than two hundred. In one morning, Iraqis' hopes for a happy Ramadan vanished. The first week of the holy month passed in gloom and foreboding. That Friday, a poet friend of Hazem's named Reem had a birthday party for her daughter, Laylak, and we stopped by with Hazem and Maher and Ali, an Iraqi newspaper editor who was also a poet.

Reem had kept her daughter home from school since the Red Cross bombing; many Baghdad parents had done the same. She promised her daughter a fabulous birthday party, with a spectacular cake, to make up for the week of being grounded. But the morning of the party, a leaflet began to circulate throughout Baghdad. It commanded all schools, offices, and shops to close for three days and threatened the lives of any who disobeyed. Reem drove all over town, defying the flyer with its sinister warning, but she couldn't find a cake: all the bakeries were closed. Even worse, all the guests had canceled.

That afternoon, when she heard her aunt and cousins weren't coming, Laylak burst into tears. "No one is going to leave home today!" she shouted. She ran to her room, tore off her party dress and put on her floppy pajamas instead. She stalked back out into the living room and wailed, "This is not a birthday—it's a Day of Blood!"

Laylak was thin, with a dark, serious face and that apologetic way of hunching her neck into her shoulders that seems almost universal among eleven-year-old girls. By the time we got there, she had more or less given up on her party. She sat down, smiled shyly at us, and told me quietly that she liked school.

Poor kid, I thought. Grounded by terrorists, then sentenced to spending her birthday with her parents and their boring grownup friends.

"It's so sad that she can't go to school," I whispered to Mohamad, when Laylak went back to her room.

"You should write a story about it," he said.

He was right. Forget the armies, the insurgents, the politicians—half the reporters in the world were elbowing one another to get to those. The first story I wrote from Baghdad was about a little girl who wanted to go to school and couldn't.

The cake Reem had eventually found was several days old. It was beginning to go dry, the white frosting picking up a slightly chemical taste from the hard sugary buttons of red, green, and yellow candy that had begun to crack and leak into the frosting. It had been ordered and baked in a more hopeful moment, before the Red Cross bombing, lovingly frosted, studded with sugary candies—and then sat growing staler and staler while it waited for an *iftar* that would never take place.

At its best, Ramadan is a balance: deprivation by day, celebration by night. By taking away Baghdad's nights, its ability to get together and share food, the terrorists reduced Ramadan to a season of fear and fasting. Laylak's lonely birthday party was one of thousands of isolated dinners that night. In 2003, instead of strolling down Abu Nuwas, shopping in Inner

Karada, eating ice cream at the famous ice cream shop Faqmah, or staying up late talking to cousins and aunts and uncles and long-lost friends—all the normal Ramadan things—a city of five million people sat down to a meal they had never had before, not even in the darkest days of the Iran-Iraq War: *iftar* alone.

We left early. Ramadan was just beginning, and everyone anticipated other attacks before the month was through. At the gate, Reem broke off a small branch of night-blooming jasmine and handed it to me. "Take this with you," she said. "Its smell is very good."

People in Baghdad often said good-bye by handing you a flower—jasmine, gardenia—an echo of the ancient custom of rubbing a visitor's hands with rosewater at the moment of departure. The ghostly fragrance wove around us, past checkpoints and armed guards, fending off the smell of sewage and burning garbage and generator fuel, an invisible guardian as we walked home through the insurgent night.

Chapter 12

Chicken Soup for the Iraqi Soul

Have you ever seen a garden that will go into a man's sleeve,
an orchard you can take on your lap, a speaker who can speak
of the dead and yet be the interpreter of the living?

—Abu Uthman Amr ibn Bahr al-Jahiz

TWO WEEKS LATER, Hazem and Maher left: Hazem for Beirut, and Maher for Paris, where he lived. (Oday and the other *Najeen* boys asked him to lay a bouquet of roses on Jim Morrison's grave, a mission he gallantly accepted.) I missed them terribly. But by then the search for food and drink had led me to Mutanabbi Street, named after the famous tenth-century Iraqi poet who had once boasted his verse was so powerful that the blind could read it and the deaf could hear it.

The Persians represent Paradise as a walled garden. My idea of paradise is more like Mutanabbi Street, in Baghdad's old city: an entire city street with no cars, just books and cafés. Every Friday, book and paper merchants laid down blankets and sheets of plastic, covered them with books, magazines, and newspapers, and hawked the written word as if it was potatoes or watermelons. The entire street and parts of the sidewalks were paved with books used and new—books of spells, religion, poetry, proverbs, and propaganda. It was like a giant horizontal library, an earthly garden of books. And not just books! In Mutanabbi Street, you could buy anything and everything that had to do with writing or paper. Green-and-gold-embossed Qurans. Giant posters of Imam Hussein holding his dying infant son, pierced with arrows by the soldiers of Yazid at the battle of Karbala. Glue sticks, pens with fuzzy feather heads, and inflatable armchairs for children. Spiral notebooks with fluffy white kittens, gamboling puppies, and vampy women batting dark-lashed eyes. Engineering textbooks. *The Oxford Guide to Phrasal Verbs.* Teach-yourself-English phrasebooks nestled among handbooks of archaic tongues like PASCAL and BASIC and COBAL; and, for reasons I never divined, copy after yellowing copy of *The Journal of Heat Transfer.* Rows and rows of vintage *Time* and *Newsweek,* a few of them old enough to have Nixon on the cover. Ancient copies of *Playboy* and *Hustler* jostled for sidewalk space with back issues of *Flex* and other bodybuilding magazines. Mutanabbi Street was also known for books of spells and sorcery for putting curses on rivals or enemies. They were banned under Saddam, who feared black magic might succeed where CIA-backed coup attempts had failed, and according to my friend Usama some of them sold for thousands of dollars.

The Baath Party had imposed controls on book imports in 1970. After that, no books could enter the country legally without government approval, and the number of books coming into Iraq dwindled. The booksellers still came to Mutanabbi under the Baath, but the books they could sell were more tightly controlled, and some were contraband. My favorite books in Mutanabbi were the samizdat copies of books that used to be outlawed, like *1984* and *Animal Farm.* They were tiny, the size of poetry chapbooks, easy to hide or jettison if necessary. Mimeographed on cheap shiny paper and stapled together crookedly, they were barely more than the idea of a book, stripped down to the barest element of thoughts moving on paper. It was hard to believe that these faint purple words, already fading, once held the power to jail or even execute their readers. And yet people had read them nonetheless. The crowds that packed Mutanabbi Street every Friday showed how hungry Baghdad was to sample these formerly forbidden fruits.

Most of the books were in Arabic, but inside the dusty little bookstores you could find plenty of English-language paperbacks piled in perpetually collapsing towers: E. M Forster; Herman Melville; English translations of famous Iraqi writers; even Wilfred Thesiger's classic ethnography of southern Iraq, *The Marsh Arabs*. Then there were stacks and stacks of dusty, faded romance novels from Mills & Boon, Harlequin's British cousin.

The first time we went to Mutanabbi, Roaa bought a six-inch pile of battered 1970s romance novels. Their covers blazed with craggy men and bosomy women clinching in front of purple mountains and heaving seas. "People laugh at me for these," she said, putting them in her bag. "But in fact, it is from these books that I learned how to speak English."

Roaa had not been able to attend the English-language high school, where the sons and daughters of Baghdad's elite chattered in perfect American accents. But Mutanabbi's bookstores functioned like lending libraries: for a small deposit, she could check out a book or two, devour them at home, then bring them back the next week and trade them in for more. After years of studying her borrowed bodice rippers, she spoke English as fluently as any Baathist apparatchik's daughter. Mutanabbi Street was a great equalizer.

The heart of Mutanabbi was its cafés, the most famous of which were Hassan Ajami and Shahbandar. Like those on Abu Nuwas Street, the cafés housed a culture of intellectual curiosity that cut across sectarian and ethnic identities. They were part of a tradition of public discussion and debate that stretched back to medieval Baghdad.

Shahbandar was my favorite tea house, close to a century old, on the corner of Mutanabbi Street. Inside the café, birdcages hung from the high ceilings. Gossip floated upwards on cigarette smoke, staining the lofty light-blue-and-white-painted walls with the fumes of ancient literary feuds. The whole room was glazed a comforting sepia from a century of nicotine. On the walls there were colorful paintings of old Baghdad streets, with their overhanging balconies; pastel paintings of mosques; a drawing of the Grand Mosque in Mecca, inscribed with the *shahadah*, the Muslim profession of faith; a watercolor of the family tree of the Prophet Muhammad, in reds and blues; and the ninety-nine names of God printed in Arabic calligraphy. Faded black-and-white photographs told the story of Iraq's tragic twentieth century: here was a picture of King Faisal I, the Hashemite chieftain the British installed as Iraq's king in 1921, his reward for leading the Arab Revolt against the Ottomans. Next to it hung a picture of Faisal's young son Ghazi: a little boy dwarfed on a great throne, his feet barely reaching the ground. A little farther down the wall, another photo showed the massive

1939 funeral of the flamboyant, beloved twenty-seven-year-old Ghazi, by then king of Iraq, killed in a convenient car crash as he grew increasingly critical of British control over the supposedly independent Iraqi state.

I always ran into somebody I knew at Shahbandar. Basim the sculptor; Nassire, a poet I knew from the *Najeen* group; Reem's husband Sadiq; and always, holding court in his usual spot on a worn white wooden bench against the back wall by the kitchen, Abu Rifaat, otherwise known as the Professor; Graffitiman; King of Graffiti; Wall Hunter; and the Virgil of Baghdad.

When I look at my photographs of Abu Rifaat, I don't see a person so much as a hurricane. He could never stay still long enough to have his picture taken, and so a lone eye peers distractedly out of a blur of whirling cheeks and chins. The pink tip of a fleshy nose holds a graying mustache in place; the rest of him reels as he turns from one side to the other in midsentence, the better to speak to everybody at once. Black plastic glasses jammed crookedly across his nose, black watch cap mashed down over his bald pink pate, muffled in layers of ragged sweaters and jackets like a woolly snowman.

"This you must try!" he decided, on my third or fourth visit, after peering at me for a few seconds and trying to remember which of his courtiers I was. "It is a traditional tea, an Irrraqi tea;"—rolling the "r" in Iraqi, holding up a finger—"the very best tea of all!"

In vain I protested that I had already ordered and drunk an ocean of tea. I was speaking to the air. He was already gone.

He bustled back in with a glass of pale tea. "This," he said, presenting it to me with a flourish: "this—believe me!—is the *real* tea of Iraq!"

It looked oily, dense and yellow, like a glass of melted topaz. It tasted musty and bittersweet—an antique taste, like drinking old history books. It was called *hamudh*, which means sour, and it was made from *noomi Basra*, little sun-dried key limes historically imported from Persia through the southern Iraqi port of Basra.

Abu Rifaat had spent most of his life as a radar operator in the Iraqi army. Once he retired, he became a full-time scholar of the word. Medieval Iraqi poets went to the Basra *souq* to learn the desert Arabic of the Bedouin; twelve centuries later, Abu Rifaat haunted the cafes and streets of Baghdad, compiling massive, heavily annotated guides to the strongly flavored expressions of Iraqi speech—the proverbs, idioms, jokes, graffiti, and slang. "All of them are alive," he told me, as we sat in Shahbandar, waving his hand around the café, "because they are circulating in places like this."

I never saw Abu Rifaat without a stack of books. He would pile them on one of Shahbandar's little linoleum tea tables: a rusty old copy of *Cricket* magazine with the cover torn off; a ragged 1950s-era primer on *Business English*; and *Chicken Soup for the Soul*. This he considered second only to *Uncle John's Bathroom Reader,* a compendium of trivia, stories, and odd little facts that he often held up as proof of the beauty of American literature.

"They write things that are so beautiful, you cannot find anything like this in any other country!" he told me. "For example, the *Bathroom Reader*. It is so beautiful. It is not a book—it is a university! It contains everything beautiful."

In the Middle East, folk stories chronicle the misadventures of a wise fool, a trickster named Juha or Nasir id-Deen, or, in Lebanon, Abu Abed. In America, the storytelling tradition lived on in compilations of urban legends and little self-help fables, like *Chicken Soup for the Soul.*

Abu Rifaat loved America and everything it produced. His father started it: if an American movie aired at night on television, he would wake up the children, shaking their shoulders gently: "Look, watch—James Cagney! Jimmy Stewart!" Later, Abu Rifaat discovered something even better than Hollywood: American literature—Jacqueline Susann, Harold Robbins, Sidney Sheldon, and Barbara Taylor Bradford. Books were his key to America, the dream world that kept him going through the long, lonely years in the army.

"We need the artists, because they make life so beautiful," he sighed to me once, in Shahbandar. "I don't know why the journalists laugh at me when I tell them I love Sidney Sheldon. His writing, it is so beautiful. You know, one of his books, I read it twenty-two times before I was satisfied!"

I never made fun of Abu Rifaat's taste in books. In Baghdad you read whatever you could find. I scored an old paperback of *Moby-Dick* in Mutanabbi Street, and John Dos Passos's entire USA trilogy in one volume. But I was equally excited to find a flaking old copy of Budd Schulberg's boxing novel *The Harder They Fall,* with a pulpy cover that growled, "Rough and

Tough, Smelling of Blood and Lust." That was America too, and we all need to escape sometimes.

Late fall in Baghdad felt like spring in the Midwest. It was warm instead of hot, and after it rained the fragrance of orange and lemon trees would temper the stench of burning garbage and generator fuel. I started driving around with Abu Zeinab, and sometimes Roaa, and exploring different parts of the city: Hurriya, Kadhimiya, Bab al-Muadham, Baitaween; Mustansiriya University; the art gallery Hewar ("Dialogue"), with its green sculpture garden and outdoor café. But there was one place I had been avoiding. Aside from a late-night trip to the American military hospital when I was sick, I had never been to the Green Zone.

The Green Zone was surrounded by concrete barriers, concertina wire, armed guards, sandbags, and checkpoints where you had to stand in line for hours, every minute of which you were a sitting duck for suicide bombers; all to attend press conferences where U.S. occupation officials would read prepared statements about how well everything was going in Iraq. By mid-November, I felt safer drinking tea at Shahbandar than approaching the citadel of American power. Mutanabbi Street felt less alien.

But shortly before Thanksgiving, a friend told me to look up an American colonel she knew named Alan King. She introduced us over e-mail and suggested we get together. I invited him to lunch—thinking, naively, that I would take him to Karada for *masquf.*

He e-mailed me back right away. Lunch was great; as for location, he wrote, "since I have a price on my head I try not to go to too many public places." He asked me to meet him in the Green Zone.

Alan King was thick as an oil drum, solid, and so blond his hair looked white. He had a round, red, sun-seared face that he screwed up in a perpetual squint, as if blinded by his own blondness. He looked like he was designed for colder climates. But he was from northern Virginia, and he had spent the 1980s and '90s in places like Egypt, Bosnia, Honduras, and Panama. He seemed to feel right at home in the brick-oven heat of Baghdad.

"Betsy said you were a good journalist," he said, and gripped my hand with what felt like a cinder block. "I'm real pleased to meet you."

Alan headed a civil affairs battalion that was responsible for building relationships between the U.S. military and the local population. As the military marched through the south and up into Baghdad during the invasion,
Alan realized that the tribes had a lot of influence, especially outside Baghdad. He built a Rolodex of Iraq's tribal sheikhs, and made it his mission to
build alliances with these leaders and their far-flung networks. He studied
all the tribal divisions in Iraq, from the overarching confederations to the
smallest unit of five generations in one family. He got a copy of *Arab Tribes
of the Baghdad Wilayat*, a guide published in 1918 by British colonial authorities, and began learning the history of the major tribes. He held weekly
meetings with an Iraqi historian, and they amassed a list of all of the tribes
in Iraq. He punched them into his Palm Pilot, indexed into tribe, sub-tribe,
clan, sub-clan, branch, and family. He memorized every line and verse of
the Quran, especially those that had anything to do with relations between
Muslims and "People of the Book"—Christians, Sabaeans, and Jews. In
conversation he would rattle off verses of the Muslim holy book and follow
them up with biblical scripture.

All this homework paid off when he met Hussein Ali al-Shaalan, a Shiite
from the southern town of Diwaniya. Sheikh Shaalan led a branch of the
Khazail, a historically rebellious confederation with branches across the
Middle East. Sheikh Shaalan fled Iraq after the 1991 uprising, when Shiites in
the south rebelled against Saddam at President Bush's urging. After a year in
Saudi Arabia, he was granted political asylum in London and studied law at
the American University there. He returned to Iraq after the 2003 invasion.

In a show of respect, Alan invited Sheikh Shaalan to meet with him three
times. Shaalan waited for the third invitation before he granted the American officer an audience. When they finally met, Alan related a centuries-old
Iraqi tale about Shaalan's tribal confederation crossing a river. That was an
even greater compliment than the three invitations. "This knowledge that
he had, he either knew it or he found it out," Shaalan said, nodding gravely,
when I met him. "In both cases, this shows that he is doing his duty."

Learning the tribes, knowing their history—those gestures showed the
kind of mutual respect one warrior caste expects from another. But one of
the most important acts of diplomacy an American soldier could perform,
as Alan soon discovered, was simply to eat. Eat the sheep a tribal sheikh

has slaughtered. Eat mountains of rice scooped up with three fingers. Eat gobbets of fat with relish, and not a moment's hesitation, because your host would normally save this delicacy for himself and he is offering it to you *min eedu*, from his hand. Eat sitting at tables in gilded overstuffed dining room chairs, reclining on cushions in a *diwan*, or kneeling on a concrete floor around a sheet of plastic weighed down with bowls of *kubba*. The path to hearts and minds led through the stomach. *You have to eat the meal.*

This was proving just as true for me. Food and drink were like truth serum. People would say one thing when you first met them. After a cup of tea or coffee, a plate of pastries—gradually, bite by bite, they would reveal what they really thought.

"We are outraged by the despicable events in Abu Ghraib!" they might rail at first, politely supplying the bluster they believed I was after.

After a cup of coffee, the outrage over Abu Ghraib would turn into "Well, we are not surprised." By the end of a meal, it might be an incredulous shrug: "Do you think we care if the Americans torture these people? Those Baathists tortured us for years. Forget Abu Ghraib. What I really want to know is: when are we going to get electricity?"

Every place in the world has a shibboleth, a question for sussing out who you are and where your loyalties lie. Classical Greeks would ask strangers which city-state they were citizens of: the Cynic Diogenes hated this question so much he came up with the famous retort "*Kosmopolites eimi*"—"I am a citizen of the world."

Like all questions, these also contain an answer. When you move to a new place, you do well to learn its question right away, because the question tells you what its people value (or fear) above all else. During my two years in Clayton, Missouri, I got used to the question: "What parish are you from?"—because being Catholic was apparently, in some circles, a given. In New York, it was "What do you do?"—because in New York everyone must do something.

In Iraq, the question is *"Min aya aamam?"* "Which tribe are you from?" Literally, *aamam* means "paternal uncles": the tribe—called *banu*, the plural of *ibn,* which means "son"—is a very extended family that serves as the guarantor of lineage and honor.

The tribes of the Middle East emerged long before Islam or Christianity. Tribal identity cuts across sectarian lines and supersedes national boundaries; a tribe might be Shiite in some places, Sunni in others. A tribesman from western Iraq might feel more loyalty to kinsmen across the border in Syria than he did to an Iraqi from Basra. Some of the larger tribal confederations, made up of numerous tribes aligned for purposes of war, spanned the entire Arabian Peninsula.

Historically, one of the tribal leader's most trusted attendants was his coffeemaker, the man in charge of hospitality. Tribal sheikhs often formed alliances over a massive dinner feast. They would eat and talk for hours in courtly monologues that eventually corkscrewed into concrete demands. More often than not, they would seal their agreement with another ceremonial meal: roasted lamb, chickens, *tanoor* bread, stews of lamb and tomatoes and eggplant and zucchini for pouring over the obligatory galaxies of rice. The meal and the business being conducted were both essential parts of the same ritual.

Alan met with sheikhs in desert tents or cement mansions. Complicated negotiations around irrigation rights, oil pipelines, and security agreements would unfurl over the course of the meal. Once, as he met with a sheikh inside his house, Alan's team leader ran in from outside in a panic. "Sir, they're slaughtering a sheep out there!" he whispered. "What do we do?" Laughing, he told the soldier to stand down. "I knew then," he said later, "we were going to have to stay for lunch."

He was learning one of the first, most basic lessons about Iraq: never, ever turn down a meal. So when Alan invited Mohamad and me to a dinner hosted by Sheikh Shaalan, I figured saying no would be an act of unforgivable cultural insensitivity. And if we were obliged to eat a Brobdingnagian feast in the interests of cross-cultural understanding, then I was prepared to make that sacrifice.

That is how Mohamad and I ended up in the back of a four-by-four with Alan and a Philadelphia judge named Daniel L. Rubini, roaring down the middle of Palestine Street in a two-car convoy that was painfully, conspicuously, deafeningly American.

Alan was edgy. Leaving the Green Zone was as dangerous and stressful for him as entering it was for us. He had to get permission to venture out into the Red Zone, and he had to take a security detail wherever he went: in this case, two men he introduced vaguely as "friends," but who had the quiet watchfulness of spies. He stopped to make several urgent, whispered phone calls (Iraq still had no cell phone service, but military and occupation officials had a special telephone network). Finally he told us what the problem was: he had thought the dinner would be at Sheikh Shaalan's villa, but somehow signals had crossed, plans had mutated, and apparently we were on our way somewhere else—a Lebanese restaurant called Nabil.

For the military, restaurants were dangerous. Like checkpoints, they were an intimate point of contact among occupiers, occupied, and everybody in between. Food and the public spaces where you bought or consumed it—hotels, restaurants, cafes, and markets—were theaters for all the ambiguities and frustrations between Iraqis and foreigners, which is why these places were among the first to be attacked.

As we walked inside, I could see Alan and his security detail dissecting the dining room with their eyes, measuring the line of sight from the tables to the windows and the quickest path from the front to the back. Several hushed consultations later, the waiters ushered us into a windowless back room.

Sheikh Shaalan was tall and moved very slowly. His face was tanned, with heavy-lidded eyes that often carried a weary expression, as if he was going through motions he knew would be useless but nevertheless felt obligated to pursue. He had the bearing of a man born into a position of command, a way of speaking and watching as if everyone were waiting for him. He wore bespoke wool suits, occasionally pinstriped, cut by skilled tailors into flowing Middle Eastern designs. He talked in long, ornate sentences that would have made Henry James proud.

The sheikh sat down in the middle of a long banquet table, with Alan's translator Faisal next to him, then Alan, and one of his bodyguards. I sat across the table with Judge Rubini, Mohamad, and the other bodyguard. Waiters rotated in and out, depositing plate after plate of hummus, tabbouleh, *baba ghanouj*. Great oval platters of grilled lamb, chicken, and *kafta,* all blanketed tenderly with bread soaked in tomato juice. Mountains of fresh cucumbers, radishes, and green onions, whole heads of romaine, and delicate, opalescent peeled white onions. In keeping with the rules of hospitality, they brought more than one plate of each kind of food so that no one would have to reach across the table.

We hadn't eaten before going to meet Alan. The hours of waiting in traffic, then standing in line at the Green Zone, topped by the adrenaline-fueled ride through Arasat—all of it had left my blood screaming for sugar. The restaurant had grilled the dish of meat with onions and tomatoes, and the smoky smell of charred tomato skins wrapped around their melting red insides, the iron smell of grilled meat, still bloody inside, impaled on long metal skewers, was shooting urgent animal commands—*seize, kill, eat*—across the already raw fight-or-flight circuits of my brain.

But as soon we arranged ourselves around the various delicacies, Sheikh Shaalan looked around, nodded, and started to speak. "Saddam," he began, waving his wool-draped arm with an ominous air of enumeration, "did many wrong things."

I got out my notebook. This was going to be epic. To lunge across the table and grab a mouthful of food while the sheikh was speaking—even to surreptitiously tear off a tiny scrap of the bread so close to my hand—would be unthinkable disrespect to our host. Only the ugliest of Americans would commit such an insult. And so we settled in to listen to the sheikh. For the time being at least, we would eat history.

The Ottoman Empire, which ruled Iraq off and on for centuries, left its tribal leaders more or less alone until the nineteenth century, when it imposed land reform and a penal code that eroded their power. But when the British Empire occupied the country, after World War I, the colonial administrators decided to promote the rural sheikhs. British officials believed the sheikhs could be more easily controlled than the educated urban Iraqi upper class, whose members were beginning to mutter that Iraqis might want to rule their own country. Britain's needs in Mesopotamia (read: oil) would be better achieved by "a veiled rule" through the sheikhs, wrote the colonial political officer Bertram Thomas, than by a "premature experiment" in native government.

In 1918, British administrators gave tribal sheikhs the power to settle disputes and collect taxes. Iraqis might have desired a more modern, egalitarian system, but tribal law, said Thomas piously, had "the sanction of immemorial custom." Over the following decades, the empire expanded the sheikhs' control so much that Iraq's peasants became virtual slaves. By the time the Tribal Disputes Regulations were finally repealed, in 1958, many sheikhs had amassed unprecedented wealth and power.

At first Saddam saw the sheikhs as a potential threat to his hegemony. But then he realized they could be useful. During the 1980–1988 Iran-Iraq War, soldiers began to desert the army and return to hide among their tribes. Saddam enlisted sheikhs to turn in deserters. Just as the British had before him, he replaced those who did not cooperate with pretenders. People called them "fake sheikhs," or "Swiss sheikhs" for the cars, gold, and currency that Saddam lavished on them. The regime kept a detailed list of all the sheikhs, fake or genuine; at one point they numbered 7,380.

The tribes of Iraq, as the historian Hanna Batatu points out, have always thrived as its cities have suffered. When the country's civil institutions began to crumble under the Baath dictatorship, the sheikhs regained much of the influence they had lost. As the rule of law grew weaker, tribal law gained strength: when Iraqis had a dispute, they turned to their sheikhs instead of the corrupt judges or policemen.

"You have a conflict—land theft, irrigation rights, car accident," Adnan al-Janabi, a tribal sheikh who trained as an economist and was an OPEC official in the 1970s, told me. "The tribes of both parties try to meet, and to make an agreement. If not, you go to the courts: the policemen will blackmail you, the judge will take the rest, and in the end somebody from the government will have the judgment overturned. Even if you get a judgment in the court, you can't enforce it. In some cases, it will go into this cycle for years—if vendetta doesn't break out, which is very likely."

When tribal mediators reached an agreement, they brought both sides together, almost always over a meal. Sometimes they even shared the ceremonial bread and salt. "The role of tribal leaders is to bring the two parties together very early on," explained Janabi. "And we end up by breaking bread, kissing each other—and more often than not, the matter is resolved."

Back in the 1950s, Janabi's father agitated to replace tribal law with a civil code. Janabi himself took a dim view of the supposedly hallowed Iraqi custom of settling disputes through the tribes. "The British imposed it—they brought it with them," he told me, rattling his prayer beads impatiently. "Inshallah, if we have a civil society, I can rest at home and get a good night's sleep. But my hopes for a quick resolution into a peaceful and civil society, I must say, are being dashed."

He added sadly: "I was thinking that it would take a couple of months."

By the time we sat down to dinner with Sheikh Shaalan, Iraq's judicial system was in shambles. Police, investigators, and judges would wait for a bribe before opening a case. Honest judges were afraid to try cases for fear that those they ruled against would have them killed. A week before we had dinner at Nabil, Judge Rubini had written a memo to officials at the American-led Coalition Provisional Authority, where he worked as a senior adviser to Iraq's Ministry of Justice. He pointed out that while criminal courts had been open for seven months, there had only been twenty criminal convictions in Baghdad—a city already descending into anarchy.

If Iraq's new Ministry of Justice had any hopes of rebuilding the country's legal system, it made sense to talk to the tribal sheikhs who had been serving as de facto judges for decades. That was why Alan had brought Judge Rubini to meet Sheikh Shaalan.

"I speak from a point of ignorance," said the judge, who had been carefully coached by Alan. "I know courts, but I don't know tribes. I know you have 10,000 years of history. My country has only 225 years of history."

Smiling slightly, Sheikh Shaalan inclined his head.

"You have the power—you and all the national tribes—and you have a lot of enemies, from without and within," Judge Rubini continued. "The country is falling apart from corruption, there is tremendous power . . ."

"That is very true, our country has 10,000 years of history," said Sheikh Shaalan, interrupting smoothly. "You mentioned that your country has only

225 years of history. But in that 225 years, you have managed to achieve many things . . ."

He paused, magnificently, and Judge Rubini nodded.

"And here comes the role of the tribes, if they take their duty seriously," said Sheikh Shaalan. "By practicing their role, they will be better because of these following reasons, which I am about to explain."

It would be years before we could eat. Everything Sheikh Shaalan said had to be translated into English; everything Alan or the judge said had to be translated into Arabic. I looked past the judge at Mohamad. He looked hungry. Ever so slightly, with a movement only I would be able to read, he rolled his eyes.

"We would like to have a relationship that is on a good foundation, so that we can take full advantage of your presence here," said the sheikh. "It is a correct step. We know you are leaving"—

Here the sheikh paused, looking around the table, as if to underline that point—"but before you leave, we want to take advantage of your presence here. We have to make things run quicker than before, so that we can be ready when all these changes come. There is a constitution-writing council, as I'm sure you're aware." He waved graciously at Judge Rubini—

"Painfully aware," said the judge.

Everybody laughed politely, a bit desperately. The long-awaited constitution had not yet been written, but the question of who would write it, and how they would be selected, was already causing bitter conflicts.

"But we want to make these changes happen quicker," said Sheikh Shaalan, frowning slightly. "We should be ready for rapid changes. The work that Colonel King is doing is one of the most important things for the CPA to get a true picture of what's going on in Iraq . . ."

Suddenly the lights blinked off. There was a second or so of shocked silence. In the small, windowless room, the darkness was absolute.

Power outages were constant in Baghdad, and usually no cause for alarm. But Alan had said something about having a price on his head. If the wrong people had seen the four-by-four—if the wrong people knew an American officer was eating dinner here, along with two spooks, a tribal sheikh, and a couple of interlopers, then this would be the moment to attack.

In the darkness, I was doing a risk analysis of my own. If we were going to be attacked, I thought with the feverish intensity of low blood sugar, I don't want to face it on an empty stomach. I had been watching the food for what felt like hours; each plate of hummus, each skewer of meat was burned into my brain. I could reach out, grab a flap of bread and a mouthful of hummus, and no one would know who had committed the crime.

At that moment, the "bodyguards" each clicked on a tiny but powerful penlight. They watched in silence, their faces lit from below.

"And if some of these tribal leaders were to fail," continued Sheikh Shaalan, resuming his speech as if nothing had happened, "if they fail in their mission, they will be shamed, deeply shamed, and blamed. Because they will be accounted for in front of their tribes, in front of their families, in front of the people in their area . . ."

The lights blinked back on. The bodyguards clicked off their penlights. In perfect Levantine Arabic, one of them murmured *"Alhamdulillah"*— "Thanks be to God."

Sheikh Shaalan's head snapped toward the sound. "And what a wonderful surprise," he declared, smiling broadly, throwing his arms wide, "to discover that our friend speaks Arabic!"

We all muttered that it was wonderful. Sheikh Shaalan smiled and tactfully resumed his oration. But before he could settle back into his speech, Mohamad tore off a piece of bread, reached his hand across the table, and dipped it into the hummus.

Sheikh Shaalan froze, arm outstretched, in the middle of a multi-clause sentence. Alan frowned. Faisal, Alan's elegant, British-educated translator, looked aghast. Even the bodyguards allowed themselves slight facial twitches. Mohamad looked back at us, chewing calmly, completely unapologetic.

I glared at him. We were there to witness this alliance. Not to eat. Also it was my job, not his, to be the greedy one.

"And I wish," said the sheikh, placing his hand on his heart, and shaking his head with infinite sorrow, as though we had refused his food, "that our guests would eat something, and not wait for me."

Six days after our dinner with Sheikh Shaalan, a few days before Mohamad and I were supposed to leave, word rippled through Baghdad: the American military had finally caught Saddam. On December 13, 2003, U.S. troops captured him in a little hole in the ground outside the village of al-Dour. The next day, after he'd been debriefed and deloused, U.S. officials released a video to all of Iraq and the world: the great dictator dirty and defeated, following his captors like a senile child; ducking his head for the lice check; and opening his mouth, obediently, to receive the American flashlight.

Shiite clerics passed out candy at prayer time. The Iraqi Communist Party raised red flags in jubilation. Sporadic happy fire rang out. In the streets, people burned the old Iraqi dinars printed with Saddam's face. The celebrations ended early, when most of Baghdad rushed home to hide from gunfire and retaliatory attacks, and I called Roaa.

When U.S. occupation authorities showed the Saddam footage at a press conference, one of the Iraqi journalists had leapt to his feet and shouted "Death to Saddam!"—words he had probably been waiting his entire life to say. I had thought of Roaa immediately: I was excited and happy for her. This would be a cathartic occasion, the moment when her freedom would finally feel real.

She answered the phone sobbing.

"I thought you'd be happy," I said, feeling stupid.

"Happy?" she said. "When we saw this small movie of him, looking like this, it was something terrible."

Her voice had a flat quality that alarmed me. Normally it leapt from one syllable to another, lilted with unexpected accents. Now it sagged in a hopeless monotone.

"I was sad because our whole lives were just wasted by this man," she said. "And for what? For nothing."

Roaa and I spent the next day walking around the city, talking to people we met. They were torn between happiness, humiliation, and rage. A woman whose father had been killed by Saddam said she was angry that he had been captured by Americans. Another woman, who had lost twelve relatives to Baathist purges, said she didn't know how to feel. The flavor of freedom was more complex, more bitter than we imagined.

Finally a theater director in his late thirties said what everyone was thinking: *Thank you, America. Now go.*

"When are the Americans going to leave?" he asked. "They said they wanted the weapons of mass destruction. There were no weapons of mass destruction. They said they wanted the regime to fall. It fell. They wanted to find Saddam. They found him. Now what? What reason are they going to use to stay now?"

Mohamad and I had been in Baghdad for two and a half months, and the honeymoon was over. I wasn't sure where home was—we didn't live here, or in Beirut, or in New York anymore—but I felt homesick. Suddenly I wanted to be in Chicago, where it would be Christmas, and the houses would be strung with colored lights. Instead, a few days before Christmas, Mohamad and I flew back to Beirut.

Chapter 13

The Devil's *Hijab*

B Y THE TIME Mohamad and I returned to Baghdad in March 2004, a deep gloom had settled over the city. There was an undercurrent of fear in people's conversations, a subtle change that had been building gradually in the past several months. People would disappear in broad daylight, their bodies found days later marked by signs of torture. Everyone knew someone—a friend, a relative—who had been killed. It was nothing compared to the sectarian slaughter that would come in the next few years, but at the time it seemed unimaginable.

An American company had rented the entire Sumer Land and refused to accept any new customers. We moved into the Andalus, a small hotel off Abu Nuwas Street. It was just down the street from Firdous Square. On the other side of the square was the beautiful blue-domed mosque that most of the television correspondents tried to work into the background of their live shots. Across from the mosque were the Sheraton and the Palestine, two tall hotels surrounded by several layers of blast walls and checkpoints. Together they made up a compound, a locked-down fortress where the big television networks and wire services put their reporters. The Palestine had a pool and a panoramic bar where people said Saddam's son Uday used to drink. I went there a couple of times: it was full of drunken contractors, and this, plus the underlit tables and retro 1970s lamps, gave the place a feverish, menacing glamour. From the windows I could see the Tigris, a dark snake dividing the city, and on either side, flickering orange lights kept alive by a thousand and one generators.

Outside the Palestine and the Sheraton's first line of checkpoints and concrete blast walls there was a small street with a couple of smaller, cheaper, and less secure hotels, including ours. The Andalus was an octagon inside a square: an eight-story atrium extended to the top of the building. Rooms radiated off the atrium, fitting together in strange shapes like puzzle pieces. Our room had no kitchen, but there was a tiny refrigerator and a sink in a narrow hallway outside the bathroom. I bought a Korean hot plate from Karada, perched it hazardously on top of the fridge, and made scrambled eggs. I filled plastic bins with onions and apples and Iraqi dates. We stayed on the fourth floor for most of the summer of 2004. We ate a lot of canned hummus at the Andalus.

By the time we got to the Andalus, Abu Nuwas Street had changed yet again. Saddam's old palace grounds across the river were now part of the Green Zone. Militants would fire mortars across the river into the Green Zone; the U.S. military would return fire. The few surviving *masquf* restaurants, which were hardly ever open, would occasionally get hit.

Checkpoints and concrete blast walls and American tanks blocked off Abu Nuwas for most of the summer. Neighborhood street kids hung out practicing their English with American soldiers. Aging checkpoint ladies flirted desperately with young reservists. Boys as young as eight or nine, orphans of wars past and present, sniffed glue and offered to pimp their sisters. It was dusty and depressing. Abu Nuwas would have stopped and wept.

But early some evenings, when the sun was setting over the long silver necklace of the Tigris and the remaining palm trees stretched their arms against the sky, people did still come to the river. Old men would sit quietly smoking and look out over the shining water. Watching them silently contemplate the river, I liked to think that life along the Tigris, which had seen much worse over the years—floods, plagues, Mongol invasions—would survive.

A few days after we returned, I went to the Sumer Land to visit the staff and see if Layla was still there. The man at the front desk bought me a cup of tea. I asked him how everyone was doing.

"Many problems," he said, and shook his head. "After you and Mr. Mohamad left, we had many problems."

I asked him if I could buy a newspaper. The hotel usually sold them from a little rack in the lobby, but now it was gone.

"No more newspapers," he said. "When I go to the bathroom, they steal them."

"Who? Who would steal a newspaper?"

"Americans," he said bitterly.

Upstairs, Layla and her daughters felt as if they were living in lockdown. They weren't comfortable eating in the restaurant downstairs, which was full of drunken contractors every night. They didn't go to the Internet café anymore. But the bitterest loss was the pool.

Before the war, Layla had gone swimming at the Olympic-sized pool in Qadisiya, which set aside one day a week for women. After the war, she told me, "the Americans" took over the pool, and there was no more women's day. For a while she and Shirin had splashed around in the tiny, kidney-shaped pool behind the Sumer Land, no bigger than a truck bed. Then the contractors came.

"Now the only place I go swimming," she said, making sad little breast-strokes, "is in the shower."

As we sat talking, a fleshy man with a crew cut and a red face came out on to the balcony across from her window. He was wearing a white polo shirt and khaki cargo pants. He looked at her window and waved.

Layla did not wave back. "You see this man?" she said, tipping her chin and curling her lip at him with hatred. "He is a fool."

He waved again. He stood on his tiptoes and shaded his eyes, trying to peer in her window.

"When we see him in the hotel, he always says, '*Salaam aleikum, salaam aleikum,*' " she said with disgust. "And he is wearing a dishdasha and dressed like a sheikh."

One night, Layla said, the contractor knocked on her door and tried to invite himself in. She was having a small party in her room: some relatives had come over, and they were playing music. She tried to shut the door so he wouldn't see her daughters and her relatives, and they wouldn't see him. But he'd stuck his foot in the door and tried to look in over her shoulders.

"He said, 'Hey, how come you didn't invite me? We're *friends*!' " She spat out the word "friends."

Maybe the guy didn't realize what he was doing; maybe he was just trying to be friendly. Maybe not. But there was no way for Layla to reconcile Rachel and Ross with this very different kind of American friend. No way this contractor would have grasped that Americans were not guests but occupiers, and that hospitality was out of the question.

By now I was filing stories regularly for *The Christian Science Monitor*. My editors were particularly anxious for one about Fern Holland, a thirty-three-year-old American woman who had been trying to set up women's centers in southern Iraq.

On March 9, Fern visited the women's center in Karbala with her assistant, Salwa Oumashi. In the late afternoon, Fern and Salwa got in their car with a press officer named Robert Zangas, and headed back to their office in Hilla. As they were driving, a car full of gunmen forced their car off the road and machine-gunned all three of them to death. Hours after the killings, Coalition investigators arrested six suspects. Four of them had valid Iraqi police identification cards.

Those three people were casualties in a larger war, one against Iraqi women. There was no way to know if they had been specifically targeted for promoting women's rights, but it seemed likely: I had already interviewed Yanar Mohammed, an outspoken feminist who had received several death threats, and she was not the only one. The Coalition had announced that it was going to shift the management of the women's centers to the local staff. I wanted to focus my story on those Iraqi women. To do that, I would have to go to Karbala.

I had never been to Karbala, and neither had Roaa. She could speak three languages fluently, but she had never ventured outside Baghdad or the northern city of Sulaimaniya, in Iraqi Kurdistan. "I'm twenty-three years old, and I still don't know the rest of Iraq!" she said.

This isolation had left her with some interesting ideas about Shiites: they were bad Muslims who did not pray enough; they used Shiite trickery to weasel out of religious obligations, such as fasting for Ramadan; their

1991 uprising against Saddam had failed due to their own shortcomings, not because the Americans had abandoned the southern rebels after calling on them to rise up. (The Kurdish rebellion, according to her, had succeeded thanks to Kurdish ingenuity and not the military assistance of a no-fly zone patrolled by U.S. and British fighter jets.)

I used to argue with her about this kind of thing for hours. I would point out that some of her closest friends were Shiites: she adored Usama, another young student at the Institute for War & Peace Reporting. And she liked Mohamad, especially after the *hijab* incident.

Before we left Beirut, Umm Hassane had given me a black-and-gray polyester *hijab* for the car ride through Anbar and other situations where I would need to look Iraqi. As she showed me how to tie it beneath my chin, a crafty smile stole across her face. "Maybe you'll like it," she said, casting her eyes upward with a wistful sigh, "and you'll start wearing it all the time."

I lifted an eyebrow in Mohamad's direction. He replied with a baleful stare that said *Over my dead body.*

Mohamad objected to *hijab* on philosophical grounds, but I suspect this reaction was also partly aesthetic. The minute I put on a *hijab*, a remarkable transformation occurs. As the telephone booth turns mild-mannered Clark Kent into Superman, so do I, in *hijab*, transform into a sullen Albanian peasant woman. My round face turns doughy and stolid, resentful, and stunningly ugly. Jowls emerge. I find myself hating men, all of them. I look so hideous in a *hijab* that everything I look at turns ugly too, out of sympathy. Mohamad hated this metamorphosis so much that after we moved to the Andalus I sometimes found myself in the feministically awkward position of arguing that I needed to wear the damn thing for safety.

Roaa refused to back me up: she was completely on Mohamad's side. "For an Eastern man, to not want his wife to wear *hijab*—this is something wonderful," she exulted. "This is something really fantastic."

Roaa was a devout Muslim. She prayed five times a day, as she had done her entire life, and set her watch to give an alarm at prayer time. If we were working, she would make up her prayers in the evening after going home. But she was not conservative: her best friend was a guy her age, a Christian, and they talked on the phone almost every day. She didn't wear *hijab*, and she dressed in jeans and bright, butterfly-colored shirts—pinks and yellows and light blues—that always matched her eye shadow. "Annia, for sure they can tell you are a foreigner, because you never wear enough makeup," she scolded me once, laughing and rolling warm brown eyes that were dusted iridescent blue that day. "Iraqi women, we like to wear a *lot* of makeup!"

Yet it was Roaa who taught me the proper way to wear a headscarf. We both put on headscarves and *abayas* before leaving Baghdad. In the car, Roaa showed me how to pull up one end of the headscarf and pin it to the side, so I could look like a good Muslim girl who wore it often enough to give it a little style. We needed to look as unobtrusive as possible: the road to Karbala was one of the most dangerous in Iraq, and people called the area it passed through the "Triangle of Death."

Roaa confessed that she had not been able to sleep at all the night before. I was nervous too: a week before Fern and Salwa had been killed, on the Shiite religious holiday of Ashura, Sunni extremists had launched nine simultaneous attacks in Karbala that killed about a hundred people.

I had e-mailed a Coalition adviser from the Hilla office and told him I wanted to visit the center. He told me flatly that it was not a good idea to go to Karbala. I decided to ignore him: if you listened to the Coalition people, you would never go anywhere but the Green Zone.

Before we left, I called my friend Manal Omar. She worked for Women for Women International, an aid group that helps women in war zones become self-sufficient. Fern and Salwa had been friends of hers. Manal warned me to be extremely careful on the drive. "We can't get out there because of the security risk," she said. "And it's tearing me apart, because I know Fern and Salwa would have wanted us to carry on their work."

Manal told me to turn back if the military had blocked the main road, as they often did after attacks. "There's a little road, a side road that you have to take when they block the main highway," she said. "There's a sign—I forget the name—but if the main road is closed, don't take that road. Just turn around and come back."

I did not notice the signs. One minute we were on the main highway, which went through the small Sunni towns south of Baghdad. And then the main road was closed, and suddenly we found ourselves on one of the small side roads that wound through the lush irrigation canals of the Euphrates. I could not tell if this was the route that Manal had warned me about or not.

Karbala is famous for sweet pudding, *fesenjoon,* and a story that dates back to the early years of Islam. After the prophet Muhammad died, a civil war broke out over who should become caliph—a relative of the Prophet, or one of his closest companions. The conflict between these two camps eventually divided Islam into the Sunni and Shiite sects.

In the year 680, the Prophet's grandson Hussein rebelled against Yazid, the caliph in Damascus. He set out with his family and a small band of followers for the southern Iraqi city of Kufa, whose people had promised to support him. Yazid's army intercepted Hussein in the Iraqi desert. It surrounded Hussein's caravan and cut it off from the waters of the Euphrates. After a bitter siege of ten days, during which the children of Hussein's family begged for food and water, the caliph's men killed Hussein and cut off his head. They took the surviving women and children back to Damascus, where the caliph displayed the captives and the severed heads in his court. But Hussein's sister Zainab refused to acknowledge Yazid's rule. In a passionate speech, she denounced him for killing her brother, the Prophet's grandson. By secretly saving one of Hussein's sons, she preserved the Prophet's bloodline, and to this day millions of Shiites make the pilgrimage to the dusty town to visit the grave of Imam Hussein. Shiites believe that the blood of Hussein soaked into the soil of Karbala, leaving the very earth smelling sweet.

When we got to Karbala, the shrine was overwhelmed with Iranian pilgrims. Most of them were women. They were wearing jeans. Their robes flapped open to reveal swaths of rainbow-colored fabric cinched around their waists. They wore the kind of headscarves that some of the more dogmatic Iraqi Muslims called *al-hijab al-shaitany,* "the Devil's *hijab*": filmy floral pinks and greens that floated far back on their heads, arranged to reveal swirls of artfully fluffed hair. They chittered in Farsi as they stalked through Karbala's muddy streets. One teenage pilgrim wore skintight purple jeans and high-heeled boots.

Roaa glowered at her from inside her black hole. "We are wearing these terrible things, and just *look* at the Iranian women," she hissed. "While it is *their fault* we are wearing *abayas*!"

At the Zainab al-Hawraa Women's Center, named after the Prophet's granddaughter, the Iraqi women who were supposed to be taking over the management felt isolated. They missed Fern and Salwa, who used to visit them almost every week, bringing falafels from the *souq* and other little gifts. They reminisced about Fern and Salwa's last day: one of the Iraqi women at the center had made *fesenjoon*, the spectacular Iranian dish of chicken stewed in a sweet-and-sour pomegranate sauce thickened with ground walnuts, and the women had all eaten it together.

Two weeks after Fern and Salwa were murdered, the women were under siege. They had not had many visitors, they said, because of the dangerous roads. All of them had received multiple death threats. Some of the threats came from mysterious callers, but others were from people they knew— local religious women who would call them at night, or come to their houses and warn them that the women's center was run "by Jews" and it was not good for a woman's reputation to go there. The latest death threat came that very day, delivered by a young clerical student who knocked on the door while Roaa and I sat speaking to the women inside. The manager tried to dismiss the incident, not wanting to alarm us, but the look of fear on her face was more frightening than anything she could have said.

It was beginning to dawn on me that this trip was more dangerous than I had thought, not just for me but for others. I wanted to try the famous Karbala sweets, which Roaa and others had told me about. But we had to get out of the city before nightfall. And we had one more stop to make before we could go.

A young Shiite cleric named Muqtada al-Sadr had been denouncing the American-led occupation from the beginning. In the weeks before the killings, Sadr's clerics had been criticizing the women's centers. I wanted to see what his representatives in Karbala had to say about the murders.

The cleric who managed the office, Sheikh Khidayer al-Ansari, showed us into his visiting room. Pictures of Shiite martyrs hung on the walls, including Sadr's father, a grand ayatollah who had been assassinated by Saddam's regime in 1999. We took off our shoes and sat down on the floor with the sheikh.

Sheikh Ansari approved of the women's centers: they taught sewing and computer skills and this technology, he said, was good for the people. He condemned the murders. "I can't see how this is helping," he sighed, looking unhappily at the floor.

But he grew angry when he remembered how L. Paul Bremer, the American viceroy in charge of Iraq, had inaugurated the center the previous month with an elaborate photo op. "When Bremer opened this center, we heard that Bremer said, 'We intend to give Iraqi women their full freedom,' " he said, and added ominously, "and you can put two lines under 'full freedom.' "

During this conversation, he kept his eyes on Roaa, who was translating, and I could see that his relentless stare was making her nervous. "They pretend that they have freedom and democracy and they brought it for women," he said angrily, "and that is a lie because they have not permitted democracy to this day."

That was hard to argue with. In the summer of 2003, occupation authorities had canceled local elections, which most Iraqis desperately wanted, and installed former Iraqi military and police officials as local leaders instead. Then U.S. authorities started setting up women's centers—many of them, like the one in Karbala, in former regime offices that Iraqi political parties coveted for themselves. In Karbala, American authorities had kicked a local Shiite political party out of the building, and later sent Bremer to be photographed with Iraqi women at the center's opening. To men like the sheikh, the message seemed clear: women's freedom came at the expense of Iraqi society. That the women *were* the society was something no one but Iraqi women—and a few rare outsiders, like Manal Omar and Fern Holland—ever understood.

Suddenly the sheikh thought of a way to illustrate his point. Sitting up straight, he placed one hand on his knee, and unfurled the other hand theatrically in my direction.

"Ask her this," he said intently, still looking at Roaa. "Do you know why Marlene Monroe killed herself?"

It had been a long, depressing day. The road from Baghdad, which we would have to take back, was lined with graffiti saying TO THE JIHAD, O MUSLIMS, and whoever had written it did not intend jihad in the sense of "struggle" or "striving." When the women heard we had driven down from Baghdad on our own, they looked at each other with alarm. One of them had lost a nephew on the same road earlier in the week. They told us to get back as soon as possible. The sun was slipping down toward the horizon. It was time to go. And now Muqtada's man in Karbala wanted to talk about "Marlene" Monroe.

"No," I said. "Please tell me."

Settling his thighs into the floor, he began what was clearly one of his favorite stories.

"Marlene Monroe had many fans," he recounted, in the singsong story-telling cadence of classical Arabic. "And these fans, they would write her many letters. These fans would ask her questions like 'How did you become a star? What did you do to become so famous?' "

One fan, said the sheikh, got a letter back from Marlene. On the envelope the movie star had written instructions to open it only after she was dead.

After she committed suicide, the faithful fan, who had obeyed her wishes, finally opened the letter. This, according to the sheikh, is what it said:

> It is true, I am a star, and famous the world over. But all I ever wanted was a family. I tried to raise a family decently, and with honor, and I failed. So do not forget this: Fame is not worth it if you lose your honor, and lose Paradise.

He looked at us in triumph.

"These women's centers are very good for women, but the most important thing for Iraqi women is to raise a family with honor," he concluded, in case we had missed the point. "The Iraqi woman should keep her honor— she shouldn't lose Paradise and throw away her whole life for what they call 'freedom.' "

Politely, we thanked the sheikh for this lesson. Adjusting our *abayas*, tucking away every disobedient hair, we headed back up the road to Baghdad.

Chapter 14

The Free One

B Y APRIL, AMERICAN troops were battling two rebellions in Iraq: one by Sunni militants in Fallujah, and the other by Muqtada al-Sadr's militia. He named it the Mahdi Army, after the Shiite imam who vanished mysteriously in the ninth century, and whom many Shiites believe will return on Judgment Day. On April 3, the U.S. military arrested one of Sadr's top lieutenants. The next day, Sunday, the cleric's supporters poured into the streets in cities all over Iraq. Eight U.S. soldiers were killed in clashes in Sadr City, a Shiite neighborhood of Baghdad that was home to almost half the city's population. In Firdous Square, just down the street from the Andalus, hundreds of young men began to gather.

We went outside to see what was happening. A crowd of men dashed down Saadoun Street shouting *Muqtada! Muqtada!* Shots rang out from the direction they were running in, and the men turned and ran back, much faster this time, not shouting anymore. An open truck thundered past with several dozen men in the back of it, all dressed head-to-toe in black and holding black banners, shouting and heading toward the gunfire. I had seen riots before, back in America, but nothing like this. Nothing where people would drive into gunfire.

Two days later, the U.S. military surrounded the city of Fallujah. That same day, occupation authorities announced that they would arrest Sadr for his involvement in the killing of another Shiite cleric a year earlier, in April 2003. Three members of the Iraqi Governing Council threatened to resign. One of them was a woman, Dr. Salama al-Khafaji.

* * *

On April 9, the one-year anniversary of the fall of Baghdad, a Humvee circled Firdous Square all day, blasting a curfew warning in Arabic at psyops-
level volume: "THIS IS A MILITARY AREA. THIS AREA IS CLOSED
BY ORDER OF THE COALITION FORCES. IF WE SEE ANYONE
ENTERING THIS AREA, HE WILL BE INSTANTLY SHOT."

Then, in case that seemed unlikely to win Iraqi hearts and minds,
the voice of America added: "IF YOU ARE ANGRY TODAY, YOU
SHOULD BE ANGRY AT THE MAHDI ARMY, BECAUSE THEY
DON'T HAVE THE BEST INTERESTS OF THE IRAQI PEOPLE
AT HEART."

That day, Mohamad and I went to Sadr City for Friday prayers. Mohamad and Abu Zeinab went to the mosque. I went around interviewing
people with Usama, a young journalism student we had hired as a translator. Everybody mentioned Dr. Salama, as they called her. "She is braver
than many men," grizzled men would say, in admiration. "Her shoe is worth
more than the entire Governing Council," one of Sadr's aides thundered to
tens of thousands of supporters during prayers at the mosque.

Dr. Salama was Iraq's most popular female politician, according to one
poll, which also ranked her as the tenth most popular figure overall. Because
she had wide support among Sadr's followers, she was mediating between
them and the U.S. military—an essential but extremely dangerous form of
shuttle diplomacy. Not long afterwards, Sheikh Hussein Ali al-Shaalan took
Mohamad and me to meet her.

We sat in Dr. Salama's office with her adviser, a Shiite cleric named
Sheikh Fatih Kashif al-Ghitta. The two sheikhs were friends, but as soon as
we sat down they launched into an argument over women's rights.

Women were demanding a 40 percent quota in the new parliament,
the legislative body that would succeed the Governing Council. The idea
of women holding political office had wide popular support, particularly
in Shiite areas. But some politicians were objecting to the quota in the
name of tradition. Our friend Sheikh Shaalan, unfortunately, was one of
them.

"I want for women in Iraq what exists in other countries, but within Islamic bounds," argued Sheikh Shaalan, leaning back in his chair. He was resplendent, as usual, in a robe of rich dark brown wool.

He pointed out, quite accurately, that most of the countries in the U.S.-led "coalition of the willing" had only a handful of women in their own governments.

"How can we possibly exceed those countries that are coming in with their rhetoric of freedom and democracy and human rights," he asked, smiling, "when in those countries, women's political participation barely exceeds twenty percent?"

Crafty bastard, I wrote in my notes. Mohamad was translating most of the conversation, although Dr. Salama and Sheikh Fatih occasionally switched into English, and I was taking notes for both of us.

"The system that I would like to see, personally, would be one where the person who is most able—regardless of sex or religion—would be the one in government," said Sheikh Shaalan. "Of course, taking into consideration that we're an Eastern society. I don't call for backwardness, or being frozen in time. But I also don't favor a wide openness that would lead to confrontation, and lead to a society that is not an Eastern society, nor a Western society, but a society in turmoil."

Sheikh Fatih looked at Dr. Salama. She smiled.

Sheikh Fatih was wearing a long robe and the white turban that identified him as a Shiite cleric. The fleshy face under his turban ended with a trim, graying beard. The deep grooves under his eyes gave him the weary look of a man whose health you might worry about. But when he smiled or made goofy puns, which he did often, he resembled a genial college professor.

Dr. Salama's eyes usually held an expression of patience, with the slightest hint of humor. With her oval face and hooded *abaya,* she looked like a black-robed madonna. She was forty-six years old.

"We are a picture of Iraq," said Sheikh Fatih, meaning: religion, tribes, and women. "And I like the way we are sitting."

Dr. Salama was sitting behind an enormous desk in a padded black office chair that was taller than she was. There was a large flat-screen computer screen at her back and a gold Quran in a green velvet case on her desk. Some newspapers lay open where she had been reading them. The two sheikhs—one religious, one tribal—sat before her like supplicants.

Sheikh Shaalan laughed indulgently. "I'm not going to say anything about that, but I want things to go the natural way," he said, in a tone that indicated the discussion was over. "Let's see what happens. Don't close any doors, and maybe women will take fifty percent!"

(*Consummate bullshitter,* I noted.)

But Sheikh Fatih was not willing to let the topic drop. "The twentieth century was a man's century, and we had four or five wars," he persisted. "Let's give the twenty-first century to the women, and see what happens."

"Very well, but how many Dr. Salamas are there?" said Sheikh Shaalan frowning. "I'd be worried about how many are out there and how good they are."

"It's true that many of the women that I work with don't have political experience," said Dr. Salama, who had been quiet up to this point. Her dark brown eyes were following the argument from side to side.

Sheikh Fatih sighed and rolled his eyes. "Sheikh Hussein," he said, using Sheikh Shaalan's first name, "Nisrine Barwari, in the Ministry of Public Works, is worth ten ministers. I have experience with women all over Iraq—Basra, Amara, Kut—and you don't have to worry, there are women *even better* than Dr. Salama all over Iraq. If I was an extremist, I would call for sixty percent!"

"Forty percent will be a social shock that society isn't ready to accept," said Sheikh Shaalan. He was not smiling anymore.

"Sheikh Hussein, in the current crisis, in Fallujah and Najaf, who is losing? The loser is the women."

"No, it's the entire society."

"No, let's be honest: it's the women," said Sheikh Fatih, whirling his prayer beads, almost shaking them at his friend. "Who is the social base who will be pressured the most? The woman. She has to balance between her child, her house, and her cause."

"We should have a bigger debate," said Shaalan, flicking the conversation away with his hand, smiling a smooth urbane smile that seemed to say *Enough of this nonsense, let us men move on to the real issues.*

But Sheikh Fatih still wasn't ready to let it drop. "We've talked about this a lot!" he said, leaning forward for another round.

I looked at Dr. Salama. Her mouth held a watchful, nearly imperceptible smile.

She has a thing or two to say about this, I thought. But she's going to let them wear themselves out fighting each other first.

There was an analytical hum to her quietness, a sense of wheels churning beneath the surface, that reminded me of Mohamad. And Sheikh Fatih, unwilling to let an argument drop until he had convinced his opponent, or at least browbeaten him into submission, reminded me a little of myself.

Our first meal with Dr. Salama and Sheikh Fatih was a working lunch. A week or so after we met, she invited us for *masquf* in her office. They spread a tablecloth over one of her work tables, and we ate *masquf* and talked about Sadr's uprising.

It was a challenge to pick tiny bones out of the smoky fish and write notes at the same time. But as we discussed the upcoming "transfer of power" to a transitional Iraqi government, and the awful living conditions in Sadr City, I had a strangely comfortable feeling of déjà vu. Dr. Salama was talking about the same things people talked about in Buffalo, Chicago, or any of the other places I had lived: toxic waste dumps too close to people's homes, bad sewer systems, the need for better schools and hospitals. They reminded me of civic leaders I knew back in the United States, of church basements and mimeographed flyers and community meetings; except the community, in their case, was Sadr City.

Salama Hassoun al-Khafaji's father was a carpenter—a religious man, but self-educated, a reader. He loved logic, and taught his daughter the importance of reading books and asking questions. At the age of fifteen, she started wearing the *hijab*, which was frowned upon by the secular Baath regime. She did it anyway. "I was not a calm woman," she told me once—speaking calmly, as she usually did, but with a firm expression that made me believe her.

Like practically every Iraqi I met, she had wanted to be an artist. As a young woman, she also wanted to be a doctor or an oil engineer. When the Baath educational system had ruled out those ambitions, she had studied dentistry instead. "I found myself in it," she said, "because I like sculpture, and dentistry requires sculpting and taking a picture." She got married and had four children.

But every week, wrapped in her black *abaya*, Dr. Salama would slip out of the house without telling her husband where she was going. If he asked, she would say she was visiting a friend's house for lunch or tea. Finally, one day, he demanded to know what she was up to. Lowering her eyes, she gave him the enigmatic reply, "I am doing what is right."

She was studying in an underground *hawza*, or Shiite religious academy, for women. Informal salons and study groups have been a tradition in Iraq for centuries; during the Abbasid caliphate, philosophers would meet in the mosques of Basra and Baghdad to drink tea, steal food from each other's plates, and debate the latest translation of Greek philosophy. But under Saddam, the practice went underground, and by the time Dr. Salama started attending it was extremely risky. She did not tell her brothers or even her husband where she was going, "because I was afraid that someone might ask my child, and we would be in great danger."

The women who studied with Sheikh Fatih and his mother, Dr. Amal Kashif al-Ghitta, told their husbands, brothers, and children they were going to ladies' luncheons—harmless gatherings where women ate and gossiped and drank tea. Instead they were studying economics, social sciences, logic, rhetoric, humanities, comparative legal systems, and Islamic law—a kind of book club for religious women.

"We didn't hide the fact that we were gathering, we didn't hide the fact that we were students," she told us. "But we would do things like say 'Today, we are going to have lunch' at one person's house. Another day we would have tea at another's house."

It was the mid-1990s, at the height of Saddam's "faithfulness campaign." After the first Gulf War, Saddam began courting Islamic hardliners in a bid to shore up support. The Baath Party was still nominally secular, but Saddam became a master at using Islam as a tool of political repression. He beheaded women—in many cases, apolitical women whose male relatives were accused of belonging to banned political parties—under the pretext that they were "prostitutes." Many men responded by keeping their wives, daughters, and sisters locked in the kitchen. Such women often turned to religion: it was an identity their men couldn't criticize. (I suspect they also wanted to be able to quote the Quran and its interpretations back to husbands and fathers who told them such-and-such was Islamically ordained.)

But Shiite women were at a disadvantage when it came to learning their own religion. Public academies taught only government-approved Sunni doctrine. Saddam could not close the Shiite religious academies, which had been the center of Shiite learning for centuries. But the *hawzas* did not admit women. And anyone who taught Shiite principles in private places, even at home, risked imprisonment or death.

Despite the danger, Sheikh Fatih and his mother decided to teach women at their home. Their informal *hawza* was grounded in the Shiite seminary tradition of studying a wide range of fields as part of a religious education. They followed the same course of study that men followed at the *Hawza al-Ilmiya* in Najaf, where most of Shiite Islam's grand ayatollahs had studied. So dangerous was this knowledge—philosophy, rhetoric, logic, history— that Sheikh Fatih would teach the women from behind a screen or through a microphone from another room to protect their identities. They would ask him questions "because in our *hawza*, questions are more important than the lessons." But he never saw his students, and they never saw his face. "I didn't want to know who my students were," Sheikh Fatih told us. "Because under torture, I would be forced to give their names, and I didn't want to do that. They would have captured all of my students."

Despite all these precautions, Sheikh Fatih got caught. In 1998, he was arrested and sent to Abu Ghraib prison, charged with instigating opposition to the regime. Dr. Amal continued the lessons for a while, but eventually she had to stop. She was living confined to her home, subject to constant surveillance, and she worried that the Baath Party would execute her son if she caused trouble. She passed the time by writing books.

Eventually Shekih Fatih was sentenced to death. Dr. Amal and the *hawza* students pooled what money and jewelry they could scrape up, including about a pound of gold. It amounted to $20,000, about $8,000 of which went to bribe the judge and the rest to other officials. The money didn't get him out of prison. But it was enough to buy his life.

"He's worth it!" Dr. Salama exclaimed, as they told us the story. "He's worth more than that. One lecture from him is worth that."

"Well, everyone is worth that," Sheikh Fatih said gently. "Many others have died in Abu Ghraib, and they were worth that too."

In December 2002, as the U.S. invasion loomed, Saddam granted an amnesty to some political prisoners (except for those he executed). The day Sheikh Fatih was released, Dr. Salama went to the prison with Dr. Amal and three other students. But they did not actually meet face-to-face until after the fall of Saddam; she saw him walk out of Abu Ghraib, but he did not see her watching in the crowd.

Dr. Salama and Dr. Amal still held the *hawzas*. No longer clandestine, they were more like book clubs now—talking circles where women discussed ideas, politics, and everything else. In early May, Roaa and I attended one of the sessions.

Sheikh Fatih and his mother lived in Hayy al-Jamia, the university neighborhood, in a house surrounded by a garden of palm trees and flowering shrubs. We sat in the living room while eight women, ranging from their twenties to the sixty-year-old Dr. Amal, discussed jobs, politics, elections, and how they didn't feel safe in the universities or anywhere else. One woman shared the kind of story that was becoming commonplace: her brother was an Iraqi policeman. He had shot a thief who was trying to escape, and now the thief's family was demanding blood money under tribal law. "We must have a system that protects the police," said one of the women firmly. A woman in her late thirties got into a fight with a young civil engineer who did not believe *hijab* should be compulsory. They all agreed on the need for more education, especially for women. Dr. Amal gave a short lecture defending freedom of thought, which she illustrated with an Iraqi-sounding version of the Watergate story, in which Nixon was an unjust ruler led astray by wily advisers.

Afterward the women clustered around Dr. Amal, addressing her as *Sheikha*. I asked her about the books she had written.

"My favorite is *Torn Bodies*," she said. "I wrote this while my Fatih was in prison. I was inspired by Franz Kafka—do you know Kafka?—and Edgar Allan Poe. It is narrated by each of the parts of a man's body: arms, legs, and, excuse me"——here, she assumed a severe expression——"sexual organs. It is a metaphor for the Iraqi society."

She disappeared and came back with a copy of one of her books. She pressed it on Roaa.

"Next time I see you," she said sternly, "I want you to discuss it with me." Roaa nodded and looked terrified.

We went outside and got ready to leave. Dr. Salama and I stood in the yard under a palm tree with her daughter, a shy thirteen-year-old with her mother's moon-shaped face. Dr. Salama and I were discussing the legacy of fear left behind by the old regime.

Her daughter tugged at her sleeve. "Mama," she whispered anxiously.

"What is it?" Dr. Salama asked, turning to her and leaning her head down to listen.

"What is this regime? Will it help me lose weight?"

Régime, a French word people often used in Iraq, can also mean diet.

Dr. Salama burst out laughing. She put her arms around her daughter and hugged her, drawing her close into the billowing black fabric of her *abaya.* "No, my dear," she said, smiling, "that's not the kind of regime we're talking about."

Dr. Salama was a conundrum to me. She was intelligent, outspoken, and independent. She opposed *wilayat al-faqih,* the doctrine of absolute rule by the clergy that is applied in Iran. She defied the Iranian-influenced Islamist parties to endorse Ahmed Chalabi, a Shiite secularist, for prime minister. (He lost.) She and Sheikh Fatih consistently pushed for a more democratic transition of power, for more female ministers, and for more political representation of Sadr and his followers (a tactic that could have defused some of the momentum of his uprising if it had been pursued at that time). And yet she supported Resolution 137, a proposal to replace Iraq's 1959 Personal Status Law with a decentralized system that would allow religious authorities to control personal matters—including family law like divorce, marriage, child custody, and inheritance rights.

Most Westerners made the mistake of classing Dr. Salama with the hard-line Islamists. (Hillary Rodham Clinton once denounced her as "ultra-conservative.") But the reality was more complicated.

The majority of Iraqis were Shiites. Thanks to years of war and mass killings of men, the majority of Iraqis—some estimates went as high as 55 percent—were also women. Shiite women were the face of Iraq, the largest demographic group in the country. Most Iraqis supported some form of Islamic law; at the same time, most Iraqis also supported women's rights to work, education, and political power. In July 2004, Gallup released a poll finding that Iraqis supported women's right to hold national political office by a two-to-one margin (except in heavily Sunni areas, where support for women's rights was much weaker). Like many Iraqi women, Dr. Salama believed that Islam allows women to wield power in the public and private spheres.

In theory, this is true. One of the uncomfortable truths in Iraq, as in much of the Muslim world, is that women don't have the status that the Quran says they should. Political and religious leaders invoke Islam—often using misogynistic interpretations of ambiguous and highly contested Quranic passages and *hadiths*—to justify pre-Islamic tribal practices such as honor killings and genital mutilation. Ira Lapidus, the respected Islamic scholar, put it best in his definitive book *A History of Islamic Societies:* "The Quranic ideal and Muhammad's example," he wrote, "were probably much more favorable to women than was later Arab and Muslim practice."

In 1959, when Iraq passed its landmark Personal Status Law, Iraqi women got civil protections that were among the best in the Arab world. But the Baath Party weakened those rights in the 1960s, and Saddam eroded them even further during the faithfulness campaign of the 1990s, when he segregated schools and decriminalized polygamy and honor killings. For many Iraqi men, Saddam's repression provided a convenient justification for the disparity between women's status on paper and in practice. Once that excuse was gone, Shiite women wanted to reenter the public sphere. They saw Islam as their way in.

There was some precedent for this idea. In Morocco, feminists had pressured the government to work with Muslim scholars on reforming the country's restrictive family law. The result was a new Islamic family law that promised women more rights than previous interpretations of *shariah*. But the question, in both countries, was whether women would ever get those rights in practice.

I called Amira Sonbol, a Georgetown University professor who has written several books on women and Islamic law, history, and society. "I'm one of the very first to advocate the Islamic discourse to change the law," she said. "It's the only hope for Muslim women in the future. But it has to work under conditions where women really have a chance. And women in Iraq right now really don't have that chance, because of the political situation in Iraq."

Sonbol predicted that women's rights would end up being a bargaining chip in negotiations between male-dominated political parties. "The waves pull you where you don't want to be pulled," she said. "The Shiite women in Iraq do not know that they are going to be a pawn in the division of Iraq, and that they are going to be expendable."

Around that time, Roaa got a job at Al-Hurra, "The Free One," the Arabic-language satellite channel set up and funded with American tax dollars. She was making real money—$800 a month, an excellent salary (even with the six-day work week that was common in Iraq). She covered car bombs and political meetings and did street reporting for stories about daily life. Our poet friend Ali, from Laylak's birthday party, which seemed like years ago, was appointed news director a few weeks after she started; he would be her new boss. This was the career she had always wanted.

During those months, we would meet for coffee and have the kind of career-girl conversations I would have with my girlfriends back in New York: we would complain about bosses and boys, talk about marriage and relationships, confide our ambitions for the future.

Like Layla, Roaa longed for the days when boys and girls could spend time together as equals, without gossiping tongues ruining their reputations. But unlike some of her friends, she didn't believe in premarital sex or even premarital kissing: freedom, for her, meant freedom to explore the world and different ways of thinking. "It's not that I'm liberated," she said earnestly (this made me smile), "but I have a hard time finding someone who thinks the way that I do. I have my own ideas. I have male friends."

Being a young Muslim woman with independent ideas was lonely. Added to that were all the usual barriers to marriage for young Iraqis: lack of money, instability, and the fact that as a Kurd, it would be difficult for her to marry an Arab. "This is the problem," she sighed. "I've never had love!"

One day, after we finished our little cups of thick Arabic coffee, she flipped my cup facedown on the saucer. After a few minutes, she read my future in the dark slurry of sugary coffee grounds. I would go places, she predicted: in my cup, she saw rivers, trees, and a looming black giant with a pure white heart.

And her future? "You can't read your own grounds," she said. "It's bad luck." But we wanted the same things: travel, careers, advanced degrees. Parties where men and women could sit together and talk. The freedom to see the world. During those conversations, I often had to beat back the urge to promise her all the travel, education, and adventures that she longed for, all the things I wanted her to have, if only they were mine to give.

We all struggle to reconcile these two sides of our natures: the nomad and the homebody, the mother and the movie star. I wanted Roaa to have them both. In another Iraq—the one that "we" had promised "them"— perhaps she could have.

"I had this dream of knowing people from other cultures," she said. "I hope to do this someday. Because we were blocked from the whole world for so long."

"Do you still want this? Even if it's dangerous?"

"I still have that dream," she said. "And it's very hard to make this dream come true. But maybe, someday, if Iraq settles down, I could do it."

We were sitting in a restaurant that faced Abu Nuwas, looking out toward the Tigris. Even surrounded by tanks and barbed wire, the river had a sluggish, iridescent grandeur. The date palms leaned over and admired their reflections on the river's gleaming skin. Inside, we sprawled on worn wooden divans covered with Ottoman-style cushions. The ceiling of the restaurant was woven with reed mats that gave off a wheaty, sun-baked smell in the dry heat. By the doorway a brass pot of tea simmered on a gas ring. We were the only customers.

Suddenly she shook her head, as if waking from a dream or in surprise at some private thought.

"Do you know, Annia?" she said, looking at me with a quiet, intense wonder. "I never imagined, not even after the war ended, that I would be sitting with a foreigner and talking about these things."

On May 13, Mohamad left Baghdad for Beirut. I was supposed to go with him, but at the last minute the *Christian Science Monitor* editors asked me to stay and fill in for one of their staff reporters who needed a break.

That morning, we packed up our little room at the Andalus. We took the hot plate and the plastic bins and the apples and onions and the various packets of dried soup and pasta, and gave them to Abu Zeinab. I moved everything else to the *Monitor*'s room at the Musafir Hotel. Later that afternoon, the *Monitor*'s driver, Adnan, drove Mohamad and me to the airport. We held hands in the backseat as we drove down the highway that led to the airport, which was by then one of the most dangerous roads in Iraq.

Mohamad got out at the first checkpoint to wait for the shuttle bus that would take him to the terminal. Adnan stood outside the car and shook Mohamad's hand and kissed him on both cheeks. "Mr. Mohamad, don't worry," he said in Arabic. "I will take care of her like I would my own sister."

Once we drove away, I started weeping in earnest, big choking sobs. Adnan looked over at me in distress. "Mrs. Annia," he said, struggling to find the words in the new language he was learning. "When I was in the Iraqi army, I went away for nine months—my wife, alone like you."

Nine months at a stretch fighting the Iran-Iraq War. I could survive twelve days in Baghdad on my own.

"I tried to be like this"—here, he turned back to the wheel, gripping it with tight fists and stiff straight arms, as if trying to thrust it away from him, and thickened his neck in a parody of manliness—"but inside, I was crying."

He turned to me, taking both hands off the wheel and balling them into fists and putting them over his heart: "I am sorry," he said. "But after he is gone, more love."

The next day I went to Shahbandar. I ran into Nassire, a handsome young poet I knew from *Al-Najeen*. He had once had a perfectly chiseled nose, but now the entire front of it had been sheared off. He held his head awkwardly to the side, trying to hide the hole where his nose had been, but you cannot hide a missing nose.

"What happened to you?" I said stupidly, so shocked I forgot my manners.

"They held me down and sliced off my nose with a paper cutter," he muttered, looking down at the floor.

I didn't ask him who "they" were. It was irrelevant. Everyone I knew felt lucky just to be alive. Abu Rifaat had been robbed and beaten six times; being Christian made him an easy target. He felt betrayed by America, by the culture he loved, and most of all by the man he had once idolized—the liberator George W. Bush.

"He said he was going to turn Iraq into an oasis," Abu Rifaat said, pronouncing it like "Onassis." His voice was raw with bewilderment and pain. "In the past several months, I have been attacked six times by thieves. One of them hit me on the head with a bottle."

He leaned over and pulled off his watch cap, exposing a deep dent in his soft pink skull.

"So is this the situation of the happy people? Where is the security, where is the happiness, where is the oasis of Mr. Bush?" he cried. "This is an oasis where bottles are smashed on your head!"

As we spoke a thin, hunched man came up to us. He had a brown mole in the middle of his cheek and his eyes glittered and danced. He stood in front of me, leaned his face into mine, and shouted, "You tell her that we reject this new American-Israeli flag!"

Since everything else was going beautifully, the Governing Council had turned its talents to the country's most pressing problem: designing a new Iraqi flag. The new flag's dominant colors were white and pale blue, and this resemblance to the Israeli flag did not go over well with the Iraqi public. And it got rid of the words *Allahu Akbar,* God is Great, which Saddam had added to the old Iraqi flag during his faithfulness campaign—words that are always easier to add than to remove.

"You tell her that if they try to hang their new Iraqi flag in Fallujah, in Ramadi, we will kill them!" the man railed. "We will take down their flag and we will hang them up in its place!"

"But she is not American!" lied Abu Rifaat. "She is Lebanese! A Lebanese journalist!"

"She is a spy!"

"She is a journalist!" pleaded Abu Rifaat. "A French journalist!"

The conversation deteriorated from there.

After the man disappeared, a thin, kindly old man in a dishdasha and a white knit prayer cap came and stood over me. He was the manager. On behalf of the café, and the people of Iraq, he apologized for the angry man.

"You are a guest here, you are welcome here," he said. "We know you, and you are a friend of Abu Rifaat, who is well known here; we know that you like Iraqi poetry, and we like this, and I am sorry that this man has spoken rudely to you."

He would not let me pay for my tea.

The next time I saw Abu Rifaat, he was still apologizing. "After you left this place, myself and the owner of the café, we spoke very strongly to this man," he told me. "And this man, he became very ashamed of himself, and he felt very badly for what he had said."

I doubted that. I knew that Abu Rifaat and the old man would have welcomed me if I returned. But hospitality was a double-edged sword; I didn't want my pleasure in books and the company of poets to identify them with the "enemy," which was what I had by then become. So although Shahbandar was my most favorite place in Baghdad, and possibly the entire world, I stayed away from Mutanabbi Street and Shahbandar Café after that. Every Friday I would stay home, and think: this is what it must feel like for Roaa, for Laylak, for all the Iraqis who can't go see their favorite friends or sit in their favorite places; except it's much worse for them, because I can leave and they cannot.

I went back only once, to say goodbye. I sat in the back, talked quietly, and left after five minutes, and I never saw Shahbandar Café again.

A week later, Abu Rifaat came to visit me at the *Monitor*'s bureau in the Musafir.

"Books!" he shouted, when he saw the bookshelf in the office. He walked to the shelf, stood in front of the books, threw his arms open wide, as if to embrace them all, and shouted, "I am weak before books!"

He was rattling on about something or other, graffiti or magazines or poetry, when he noticed I was not saying anything. He stopped short and peered at me over his glasses.

"Would you like something to eat?" he asked suddenly.

Earlier that week, the head of the Governing Council had been assassinated, I had talked to several men tortured in Abu Ghraib, and I was finishing a story about female prisoners who had been psychologically tortured. An Iraqi from Fallujah had brought me a floppy disc people were passing around in insurgent circles, supposedly pictures of American soldiers torturing and raping Iraqi women. The photographs were fake—they had actually been lifted from a Hungarian porn Web site—but they were a graphic reminder that all sides were using women's bodies in a dangerous game of political symbols, and when I saw them I lost my appetite for days. Every time I ate more than a mouthful of anything, a panic would come over me: a message from my stomach of extreme stress, my body completely rejecting food, and although I was not sick I would feel the urge to throw up. I had lost about ten pounds in ten days.

"Maybe a cigarette," I said.

He frowned at me, and I remembered that before his wife moved to Canada with their two sons, Abu Rifaat had been a father.

"You are always working and smoking too much," he said. "You work too hard, for you love the Iraqis too much, and you love your job more than you love yourself. And you are always eating in restaurants, and this is not good. The food in restaurants, it is not healthy. I cannot take you to my house, because it is not safe"—he lived with a couple of maiden aunts in a working-class neighborhood—"but I will take you to lunch, and I will show you the *real* food of Iraq."

Down the street there was a small kebab shack. As Iraq's fortunes had fallen, the kebab shack's had risen: by now it had grown from a small wooden cart to a gleaming corrugated metal shed that you could actually walk inside. A tiny television played from a shelf on the wall. Abu Rifaat sat me down next to it and bustled off to get us food.

At the counter, he held an urgent conference with the cook, a plump young man in a dirty dove gray dishdasha. The cook laughed with amazement at what Abu Rifaat requested. When he saw that the old man was serious—the *ajnabieh* was really going to eat this thing—he set to work.

Instead of making the usual grilled kebab, he took the ground meat off the skewer and sizzled it over a very high flame in a little battered iron cooking pan. At the same time, he chopped a fat, juicy tomato into chunks and threw it into the pan together with some onions and a hint of hot pepper. He sautéed the vegetables in the fat and spices from the meat. The meat, in turn, soaked up the spicy hot tomato sauce. In Baghdad they called this *banadura shamee*, "Damascene tomatoes," or sometimes "chili-fry."

"This," said Abu Rifaat, as he bore it to the table, "this is the *real* food of Iraq!" He showed me how to scoop up dripping hunks of meat with scraps of *tanoor* bread. He watched me, beaming, as I ate all of it. We mopped up the last of the sauce with more bread.

Over tea Abu Rifaat expounded on education, his favorite topic. According to him, the Iraqi people needed education more than anything else, "because from thirty-five years ago, these people were separated from the rest of the world. And this separation killed a great proportion of his manners, his morals." And they needed travel, he added: "To travel around the world, which will make them feel they are citizens of the world, not of just one country."

After the food, I felt exhaustion creeping back. But Abu Rifaat was unstoppable. "I love tea!" he shouted, and ordered another cup. When it came, he demonstrated the correct way to stir the tea without rattling the spoon inside the glass.

I couldn't help laughing. I needed to get back to the office and finish my story, but Abu Rifaat always cheered me up.

Suddenly he realized I was waiting for him. "I will show you the *Irrraqi* way of finishing your tea quickly!" he declared. "You do like so"—pouring his tea into the tiny glass saucer, he swirled it around a few times to cool it quickly—"and then you drink it like this!" He tipped the saucer up to his lips and sucked down the tea in one long slurping suck. It was not pretty, but it was the essence of good manners.

* * *

Thanks to Abu Rifaat, my appetite was completely restored. The next day I went to the Sumer Land restaurant, which was still occasionally open to the public, for my usual plate of *shajar, jazar, wa qarnabeet.* For some reason the chef had chosen that particular moment in late May 2004—during the Mahdi Army uprising, the first Marine assault on Fallujah, and the Abu Ghraib court-martials—to make a chicken roulade stuffed with cream sauce.

It was a beautiful thing. A gesture that might, like Layla's manicures, have seemed pointless to some; but to others it might contain the whole of civilization, or at least a reminder of normal life. I went back to the kitchen to thank him.

He sat slumped in a chair, sweating, surrounded by bedraggled pots and pans. Dirty knives lay on the counter next to him, attended to only by the flies. The air-conditioning was off. The generator must have failed, or maybe they just didn't care any more.

"Why?" I asked. "Why make such a beautiful thing at a time like this?"

He shrugged. An expression of pride and despair, halfway between a smile and a sigh, flickered across his face.

"It's what I do," he said.

Chapter 15

Even a Strong Person
Can Ask for Peace

A FTER HE BECOMES human, Enkidu goes straight to Gilgamesh, who beats the tar out of him. That makes them best friends, just like in a good martial arts movie, and Gilgamesh decides they should go on a road trip.

Gilgamesh wants to slay a monster and drive out evil from the world. Enkidu has a bad feeling; he tries to talk his friend out of it, but Gilgamesh won't listen. They get their weapons. The old men sigh. The young men cheer. The two friends walk all the way to what is now modern-day Lebanon and kill the monster Humbaba, who guards the cedars.

Unfortunately you're supposed to consult the gods before you kill their monsters. Somebody has to pay for this act of hubris. The trip was Gilgamesh's idea, but the gods kill Enkidu.

Gilgamesh cannot believe that his friend is dead. He holds Enkidu in his arms for six days and seven nights and speaks to him as if he were still alive. On the seventh day, a maggot falls out of Enkidu's nose, and Gilgamesh finally understands that his friend, the mighty wild man, is nothing but rotting meat. He wanders the wilderness for days, disheveled and haggard, dressed in the skin of a lion. Finally he arrives at the ocean, whose shore is also the edge of the world.

Luckily, just at the world's outer limit, right where a wandering soul needs it most, is a bar where he can get a beer.

The bartender sees him coming, locks the door, and runs up onto the roof. "Who are you?" she shouts down at him. "You look like hell."

Gilgamesh pounds on the door of the tavern. "My friend whom I loved has turned to clay," he cries out. "Am I not like him? Will I lie down, never to get up again?"

Siduri, the bartender at the end of the world, looks at him with compassion. She solves a lot of existential crises in her line of work.

You will never find immortality, she tells Gilgamesh, because the gods kept it for themselves. So stop running after what you can't have and enjoy the things you can:

> *Now you, Gilgamesh, let your belly be full!*
> *Be happy day and night,*
> *of each day make a party,*
> *dance in circles day and night!*

* * *

Mohamad and I were in Beirut, taking a two-week break in between stays in Baghdad, when we heard the news: insurgents had tried to assassinate Dr. Salama as she drove through the Triangle of Death. She had survived. But her seventeen-year-old son and one of her bodyguards had been killed.

As soon as we returned to Baghdad, we went to pay a condolence call to Dr. Salama at her office. We had made an official appointment, but for some reason the U.S. military guards refused to let us in. So Dr. Salama, still in mourning for her son, made a clandestine visit to the Andalus.

We met her in the lobby and took her upstairs to our room accompanied by several bodyguards, serious-looking young men who waited outside the door. I made tea, and we drank it while she sat on the chair in our tiny front room and told us what had happened.

She had gone to Najaf to talk to people there as part of her mediation between the Mahdi Army and the U.S. military. That evening, U.S. troops had blocked the highway, so her two-car convoy was forced to take the smaller, lethal side roads. At about eight in the evening, a red Opel drew up behind them and then spun away. A few minutes later, it returned, and whoever was inside opened fire. Her driver sped away. She saw the car her son was in veer off the road. She begged the driver to turn back, but it was too dangerous.

She hoped that her son might be alive. But later that night, she found out that her bodyguard had died. "I thought that night about his mother, his wife, his young child," she said. "I was very upset. So the next day, when I received the news about my son, it made it a little easier to accept it."

In Najaf, she had met many women who had lost their sons, husbands, and brothers in the fighting between the U.S. military and the Mahdi Army. "Such simple things they wanted: to live peacefully and to have their families," she said. "I think that in this occupation, it is the women who have suffered the most. And I think that this is why it is the women who want peace. I found this such a simple thing, yet the governments—the American government—didn't understand it."

She talked about the work she was doing with Sadr's supporters, trying to convince them and the U.S. military to come to some kind of cease-fire. "The people say that because you are asking for peace, that means you are weak, you cannot fight," she said. "So I told them, 'No; even a strong person can ask for peace.' "

We were terrified that someone had seen her—that someone would send a message to the wrong people, who would try to assassinate her on her way back from the hotel, and that it would be our fault. But no one in the hotel even recognized her. In the *abaya*, she was completely safe: just another anonymous Iraqi woman.

Things got worse all summer. At night we left the door to our room open to let out the heat. One night a large rat ambled down the corridor, stopped at our door, and looked in hopefully, as though we might invite him in for tea. We kept the door shut after that.

Mohamad and I were both working all the time, exhausted and stressed and fighting constantly. The fights would flare up before we could catch them. The electricity would go out, there would be no water, and suddenly we would be fighting over who had forgotten to fill the gallon jugs. At the grocery store, if we were lucky to find two kinds of pasta, we would fight over which one to buy. And that was nothing compared to the serious fights like whether we should move to a "safer" hotel.

On Father's Day, I borrowed Mohamad's satellite phone and called my grandfather. He was ninety-two and deaf as a post. I lied and told him I was in Beirut, but I don't think he bought it.

"Don't stop any bullets!" he said, and chuckled. It was his favorite line from World War II, when he had been a radio operator in the Merchant Marine. His other favorite line was "Praise the Lord and pass the ammunition."

My mother got on the phone. Grandpa's sister Connie had joined the WAVES (Women Accepted for Volunteer Emergency Service) in World War II, and my mother had called her for advice on life during wartime. "Aunt Connie said you should take lots of calcium, and magnesium, and zinc," she said. "And vitamin B for stress, and vitamin C too!"

Vitamins, in Baghdad: that's my mom. If we could eat like kings when we were broke, homeless, and living out of our car, then why sacrifice proper nutrition in a war zone?

"Mom, it's Baghdad. They don't have Walgreens here. You can't get vitamins. Most of the time you can barely get medicine."

"Didn't you say your driver gets vitamins from Germany?"

This was true: Abu Zeinab's brother lived in Germany, and he had once offered us some European herbal supplements. I had forgotten all about it. But my mother remembered.

"And another thing," she said. "Don't fight with Mohamad—he's a wonderful person, and we love you, and he loves you too. And the other thing is, it's a war! What could be more stressful? Of course, you're fighting. But I'm just so worried—I thought, Oh my God, these two people are arguing, and they're going to step on a roadside bomb, and they'll still be arguing!"

This was such an accurate description of us that I had to laugh.

"Also, make sure you exercise," she said. "Keep track of your exercise, and your vitamins, and you won't fight."

I hear it all the time from Lebanese friends who lived through the civil war: In those days, the drinks were stronger. The music was louder, to drown out the shelling. The men were more tender, the women more brave. They stayed out dancing all night long because it was safer than driving home. "Every half hour was a new life," is how my friend Adessa put it. "In that half hour, you had to reinvent yourself. And if you made it to the next bomb, you would reinvent yourself again."

One of the secrets of life during wartime is that your senses become unnaturally sharp, more attuned to pleasure in all its forms. Colors are brighter, more saturated. Smells are stronger. Sounds make you jump. Music makes you cry for no reason. And food? You will never forget how it tastes.

In Baghdad, our friendships began to thrive just as the public sphere began to shrink. It became dangerous for Iraqis and foreigners to meet in public. And so instead of meeting our friends in hotels and restaurants, which was dangerous for them and for us, we ate in their homes.

Almost all of the food served in restaurants and hotels was social food: grilled meats, hummus, tabbouleh, kebab. But there was an entire universe of food—what Abu Rifaat might have called the "real" Iraqi cuisine—that you never tasted if you only ate out. This other cuisine was part of a hidden Baghdad, a life that people cultivated behind closed doors. Iraqis were still fighting to defend public life, but they were losing, and they knew it. And so people began to conduct their lives in private. They studied in living rooms instead of in universities; got their hair cut at home instead of in barbershops and beauty salons; and instead of going to plays or concerts, they watched the dizzying parade of Iraqi soap operas and reality TV shows that, for many, had replaced real life.

The history of a country is written in its food. Most Americans think of Arabic food as hummus and tabbouleh, the social appetizers of the Mediterranean. But Iraq had its own cuisine, a fusion of different culinary traditions that had evolved over centuries of migration and war. The Sumerians gave way to the Akkadians, then the Assyrians, whose empire spanned Iraq, the Levant, and parts of Turkey, Egypt, and Iran. The Assyrian emperor Ashurnasirpal, a master food propagandist, once threw a ten-day banquet for 69,574 guests. (A later Assyrian ruler dined underneath the severed head of an Elamite king mounted on a pole above the dinner table.) Then came a series of conquerors: Babylonians, Persians, Greeks, Parthians, Romans. In the eighth century, when the Caliph al-Mansur founded Baghdad and made Iraq the center of the Abbasid Empire, he initiated what people still refer to nostalgically as the Golden Age of Islam.

To the Abbasids, whose scribes translated Greek and Persian texts, cuisine was a science—a branch of medicine as well as an art. The Abbasids transformed the banquet from a display of raw power into an elite salon. The caliph would flaunt his knowledge of cuisine as well as that of painting, poetry, music, and history. Cooking was a social art: poets would recite long, flowery descriptions of banquets to win the caliph's favor. One caliph even staged a cook-off between his courtiers, like a medieval Iraqi version of *Top Chef*.

Like the rulers of any empire, the Abbasids were cruel, repressive bastards. But they were bastards with style. They presided over an explosion in agriculture and trade that historians describe as a medieval green revolution, taking spices and fruits from Asia to Europe and spreading agricultural innovations to the countries they ruled. They fused the indigenous desert foods with Persian and Byzantine court cuisines to create a culinary revolution that forever changed the way the world ate.

As Islam swept out from the Arabian Peninsula and across the Middle East, it picked up the cuisines of its converts. The classic Bedouin food—roasted goats and sheep, grilled camel, bread cooked in ashes—mixed with Indian spices, Persian pilafs, Turkish yogurt cooking, and Byzantine vegetables.

Arab writers churned out treatises denouncing the fruity, effeminate Persian pilafs and praising manly Bedouin fare. But it was a losing battle: the traditional diet of the desert Arabs was transforming, picking up Persian touches like spicy rice with nuts and raisins, broth flavored with *noomi Basra*, the little dried limes, and the sweet-and-sour sauces that distinguish Iraqi cooking to this day. The Arab Muslims conquered infidel souls; but the non-Arab converts took over the Islamic palate. Ibn Khaldun's endless struggle between Bedouins and urbanites, it turned out, made for a rich and varied cuisine.

The Abbasids went the way of all empires in 1258, when the Mongol chieftain Hulagu, the grandson of Genghis Khan, sacked Baghdad. Medieval chroniclers tell how the Tigris ran red with blood on the first day and black with ink the next, when the Mongols eviscerated the Abbasid libraries and tossed the books into the river. But the Mongols couldn't destroy the food: the Abbasids had already exported their cuisine to Europe, where its influence remains to this day, especially in Spanish cooking. *Escabeche,* the marinated fish or chicken that is a staple of Spanish and Latin American cuisine, descended from the piquant Persian condiment *sikbaj.* The little Spanish meatballs called *albóndigas* began as *al-bunduqieh,* from the Arabic *bunduq,* "hazelnut," a playful name for the tiny, filbert-sized meatballs that Arab cooks would put in soups. And when you drink a mint julep, think of its great-great-ancestor, the syrupy *julab,* from the Persian for "rosewater."

After the Mongol rampage, Baghdad became a backwater where various tribes and dynasties—Seljuks, Mamelukes, Persians, Ottomans—fought back and forth for centuries. The irrigation system collapsed. The fertile plains became deserts. The Ottomans finally took control, only to be supplanted after World War I by the British, who stitched together a nation out of the fragments of vanished empires.

A map of modern-day Iraq will not tell you this history, but its food will. Each empire imposed its influence on the country's cuisine, which is why stuffed vegetables are called *dolma* in Iraq, as they are in Greece and Turkey, and not *mehshi,* the Arabic word for "stuffed"; it's why Iraqis drink out of *glassat,* the Arabized plural of the English word "glass," and Iraqi pickles are sometimes called by the Farsi word *turshi.* To this day, the boundaries defined by food and language often reflect the differences between people much more accurately than the lines drawn arbitrarily on maps.

Iraq's cuisine echoes its position at the intersection of vastly different regions: the Levantine world, the Arabian Peninsula, Turkey, and Persia. Baghdad was the table where they all sat down. *Fesenjoon,* the sweet-and-sour pomegranate dish with walnuts, came from Persia. *Tashreeb,* the bowl of broth-soaked bread with chicken or lamb, was an old desert meal from the Arabian Peninsula—now flavored with Indian spices and *noomi Basra.* Karada street vendors fried their catfish in sunflower-gold curry powder, rich with turmeric, a fleeting aftertaste of the historic community of Iraqi Jews who once traveled between Baghdad, Bombay, and Calcutta. The old Mesopotamians still lurked in places like Khan Dajaj, Chicken Inn, a simple working-class restaurant where everybody got a whole roasted chicken swaddled in a shell of Iraqi bread that you unwrapped and then ate from like a Sumerian king.

In the end, I realized that the beauty of *masquf* lay in its intersecting lines of descent—in the very fact that I couldn't pin it down. Its origins didn't matter half as much as what people thought they were. If every Iraqi I asked spoke of *masquf* as a dish that belonged to another group, perhaps that was precisely the point: it was a national dish, the cuisine of a place and a time where identities—ethnic, sectarian, ideological—dissolved, at least for the golden hour of waiting for your fish to be prepared. It didn't matter whether *masquf* was invented by the Sumerians, or the Assyrians, or the Christians, or the Muslims, or the Jews. What mattered was that everybody thought of it as somebody else's dish and yet also entirely their own.

Sami Zubaida is a professor emeritus of politics and sociology at the University of London's Birkbeck College, and one of the world's foremost scholars on comparative food and culture. He grew up in the Baghdad neighborhood of Baitaween in the 1940s. In those days, Zubaida told me, hummus was practically unknown in Baghdad. But in his neighborhood, which was fairly cosmopolitan, it was common for families of different faiths and backgrounds—and hence, different food traditions—to send their neighbors plates of food. Zubaida's Iraqi Jewish family had friends from Syria, where hummus was a staple; the men did business together, and the women exchanged food. "That was my first experience of hummus," he told me, laughing. "They would send us that and tabbouleh. These were novelties to us."

I asked Dr. Salama if Iraqis of her generation had grown up eating *meze* like hummus, tabbouleh, and *fattoush*. "Grilling bread and putting it on a salad?" she said, laughing. "No, we never did this. All of these salads— tabbouleh, *fattoush*, even this, what do you call it"—we were sitting at a table spread with *meze*, and she pointed to a round dish of *baba ghanouj*, which many Lebanese call *mtabal*—"this *mtabal*, all of them were new to us. When I was a child, we didn't eat them. We had *jajik* and the cucumber and tomato salads. Those were the famous Iraqi salads."

After 1948, Palestinian refugees who moved to Iraq made Levantine food more familiar. But it was during the oil boom of the 1970s, when middle-class families like Roaa's earned enough money for vacations abroad, that Mediterranean food became widespread. Families traveled to Turkey, Syria, or Lebanon and came back with a taste for little Mediterranean salads. "By the end of the 1980s, we started to have little shops selling these dishes," said Dr. Salama, "and people would have them for dinner."

On the surface, my first awful meal at the Hamra Hotel might seem like evidence that Iraq had no cuisine. But once I dug a little deeper, I found a different story altogether: the *fattoush* spoke of a precious, fleeting era when ordinary Iraqi families could travel to the Mediterranean. The hummus without olive oil reminded you that Iraq's indigenous vegetable oil, as Herodotus pointed out, came from the sesame instead of the olive. Even the shish kebabs contained layers of meaning: chicken kebabs are *shish taouk* in Beirut and most of the Levant, *tikka dajaj* in Baghdad. According to Zubaida, *tikka* is an old Persian word (no longer used in Iran but common in South Asia and Iraq) for single or odd-numbered pieces of meat. A simple skewer of meat; but in its various names, a tale of empires fighting to dominate the land where civilization as we know it began.

When I talked to Zubaida and Dr. Salama I finally realized why the food at the Hamra had been so bad: it wasn't Iraqi. The food foreigners were eating in hotels and restaurants was not Iraqi at all but a series of murky transliterations of Mediterranean food. To judge Iraqi food by the *meze* in Baghdad's upscale hotels and restaurants—unhappy émigrés from the empire of olive, fig, and vine—was like denouncing midwestern cuisine after trying chop suey in a suburban Indianapolis mall.

During the summer of 2004, we often visited Sheikh Fatih and Dr. Salama for lunch. Sometimes they fed us *masquf;* sometimes chicken and lamb. Roasted meat is ceremonial, the food traditionally served to honor a guest. But on our last visit, we got a taste of something different.

Dr. Salama sent two of her young bodyguards to pick us up. One was skinny, with a craggy, narrow face and an angry squint. The other was just a kid, with baby-fat cheeks underneath his fluffy beard. They greeted us by putting their hands on their hearts. When they smiled, their desperate faces transformed, and they looked almost hopeful. Then they ushered us to a bulletproof black Mercedes.

Inside the car, the younger bodyguard slid a cassette into the tape player. It was *latmiyat,* the rhythmic throbbing songs that commemorate the massacre at Karbala. As we drove through the streets, he began to chant softly along to the tape. Mohamad and I looked at each other and wordlessly took each other's hands.

At the house, the bodyguards drove through the gate, closing and locking it carefully before we got out. A crowd of more security guards stood in the grassy courtyard outside.

Sheikh Fatih met us at the door and showed us into the sitting room where the ladies' meetings had taken place. The Kashif al-Ghittas came from a long line of clerics, an old religious family whose name means "uncovering that which is covered," and Dr. Amal showed us portraits of relatives from Najaf and a beautifully painted family tree. We sat and talked politics in Sheikh Fatih's study, which was lined with books, and then we went down to lunch.

The table was heaped with food: steaming trays of fluffy golden rice. River fish baked in a sauce of tomatoes. Chicken roasted with saffron. *Tebsi baitinjan,* my favorite Iraqi stew—eggplant, tomatoes, potatoes, bell peppers, and spices, meant for pouring over rice.

"Try this," said Sheikh Fatih, holding out the platter of fish. "It's a Najafi specialty, something we learned from there. It is very delicious."

Like so much southern Iraqi food, this meal was heavily influenced by Persian cuisine—the saffron flavoring the chicken, for example. For dessert, we ate *sohan,* the burnt-sugar pistachio brittle from the ancient Iranian holy city of Qom. The food and religion of Iraqi Shiites are so bound together, in fact, that Saddam's father-in-law once contemptuously called them *ahl al-mutah wal fesenjoon*—"the people of temporary marriage and *fesenjoon.*" (Had he been lucky enough to enjoy either, he would have realized that this was a compliment.) You could not find this kind of food in Baghdad's restaurants. Sheikh Fatih's wife made this meal especially for us and our friend Moises, a Spanish photographer whose nationality summoned a sudden recollection from Sheikh Fatih.

"I was in Spain once, many years ago," he confided, ebullient. "It was a wonderful place."

Like his mother, Sheikh Fatih had studied science and philosophy along with Islamic jurisprudence. He had traveled in his youth: Spain, Switzerland, Italy, and Lebanon. In Rome he had eaten spaghetti. In 1978, at a photography exhibit in Switzerland, he had seen a picture of a man kneeling before the Yugoslavian dictator Tito and tying his shoe. He never forgot the image. "It taught me the beauty of ugly things," he told us, "something which is very complicated but which helps you understand."

In Spain he had eaten Spanish food at a restaurant. "I remember, I had a very excellent drink there," he mused. "It was very delicious. I believe it is a sort of national drink of Spain."

He smiled and wrinkled his forehead, looking toward Moises. "What is it called, this national drink of Spain?"

Nobody said anything. I could tell from Mohamad's face he was thinking the same thing I was: Sangria. If the sheikh had drunk wine without knowing we did not want to call attention to it. Silently, we telegraphed Moises the urgent message: Please, Moises, don't say sangria.

Moises was quiet, a little hung over maybe, hunched above his plate. "The national drink of Spain is wine, man."

Sheikh Fatih laughed indulgently. "No, no, it was not wine!" he scoffed. "It was sweet! Very sweet, very delicious."

Maybe it wasn't sangria after all. Maybe it was *horchata,* or something else. Maybe there's some other national drink of Spain.

"What did it taste like?" I asked.

"Ahh . . ." he replied, looking into the distance, savoring the memory of travel. "I remember it was red; it had fruit in it. Very delicious, very sweet."

The Najafi fish was delicious, I told them, hastening to change the subject. And because we were among friends, I remarked that my grandmother was Greek and that it was very similar to one of the many Greek ways of making fish—stewed in a tomato and onion sauce.

"Greek?" said Dr. Amal. "Have you read Aristotle? I am very inspired by the Greeks."

"We read Aristotle in our *hawza*," Sheikh Fatih said.

"And *The Frogs* by Aristophanes," said Dr. Amal. "This is an excellent description of politics. It could be describing politics in Iraq to this day. Have you read it?"

"Yes, and *The Clouds*!" I said. "Aristophanes is my favorite Greek playwright! But forget about *The Frogs*—have you read *Lysistrata*?"

Dr. Amal shook her head. She frowned and looked around at Sheikh Fatih and Dr. Salama. Nobody had read *Lysistrata*.

"It's my favorite Greek play!" I said, oblivious to the cliff I was galloping toward. "It's about this time when the Greeks were at war for—I don't know, years—and the men won't stop fighting each other. So the women all get together and tell the men that until they stop fighting . . ."

I stopped suddenly when I realized what I was about to say. I looked around the table. They looked back at me expectantly: Dr. Salama in her black *abaya*; Sheikh Fatih in his clerical turban; and Dr. Amal, his elderly mother. These were deeply religious people, no matter how much Greek philosophy they read. How could I describe *Lysistrata* to them—a play turgid with raw sexual jokes, originally performed by men wearing giant leather phalluses? A play whose plot hinges on women telling men that until they stop the war they can forget about getting laid?

I shot a desperate glance at Mohamad. He had not read *Lysistrata*. He was waiting for me too.

"The women get together, and they make an agreement that until the men stop fighting, to, uh, not have anything to do with them," I concluded.

Dr. Amal and Dr. Salama looked at each other, their eyes round with astonishment. They looked back at me.

"This is wonderful!" said Dr. Salama. "I must read this play! This is *exactly* what we are trying to do with the women of Sadr City!"

By the end of July 2004, a month after L. Paul Bremer transferred power to the interim government of Iraq, our poet friend Ali's brother and nephew had been murdered in an ambush intended for him. Someone—militants, criminals, there wasn't much difference—had tried to kidnap Sheikh Fatih's wife. Another friend's uncle had been shot, for no reason that anybody knew, as he stood in his front yard. Abu Rifaat and most other Iraqi Christians were desperately trying to flee the country. Even Alan King was leaving. We met him in the Green Zone for a dismal farewell dinner just before his tour of duty ended. "I feel like I'm abandoning these people," he said, his pink face looking close to tears. "Like this is a sinking ship, and I'm getting out on a life raft, and leaving them behind. We're leaving this place worse than when we got here."

As for Roaa, she had quit her job at Al-Hurra. Iraqi journalists had a very low life expectancy. One day, an old man sitting on a curb told one of her colleagues that even though he didn't agree with the insurgency, he wanted to help them kidnap "all of you who are working for the Americans." Roaa gave notice not long after that. Before we left—we would return in a few months, or so we believed at the time—she invited us to her house for lunch.

As soon as we pulled into the driveway, Roaa looked quickly down the street and drew the metal gate shut. In the short walk from her driveway to the front door, Mohamad and I were careful not to speak English to each other. When neighbors asked who had come to visit, as they surely would, Roaa would tell them we were Kurdish relatives from Sulaimaniya. I was wearing Umm Hassane's black-and-gray polyester *hijab*—I never left home without it these days—and Abu Zeinab had driven us there in his new car with the driver's seat on the right, a car that nobody would ever think was American. We had needed all this intrigue for interviewing insurgents or female activists, who lived under constant death threats from the insurgents, or for university professors, who were being assassinated one by one. But by the summer of 2004, we also needed these cloak-and-dagger maneuvers for more innocent missions such as eating lunch with an Iraqi friend.

I had thought that lunch would be a casual affair. But when we walked in the house, we saw that it was something else: a *sufrah*, a spread. *"Beitik aamra, sufrah aamra,"* goes an Iraqi expression that means something like "May your house be always open to others, may your table be always full of food."

Roaa had cooked a farewell feast of all my favorite local dishes. Starting the night before, she had made an enormous *dolma*, the characteristically Iraqi mixture of stuffed vegetables—not just grape leaves and zucchini, but also tomatoes, green peppers, eggplant, and even onions and swiss chard; all stuffed with fragrant rice and meat and stewed together for hours in a pot with a layer of lamb chops at the bottom. It dominated the table, a steaming mountain of purple, dark green, and red, the colors brooding and saturated as in a Braque painting. She made a northern Iraqi dish called *kubbet hamudh,* oblong patties of ground farina stuffed with spiced meat, then simmered like matzo balls in a tangy tomato broth. She had also made *tebsi baitinjan,* because she knew I adored it. (She had laughed at me when I told her how much I loved it: "You know, Annia, in fact it is very easy to make.") And in a nod to Mohamad's nationality, she served tabbouleh, fluffy and fresh, with the bulgur slightly crunchy, the way they make it in Beirut.

"I had no idea you could cook like this," I said, as we sat down at the table. Roaa wanted to be a diplomat, an ambassador. Not a housewife.

She smiled sideways at her mother. "We have a saying: that whoever learns from a good teacher will turn out even better than the teacher."

Her mother smiled back, proud despite the teasing nature of the compliment. She might have taught her daughter to cook, but she also raised her to speak her mind.

We sat down at the table. Roaa's quiet, protective elder brother, Schwan, was there too. I finally met Roaa's younger brother, Shko, "a genius at computers" whom I had been hearing about for months. He was shy and plump and smiled instead of speaking. "I'm encouraging him to apply to good colleges," she said, "because now there are no more extra points, no more president's friends."

Only Roaa's father was absent. At the age of sixty-seven, he was in Jordan looking for work. "We don't like this idea, because he's old now," said Roaa. "But it's hard for him to sit and do nothing."

I thought that it must be hard for her too, but I did not say this.

After we had demolished as much of the mountain of dolma as we could, after there was no more *tebsi* to be consumed, Mohamad and I looked at each other and said something about leaving.

"Where are you going?" said Roaa. "We haven't had dessert!"

Disappearing into the kitchen, she came out with a covered pie plate. We migrated to the living room to drink coffee and tea on wooden chairs and sofas by the window. She uncovered her masterpiece: a banana cream pie, topped with a layer of clear cherry-red Jell-O. Festive banana slices hung suspended in the glassy red gel like little moons.

"How did you learn how to make this?" I asked, dumbfounded, forgetting that recipes, unlike people, can cross national boundaries whenever they please.

She tucked in her chin and raised an eyebrow at me, looking for a moment exactly like Umm Hassane. "You know, Annia," she said, laughing, "we do know how to make these things. This is a specialty of ours, in fact."

The food Roaa cooked for us that day inherited a cosmopolitan idea, a convergence of cultures that was still encoded in its DNA. The *kubbet hamoudh* took the old indigenous grains, refined them, and mixed them with meat. It absorbed the tomato, the turnip, and other invaders from Asia and the Americas. Under the Ottomans, the Byzantines before them, and the Parthians and Sassanians before them, the stuffed vegetables had traveled over mountains and along rivers, from the Mediterranean basin to Mosul, Aleppo, and Anatolia, where it was known by the Turkish name, *dolma;* they visited the kitchens of Muslims, Christians, and Jews; of Kurds and Armenians, Sufis and Salafis, speakers of Arabic and Aramaic, kings and commoners, Ottoman pashas and British sahibs, until it reached the table where we sat with Roaa in Baghdad in late summer of 2004.

For Roaa, the hours at home cooking made for a dubious salvation: a prison, but also a refuge. She had once dreamed of traveling to other countries. Now she couldn't even drive across town. Trapped in their kitchens, Iraqis like her still longed to explore the world. By the millions, they went through the same motions: they boiled rice and sealed the pot with tinfoil—or, for the post-sanctions generation, a plastic bag—just as the ancients had sealed theirs with bread dough. They salted eggplant and then submerged it in water, weighed down with a plate. They washed chicken and meat, perhaps whispering, "Thanks be to God" as they picked up their knives to cut the flesh. They cored out zucchini, tomatoes, green peppers; millions of hands rolled grape leaves in Basra, Mosul, Baghdad, Sulaymaniya, Erbil, and a thousand villages across Iraq. Through the universal act of handing down recipes, they also handed down the memory of other places, other worlds. As long as that memory existed in any form—cookbooks, recipes, a banana cream pie—it would survive.

PART III

Beirut

Beirut is boiling like a cooking-pot!

—Tawfiq Yusuf Awwad, *Death in Beirut*

Chapter 16

Republic of *Foul*

A FTER A MONTH in New York and another month of pointless apartment hunting in Beirut, I missed Baghdad. I missed the
date palms, the dry yellow heat, and the hard consonants of Iraqi
Arabic. I missed Roaa, Dr. Salama, and Abu Rifaat. In October 2004, *The
Christian Science Monitor* had asked me to join its regular rotation of Iraq
correspondents in mid-October, and I was looking forward to going back.

There was just one problem. In the two and a half months we'd been
gone, nine foreign journalists had been kidnapped, most of them freelancers
like me. A group calling itself "the Islamic Army in Iraq" had executed an
Italian freelancer and sent a videotape of his body to Al-Jazeera. Militants
were still holding two French reporters, one of whom we knew. An Aus-
tralian journalist was snatched immediately after he left the Hamra Hotel,
and it seemed clear that somebody in the hotel or just outside it had tipped
off his kidnappers. They targeted freelancers or small news outlets with no
security, like the *Monitor*.

Two nights before my flight to Amman, I was watching a grainy video
on Al-Jazeera. Masked, hooded figures stood in front of a black banner with
white Arabic calligraphy. Their mouths opened and shut soundlessly as they
shouted. A captive was kneeling in front of them. With no emotion, just a
flicker of curiosity, I noted that it was me. One of the masked men grabbed
the captive's head and tipped it back, and at that point I woke up. I did not
feel afraid, but I knew this dream was telling me that I should.

"Look, Annia, I know you love working for the *Monitor*," said Mohamad. "And if you really want to go, I'm not going to stop you. But just remember that you don't have to prove anything to anybody. I know you're a good journalist."

"I'm not trying to *prove* anything." I was angry; everyone seemed to think this was some kind of emotional issue, but as far as I was concerned feelings had nothing to do with it.

"I know you feel like you're abandoning the story if you don't go back," he said. "I know how that feels. I know it's not about ego. But just remember that no story—nothing you could *possibly* write about—is so important that it's worth dying for. And you're not going to be helping anybody, you're not going to be bringing anyone's attention to the story, by being there and getting kidnapped."

The day I was supposed to leave for Amman, the *Monitor*'s staff reporter Scott Peterson called me. "Listen, Annia, things are really not good here," he said. He spoke very quickly and sounded distracted. "Margaret Hassan was kidnapped this morning."

Margaret Hassan was an Irish woman who had married an Iraqi, converted to Islam, and lived in Baghdad since 1972. She worked for an international charity and had spent decades helping Iraqis get health care and clean water.

"We don't know what happened. Maybe she wasn't kidnapped. It's not clear. But it's not good. It's not good. Are you sure you want to come?"

"No," I said.

Mohamad's parents invited us to stay with them until we got our own place. But we needed a more central location to start apartment hunting in earnest. Our friend Hazem, the writer for *Al-Hayat* with whom we had spent Ramadan in Baghdad, helped us get a discounted room. It was at the Berkeley, a small hotel on Jeanne D'Arc Street in a neighborhood called Hamra. We didn't think we'd be there long.

Beirut juts out from the eastern Mediterranean coastline like a giant goat butting into the sea. The northwestern corner of the city sticks out even more, a stubborn little hump called Ras Beirut, "the cape of Beirut," and this is where you will find Hamra, the famous street that gave the neighborhood its name.

Hamra was historically a mixed area, with Muslims, Maronites, Armenians, Greek Orthodox, and even American Protestant missionaries. It was a rebellious, cosmopolitan quarter from the beginning—one of those places where fact and fantasy converge, which is probably why it has always attracted writers. A disproportionate number of novels are set in Ras Beirut, especially those about the civil war or the period before it, when Hamra Street was the city's most glamorous shopping drag. Here was the store where our friend Leena came to buy panty hose during the civil war, even as militiamen stalked the streets; there was the famous Wimpy restaurant—in 1975, the height of fashionable prewar Beirut. Now it was a dusty time capsule where old men sat on cracked orange plastic chairs and smoked over the same cup of coffee all day like patient gray lizards.

A journalist friend of ours named Mansour was sitting in one of Hamra's famous cafés one day with a friend. They started speculating what would happen if there were another civil war: Each café would have its own militia, they joked. The Café Younes fighters would join forces with the Baromètre Brigades! Regusto's regulars would march against the habitués of Starbucks! The image of Hamra's eternal coffee drinkers rising up made them laugh.

An old man chain-smoking at the next table heard them. He turned around and fixed Mansour with an ancient mariner stare.

"I was here during the civil war," he said. "I fought in Hamra. And you may be laughing now, but I can tell you, that is *exactly* how it was."

Our little two-room suite at the Berkeley was shabby but clean. The door opened into a narrow living room with a brown vinyl loveseat, a television, and one chair. (Above the loveseat hung an engraving labeled *L'Arrivée des Mariés,* of a nineteenth-century couple alighting from a horse-drawn carriage, which seemed to indicate it was the honeymoon suite.) To the right of the door, a tiny sink and a mini refrigerator were tucked into an alcove about four feet deep. On the left, past the television, a door led to a small bedroom with a bed, a bathroom, and a small vanity table that we used as a desk. It was not remotely luxurious: more like a very small apartment without a real kitchen. But the beauty of the Berkeley was its balcony, which was bigger than both rooms put together.

Beirut is a city of balconies. The million and a half residents of Greater Beirut had only a handful of tiny, pocket-sized public parks, none of them particularly green. And so, like Nebuchadnezzar, people created hanging gardens. Balconies and rooftops overflowed with greenery: geraniums, bougainvillea, rosemary, and frangipani. A city of gardens in midair.

From the top of the Berkeley, I could see one rooftop garden plush with teak furniture and potted palm trees that must have cost a small fortune at Exotica, the upscale tropical plant store. Across the street, tomato and basil plants burst out of rusty olive oil tins, and old men layered in moth-eaten sweaters sat smoking on old packing crates in the evenings. A rooster strutted around with a lordly air, casting a beady eye from side to side as if supervising his serfs.

Beirutis still kept pigeons on their roofs, an ancient practice the Arabs used during the Crusades to send messages from besieged cities (and once, in the tenth century, to send fresh cherries from Lebanon to the Fatimid caliph in Egypt). One Hamra pigeon keeper had dyed the lead bird of his flock a deep fuchsia, the same fluorescent pink as the turnips pickled in beet juice that Beirut restaurants served. Whenever I saw the white birds swooping across the blue sky, following their borscht-colored leader, I thought of the Beirut militia that reconciled war and fashion by dressing in hot pink uniforms. Perhaps some small postwar demigod turned the fighters into pigeons when the war was over. From the balcony, anything seemed possible.

Our room was seven stories above the street; from that high, the car horns sounded like the faraway bleating of sheep. We could see hectic Hamra Street and the taxi stands and the men who sat arguing outside the Royal Flush gambling den and the Barbarella Amusement Center. We could see the mountains capped with snow in the winter sun and wreathed in fog in the fall rains. We could see the city's gaudy flamingo-and-apricot sunsets. When dusk settled over Hamra, we could see the dancers from Morocco and the former Soviet republics file out of the Pavillon Hotel, shrink-wrapped into purple spandex hot pants, and climb into the minibuses that ferried them up the neon coastline to the super-nightclubs.

I still flinched when walking past parked cars. I jumped every time I heard loud noises. I crossed the street to avoid garbage cans, which might contain IEDs, and in cafés I sat as far away from the cappuccino machines as possible. Walking past our peaceful neighborhood mosque, I kept half-expecting to see thousands of men pour out of it waving their arms and bellowing *"Muqtada! Muqtada!"* In early October, a small bomb had blown up a politician's car as it drove through Ras Beirut. He survived, but his driver did not, and the explosion reinforced my belief that everything—slamming doors, backfiring trucks, children setting off M-80s—was a bomb.

But the more I prowled the streets of Hamra the more these fears receded into the angry past. Somehow in the months of back and forth, of driving and flying from Iraq to Lebanon and back again, Beirut had become home.

A few weeks after we returned, a real estate agent offered to show us an apartment in a neighborhood on the other side of downtown. We walked through Hamra to the American University of Beirut, past the banyan tree at the Medical Gate, and down John Kennedy Street. Past the pale ghost ship of the Holiday Inn, still empty and bullet-scarred from the War of the Hotels, one of the many small, bloody conflicts that made up the fifteen-year civil war. Across Fakhreddine Road, and into Bab Idriss—the Gate of Idriss—a neighborhood named centuries ago when the city still walled itself in against invaders. We walked through Wadi Abu Jamil, the old Jewish quarter, past the few doomed Ottoman mansions, soon to be demolished, and the sleek reconstructions rising in their midst. The old buildings smelled of wild rosemary and chamomile. Bats flitted across the blue glass sky of early evening. We walked across Bank Street, past the Parliament building, and into the middle of downtown Beirut.

Downtown revolved around Sahat al-Nijmeh, Star Square, which was actually circular, a wheel of cobblestoned pedestrian streets intersecting in an open space with a tall art deco clock tower at its center. (Lebanon was under French control from the end of World War I until 1943, and the square was designed during the French Mandate years as a miniature of Place de L'Étoile, the axis of Haussmann's radial plan of Paris.) In the large open circle around the clock tower, teenage girls and boys strolled around pretending not to notice one another. Children rode tricycles and threw rubber balls. Nannies from Sri Lanka and the Philippines ran after them, while parents lounged at open-air cafés and smoked water pipes. Chairs and tables spilled over into the streets, packed with people eating and talking and laughing. Aside from the Corniche, the road that skimmed between the edge of Ras Beirut and the sea, Beirut had very little public space. It was a pleasure just to be surrounded by people.

Before the civil war, the city center was a massive *souq*. People came from all over Lebanon to buy everything from food to furniture: clothes, coffee, newspapers, spices, books. Just as caravans had once connected to regional trade routes in the Roman colony of Berytus, the country's prewar downtown was a gathering place where all Lebanese could sample the pleasures of cosmopolitan life. They could watch movies, chase prostitutes, join in demonstrations, sell their tomatoes, buy used books, or listen to a *hakawati*, a traditional storyteller. There were even informal coffee stands where villagers from the same area could congregate and drink coffee, waiting for shared taxis to ferry them all back to their hometowns together.

During the war, the Green Line ran through downtown. Snipers aimed at one another and any civilians in between. The beautiful old buildings with their Parisian arcades were torn and smashed. The streets were full of rubble and barricades. Two years after the war ended, Lebanon's prime minister, Rafik Hariri, proposed a dramatic renovation of the old downtown.

Hariri was a billionaire construction tycoon who had made his fortune in Saudi Arabia, working for the royal family. He dreamed of restoring Beirut to its prewar status as a glittering commercial and banking hub—Dubai on the Mediterranean. He kicked out small shopkeepers, coffee stalls, grocers, booksellers, restaurateurs, and most of the area's residents, and compensated most of them with stock in a brand-new company called Solidère. Many downtown tenants and property owners alleged that the company had deliberately undervalued their property, but there was nothing they could do: Solidère's takeover of downtown was negotiated between Hariri's company, Hariri's government, and one of Hariri's former employees, who was head of Lebanon's reconstruction authority.

Hariri turned the ruined city center into a plush pedestrian mall where the global rich could nibble on sushi flown in from Asia, try on $100 feather-trimmed thongs at La Perla, and buy a thousand-dollar telephone shaped like a banana at Bang & Olufsen. Solidère and its top shareholders made billions as Lebanon's debt skyrocketed: by 2005, Lebanon's ratio of public debt to GDP was the second highest in the world (after Malawi), and Hariri, whose net worth by then was $4.3 billion, had ranked 108th on *Forbes* magazine's 2004 list of the richest people in the world.

But Hariri rebuilt what others had destroyed, and for this people were willing to forgive a lot of corruption. The son of a Sunni fruit picker from Sidon, he was a self-made man—charismatic and blunt, given to lavish gestures—and few other Lebanese leaders had articulated a vision that transcended sect and neighborhood. He had never been a warlord, never had a militia. People grumbled at how he had taken over downtown, but many, even some who had lost their family homes or businesses, loved him anyway. The apartment we were to look at was in a neighborhood his company had reconstructed, a place called Saifi Village.

Beirut still had neighborhoods where old men wheeled up every morning on bicycles hung with hoop-shaped sesame breads called *kaak,* shouting *"Kaaaaa-EEK!"* Women would come out on their balconies, lower money down in baskets to the old men, and reel them back up filled with bread. Old men would push carts of fruits and vegetables through the streets. Shopkeepers would feed stray cats on the sidewalks. Lottery ticket vendors would walk up and down bellowing, "This is the day! This is the day!" Tiny old women in high heels would march down the potholed sidewalks every morning to the grocery store. Idlers would take over the sidewalks for their open-air salons but step aside whenever a woman sailed past, and sometimes croon a few bars of a love song, so that on some days, as you walked down the street, it seemed like the entire city was singing one continuous serenade.

Saifi Village was not that kind of neighborhood. During the war, the area had been a front line. Now it was a stucco fantasyland of pink and yellow pastel villas with white filigreed shutters. It was surrounded on all sides by highways and parking lots, making it virtually unreachable by foot. The empty streets made you feel like you were trapped inside an architect's plaster model. Little gardens were closed off to the public by locked gates. Boutiques offered handcrafted leather purses that cost three or four times

Lebanon's monthly minimum wage, which was then $200. No way could we afford to live here, which was fine with me.

The real estate agent was gloomy, with a defeated slouch, and he shuffled us morosely through the overpriced apartment that all of us knew we would not rent. Then, as we stood outside the quaint little boutiques, Mohamad mentioned that we had been to Baghdad.

"Baghdad?" said the agent, suddenly standing up straight. "They have car bombs there! All the time! Just like here, during the war!"

He pointed across manicured shrubberies to the parking lot. "You look at a car—BOOM, it blows up!" he said, throwing open his arms to illustrate the explosion. "This car here; that car there! You never know which car! It could be any car! Two, three car bombs a day!"

He dropped his arms back down at his sides and beamed at us, sighing happily. He missed the car bombs.

I knew how he felt. It wasn't that I liked war, exactly. I had longed for a normal life the whole time we were in Baghdad. But when it came, I was left with a feeling of unreality: we went through that, survived all that—and for what? So people can buy $700 artisanal handbags? Neither world—neither the car bombs nor the pink pastel reconstruction—seemed real.

Things were getting worse in Iraq. Roaa had another job, but she was getting anonymous instant messages urging her to "the jihad" and insinuating that women who worked with "the occupiers" were . . . she didn't use the word, but I could imagine what it was. I wanted to grab everyone and shout in their faces that the war was still going on. I wanted to have a normal life, but I did not want the Iraqis, who were struggling just to have any life at all, to be forgotten.

Beirut seemed to offer a kind of solution. The economy was a mess, the political system a shambles. After the civil war ended, the Syrian regime ran Lebanon as a satellite state. The Assad family and its cronies funneled money and goods out of the country, extorted Lebanese business owners, and beat or jailed Lebanese who protested their policies. Lebanese politics was punctuated by a string of unsolved assassinations that started during the war years and continued into the oughties. Nobody knew how much money had disappeared from the Lebanese economy—an unfathomable entity even before the war—only that it was a lot.

But fifteen years after the war ended, you could walk down the street and buy a loaf of bread without being killed. People rarely talked about the war. It was surreal to see people paper over old hatreds, but it also gave me hope that life could resume after a war. People didn't have to love each other, or even like each other; all they had to do was join in the unspoken agreement to live together, to make it work somehow. And if you looked at the rhythms of daily life in Beirut, it was working.

If Lebanon could get over its civil war, I would tell Roaa and Oday and Salaam and Usama, then so could Iraq. It might take a while, but we would wait. In the meantime, I would settle down, start taking Arabic classes, and we would find an apartment.

A faded, smoke-stained, black-and-white photograph hangs behind the counter of many a small Beirut business. In it, an old storefront is usually surrounded by bustling suit-hatted men, streetcars, gracious old buildings. Perhaps a proud owner is standing outside in a butcher's apron or inside behind a cash register—the family business back before the war, when it was located downtown.

When the center of Beirut fell apart, the small shops that made up its commercial heart spun out into all corners of the city. Every neighborhood got a little piece of downtown: Hamra had the famous dessert maker Intabli and Café Younes, which filled our neighborhood with the aroma of roasting coffee beans, and many others.

With the center gone, the city's collective mental map fell apart. The fighting had confined people to certain neighborhoods or sides of town. When it was over, a willed amnesia about the war spread across the entire city. People gave directions for a city of the past: pass by "Al-Nahar building," where the newspaper of that name no longer publishes; turn the corner where Modca Café used to be; or drive down Nazlet al-Piccadilly, named for a movie theater closed for decades. The snipers were long gone, but people still avoided certain neighborhoods or streets without remembering why.

The foreigners who came to Lebanon learned one set of names—the written street names, which were useless. Beirut had hardly any street signs. The few it did have tended to hang bashfully on the sides of buildings, European-style, and were roundly ignored. The street labeled "Baal-bek Street" on maps and street signs was better known as "Commodore Street," after the Commodore Hotel (a nerve center of the civil war, now just another one of Hamra's many hotels). My friend Paula grew up on Si-dani Street. She did not know the name of Makdisi Street, a couple of blocks away; for her it was "the street before Hamra" or "the street that the co-op grocery store is on."

I met a real estate agent just down the street from us once. She had lived in Hamra her whole life, but when I told her I had walked from Jeanne D'Arc Street, she said I was mistaken; it was "very far from here," she in-sisted, much too far to walk. I walked her over to Jeanne D'Arc, which was exactly two blocks away, and showed her a tiny, tucked-away street sign she had probably walked past a thousand times. There was *another* Jeanne D'Arc Street, she maintained—one that I wouldn't know about, of course, being a foreigner. She was correct in her way: there *was* another Jeanne D'Arc Street, a Jeanne D'Arc of her imagination, and in Beirut such streets are as real as the ones made of asphalt.

Everyone I met seemed to carry an alternate map of Beirut in his or her head, a ghost map superimposed on the physical street grid. Each of these imaginary Beiruts was different from the other, and everyone insisted that their personal Beirut was the real one. People were always getting lost, no one could give directions, and you could never tell a taxi driver where you were really going, because he was driving through a different Beirut than you were. After a few weeks I began to believe that all cities are nothing but mass hallucinations.

Fortunately there was one set of directions everyone could agree on. In the absence of street signs, a functioning government, or any semblance of a social contract, I learned how to navigate the city by food. Ask a taxi driver to take you to Sidani Street, and he may not know what you're talking about; he may very well deny such a street exists. Tell him to take you to *sandwichat* Marrouche, famous for shredded chicken sandwiches with garlic sauce, and he knew exactly where to go. The edible map was the most reliable.

There were Gulf tourists who came to Beirut knowing just one loca-tion: Barbar, the famous block-long empire of restaurants in Hamra. Barbar served everything from brain sandwich to fruit cocktails named after Hitler,

Castro, Noriega, and Nelson Mandela; but it was best known for its *sha-warma* and falafel. "They say 'Take me to Barbar' as soon as they get off the plane," said Abu Hussein, a *servees* driver we knew from the neighborhood.

This system suited me just fine. I would never, ever forget how to get to Salim Hassan, the spice shop near the corner of Jeanne D'Arc and Makdisi, because it stocked black mustard seeds, fenugreek, and little bags of *noomi Basra* for a dollar. "Food is the only thing that works in Beirut," our friend Bassem said once, and he was right.

I began building a map of Hamra in my head. A good day in Beirut starts with *foul* (pronounced "fool"), so that's what my map started with. *Foul* means "fava beans," but it is also the shorthand for *foul mdamas*, the soupy breakfast of stewed dried fava beans mixed with garlic, lemon juice, olive oil, and—depending on taste and location—chickpeas and spices. (In the Levant, fava beans and chickpeas are also the main ingredients of falafel, and something about the combination seems to work magic no matter what form it takes.) There's an old proverb that varies from country to country and goes something like this: "*Foul* in the morning, breakfast of kings; *foul* for lunch, food of the poor; *foul* in the evening, the dinner of donkeys." (It rhymes in Arabic.) Another proverb commands darkly: "*Ma t'oul foul hatta yaseer bil makyoul*"—"Don't call it *foul* until it ends up in your bowl," the Arabic equivalent of "Don't count your chickens until they're hatched." All of which underlines the supreme importance of *foul*.

In Beirut, every neighborhood worth the name had a *fawal*—a bean man, a maker of *foul*. Certain *fawals* were famous: the one in Zarif, behind the Future TV station, practically had his own cult. Customers lined up in front of him, some bearing their own bowls, like hopeful beggars. If he didn't like the looks of you, he'd serve everyone else first, and you'd be lucky to get your bowl of beans. (My friends called him the Hummus Nazi, after the Soup Nazi from the television show *Seinfeld*.) But I preferred my Hamra *fawal*, Abu Hadi. Down through the thicket of side streets between Hamra and Bliss, across from Moderne Butchery, sandwiched between the old porn theater and the devout Muslim greengrocer, was the narrow store-front of Bassam Badran, now better known as Abu Hadi—for my money, the best *fawal* in Hamra, and possibly all of Beirut. He called himself *Malik al-Foul*—the King of *Foul*.

Abu Hadi had a greyhound face, five o'clock shadow, and big brown eyes full of that anxious motherly expression good cooks always have— permanently preoccupied with a pot about to boil or a customer that needs to be fed. Born in Damascus in 1969, he worked as a hairdresser until an arm injury inspired him to turn his love of food into a living. "At home, I don't let my mother cook," he told me once. "In my family, everybody waits for me to get home, because they enjoy eating with me and tasting what I cook."

And then he used one of the Untranslatables: "*ana bshaheeyun*," I awaken their appetites, or in this case something like "I take such pleasure in eating that it makes people's mouths water just to see me."

Watching Abu Hadi cook always gave me this feeling. His narrow store-front was usually packed with people, mostly men, either waiting covet-ously for beans or savoring them at the two small tables and the ledge across from the counter where he held court. He was constantly whipping omelets in a tiny bent frying pan, blending hummus in his ancient Moulinex, sending his prep cook across the street to Moderne Butchery for meat, and packag-ing everybody's beans with a plate of mint, tomatoes, scallions, hot green peppers, pickles, olives, and bread. He made the full range of dishes you can expect from a good *fawal: foul*, hummus, and hummus with meat; *msabbaha* (the swimming), whole chickpeas bathed in lemony garlicky tahini sauce; *balila* (the wetted), whole chickpeas mixed with garlic, salt, and cumin. But my favorite was *fattet hummus*, one of the many exquisite Arabic dishes that revolve around day-old bread. He would crush a clove of garlic into a paste in a bowl with salt, whisk in a generous ladleful of soft stewed chickpeas from the tall brass amphora simmering on top of his two-burner gas ring, and dump the mixture into a metal takeout container almost in the same motion. Somehow, simultaneously, like a multi-armed Hindu goddess, he would whip tahini into yogurt and top the beans with it. He'd throw a bent and blackened aluminum pot on the other burner, cut half a stick of but-ter into it, reach under the counter for a pinch of pine nuts and a handful of dried pita shards, and set them to sizzling in the hot butter. Once they blushed caramel, he flung them on top of the yogurt, where they formed a buttery puddle, and dusted the whole landscape with dried mint, cumin, and paprika: a miniature mountain range, sharp cliffs of crisp golden bread, valleys brimming with butter, snowed in by white yogurt spangled with green, brown, and dark red.

"I only use the best ingredients in my *fatteh*," Abu Hadi told me, and to prove it he held up a white plastic vat of Taanayel yogurt, a foil pack of Lurpak butter. But he didn't have to prove anything. I could taste it in his *fatteh*.

After a breakfast of *fatteh* or *foul* I felt ready for anything, even Abu Ibrahim. I would head back up Makdisi, past Book Sale and its posters of Stalin, Marx, Che Guevara, and Hugo Chávez. I would stop by Smith's, the famous grocery store that had stayed open during the civil war, to pick up salad greens and a few other staples. A block back down Makdisi, then a right on Gandhi Street, across Hamra, and I would be at Abu Ibrahim, the *khadarji,* or greengrocer, who sold the freshest fruit and vegetables.

Abu Ibrahim was born Mohamad Ali Sadi Gul in 1953 in Mardin, Turkey—"the most beautiful country, the best mountains, best buildings, best streets." His parents died when he was only nine, leaving him an orphan. So he moved to Lebanon to join his grandfather, one of about a hundred thousand Kurds who migrated to Lebanon during the twentieth century. Now he had a thriving business: a cool little cave in the side of a building, packed with zucchini, eggplant, lettuce, tomatoes, and whatever fruits were in season. He piled up boxes of parsley, mint, romaine, and cilantro on the sidewalk so they spilled over the pavement in a green wave. Customers clustered around him, haggling and badgering and elbowing one another for his attention. He weighed their purchases against octagonal iron weights he piled on the two arms of a bent metal scale. He swaggered up and down the sidewalk shouting huskily at his children, who helped him sell vegetables. He had twenty-six, he told me once—yes, twenty-six, he said, sticking out his bristly chin—"from the same wife!"

A pale, balding man standing behind him with a head of lettuce rolled his eyes and snorted with disbelief. But I believed Abu Ibrahim: he was tough as an old tree, and I could imagine him having a wife even stronger than he was.

I set down my shopping bags. It was avocado season, and he had a box of them laid out on the sidewalk. I stroked their glossy reptilian hides and dreamed of avocado cheesecake. Meanwhile, Abu Ibrahim went rooting through my groceries.

"What is this?" he roared.

I looked up to see Abu Ibrahim's son emptying out my shopping bags from Smith's. Abu Ibrahim himself was holding up my cellophane pack of salad greens. It was marked 1,250 Lebanese lira, which is less than a dollar.

"Lettuce for one thousand, two hundred and fifty!" he howled, as if he were the one being robbed. "I sell it for five hundred! Tomatoes for three thousand! I sell them for fifteen hundred!"

An old woman looked up from the eggplants and frowned at me sharply over her glasses. The men who lounged across Mahatma Gandhi Street, outside the building where Moroccan prostitutes were said to live, watched with interest.

"This is special lettuce, special tomatoes," I protested in wilted Arabic. "No not-good thing inside." I didn't know the Arabic for "organic" or "no pesticides." I definitely didn't know the Arabic for "community-sponsored agriculture project that benefits small farmers."

"Why are you paying such prices?" he bellowed. "Why do you buy vegetables from these thieves? You should buy them from *ME!*"

I couldn't blame Abu Ibrahim: he was just trying to protect his monopoly. Lebanon was a nation of monopolies, a country founded by bankers and merchants, where laws awarded the right to sell foreign goods to one holder exclusively. If you bought Lipton tea, Kraft cheese, or Lindt chocolates, you were buying them from the same family, because nobody else had the legal right to import those goods. (Hariri had tried to abolish the exclusive agency law, but even he could not prevail against the oligopolies that had run the country since its founding.)

My other local *khadarji* explained it like this: "If I want to buy potatoes, I have to go to somebody from the X family, because he controls all the potatoes. He goes to the Bekaa Valley, where the potatoes are grown, and he tells the farmers: 'Here is some money—grow your crops, and when they are grown, you will sell them to me.' And the poor man is in debt to him; what can he do?"

He sighed heavily. "The whole Middle East is like this. The whole world!"

* * *

In January 2005, Mohamad went to Iraq to cover the historic parliamentary elections. I stayed in Beirut and made appointments with real estate agents and *simsars,* the neighborhood fixers who act as informal brokers. I even made an appointment with Solidère's rental agent, who made it clear he would rather rent to Gulf millionaires than to Lebanese expats and their foreign wives. But he grudgingly admitted to having some apartments. If we came back the following Monday, they might let us look at a few.

On Sunday, Mohamad flew back from Iraq, exhausted but exhilarated by the jubilation of the Iraqis at their first real election in decades. Monday he slept late. I went out to the balcony and watched the midday sunlight play over the zigzag jumble of satellite dishes and rusty antennas. I imagined what it would be like to have our own apartment, how it would feel to settle into Beirut after the wanderings of the past year and a half. Perhaps we would keep a cage of canaries on the balcony, as people did here, and potted hibiscus and bougainvillea, our contribution to the network of gardens suspended in midair. I would plant tomatoes in big buckets.

A sudden thunderous boom cracked through the city. Startled pigeons ruffled the air.

"Mohamad!" I ran into the dark bedroom and shook his shoulder. "Sweetie, did you hear it? There was a huge explosion! I think it was a car bomb!"

He whimpered the way men do when you wake them up. If he heard anything, he'd absorbed it into his dreams. I shook him again.

"Why did you wake me up?" he groaned.

"There was a car bomb!"

"Annia, you think everything is a car bomb," he said. "It was just a truck backfiring. I'm going back to sleep."

I went back out on the balcony. Seven stories below, a lone car sped silently down Hamra Street. Jeanne D'Arc, normally clogged with honking cars at midday, stretched empty. A man ran down the sidewalk shouting hoarsely.

I went around to the other side of the balcony, the one that faced the mountains and the Mediterranean. Across the far rooftops, between our balcony and the rippling raw silk of the sea, a black cloud of smoke began to rise.

Chapter 17

The Green Revolution

O N FEBRUARY 14, 2005, a truck bomb filled with one ton of TNT ripped through Rafik Hariri's armored motorcade as it drove along the Corniche. Soldiers and policemen gathered around the enormous crater the bomb blasted out of the road. Rescuers dragged charred bodies from flaming cars. On Future TV, the anchor wept as she announced that Hariri, the billionaire former prime minister who owned the television station, was dead. Angry crowds gathered at Hariri's mansion, just up the street from the Berkeley, chanting anti-Syrian slogans. Outside the hospital where the victims were taken, women rocked and sobbed and held one another. Just hours after the killing, opposition politicians gathered at Hariri's house and drafted a statement accusing the Syrian regime and Lebanon's reigning pro-Syrian government of his murder.

I took a *servees* downtown that night. Streets that usually bustled with cars were empty except for the occasional speeding taxi. Intermittent cavalcades of young men roared through the darkened city on mopeds fluttering with pictures of the murdered tycoon. In Zuqaq al-Blatt, a historic neighborhood with Ottoman and French Mandate buildings, they had smashed the windows of the few shops that remained open. Glass glittered on the sidewalks. The restaurants downtown were dark, their $200 prix fixe Valentine's Day dinners forgotten. Within hours, the bombing stripped away the fairy tale we had wanted to believe—that Lebanon had recovered, that daily life had resumed, that the war was over.

* * *

Like many wars, "the Lebanese civil war" was not a single conflict so much as an epoch, a long twilight of battles that flared up and died down just unpredictably enough to keep civilians unsettled. Proxy wars between Syria, Israel, Iran, and others played out as a series of neighborhood gang wars between heavily armed militias: the War of the Mountains, the War of the Flags, the War of the Camps. Most of the Lebanese people I knew had referred to the war, while it was happening, with an astringent little euphemism that recalled Northern Ireland and its endless "troubles." They called it "the events."

For most Americans, the defining moment of the Lebanese conflict came in October 1983, when a suicide attacker slammed a truck bomb into the U.S. Marine barracks outside the Beirut airport and killed 241 servicemen. The American military investigation concluded that Shiite militants had carried out the bombing. These militants would later coalesce into Hezbollah, the group whose name means "Party of God."

In 1989, Hariri had helped organize a summit in the Saudi resort town of Taif, where he had built a luxury hotel for his royal patrons. Lebanon's political and militia leaders signed a Saudi-brokered peace deal that redistributed power among the major sects and installed the Syrian regime (with America's blessing) as the guarantor of peace in Lebanon. The end of the fighting and the postwar agreement raised high hopes: Government jobs would be distributed according to merit, not sect. A bicameral legislature would be formed. Syrian troops, which had been in Lebanon almost continuously since 1976, would redeploy and ultimately leave. By early 2005, none of these things had happened, Syrian troops still remained, and the small anti-Syrian opposition had begun to grow. Hariri had never officially joined the opposition, but he was planning to run an independent slate in the upcoming parliamentary elections, and opposition politicians believed the Syrian regime killed him in order to prevent him from challenging its rule over Lebanon.

Hariri's family decided to bury him downtown. They located his funeral tent between the Virgin Megastore and a mega-mosque he had built just on the edge of Martyrs' Square, the big open area that lay a short walk to the east of Sahat al-Nijmeh. During World War I, when the country was racked by famine, the Ottoman military governor Jamal Pasha (known in Lebanon as "the butcher") executed Lebanese nationalists in the public square. Later it became a gathering place lined with movie theaters and cafés; then a front line in the civil war; and afterward, a large empty space where protesters would gather. In the 1990s, Lebanon's Syrian-controlled security forces had beaten and arrested demonstrators in the square. But they could not prevent people from assembling there now that it was a grave site. The funeral procession attracted thousands, and Martyrs' Square became a magnet for mourners.

A week after the assassination, the opposition called for a massive demonstration. No party banners, instructed party leaders, only the Lebanese flag. Employees of global advertising agencies unveiled a brand: a red-and-white color scheme and the word "Independence" in English, Arabic, and French. Thousands of protesters marched toward downtown holding signs: STOP SYRIA. SYRIA OUT. TRUTH, FREEDOM, INDEPENDENCE. One massive sign said simply, in giant block letters: HELP. Once the crowd arrived in Martyrs' Square, they set up a tent city and vowed to remain until the government fell and Syrian troops left Lebanon.

For the next few months, downtown Beirut hosted something between a wake and a rave. Money, posters, flags, and food flowed in from political parties. Teenagers pounded tent stakes into the earth. Middle-aged men wearing bespoke suits walked around clutching bags from Patchi, the upscale chocolatier, and passing out flagpoles. At night, singers and emcees would shout slogans from a giant stage. Hundreds of people strolled up and down, mostly young girls and boys dressed in their best, strutting and preening like joyful, revolutionary mall rats. The Lebanese called this peaceful uprising the *independence intifada*. The Bush administration declared it the "cedar revolution." American pundits proclaimed it proof that the Iraq war had been worthwhile: the Iraqi elections had awakened an "Arab spring," a wave of democracy that would sweep through the region, starting with Beirut.

Mohamad and I spent most of our nights downtown that spring. Dinner downtown became a ritual: We would eat dinner at Al-Balad, a restaurant just off Sahat al-Nijmeh that served Lebanese country food, and then walk around talking to the young people that filled the square. They were thrilled to be part of a mass movement; they spoke eagerly of throwing off years of humiliating Syrian rule. Most of them believed that once the Syrians left, all of Lebanon's economic and political problems would leave with them.

By now I was beginning to see the deep vein of depression that ran through Beirut, even among those young enough to have missed most of the civil war. Lebanon was particularly cruel to its young: about a third of college-educated Lebanese had to migrate abroad to find salaries that matched their qualifications and the high cost of living in their own country. Zuhair al-Jezairy, the Iraqi journalist who spent part of his own exile in Lebanon, described it mournfully as "not so much a country for its children as a staging post for their future exile."

The income from Lebanese working in other countries made up almost a quarter of Lebanon's GDP. But the young people who were forced to leave their own country in order to keep its economy afloat were not even allowed to vote from abroad. This was partly a product of Lebanon's feudal political system: the Parliament was still stacked with *zaeems*, hereditary clan chieftains who passed down seats to their sons and nephews. The result was a legislature in which many members, as a Lebanese good-government group once dryly put it, "lacked experience in drafting laws." A new class of warlords had arisen during the civil war, militia leaders or military men of humble origins, and if anything, they were more corrupt than the hereditary *zaeems*.

Once the intifada was a few months old, our friend Rebecca came to visit. Her brother Rudy had spent most of the spring camped out in Martyrs' Square. But she had missed the revolution—she was still working in Baghdad, one of the many young Lebanese abroad, making better money than she would ever get in her own country. We went to dinner downtown and talked about the parliamentary elections coming up in May and June.

Rebecca was from Bikfaya, the hometown of Christian warlord Bashir Gemayel, who was assassinated in 1982. Her family had always been loyal to the Gemayel dynasty. But that spring, as Lebanon prepared for its first postwar elections free of Syrian dominance, she began to question the logic of hereditary leadership. "Why does it always have to be a *zaeem*, or the son of a *zaeem*, who runs for Parliament?" Rebecca asked us over *kibbeh* and tabbouleh at Balad. "Why not me?"

* * *

Dinners were for downtown. Lunches were for *dahiyeh*, a fifteen-minute drive (on a good day) and a world apart from Martyrs' Square. Every weekend, Mohamad and I went to Umm and Abu Hassane's for a home-cooked meal.

Going to *dahiyeh* was like traveling backward in time. We would catch a *servees*, one of the dilapidated old taxis that careened around Beirut blasting their horns at unwary pedestrians and picking up multiple passengers for a dollar each. As we rode up Bishara al-Khoury Street, along the old Green Line, downtown and its nightclubs slid away behind us. The moth-eaten buildings of the civil war, the Beirut of snipers and militiamen, lumbered up ahead. At the end of the drive, past the fenced-off Pine Gardens and the walled Hippodrome, under the giant hand-painted billboard of Musa al-Sadr, a Shiite leader who disappeared the 1970s, we entered *dahiyeh*.

Literally, *dahiyeh* means "the suburb." But over time, in Beirut, the word evolved into a shorthand for the constellation of neighborhoods—including Haret Hreik, Tayuneh, and Shiyah—just outside the city limits. In the 1940s, a French urban planner conceived Beirut's suburbs as a genteel, spacious area where middle-class families could raise children amid trees and courtyards and little green parks. Alas, the well-intentioned Frenchman did not anticipate the demographic upheavals that would follow World War II. The economy of southern Lebanon depended heavily on trade with Palestinian cities like Haifa and Acre. In 1948, war broke out after the creation of Israel, southern villagers were cut off from their primary markets, and the economy of the south all but collapsed. For this and other reasons, villagers migrated to Beirut and its outskirts throughout the second half of the twentieth century—among them, in the late 1950s, Mohamad's parents.

In March 1978, after a series of attacks on northern Israel by Palestinian guerrillas, the Israeli military invaded southern Lebanon and set up a "buffer zone" manned by mostly Christian Lebanese militiamen. More Lebanese Shiites migrated to the outskirts of Beirut, joining thousands already displaced from the south, and by the early twenty-first century a country that had been 88 percent rural in 1950 had reversed its demographics almost completely and become 87 percent city dwellers. By the late 1990s, *dahiyeh* was home to approximately half a million people, many of them Shiites from the south. The area was largely controlled by Hezbollah, the Iranian-backed Shiite militia that had emerged during the war and became one of the most powerful political parties in Lebanon. It was also a Syrian ally.

Fifteen years after the war ended, the government had rebuilt very little in Beirut's outlying suburbs. Electricity still went out for up to eight or even ten hours a day, because Lebanon's electrical company could not meet the population's demand. Water taps ran dry for days in the hottest months of the summer. These shortages were not unique to *dahiyeh*—friends who lived in other suburbs had the same problem—but they were worse there.

I was curious to find out whether the intifada would inspire people in *dahiyeh* to vote their corrupt leaders out of office—if, having thrown off the Syrian overlords, Lebanon would finally elect politicians who could provide basics like water and electricity.

"Umm Hassane, are you going to vote?" I asked her at one of our lunches.

"Why should I vote?" she asked, setting down a plate of stuffed zucchini and grape leaves. "Nobody deserves it!"

In Bint Jbeil, the village where Umm Hassane grew up, politicians would pass out bread, meat, vegetables, and olive oil a few days before the elections. The village women would spend the next two or three days making every dish in their repertoires: *kibbeh, kusa,* grape leaves, *maqlubeh,* and more. On election day, everyone would gather in the town square, stuff themselves, and vote for the *zaeem* who had passed out the food. Umm Hassane regarded elections with a certain cynicism.

But what about here in Beirut? I asked her. Surely it was different here. Whom would she vote for?

She looked at me like I was crazy. Umm Hassane had lived in *dahiyeh* for almost half a century, but thanks to Lebanon's arcane election laws, she could not vote there. Because her residency was still in Bint Jbeil, where she had been born, she had a choice: she could spend hours on a hot, diesel-fumed bus, rattling down to the village she left behind decades ago, all for the dubious pleasure of casting a vote for politicians who did not represent her. Or she could stay at home, spend the day coring zucchini and stuffing grape leaves, and actually end up with something to show for her time.

This Hobson's choice was a function of Lebanon's "confessional" system of government. As the French were leaving in 1943, Lebanese elites put in place an unwritten agreement that the president would always be a Maronite Christian, the prime minister a Sunni Muslim, and the speaker of Parliament a Shiite Muslim. Parliamentary seats were divided among eighteen officially recognized sects (with the smaller ones bundled into a "minority" seat). Initially, seats in Parliament were divided on a 6-to-5 ratio of Christians to Muslims, based on a 1932 census that showed Maronites as the majority in Lebanon. By the 1960s, Muslims began to outnumber Christians, but the government refused to hold a new census, and the Muslim desire for a proportional share of power became one of the flashpoints of the civil war.

The idea behind the system was that the balance of religions would keep the larger sects from overpowering the small ones. But by making religion the basic element of citizenship, and placing the different sects in a zero-sum relationship with each other, the confessional system made it virtually impossible for people *not* to have religious conflict: if Muslims gained a seat, Christians had to lose.

After the civil war, parliamentary seats were redistributed equally between Christians and Muslims (a ratio that still favors Christians, who now make up about a third of the population). The Parliament was supposed to approve an election law "free of sectarian restrictions," but it never did, and by 2005, Lebanon had still not conducted a census since 1932—as it happened, the year Umm Hassane was born. If the people of Lebanon were allowed to vote on a non-sectarian basis, the current coterie of warlords and *ʒaeems* (including the two major Shiite parties, who had much to gain from the status quo) would risk losing its monopoly on power. Until that day, Umm Hassane and hundreds of thousands like her would not be able to vote in the capital where they lived, worked, went to school, slept, bought groceries, and paid taxes.

"Would you vote if you could vote in Beirut?" I asked Umm Hassane.

She turned around from the sink and gave us a withering look. "What do you think this is?" she asked, putting a fist on her hip and waving the other hand around the small dim kitchen, the oilcloth-covered table, the forest of concrete outside. "America?"

* * *

On March 8, 2005, Hezbollah's leader, Sayyid Hassan Nasrallah, held a massive counterdemonstration in downtown Beirut to "thank Syria" for what it had done for Lebanon. Nasrallah had been hinting that the anti-Syrian opposition was poised to sign a peace agreement with Israel—anathema to Shiites with ties to the south, where memories of the Israeli occupation, which ended in May of 2000, were still raw. Hundreds of thousands of supporters of Hezbollah and Amal, the two main Shiite parties, as well as a constellation of smaller Christian and secular parties, flocked to Riad al-Solh Square, on the other side of downtown from Martyrs' Square.

On March 14, one month after Hariri's murder, the anti-Syrian coalition responded by holding its own massive rally downtown. Hundreds of thousands gathered in Martyrs' Square, and with that, Lebanon had a new political fault line. Both sides—those who had demanded that Syria leave, and those who had rallied behind Nasrallah and his allies—claimed to represent the majority. Each side defined the other's political beliefs in the darkest possible terms: If you questioned the anti-Syrian movement or its leaders, you were a terrorist sympathizer. If you criticized Nasrallah or his allies, you were a lackey of Western imperialism. If you thought both sides had earned criticism, then clearly you sympathized with the wrong side, depending on which one you were talking to, and were hiding your loyalties out of some nefarious motive. You had to take sides.

About a week after March 14, the *khamsin* began to blow.

Every spring, a wind rises up from Egypt and the Libyan desert and blasts Beirut with its hot breath. The weather changes overnight with the *khamsin*, or "fifty," named for the number of days it can last. Some scientists and Bible scholars believe that the ninth plague of Egypt from the book of Exodus—the "darkness which may be felt"—was a *khamsin*. It is "an ill wind that blows no one in the Middle East any good," wrote *Time* magazine in 1971, adding that the *khamsin* can "madden men," cause car accidents, and increase crime rates by as much as 20 percent. A professor at Jerusalem's Hebrew University diagnosed this mysterious malaise as an overabundance of positive ions. The ions made old people depressed and lethargic, but had the opposite effect on young people, who became literally supercharged with positive electrical energy. These physiological effects, *Time* noted, corresponded to the ill winds of other continents—France's *mistral,* Austria's *foehn,* and California's fabled Santa Ana, to which writers from Raymond Chandler to Joan Didion have attributed wildfires, murder, and suicide (not to mention a rash of overheated metaphors).

But I loved the *khamsin.* The wind made me feel reckless; it promised unexpected pleasures and dangers. Overnight, the cold rain of Beirut winter turned into unearthly heat. The air smelled like sand. The sky turned orange. Suddenly it was time to switch from shoes to sandals, to go outside at night, and people would shake their heads and say: "It's the *khamsin,* the *khamsin!*" with that knowing pride people always show toward events that surprise them every year. That spring, a few days after the *khamsin* began, Hanan's friend Hassan called to tell us that he had green garlic.

Lebanon had a universe of wild edible greens that marked the seasons more reliably than any calendar. Country people foraged for them in fields, on mountainsides, and in vacant lots. Grocery stores and *khadarjis* did not usually carry these greens—they were too uncultivated, too ephemeral. But you could get them from Bedouin women who sold produce on the sidewalk. I bought my greens from Umm Adnan, who sat across from Café Younes; Hassan had introduced me to her when we first moved to the neighborhood. Umm Adnan was somewhere in her sixties—she didn't know exactly where—and she had been making her living this way for twenty-five years. She would wake up every day at four in the morning, arrive at her spot before eight, and set up shop right on the sidewalk with big black garbage bags full of greens: fresh mint, oregano, parsley, romaine, arugula, purslane, and, if you were lucky and it was in season, green garlic.

The coming of the green garlic was always an unscheduled seasonal gift. People would hold impromptu dinner parties. Friends delivered armfuls of the slender green spears to each other and sautéed them with pencil-thin asparagus and wild fennel. Or they mixed it with *sleeqa,* the grab bag of wild weeds that country people gathered in the spring. Hassan's garlic came from his family land in Khiam, considerably south, where it appeared earlier than in Beirut. On a warm windy evening in late March, we went to Hassan's place for a dinner feast of early spring greens.

A couple of Hanan's friends were there, including the big writer I had met in Baromètre, back in 2003, the one who looked like Hemingway. Hassan's five-year-old daughter ran through the apartment laughing. The pale green shoots of garlic were streaked magenta at the bottoms. He chopped them into segments and sweated them in a skillet. He had a pile of *khubaizeh* too, a hairy green mallow that grew in vacant lots, abandoned buildings, and piles of construction debris. He chopped the *khubaizeh* and braised it in its own juices with wild fennel and caramelized onions. The green garlic he sautéed with scrambled eggs, a traditional Mediterranean way of serving vegetables and wild greens, and sprinkled with ground coriander. He loaded a plate with radishes, scallions, hot green peppers, and goat yogurt. He brought the garlic and *khubaizeh* to the table on big plates, two heaping mountains of green, and passed out pieces of flatbread. We tore into the *khubaizeh* first, the wilted leaves still thick and wet with dark green juice. Behind their fennel camouflage, the mallow tasted weedy, treelike—a leaf you could imagine giraffes or buffalos gnashing on. And then I tried the eggs, with their green whisper of garlic. Grown-up garlic dominates the plate, but this was different: hiding under the sweaty, animal smell of garlic was something grassy and almost sweet.

"This 'cedar revolution,'" said Hassan. He was speaking Arabic, but he mouthed the Bush administration neologism in sarcastic, American-accented English. "This is just more propaganda. Nothing will be different in the end. Until now, nothing has changed."

Strangely enough it was the big writer, whom I remembered as the most cynical of Hanan's crowd, who replied. *"Non, ça bouge, ça bouge,"* he said, shaking his massive head slowly from side to side. "It's moving. Things are changing at last."

Chapter 18

Death in Beirut

I SUPPOSE IT WAS bound to get us sooner or later. We didn't avoid it on purpose; it was just one of those things we kept putting off. In March, we had to cover the independence uprising. In April, came the historic withdrawal of Syrian troops from Lebanon. May and June brought the parliamentary elections. And then, one sweaty July day when we went to Mohamad's parents' for lunch, fourteen centuries of tradition finally caught up with us.

"*Maal asaf,* I can't kiss you on the cheek," said Abu Hassane as he stood in the doorway, trembling. "It's *haraam* for me to kiss you on the cheek."

Nobody really knows what happened—whether he decided this on his own, which I find unlikely, or whether some relative got hold of him (I suspected Hajj Naji). Either way, Abu Hassane had become persuaded that because Mohamad and I hadn't done a *katab al-kitaab,* we weren't "really married." Therefore, I was not officially part of the family; therefore, it was not permissible for him to kiss me on the cheek in welcome when I came to their house for our weekly lunches. "I want to," he said, anguished, "but I can't—it's not right."

Abu Hassane was not always so religious. But as he got older, he became addicted to worry. He worried about his health; he worried about the political situation; he worried, quite reasonably, about Mohamad going to Iraq. He worried about dying and going to hell.

Lebanon was a nation of worriers. During the civil war, the constant irregular diet of explosions, assassinations, and kidnappings made people reach for tranquilizers, antidepressants, Bekaa Valley hashish—anything to ease the stress. Fifteen years later, people still popped Xanax and Valium like aspirin. Most of the Beirutis I knew confessed to being *mdepress,* an Arabization of a word we all know. Doctors overprescribed everything, and even if they didn't, their patients overmedicated anyway.

At one end of the dining room table, Abu Hassane maintained a little shrine to the gods of mosque and pharmacy. A small green-and-gold Quran; a tiny velvet prayer rug, for praying at the table, now that he was too stiff to pray on the floor; a *qurus,* a small amulet made of clay from Karbala, that Shiites use to pray; and Tupperware containers of carefully apportioned pills for all the physical and spiritual maladies of old age—gastritis, insomnia, infection. Long after the illness itself had disappeared, he would continue to take the medicine in the hopes of staving off the inevitable.

His eyes were more sunken these days, his walk more labored. His skin, a pale and waxy pink, stretched over his cheekbones. His voice wheezed like a car trying to start in the middle of winter. As his body grew weaker, he put his faith in spiritual prophylactics like a second Hajj to exorcise the sins committed since the first one. (Because he was too frail to brave the crowds, his Hajj would be undertaken by proxy, at a cost of $5,000, by a minion of whatever cleric ran this racket, but he decided against it in the end.) Making sure that we were "really married" was another tranquilizer for the soul, a last-ditch defense against sickness and dying and eternal damnation.

A few days later Mohamad appeared at the door of our bedroom. I was sitting at the desk, finishing an article about the evils of Lebanon's sectarian political system.

"My dad gave me this thing," he said, frowning, holding a piece of paper about the size of a Post-it Note.

"Yeah? So what is it?"

"It's from Hajj Naji. He wants us to read it."

"Why?"

"So we'll be really married."

"Oh."

I remembered the wise judge who married us in New York. "You know,

Mohamad and Annia, on one level, this is just a contract you're making," she had said. "But if it were only a legal contract, then it wouldn't be a matter of such incredible moment in our experience as human beings; it wouldn't be so resonant, so sacramental." Slaves would not have fought for it in the nineteenth century; gays and lesbians would not be fighting for it now. So what is it, she asked, that makes this ceremony a sacrament?

I reached out my hand for the piece of paper. "Let's do it," I said.

"You think we should?" He handed over the paper as if he was relieved to be rid of it.

"Why not?"

Standing behind me, he looked over my shoulder, and we examined the document together. It was a small square of white memo paper, the kind they call "bloc-note" in Lebanon. Along the top, it bore the legend ANIS COMMERCIAL PRINTING. Underneath, Abu Hassane—presumably at Hajj Naji's instruction—had penciled in Arabic:

> I marry myself to you for a dowry in the amount of $50,000 American dollars, to be paid before the marriage.

Below that, it said in parentheses:

> (Put the amount you want.)

"Let's make it five thousand dollars," said Mohamad.

"Nice try," I said. "But I think I'm worth at least a hundred grand."

He smiled. I smiled back and crossed my arms over my chest.

When we moved to Beirut, Mohamad had given me lessons in the art of bargaining. Never accept the given price, he told me; always bring it down by at least 25 percent, and preferably 50. He was the one who taught me to tuck my chin into one shoulder, gaze up through my eyelashes with coy reproach, and coo *"ana zbuni indak"*—"I'm a customer of yours," a magical phrase that invoked an almost erotic web of obligations between buyer and seller. Properly applied, the rules of bargaining could transform purchasing a pound of eggplants into a flirtatious tango, a series of mutually choreo-

graphed compromises a little like marriage itself. But I don't think Mohamad would have instructed me so closely if he knew that someday I'd end up
bargaining with him.

He narrowed his eyes, the faintest smile around his lips. "It's not legally
binding anyway," he pointed out. Playing for time.

"Fine," I said, with a shrug, deadpan. "So we can make it a hundred and
fifty grand then."

In Iraq, I had spent a day in a Baghdad marriage court, watching brides
promise themselves to grooms for x ounces of gold, y amount of Yankee
dollars, so many Iraqi dinars, all of it written directly into the marriage contract. But some brides waived the marriage dowry and wed themselves for
just a copy of the Quran—a form of protest, a friend told me later, against
being sold like a sack of potatoes.

I found the naked mercantilism of the Islamic marriage ceremonies
alarming: the money transaction *was* the marriage contract. But I had to
admit that they had a certain upfront quality—they acknowledged the messy
truth, one we all try to avoid, that marriage is one of those places where love
and economics collide. It was precisely this contractual nature that religious
women like Dr. Salama valued. You can put anything you want into the contract, she told me once: custody, property rights, divorce. That gave women
some power—at least in theory, because like a pre-nup, what goes into the
contract in the first place depends on who holds the advantage.

As it happened, I had just heard the new Kanye West song, "Gold Dig-
ger," and it had gotten stuck in my head. " '*Holler 'we want pre-nup!*' "
I teased Mohamad. " '*Cause when she leave your ass / She gonna leave with
half!*' "

He laughed, hesitated. I pressed my advantage.

"I'm not going for less than seventy-five grand, and that's my final
offer," I said, setting the piece of paper down on my desk, leaning back in
my chair, putting my feet up on the desk, and refolding my arms across my
chest. "You want me to read this thing or not?"

This was the most important lesson of all, the one he had drummed into
me: always walk away. When you walk away—ideally storming off in outrage after a diatribe against price gouging—they will call after you with

frantic offers of lower prices. It always works. In commerce, as in romance, they don't realize how much they need you until you prove you don't need them.

"Okay, fine, seventy-five grand," he said, laughing. "You're worth it. But it's not legally binding."

Reader, I read it. "I marry myself to you," I said, in as threatening a tone as I could muster while trying not to laugh, "for the sum of seventy-five large."

"I accept," he said. And thus we were wed. We didn't even need a witness; they make it as easy for you as possible. Our Shiite shotgun wedding meant we were "really" married in the eyes of God. Whether we meant it or not, or whether that matters in the end, I leave to gods and lawyers.

The next day we went to Mohamad's parents' apartment for *mlukh-ieh*. Abu Hassane shuffled to the door in his slippers. He peered at us over Umm Hassane's shoulder, his pale anxious face floating in the gloom of the hallway.

"Did you read it?" he asked.

"We did," said Mohamad.

"Oh, I'm so happy!" said Abu Hassane, breaking into a toothless grin.

Pulling himself up straight, he placed his hand on his heart. "I'm very happy that now I can kiss you," he said, still beaming. He bussed my cheeks three times, and we sat down at the table, surrounded by sacraments and prescription medicines, to eat *mlukhieh*.

The next day was hot and humid. Over strenuous objections from his wife, Abu Hassane walked to the neighborhood pharmacy to pick up some medicine. He collapsed outside the pharmacy and hit his head on the sidewalk. The pharmacist called an ambulance, which rushed him to the hospital, but although he was conscious, he couldn't speak. A few days later he went into a coma.

Mohamad and I spent the next few weeks at the hospital, along with a constantly rotating cast of aunts and uncles, cousins, friends, and distant relatives. One night, Mohamad came home so angry that he could barely speak. He had spent all day navigating Lebanon's health care bureaucracy:

Abu Hassane was covered by the state-run medical insurance, and since the Lebanese government did not pay its bills, the top hospitals wouldn't accept its insurance. When he finally got to the hospital, a distant cousin sidled up to him and said, "I was here at the hospital this morning, and you weren't. Where were you?" To the sanctimonious cousin, Mohamad's brief absence proved that he was a bad son and made for a prize morsel of gossip—exactly the kind of toxic family rumor that had made our Post-it Note marriage necessary.

"Now I know why this country is so dysfunctional," he raged. "Because we spend all our time doing stupid, useless things just so people won't criticize us. Why do we have to do all these stupid things?"

I patted the bed and held up the blanket so he could get in. "Most of your family is nice, though," I said.

"And this is why Lebanese people who go abroad get so much more done," he said, climbing into bed, still furious. "Because they're freed of the yoke of their families!"

All of our young Lebanese friends had the same problem. Everyone loved their families, their traditions. But "tradition," in the hands of certain relatives, became a venomous form of emotional blackmail. Aunts and uncles would call up their siblings and insinuate that they were bad parents if a daughter or a son remained unmarried. Competitive cousins would smear one another with vicious innuendos. And a shocking number of families—Christians as much as Muslims, in my experience—would ostracize sons or daughters who dared to fall in love outside their sect. There was no escape from the malevolent schadenfreude of the extended family.

I hugged him. Since his father's collapse, he had come home in a rage every night: at meddling relatives, at the state-run medical system, at Lebanon. All of it perfectly legitimate, but all of it beside the point, which was that his father was dying.

Three weeks after his collapse, Abu Hassane died. The apartment in Tayuneh was rearranged for the condolences, the traditional mourning period when visitors stopped in to pay respects. The sofas and armchairs were cleared out of the living room, which was then filled with dozens of metal folding chairs to make space for a stream of relatives, friends of relatives, and relatives of friends. A tiny butternut-shaped woman was hired to channel an endless flow of coffee and tea into demitasse cups that she continually distributed on trays. Distant cousins sat in the living room for hours. Some cried, while others muttered condolences and stared sadly at the floor. Aunts and uncles traded gossip about who else was sick. Nobody brought casseroles or food of any kind, which I found hard to understand. Why wasn't anybody feeding these people? An old man showed up in a rusty black suit and began reading verses from the Quran. Nobody knew who he was. Finally someone paid him five thousand lira to go away. Later we learned there was an entire class of freelance mourners, old men who scoured the obituaries, attended condolences of perfect strangers, and remained until they were paid off—a kind of squeegee men of mourning.

Hajj Naji hired a funeral singer for a *majlis taẓiyeh*, the mourning ritual based on the passion play of Imam Hussein's death, a traditional feature of Shiite condolences. The singer was a tall, serious young man with pink cheeks under a patchy black beard. He was wearing a long white dishdasha and bearing a karaoke machine. Gravely, he plugged it in, attached a microphone, and began to sing. He stopped and cranked up the reverb, then began again. The narrative of Karbala thundered off the living room walls and echoed out the windows in long karaoke wails. He punctuated the melody with long, shuddering sobs that sounded as though some powerful force were ripping the notes from deep inside his body. I felt a flood welling inside my chest, but I didn't cry, and neither did Mohamad; it was too public, too theatrical. The sorrow spiraled inside, feeding into some waiting reservoir of tears.

Finally the tide of mourners retreated. Mohamad and I found ourselves alone in an empty apartment with Umm Hassane, Hanan, Hassan, and several dozen empty folding chairs. Somebody bought a rotisserie chicken; we tore into it with our fingers, dipping it into garlic sauce and eating it with pickles and shreds of *marquq*, paper-thin country bread. The coffee lady flung herself into a folding chair and fell violently asleep, snoring, her head tipped back to reveal an entirely toothless mouth. We cleared the table, made tea, brought one another coffee, and Hassan spoke to me in our customary mess of Arabic and English and French.

"Are you coming to Bint Jbeil?" he asked with an encouraging nod. There would be a memorial service the next day in the family's ancestral village, and the whole family was going.

"I don't know," I said. "I'm not sure if Mohamad wants me to."

This was an understatement. "I don't think you should go," Mohamad had said the night before. "I think you'll feel out of place."

This described his feelings more than mine, but I didn't point that out. He was having a hard enough time already.

"I think he's afraid of having to translate for me," I told Hassan, switching to French. "I think these family gatherings are difficult for him. I think it's difficult for him to change constantly between the two worlds, the two languages. It makes him tired. So I want to go, but I don't want to fatigue him."

Hassan nodded. After his father died, he had insisted on distributing money to the poor, in accordance with Islamic tradition; but a few months earlier, he had also brought us a bottle of Saint-Émilion from France. If this was a contradiction, it was one he seemed to reconcile with a grace that I admired precisely because it was not effortless. The constant orbit between languages and worlds was hard work, and I could tell it cost him, but he did it all the same.

"I know what you mean," he replied. "It was hard for me too when I first married Annemarie. But you'll get used to it; he'll get used to it. I'll talk to him. You should come with us."

We left Beirut under the serene gaze of Nabih Berri, at the end of Raousheh, on a billboard that until recently had been occupied by the Syrian president. Berri accompanied us all the way south, in various heroic poses—Berri resting chin on hand and looking pensively into the distance; Berri in a manly political embrace with Hezbollah leader Hassan Nasrallah; Berri shaking one finger in the air; Berri making a fist and looking like a wiseguy in black sunglasses. Berri was the leader of Amal, the speaker of Parliament, and one of Lebanon's most powerful and corrupt politicians—the godfather of the Shiites.

Amal emerged in the 1970s as the armed wing of the Movement of the

Deprived, a civil rights group founded by the visionary Iranian-born cleric Musa al-Sadr. By the late 1960s, Shiites were beginning to escape from the feudal conditions of peasant farmers or sharecroppers called *fallaheen,* and Sadr's movement sought to channel their displacement into political power. But in 1978, the cleric disappeared during a visit to Libya (his family believes he was killed by Libyan dictator Muammar Qaddafi). After Sadr vanished, his movement fragmented: its more religious members would later form the backbone of the new, Iranian-backed militia Hezbollah. Amal and Hezbollah were technically rivals, but over the years they had perfected a symbiotic division of spoils: Hezbollah got Shiite souls, and Amal got their land and money.

Once, during the civil war, thieves broke into Umm Hassane's apartment and carted away all her furniture. Most people would simply shrug, throw up their hands, and cry, "What can we do? This is Lebanon." Being Umm Hassane, she hove off to her neighborhood Amal office, with a "connected" relative she had browbeaten into coming with her, to complain. "Auntie, they didn't know it was *your* house," the local boss explained. Gallantly, he proposed a solution: her own possessions were long gone, but they would rob someone else's house, someone with no *wasta,* no connections, and give her the new victim's furniture. She declined.

Closer to Bint Jbeil, Berri began to give way to airbrushed photographs of martyrs: Shiite guerrillas who had died fighting the Israeli military since 1978, when it occupied a swath of the south that included Bint Jbeil. After the Israelis finally pulled out in 2000, Hezbollah planted triumphant reminders of its victory all over town. A rusty Israeli tank guarded the entrance to the village. Giant posters of Nasrallah and Berri flapped over Bint Jbeil's water reservoir, where Hezbollah had erected neon-yellow sculptures of rockets and hand grenades.

During the second, larger Israeli invasion, in 1982, Mohamad's family fled to Bint Jbeil. As the Israeli army advanced up to Beirut, it was safer to be in a part of the country already under Israeli occupation. They stayed with Umm Hassane's sister Nahla in her family home, a beautiful stone house that was more than a hundred years old.

Now, twenty-three years later, as we drove to Bint Jbeil, a discussion broke out inside the car: Hanan wanted to go straight to the memorial service, but Hassan insisted that we go to see Aunt Nahla first. I hadn't seen the house, he pointed out—"*Mais non,* she has to see it"—but really, I suspect he wanted to visit the old place himself.

We piled out of the two-door rental car and headed down the narrow stone streets of the old city. Past sky-blue wooden doors with Arabic calligraphy, down a long stone passageway, tantalizing glimpses of treetops brushing the sky above the walls, and then through the wrought-iron gate of octagonal stars.

Inside the courtyard, Aunt Nahla's garden blazed with hibiscus, bougainvillea, oleander, and rose geraniums. Oregano grew out of rusted barrels and olive oil tins. Cherry tomatoes spilled out over the flagstones. The courtyard was full of trees, their branches bent under the weight of green oranges and knobby green pomegranates just beginning to blush salmon-pink at the stems. The whitewashed wall enclosing the yard had an outdoor sink, topped by a sliver of mirror, for performing ablutions and preparing food alfresco.

Everything except the bougainvillea and oleander was edible. Aunt Nahla would put hibiscus petals into *zuhurat,* the infusion of herbs and flowers that people drank for colds. She boiled rose geranium leaves in a delicate syrup for pouring over pastries and distilled bitter orange blossoms into a fragrance for flavoring puddings. She melted the garnet pomegranate seeds into the sweet-and-sour molasses that gave her *fattoush* its flavor. Beyond the wall, spiky red fruits jutted out obscenely from a stand of prickly pear cactus; she would peel them, stripping the spines, and boil them into jam.

Aunt Nahla hobbled out to greet us, a tiny old woman dressed in a black polyester skirt and orthopedic shoes. She seemed mystified that we wanted to see the old house—it was just her house, nothing special. But as Hassan ran from room to room, lecturing us on each one, she seemed to swell up a little, and by the time I asked to take her picture, she was arranging her headscarf just so, and protesting that we hadn't given her enough warning so she could tidy up.

The front door led directly into Aunt Nahla's cool blue-green kitchen, which was long and narrow like a little ship's galley. Painted shelves rested on wooden brackets carved in curlicues. A wooden board was nailed to the wall, studded with metal hooks from which Aunt Nahla hung hard plastic yogurt containers that she reused as storage tins. In the next room there was a floor-to-ceiling *namlieh*, a screened wooden cabinet for keeping food safe from marauding ants. In the high ceilings, next to small windows designed to catch the breeze, were hooks for hanging smaller, dollhouse-sized *namliehs*.

"*Regarde*, Annia!" said Hassan, and grabbed an earthenware pitcher from the kitchen counter. It was round-bellied and long-necked, with a tiny little spout projecting off the side, and little crocheted doilies covering the openings. The *ibriq* was an ancient design, the same shape as the Spanish *porrón;* it kept water cool, even in the summer, and people still used *ibriqs* to share water without touching the container to their lips. Holding it far above his head, Hassan tipped it back so that the water shot out of the tiny spout and directly into his open mouth, like wine from a medieval goatskin. I tried this maneuver and ended up with water down the front of my shirt.

The old Lebanese houses were built around food. (Sometimes literally: under the Ottomans, Lebanese villagers built false walls into their houses to hide their grain from the empire's tax collectors.) Aunt Nahla's house had a room for the *saaj*, a convex metal griddle for cooking bread, and a stone for grinding grains, and a special room just for preparing and storing *mouneh*. The word *mouneh* comes from *mana*, "to store," or lay in provisions. In Lebanon it can refer to any food preserved for winter or hard times—pickles, jam, dried cheese, *makdous* preserved in olive oil, sun-dried tomato paste, honeyed fruit, even meat preserved in rendered fat. But it can also refer to the tradition of making the food. It's one of those words that encompass an entire way of life.

Every summer, and into the fall, Aunt Nahla and her neighbors got together to make *mouneh*. They stripped and skinned the prickly pear fruits to make preserves. They rendered pomegranates into the syrup that flavored *fattoush* and *lahmajin* and sometimes—depending on who was cooking—the spiced meat inside *kibbeh qras*. They spent a day making *tahweeshet kamuneh*, cumin mix, the blend of spices for grinding with *kibbeh nayeh*. Aunt Nahla's was full of pepper flakes so powerful that one whiff made me sneeze. And the women spent two days making *zaatar*, the pungent greenish-brown powder that they made with salt, sumac, sesame seeds, and the dried leaves of wild Syrian oregano (also called *zaatar*, confusingly enough, and universally mistranslated as "thyme").

Aunt Nahla made eleven pounds of *ʒaatar* every year. She would keep one pound for herself and take the other ten pounds "down to Beirut" to give to the rest of the family along with handmade muslin bags of bulgur and glass jars of *mouneh*. While they ground the *ʒaatar* leaves and roasted the sesame seeds, the village ladies drank many cups of coffee and tea, and traded in much vital gossip—some of it, I had no doubt, about her nephew Mohamad and his American wife.

The memorial service for Abu Hassane was in Bint Jbeil's *husseinieh*, a Shiite meeting hall that functions as something between a mosque and a community center. This one was a flat gray building that looked like a suburban elementary school from the 1960s. Once we entered the building, the men and women separated. I followed the women into a sprawling room with rows and rows of wooden benches, like church pews, covered with foam cushions upholstered in polyester print. Chairs and sofas ringed the walls. At least a hundred women sat on the benches, some of them young, but most of them old. Thick pillars held up the low ceiling, giving the impression of the nether regions of a ship. Red, pink, and yellow plastic flowers garlanded the pillars and the walls. At the front of the room a platform held a wooden lectern, also festooned with flowers. Behind the platform, just below the ceiling and above more flowers fastened to the wall, hung photographs of Shiite clerics, including an airbrushed portrait of a suave, bearded young Ayatollah Ruhollah Khomeini, leader of the 1979 Islamic Revolution in Iran, looking as dewy-eyed as the tanned blond Messiahs I remembered from midwestern churches.

An old woman with a meaty face walked to the lectern and planted herself behind it. Without saying anything, she settled her black robes and began to sing. The microphone crackled and roughened the sound, but the liquid of her voice came through. It billowed over us in waves, washing upward then back down, cascading through a chicane of notes until she reached the bottom and took a sucking, sobbing breath and began all over again. It was those weeping indrawn breaths that got you, ripping away your composure the way a crying baby summons panic, some involuntary response to the sound of another human body in anguish. The song's rhythm pounded at us, remorseless as the ocean. One by one, the faces of the women around me reddened and crumpled and collapsed. Tall, black-robed young women walked up and down the aisles holding out boxes of Kleenex just as Catholics pass the offertory plate during mass. Now I understood why every aisle was full of small plastic wastebaskets. Weeping women threw wet tissues into them, so many they spilled over. Tears began to surge up inside me, a tidal wave from so deep I didn't even know it was there, and suddenly I thought of my grandmother, whom I had never properly cried for—I was always going to do it later, when I settled down—and I felt myself dissolving.

Just then the old woman stopped singing and began to recite the *fatiha*, the opening chapter of the Quran. The women rustled, rippled, and began to compose themselves. She started singing again, a melodic folk song this time. I caught lines about bringing water, a well, and someone who was gone—an ancient tradition of mourning songs, going back to pre-Islamic times, often sung by women; songs that spoke of long journeys on foot, of coffee that grows cold because the beloved is not there to drink it, of the water that pours from your eyes like the water from a spring. The beat echoed the human heart but also the cadence of walking. It throbbed from verse to verse, and slowly the women began to strike themselves to the beat of the music. They thumped their chests, and thighs, and their steady *whump* was like the beating of a massive heart. I felt myself disappearing into the slow trudge of the sound, and the feeling of anonymity was strangely comforting after the weeks of hospitals and relatives. An old woman with a clever, leathery face sat next to me, pounding her chest; on the offbeat, she cupped her hand open to the sky, the heraldic gesture of an apostle in a medieval Italian painting.

The minute the song ended, she pulled out a pack of Marlboros. Half the women in the *husseinieh* lit cigarettes, especially the older ones, turning to each other for a light. A young girl down the aisle folded her Kleenex into a small precise square and slipped it somewhere inside her black robe. The relatives stood at the front of the room, their faces battered by the storm of grief. A long slow line began to ripple toward them between the chairs and sofas. People filed past them for kisses and gripping of hands. I followed the line, not sure if I was family or friend, if I would be giving condolences or receiving them, but when I got to Hanan she reached out and folded me in a tear-soaked embrace.

Aunt Khadija had set a table outside her house, next to a low stone wall and a young fig tree. A tall pine tree spread green shade over the banquet she had prepared; there was *mlukhieh,* the moss-green stew that Mohamad and I loved; *kibbeh nayeh;* and great round metal trays of *kafta bi saynieh,* spiced ground meat layered with tomatoes and potatoes, then baked so that potatoes soaked up the tomato sauce and the flavor of the meat. She had filled enormous plastic bowls with tabbouleh and *fattoush,* and heaped mint and romaine and cucumbers on plates. We drank water from a clear glass *ibriq,* and this time I managed to shoot the liquid directly into my upturned mouth.

For Mohamad, the youngest, Khadija had made *shawrabet shayrieh,* a traditional soup with angel hair noodles and spicy meatballs. It was his favorite. "I made this especially for you, Mohamad Ali," said Aunt Khadija, in her husky voice like dark brown sugar, "because your mother tells me that you like it."

Everyone laughed: he might be pushing thirty, might have covered wars and revolutions, and have a big job and an American wife; but here in Bint Jbeil, he was still the baby of the family, and famous for his finicky eating.

"That reminds me of a story," said Aunt Khadija's husband. "Do you remember the time when we all went to Aley?"

In the early 1980s, during an especially dangerous bombardment, Umm Hassane and Abu Hassane and all their children piled into a car and drove to stay with relatives in the mountains outside of Beirut. The journey was long and dangerous, with many hostile checkpoints, and when they got there hours later they were shaking with relief.

Mohamad, then just a little kid, complained that he was hungry. Umm Hassane offered to make him boiled eggs and potatoes mashed with olive oil—another one of his favorites. But when she began to boil the water, he stamped his little foot with rage: she was boiling the water in the wrong pot! The only pot he would eat from, he told them, was the one on the shelf at home. The adults all tried to contain their laughter as he demanded that Abu

Hassane drive all the way back to Shiyah, get the pot, and bring it back here to boil his egg: *Otherwise,* he shouted, *I'm not going to eat it!*

Back in the twenty-first century, Mohamad blushed as Aunt Khadija's husband told this story in front of everybody. The whole family was here, reunited for the first time since 1994. Hassan had come from Paris. Ahmad from New York. Hassane, the nonstop talker, from Barcelona. Mohamad Ali, who grew up "outside," and the only son who lived in Lebanon now. Hanan, who never left. And me.

We sat outside listening to crickets and cars and other sounds of the countryside until evening overtook us. As we ate the remains of Aunt Khadija's funeral feast, people remembered other stories from Abu Hassane's life. Food unlocked memories, connecting the family to people and places no longer with us, to the dead. Like tradition, the repetition of familiar foods created the illusion that the past was still alive: we eat this food because we ate it before, when Abu Hassane was still with us. We marry as our ancestors have always married because the people we love—fathers, mothers, perhaps even ourselves—find comfort in repetition, in going through motions that have long since stopped being necessary or perhaps never were. Some traditions we choose to reject, like segregating men and women or buying a bride like a sack of potatoes. Others, like cooking for a family in mourning or swearing to love and support each other in front of people we love, we keep.

Chapter 19

The War of the Kitchen

A FTER HARIRI'S ASSASSINATION, Mohamad and I suspended our apartment hunt—temporarily, we told ourselves, until the political situation calmed down. But the country did not settle down, and neither did we.

On June 2, the newspaper columnist Samir Kassir was killed by a bomb planted underneath his car. On June 21, former Communist Party leader George Hawi was killed by a car bomb. On July 12, Defense Minister Elias Murr survived a car bomb. On September 25, a car bomb almost killed the television journalist May Chidiac, blowing off one of her legs and one of her arms. A series of small but strategically placed bombs went off in mostly Christian neighborhoods, killing a handful of people, and as the bombings and assassinations continued over the course of the year, you could feel the hate rising off the Beirut streets like steam. Tensions between Shiites and Lebanon's other sects had been growing since Hariri's assassination. The polarization had many causes: Iran's expansionism, Hezbollah's support for Syria. But one loomed above the others: Iraq.

In October 2005, I got an instant message from my friend Abdullah, a literature professor I knew from Baghdad. He loved Hemingway, George Orwell, and George Bernard Shaw; he had a passion for Irish writers like Eugene O'Neill, and I was utterly charmed by the way his dark eyes lit up whenever he discussed books and ideas.

Abdullah was visiting his uncle in mid-September when one of Iraq's government militias swept through the neighborhood and arrested all the

men. Iraq's new Shiite-dominated government was rounding up Sunnis accused of being insurgents (often by "informants" who could be anything
from a pissed-off in-law to a neighborhood racketeer) and torturing them.
"They put us to torture very vehemently," he instant-messaged me, "and
after that they released me by saying SORRY WE ARE MISTAKEN." He
added matter-of-factly: "life in iraq is very dangerous no one can save himself."

I called Abdullah and asked him what happened. For seventeen days, he
said, they kept him and about two dozen others in a cold, dark room too
small for them to lie down. Every few minutes the guards would slam the
doors to keep the prisoners from sleeping. They were not allowed to take
baths, or even to wash their hands as part of the ablutions that observant
Muslims are required to do before prayers. They interrogated him on three
occasions, during which they used electric shocks "on all the parts of my
body," he told me, putting the emphasis on "all." They forced him to curse
Omar ibn al-Khuttab and Othman ibn Affan, the second and third caliphs of
Islam, whom some Shiites consider usurpers. And they told his uncle that he
should leave Baghdad—that the city belonged to Shiites now, not Sunnis.

In November, American troops shut down one of the "secret" prisons,
whose existence had been known to Iraqis for months, run by Iraq's Interior Ministry. The ministry was controlled by the Supreme Council for the
Islamic Revolution in Iraq, a Shiite party with close ties to Iran. The discovery added to a sea change in American popular opinion—a growing push to
get our troops out as soon as possible, to stuff the whole sorry country in the
hole marked Not Our Problem Anymore.

I asked Abdullah what he thought. "in fact the iraqis themselves are
in great bewilderment," he messaged back. "they dont want america to
leave now."

His view did not reflect the majority opinion: polls showed that most
Iraqis wanted the Americans to leave. But the majority of Iraqis were Shiites. How would they treat the minorities once they were in charge?

The Sunnis of Lebanon looked at Iraq and saw their worst nightmare:
a Shiite-dominated government, supported by Iran, where Sunnis were

forced out of public life. People were beginning to repeat the ominous refrain that sectarian tensions were higher now than they had been in 1975, on the eve of the civil war.

Lebanon's fifteen-year civil war had begun with a convergence of conflicts—over economic disparity, urban-rural migration, ideological struggles, among others—of which religion was only one. But religion had a way of flattening other differences, all the more so because it was tied to the political structure. The same thing was happening now. The Sunni-Shiite divide was beginning to eclipse pro- and anti-Syrian, Muslim and Christian, left and right. Most of the Lebanese Shiites I knew didn't have much use for the Syrian regime, but that didn't matter—their political parties were aligned with it. (It didn't help that Syria was a Sunni-majority country ruled by a family of Alawites, an offshoot of Shiite Islam.)

On December 12, 2005, a United Nations special investigator was due to issue a report on Hariri's assassination. Just hours before the report, a remote-controlled car bomb killed Gibran Tueni, a member of Parliament and the publisher of *An-Nahar,* along with his driver and bodyguard. That night, the Lebanese cabinet formally asked the United Nations to create an international tribunal to investigate Hariri's assassination and the series of other killings. Five Shiite ministers walked out of the cabinet in protest, leaving the government paralyzed for weeks.

I went to Tueni's funeral two days later with Chibli Mallat, a renowned law professor and human rights activist. Thousands of people marched behind the dead man's coffin. Giant truck-mounted loudspeakers blasted a looped recording of a pledge Tueni had made eight months earlier, during the March 14 rally against Syria: "*We swear by God Almighty,*" the dead man's voice intoned again and again, "*Muslims and Christians, to remain united forever in defense of our great Lebanon.*"

But Tueni had been talking about the last war. In Beirut, they were getting ready for the next one.

"We have, in Lebanon, some people who share the dream of the terrorists," a puppyish twenty-three-year-old named Ahmed al-Masri told me, shouting to be heard over the loudspeakers as we walked in the funeral procession. "And we will not be able to do anything as long as they are here."

Al-Masri was a follower of Saad Hariri, the son and successor of the

murdered tycoon. He offered to introduce me to some higher-ups from
Hariri's Future Movement. I said I would rather talk to him. His solution for
the Shiite problem was simple, he said: sectarian cleansing. "We should send
them all back to Iran," he shouted.

Back to Iran: they were outsiders, invaders in their own country. We
marched on, Tueni's voice reverberating in the background, endlessly invoking Muslim-Christian unity while Muslims spoke of cleansing other
Muslims from the land.

Anyone who thought that the hatred had ended with the civil war never
tried apartment hunting in Beirut with a Shiite. Even more than money, hatred was the force that determined where you lived.

"Thanks to God, we're finally getting rid of these people," said one
landlady we met, sliding a glance toward the real estate agent, who nodded
sympathetically.

These people were squatters who had moved to Beirut during the Israeli
occupation of the south. *These people,* in other words, were Shiites, and
many non-Shiites felt that they didn't "belong" in the city.

This was part fable and part true. Many of the Shiites who had fled the
south ended up squatting in buildings of families who had been religiously
cleansed—Christians who had been chased out of West Beirut by Sunni
militias, for example. Shiite militias like Amal settled the displaced families
in the empty apartments and later used them as human bargaining chips to
extort money from landlords and the government. In Wadi Abu Jamil (the
Valley of Abu Jamil), this was such a profitable game that people called it the
Valley of Gold.

When the war was over, some Beirutis hoped that the Shiites would just
leave—they preferred them in the south, forming a human shield between
Beirut and Israel. To see a young Shiite return from the United States with
an American wife, an American job, and an American expense account,
ready to rent the apartments they had just kicked his kinfolk out of—that
must have stung.

This particular landlady reconciled sectarianism with greed by demanding a grossly inflated rent with such rudeness that Mohamad and I simply got

up and walked out of negotiations. If she was this boorish now, how would she behave once we paid her the customary six months' rent in advance?

Then there was the converse: Shiite landlords who wanted to rent to a nice Shiite boy. "I have other people interested," said one landlord, probably lying, "but I want to rent this apartment to *you*, because you're *Metawali*"— a derogatory term for Shiites, dating back to Ottoman times, that Shiites had appropriated and used as a form of bonding. Mohamad frowned: this greasy sectarian complicity left a bad taste in his mouth. It was a beautiful place and cheap, but we didn't rent from that landlord.

Another apartment building was plastered with pictures of Bashir Gemayel, the assassinated Christian warlord. WHO IS YOUR ENEMY? demanded Arabic graffiti outside the back balcony, and answered: YOUR ENEMY IS THE SYRIAN.

One of our closest friends was a Syrian-American who lived in Damascus and visited us often. I wanted her to feel welcome, but the place was cheap and lovely, and I also wanted a home. Mohamad turned it down: "If there's fighting, we'll be trapped," he said. I thought he was being melodramatic—hadn't the fighting ended fifteen years ago?

Finally we found a landlord who seemed different. He was a Lebanese-Iraqi whose mother had run an exclusive prep school in pre-Baathist Baghdad. He had a pet turtle. He had class. He wooed us with multiple cups of coffee, long conversations about Iraqi art, and reminiscences of cosmopolitan life in Baghdad before Saddam.

On the third visit, after the second cup of coffee, he turned to Mohamad. "So . . . you're a Bazzi," he said, delicately. "Are you with Hezbollah or Amal?"

The great Lebanese question. Mohamad's branch of the family was known for producing stubborn, rebellious Arab nationalists, beholden to neither Amal nor Hezbollah—a legacy of that same mythical, long-lost Arab renaissance as the landlord himself. But religion flattened these distinctions: if you were Druze, the assumption was that you followed Jumblatt or Arslan; for Sunnis, it was Hariri; and if you were Shiite, of course, you must be loyal to Hezbollah or Amal. If you denied it, well, people would say, everyone knows those Shiites lie—they even have a word for it, *taqiyah*, a religious doctrine that permits Shiites to conceal their true beliefs in a hostile environment. The question of sectarian loyalty was the Lebanese equivalent of "When did you stop beating your wife?" Denials only confirmed your guilt.

Mohamad explained that as an American, and a journalist, he didn't have to pay fealty to any of Lebanon's political parties. The landlord frowned and looked unconvinced. He offered us the apartment eventually, but the sectarian screening had made both of us uneasy, and we backed out of negotiations.

Months later, some friends of ours rented from this landlord. They were a mixed group, Lebanese and American and Canadian. Taking aside the North Americans, the landlord offered them some advice: they should get rid of their Lebanese roommate, a medical student—he was a Shiite, and you couldn't trust such people.

Beirut could close its doors on us for not having enough money; for being the wrong sect; for being too stubborn to pay the inflated prices landlords charged returnees and foreigners. But there was one place that couldn't turn us away. In Beirut's geography of hate, bars and restaurants were uncontested ground.

One day, Hanan took us to the restaurant where her best friend Munir bartended. It was called Walimah, a word that means "banquet"—a massive celebration, a feast that might last for days. The restaurant was in the ground floor apartment of a graceful old French Mandate building, one of the few still left in Hamra, right down on Makdisi Street. Tall philodendrons grew up around the window. Outside the front door, a green chalkboard with the day's specials written in Arabic and English was the only indication that you were entering a restaurant and not someone's home.

We pushed open the heavy wooden door, its curlicued metal framing the scalloped glass panes. Inside, the restaurant preserved the layout of an old Lebanese house. There was a central gathering room, now a dining room, with smaller rooms off each side. Windows and archways between the rooms allowed you to see from one to the other and gave the impression of being outside and inside at the same time: the home as miniature village, with the central room as town square.

A dark wooden bar curved through the small entrance room, the wall

behind it glittering with bottles of vodka, whiskey, absinthe, and other li-
queurs. At the end of the bar, two windows cut into the wall looked into the
first dining room. An open doorway led into the large middle salon, now the
main dining room, with two large tables and a round wooden waiters' station topped with marble. A tall, glass-paned French door led to the balcony.
In the back was a third dining room, the mirror image of the first one. Deep,
seductively padded banquettes piled with rainbow-colored brocade pillows
ran along the front and back walls. Each room had high ceilings and tall
windows with wooden shutters. It reminded me of the Runcible Spoon, my
favorite Bloomington café, in an old converted wooden house that smelled
of coffee and cinnamon, with a porch and a backyard and sunny windows. It
felt like home.

"We should come here all the time," I whispered to Mohamad.

"Especially since we know the owners," he said, thinking practically.

Munir was not what I expected. He was tall and sleepy-eyed, with
shaggy silvery whiskers, a French accent, and the lazy, affectionate grace
of an avuncular tiger. He had a habit of ending sentences with "you know,"
especially when he was saying something you violently disagreed with, and
he loved arguing even more than I did. He could beat anyone at Scrabble.
He will deny it when he reads this, because he loves to contradict what people say, but the fact is Munir was a *ghanouj*—the kind of tease who flirts
shamelessly with everybody, regardless of age or gender, not necessarily
in a sexual way but out of sheer coquetry. (*Baba ghanouj* means something
like "father is a flirt.") He made allowances for beauty, but not other weak-
nesses, and he flatly refused to discuss politics:

"No, no," he would say, flicking away the sordid worlds of sect and ide-
ology with an autocratic hand. "I do not dwell on such things."

Munir's mother, Wardeh Loghmaji, owned Walimah. She was a fear-
some southerner from Tibneen. She had married a boy from her village
when she was only fourteen, and moved to Beirut, where she saw moving
pictures for the first time in her life—something so marvelous, just thinking about it decades later, she clapped both hands to her face in rapture. Her
husband died young; she remarried and moved to Hamra. When the war became intolerable, in the mid-1980s, she and her husband Ali moved to Ivory
Coast, and later Kinshasa, which was then the capital of Zaire.

In Africa, she started a catering business for Lebanese expatriates hungry for home cooking. She had found her calling; but in 1991, riots broke out in Kinshasa. Unpaid soldiers raided Lebanese businesses, Ali barely escaped being shot, and they lost everything except some money Wardeh tied around her waist under her clothes. The Kinshasa airport was closed, so they fled by boat to Brazzaville, where the Lebanese government airlifted them back to Beirut.

Back in Hamra, the neighborhood was stuck in an awkward limbo between its 1970s prewar heyday and the unromantic, morning-after wreckage of the postwar. The war had torn apart more than just buildings: families had separated, marriages were canceled or postponed, and people didn't necessarily have someone at home to cook for them. Wardeh's own migrations had taught her the power of home cooking, and in 1994 she and two friends opened Walimah to give Ras Beirut "the feeling of a home-cooked meal."

I was beginning to understand the smoke-stained old sign at Chez André, that night so long ago, that commanded: NO POLITICS! Walimah was the kind of place where a Hariri loyalist could split a plate of *hindbeh* with a supporter of Hezbollah. There was a silent understanding that you wiped your dogmas off your shoes when you walked through the door.

I hope that Wardeh will forgive me for pointing out that her non-Lebanese foods—the soufflés, the lasagnas—can most kindly be described as "uneven." The wise diner did not order anything with a European name or the creation she called "Chinese chicken." If you knew what you were doing, you studied Wardeh's printed fortnightly menus and scheduled your life around the days she made *yakhnes*.

When I thought of Lebanese food, I usually pictured *meze*: hummus, stuffed grape leaves, baba ghanoush. But *yakhnes* were part of another culinary dialect, one that most Americans had never tasted. Its apotheosis was *tabeekh,* from the three-letter root for "cook." These were meals traditionally cooked at home, often in a *tabkha*, a handmade clay pot (these days usually a pressure cooker). Like "casserole," the word *tabkha* could mean the meal or the pot it was cooked in. *Tabeekh* were gravies and stews, pilafs and sauces made of humbler ingredients than *meze*: wheat, rice, potatoes, greens, beans, lentils. It was the kind of food Umm Hassane made when we went to visit: slow food, peasant food, the cuisine of people who used what was in season and extended the little meat they had with vegetables and grains. *Yakhnes* and *tabeekh* were Lebanese soul food: *akil nafs*, "food with soul" (or, more literally, "food *is* soul").

For years, Beirut restaurants considered this food too plebeian to serve. *Meze* and *mashawi* were what people paid money to eat; *tabeekh* was what your mother and grandmother made at home. When Mohamad and I moved to Beirut, only a handful of restaurants served home cooking. Walimah was one of them. Wardeh made traditional peasant dishes like *mjadara hamra*, and bulgur wheat with zucchini and tomatoes, and bulgur with meat; she made *freekeh*, cracked green wheat, another traditional grain that most of Beirut's restaurants neglected. She made the vegetarian "olive oil" dishes, like *hindbeh*, dandelions or chicory sautéed in olive oil and topped with crispy caramelized onions; eggplant stewed with tomatoes, peppers, and onions; green beans, lima beans, or okra braised with olive oil; and my favorite, the glorious *foul akhdar*, tender young fava beans braised whole with caramelized onions, garlic, and cilantro until they fell apart. Country people made *kibbeh* with pumpkin, tomato, and potato instead of meat, and she made these too, as well as more complicated dishes, like stuffed zucchini stewed in yogurt; *sayadieh*, fish with spiced rice and sesame seed sauce; the stuffed intestines that very few restaurants were brave enough to serve. She even made *khubaizeh*.

Because they were from nearby villages, Wardeh's *yakhnes* tasted a lot like Umm Hassane's. The basic formula had not changed since the ancients: a stock made of chicken, lamb, or beef, and then an armful of vegetables— spinach, zucchini, green beans, cauliflower—finished with a burst of flavor from the cilantro-garlic pesto that you added at the end, which never failed to remind me of the Sumerians and their last-minute mixture of garlic and leeks.

That first time we ate at Walimah, Mohamad and I sat out on the balcony. We had *bamieh*, okra stew, made with tomatoes, beef, and flavored with garlic and cilantro.

"This tastes just like my mom's!" he said, with a sudden look of wonder, as if it were a magic trick.

He had a way of exclaiming with pleasure and surprise when he ate something he recognized. His tone of appreciation seemed to imply that I was somehow responsible, as if I had made it myself, even if all I had done was open a can of spaghetti sauce or sit there eating it with him. Sharing his excitement at this discovery, that day on the balcony at Walimah, was as good as cooking him a four-course meal: We had not found a home, but we had found home cooking, and for the time being, that was enough.

Our perpetual apartment hunt became a standing joke among our friends. When people heard we were living in a hotel, they imagined us reclining on satin sheets while servants bore delicacies to our bedside. "*A hotel, that must be great,*" they would say with envy. "*Room service—you don't even have to cook!*"

Even if I wanted it, room service was out. The Berkeley was far from luxurious. It was more like the small furnished apartments that students lived in than the grand tourist hotel it had once aspired to be. It consecrated these lost ambitions in a four-page room service menu, written in elegant cursive on cream-colored stock and larded with items like Chicken à la King and Steak Florentine with Potato Purée. If you ordered any of them, the staff would regretfully inform you that this particular item had just run out.

What the Berkeley had, in reality, was: bread, *labneh,* olives, and eggs. It was cheaper just to go to the corner store for that, which is what we did. But I wanted to cook. The more the Iraq war leaked into Lebanon and poisoned our lives, the further our hopes of settling down slipped out of reach, the more I felt that food was the only thing I could know for sure. It was the only reliable substance binding one part of life to another, the only tangible connection between who I was and where I lived.

I became obsessed with food. I mail-ordered back issues of obscure British food journals featuring treatises with titles like *Notes for a Study of Sectarian Cookery in Lebanon.* I stalked nutrition professors. I attended lectures on the development of Lebanon's agricultural sector and took voluminous notes. I tracked down the Food Heritage Foundation, a cabal of artists, college professors, and restaurateurs (Wardeh was a member) that preserved rural Lebanese recipes. At parties I cornered people and frightened them with interrogations about the years of hunger, the great World War I famine that killed as many Lebanese, in proportion to population, as the Irish potato blight.

I joined Lebanon's Slow Food Movement, and when some of its members founded a farmers' market in Beirut, I was there every week. Souk El Tayeb ("The Tasty Market" or "The Good Market") started out as a handful of farmers and small producers selling fruit, vegetables, and *mouneh* in the parking lot across from Smith's grocery store. Later it moved to Saifi Village, where it became one of Beirut's trendiest destinations. Lebanon's elite would drive Land Rovers to the *souq*, then line up to buy sandwiches made with *kishk al-fuqara*—"the kishk of the poor," a cheese made from wheat by people too poor to afford milk.

Many of my Lebanese friends had mixed feelings about the *souq*. But I liked the farmers and producers, I liked the food, and I felt that Lebanon's rich had worse ways to spend their money than subsidizing small farmers. The *kishk* of nostalgia fed their hunger to belong, to connect to a lost agrarian past, and I couldn't criticize them for that; I was looking for much the same thing. I spent most of my time talking to the farmers and producers anyway, which is how I met Ali Fahs.

A wiry, gap-toothed farmer with a limp and a leathery smile, Ali made every kind of *mouneh:* fig jam jeweled with sesame seeds, spices mixed with rose petals, soft balls of *labneh* suspended in olive oil as thick and sweet as dark green honey. Ali decided I was all right when I told him, as a joke, that my husband was *Metawali*. When he heard that Mohamad was a Bazzi, he intoned, "The Bazzis, they are *very* rich." It wasn't true, I protested, but Ali had already decided that we would go into business together—the Bazzi family coffers would supply the capital, and he would provide the *mouneh*.

"This market, it needs a big mind," Ali told me, taking me aside one Saturday morning. "And you can make a big money."

"How?"

He looked left to right, frowning away possible eavesdroppers, and weighed whether to divulge his trade secrets. "You find the thing that nobody has, and you charge a big price," he said, holding up a forefinger. "For example, sea plants; nobody here has them." Crinkling into a triumphant smile, he leaned over, tapped his bony chest, and revealed, "But I have them." He held up a jar of dark green pickled samphire leaves: *hashishet al-bahar,* hashish-of-the-sea.

Ali spoke a jagged, improvisational English and French, both languages that he had taught himself during his years of toiling in big industrial kitchens in Saudi Arabia. His dream was to sell enough *mouneh* to move to California and open a gas station.

"Last night, I had a dream," he told me another Saturday morning. "I was in California. I had a gas station; it was all mine. It was so beautiful."

Why California? "Because it is the basket of America," he sighed. "Just like Lebanon is the basket of the Middle East."

Ali Fahs was right: Lebanon was a garden, and the *souq* was my downfall. The mini-fridge at the Berkeley could fit only about two six-packs' worth of food, but I would see a pale-green bunch of *ʒaatar,* with its uncanny rose-petal scent and its delicate silvery sheen, and like a junkie, I would start rationalizing: I would cook it right away. I would make *fatayer* stuffed with *ʒaatar.* I would dry it out so it wouldn't have to go into the fridge. A farmer's wife gave me her recipe for fennel frond soufflé, and I headed home clutching a feathery green cloud of the liquorice-scented greens; I was all the way back at the Berkeley when I remembered that we didn't have an oven.

The more rootless I felt, the more I cooked. I spent hours in the little dollhouse kitchen, hunched over the two tiny electric burners, assembling pathologically elaborate meals: duck's breast with stewed fava beans and *freekeh,* my variation on a Paula Wolfert recipe—the toasted green wheat soaking up the rich sauce, studded with tender pistachio-green buttons I'd spent an hour podding and peeling. Omelets of garlic, fennel, spinach, and feta. Salmon crusted with roasted fennel and coriander seeds, poached in a carrot-fennel reduction, served atop a ragout of baby string beans and zucchini. Chicken breasts stuffed with ground pistachios and coriander and smothered in avocado sauce. Roasted cherries with toasted green almonds.

These ornate concoctions were a substitute for something else, something just out of reach. Umm Hassane would have said I wanted a baby, but what I wanted was much simpler: I wanted dinner with friends, and not in a restaurant. I wanted to invite friends over and serve them food—*my* food, made with my hands. I wanted a time and place where people who loved each other sat around a table and conversed. Breaking bread was the oldest and best excuse for such an occasion. It was how you created your own tribe, a microcosm of the world you want to live in.

But you can't invite people to dinner in a hotel room: We didn't even have a table, let alone chairs to seat guests. The sole armchair was permanently loaded with papers and communications equipment. And Mohamad refused to eat what he called my "fancy food." He never tried anything I made, and when I tried to tempt him, he would wrinkle his face in disgust and recoil.

It took me months to realize that it wasn't my food he loathed. It was the unexpected, anything unpredictable and new. As Lebanon changed he had good reasons for wanting to cling to what he knew—like in the story I'd heard at Aunt Khadija's house, about the time he had wanted eggs boiled in his special pot during the civil war. This was his way of handling stress. Frenzied, compulsive cooking was mine.

So at the Berkeley, I dined alone, imagining guests who would never come. I would cut the duck breast and fan it out on the plate, drizzle over the sauce, and arrange it all on the plate just so, as if I were back at one of the restaurants where I used to wait tables. I would pour a solitary glass of wine, sit down, and watch TV, because Mohamad would have long since retreated into the bedroom in a storm of protests over the smell of cooking, which he hated.

In late fall 2005, Sheikh Fatih and Dr. Salama came to Beirut for a conference. It was their first trip to Lebanon in years, and they were like giddy tourists. They videotaped everything with a tiny camcorder. They marveled at signs advertising laser hair removal, at people walking on the Corniche, at people simply walking the streets at all. It was their first trip out of Iraq in years, and showing the two of them around Beirut, I kept thinking of the moment in *The Wizard of Oz* when Dorothy opens the door of her black-and-white Kansas farmhouse and gets the candy-colored Technicolor of Oz.

Dr. Salama needed a nightgown, so we went to the ABC mall in Ashrafieh. Somehow we ended up at women'secret, a European lingerie store where half-naked mannequins were strapped into panties and push-up bras that would have made Frederick of Hollywood blush. But in the jungle of thongs and garter belts, everybody seemed to be staring at the Iraqi woman in the black full-body *abaya*.

We walked around the store, trailed by a bewildered saleslady, until Dr. Salama stopped in front of a mulberry-pink satin brassiere. She reached up one of her strong, clever hands—in Iraq, she was known for doing her own dental extractions, with no male assistant, and religious women came to her for this—and stroked the pink silk. "It is very beautiful," she said with quiet reverence, as if we were at the Louvre discussing a Renaissance painting. The bottle-blond saleslady stood at attention behind her, batting her eyelash extensions in polite shock.

After shopping, we went to the Bristol Hotel's pâtisserie for ice cream. I got chocolate. She ordered a scoop of lemon sorbet. She looked down at the pale buttery-lemon orb for a moment before eating it. Her face looked tired, but she was smiling.

"This ice cream," she said quietly, "it is very beautiful."

Everything was beautiful; earlier that day, seeing my hair in a ponytail, she had exclaimed, "You are wearing your hair, Annia, in a way which is *so beautiful*!"

In the year and a half since we'd seen Dr. Salama, she had survived several more assassination attempts. In one of them, the attackers had shot her husband in the leg, hand, and abdomen. He ordered her to abandon her political career; she refused, and they were headed for divorce. She had clashed repeatedly with the ruling Shiite political parties. She and her children were living in lockdown.

"I have learned to appreciate things that are beautiful," she said, so softly that I had to lean forward to hear her. "I have a plant in my yard, and one day it blossomed. And I said to my daughter, 'Look at this flower. Such a small, delicate thing. We should learn to appreciate such things when we have them.' "

While Dr. Salama and I ate ice cream, Mohamad and Sheikh Fatih were sitting in the Bristol's lobby. Were they hungry? asked Mohamad. We could take them to restaurants, cafés, anything they wanted: sushi, *meze*, French,

Italian—Beirut had it all. There was even a Spanish restaurant. But the Sheikh wanted something else.

"While we are here, we only want one thing," he said. "It would be an honor for us to have a meal prepared by Annia's hands."

It was like a fable from *The Arabian Nights:* the holy man, traveling in a foreign land, requesting the one favor we cannot grant him.

"Well," said Mohamad (somewhat sheepishly, he confessed later), "the problem is, we're having a hard time finding an apartment. So we still live in a hotel."

"A hotel?" inquired Sheikh Fatih, in polite puzzlement.

"But we're going to get an apartment soon," Mohamad added hastily.

"Of course, I was only joking," said Sheikh Fatih. "I only meant that we would love to eat Annia's food. It does not have to be now. We will do it whenever we can."

We had eaten so often at Sheikh Fatih's home in Baghdad. When would we have a chance to pay back his hospitality?

"Next time you're in Beirut, God willing," said Mohamad, breaking into the flowery formal Arabic he hardly ever used, "Annia will cook you a feast!"

In February 2006, Sunni extremists bombed the Askari Shrine, the tomb of two Shiite imams, in the northern Iraqi city of Samarra. The bombing, and the reprisals that followed, accelerated the sectarian conflict that was a civil war in everything but name only. On February 23, Hezbollah leader Hassan Nasrallah held a massive rally in *dahiyeh,* ostensibly to protest the Samarra bombing. He blamed the United States for the conflagration in Iraq and dared it to disarm Hezbollah. Sunnis and Shiites should not blame each other, he noted. But Beirut was even more tense than before.

The next week, Mohamad finally got fed up with all my cooking. He convinced the Berkeley's handyman to install a fan in the wall above the four-foot-high bar that set off the kitchen from the rest of the tiny living room where we filed stories, watched the news, and did practically everything except sleep.

The next day, which was March 1, I put on my rubber gloves to do some dishes and found them infested with tiny crumbs of plaster. Chunks of dry-wall coated the kitchen and everything in it: cookbooks, dried roses, bags of pasta, jars of *kamuneh*, bottles of red wine vinegar, olive oil, carefully wiped wineglasses, dried chickpeas, bulgur, chamomile, cinnamon sticks; all stacked precariously on top of one another as though I were trying to wall off this tiny kitchen from the world.

I looked at this jumble of dusty dry goods, this fragile repository of my domestic gods, calculated that we had been living in the Middle East for exactly two and a half years, and suddenly all the years of wandering, of exile from my grandmother's kitchen, of living in cars and on other people's couches, flooded up and pressed against my skull.

"You're such a *fucking asshole,*" I screamed at my husband, hurling one of the hotel glasses at the hotel wall. It shattered and sprayed shards of glass into my own shoes, which were lined up against the wall next to the door. "Do you realize we've been here for two and half years and we're still living in a *fucking hotel?*"

"Well, technically, that's not true," Mohamad pointed out, unwisely, "because we've really only been living here since January of 2005."

This was a longstanding argument between us: I maintained that we moved to Beirut in October 2003, when we left New York; he claimed we moved to Beirut in January 2005, when we left Iraq behind for good. Likewise, the Christian calendar begins with the birth of Jesus; the Muslim calendar begins in 622, the year the Prophet Muhammad made his *hijrah,* or migration, from Mecca to Medina. Sometimes I would tease Mohamad about his January 2005 "*hijri* calendar." This was not one of those times.

"I don't care!" I shouted. "I want a real apartment! I want to live somewhere! I want a *fucking kitchen!*"

Technically, we had a kitchen—the minibar refrigerator, the cocktail-sized sink, the two electric burners we had been strictly forbidden from using. (I did use them, and the staff, who liked us, looked the other way.) I measured it one day by lying down: it was exactly as long as I was tall, and not much wider, like a coffin. Calling it a kitchenette would have been putting on airs.

I slid down to the ground, hunched against the wall, and started to weep with rage. Mohamad crept toward me—hesitantly, in case I started throwing things again—and put his hand on my shoulder.

"I promise you, okay?" he said. "I promise we'll get an apartment."

I had to get out of the tiny room. I called my friend Leena and we decided to meet for a drink at Walimah. It was Thursday night—an ordinary night, or so I thought, but when I got to the restaurant I found it transformed. At night, the tall windows with wooden shutters let in breezes from the garden outside. Lanterns hung from the ceilings, and globes of milky apricot glass shone like radiant fruit. The tables were gone from the middle dining room, which was full of the twisting, whirling arms and the tossing hair of couples dancing. A husky voice was singing a circular, syncopated song that sounded like a cat stalking up on a bird. The air was a soup of sweat, and wine, and something else—*mlukhieh.*

This was Tango Night, the Thursday night *milonga* that Munir had inaugurated. I loved the word *milonga,* which means a kind of music, a style of dance, and a regular event—a rendezvous where people dance tango together. Like a floating craps game, a *milonga* is a communion that resides not so much in a physical place, or a time, but in a gathering of souls.

I sat in the front room drinking vodka and absinthe with Leena and Munir and watching the dancers ripple across the tiled floor like sea creatures. "In the past month, I've heard the kind of sectarian views that I have never heard before," said Munir, without a hint of his flirtatious manner. "And I've heard it from people that I never thought I'd hear this kind of talk from."

An angel passed over and we sat silent for a moment. Munir was projecting the Carlos Saura movie *Tango* (about the Argentine dirty war, although Munir denied this) on the wall with no sound. On the screen an old man's face wailed in wordless song, a mute and knowing moon above the dancers as they skimmed across the floor. One of the *tangueras* was wearing ruby sequined high heels that matched her cherry-colored curls. A tall woman in her late forties lounged in a chair and stretched out legs encased in thigh-high leather spike-heeled boots that managed, on her, to look elegant.

One of the dancers threw himself into a chair next to us. He was slender, with black hair slicked back over the smooth, benevolently sexy face of a young Valentino. He had been dancing for hours, and his black shirt, unbuttoned just enough, was soaked with sweat. This was Georges, the tango instructor. As soon as we started talking, I knew we would be friends.

The next Tango Night, when I dragged Mohamad with me, Leena had filled the front room with foreign journalists. In the middle, tango dancers circled across the floor. In the back room a circle of politicians sat around a table smoking, sharp-faced men in black suits with dark circles under their eyes. Husky, intimate roars of laughter flared from their table. It was covered with bottles of Johnnie Walker that glowed amber in the candlelight.

"I think we have a pro-Syrian plot being hatched in the back room," Leena murmured when we came in, leaning over. She had the rare ability to circulate between worlds, and Tango Night was made for that: you could have a table of pro-Syrian politicians in one room, and the front room lousy with American diplomats, their meat-necked security detail standing outside with little coiled earpieces, and everybody dancing in between.

One of Leena's journalists ordered *mlukhieh*. He had spent three years in Beirut and never tried *mlukhieh*, and now that he tasted it, he did not like it. He put his spoon down and grimaced at the white bowl and its primeval dark green soup.

"What is this stuff?" he asked.

"It's spinach," said an American newspaper reporter.

"It's okra," corrected a British travel writer.

"It's *mlukhieh*," said Leena, amused.

Mlukhieh is made from the leaves of the jute plant, *Corchorus olitorius*, and like okra, people either love *mlukhieh* or they loathe it. There is no neutrality on the *mlukhieh* question. Swampy, dark-green *mlukhieh* tastes like a dark, still pond in the middle of a deep woods. It has the loamy, fertile funk of wet leaves disintegrating into soil. The stew has been a famous North African dish for centuries; in nineteenth-century Tunis, it was so treasured that loyal city watchmen received five cows and a sack of *mlukhieh* every year. In Japan it is prized as a health food; in the Philippines it is made into a stew called *saluyot*.

Wardeh made her *mlukhieh* two ways: the first was Egyptian style (finely chopped leaves, accompanied by diced onions and vinegar). The second was pure southern Lebanese, the veiny, tea-green leaves stewed whole with chicken, cilantro, and hot red peppers into a garlicky morass. She served it with bread and lemon juice, over rice, and it soaked into the grains like a summer rain into dry earth.

In English, *mlukhieh* is known as Jew's Mallow (deliciously misspelled on one company's frozen packets as "Jew's Mellow"). Nobody seemed to know why. When I asked Sami Zubaida, the Iraqi scholar, he hazarded a guess that English speakers first encountered it from Jewish émigrés, which made sense. Clifford Wright, in his encyclopedic history and cookbook *Mediterranean Feast*, speculates that Jewish dietary commandments made the bitter leaf especially beloved to Alexandrian Jews; and this makes sense to me too, because I consider the eating of *mlukhieh* a minor sacrament. But *mlukhieh* tastes of the forbidden as well as the sacred: The mad Caliph al-Hakim, of Egypt's Shiite Fatimid dynasty, banned *mlukhieh* (supposedly because the Sunni Caliph Muawiya loved it), and perhaps this explains why Egyptians adore it so much to this day. Legend has it that *mlukhieh* is taboo among Druze because it's an aphrodisiac, but just as many Muslims drink alcohol, many Druze eat *mlukhieh*. For some reason—a tradition deep in the subconscious, perhaps—the few Beirut restaurants that did make *mlukhieh* all served it on Thursdays. When I asked Wardeh why, she gave a magnificent shrug and denied any meaning. This only added to the sea-green mysteries of *mlukhieh*.

I finished the journalist's *mlukhieh*, since he didn't want it, and went to the bar to talk to Munir. Georges came up, lithe and sweaty as a young faun.

"Watch out for this guy," he said, pointing at Munir. "He loves to take your dreams and *crush* them!"

"I'm *benessniss*," said Munir in Arabic, smiling. Another Untranslatable: to gossip, to stir up trouble between people. "Like Iago!" he added, laughing over his shoulder as he went off to torment someone else.

"Dream wrecker!" shouted Georges at Munir's back.

He turned toward me. "Do you know, Annia, that I have never been in love?"

"How old are you?"

"I'm twenty-five years old," he said, tragically. "What if it's too late? What if it doesn't ever happen for me?"

Georges spoke fluent French, English, Arabic, and a respectable Italian. He danced and wrote poetry. When he wasn't doing these things, all of which he performed with grace and skill, he was a neuropsychiatrist. He belonged to that precious tribe that crossed between worlds, like Leena and Munir. His only flaw was the terrible disease of being twenty-five.

"Hang on a few more years," I said, suddenly feeling very sophisticated and happy to be thirty-five. "I think you're going to fall for somebody very soon."

"Believe me, this is what I am looking for," he sighed. "I want to get my heart broken. I can't wait!"

Georges spun off onto the dance floor. The *milonga* music growled and moaned. Munir came back to the bar. I had another absinthe and confided that I didn't know what to do with this husband of mine. He wouldn't eat my food; he rejected every apartment we looked at. He didn't like tango, didn't like politics, and he was beginning to dislike Lebanon.

"Sometimes I think the only thing in the world he does like," I said, "is me."

"Listen, Annia," said Munir. "Mohamad does not like to admit that he wants a home. He will never admit this, you know. But if you find a place, and if you make it beautiful, make it furnished and ready for him, he will be very happy."

Chapter 20

The Operation

FTER TWO YEARS and eight months (by my calendar), with heroic assistance from Leena, Mohamad finally signed the lease on
an apartment in a neighborhood between Hamra and the sea. In
May 2006, we reclaimed books, clothes, and furniture from storage. Home
was on Najib Ardati Street, a couple of blocks from the Mediterranean, right
next door to the old black-and-white-striped lighthouse that gave the neighborhood its name: Manara. There was a big balcony, and a real kitchen, with
a real refrigerator and a real stove. From the kitchen window, I could see a
trapezoidal sliver of Mediterranean water, which was a different color every
day, a giant mood ring for the city.

I started going to Arabic classes on Bliss Street. My Arabic teacher,
Hayat, lived next door to us, and so extensive was the infrastructure of
neighborhood gossip that she knew exactly how much rent we were paying
before we even unpacked. I adopted a tiny, half-starved orange stray kitten,
whom we named Shaitan. And as soon as we moved in, Umm Hassane came
for an extended visit, installing herself on our couch and taking possession
of the remote control.

After the months of mourning her husband in the company of relatives,
Umm Hassane had found herself alone in the empty apartment in Tayuneh.
She began to feel mysterious pains shooting up her leg and back. She walked
with agony, grimacing with every step, and barely moved from the living
room couch. The doctor diagnosed a slipped disc and prescribed corrective
surgery.

At seventy-four, Umm Hassane had never had an operation in her life, and the very sound of the word filled her with dread. (Like others of her generation, Umm Hassane refused to name illnesses like cancer out loud; instead, she would whisper "that disease.") In Arabic, as in English, an "operation" can be military as well as medical: a battle, a raid, an attack. As the attack on her spinal column approached, she invoked The Operation as though she were going into battle and might not return.

Despite her fears, The Operation went well. She returned from it loaded with synthetic opiates and reclaimed possession of the couch and the remote control. She still could not walk without help, but she had more color, and even her litany of suffering had regained a certain vigor. But when we asked how she felt, she would scowl and announce, "The Operation failed."

After a while she recovered enough for me to take her out on little excursions. She complained bitterly—"How can I walk with all this pain?"—but she never said no to a stroll. She would grip my arm as she limped up the street, looking around at new streets, new butchers and bakeries, new greengrocers; a whole new neighborhood of victims. Umm Hassane regained her strength by terrorizing local merchants and anyone else who crossed her path.

We were walking along Makdisi Street one day when a beggar woman approached us with an outstretched hand. Hamra was full of beggars—men, women, small children. Most people skirted neatly around them, looking away as if they were invisible. Umm Hassane flew toward this one like an avenging rooster.

"Get out! Go!" she hissed, flapping her hands in the woman's face. The theatrical entreaty on the woman's face changed to terror, and she scuttled off down the street.

"Umm Hassane, *haraam*," I said. "What if she needs the money?"

"Needs the money?" she said, scowling. "Let her work!"

"Maybe she's Palestinian or Bedouin," I said. "Maybe she can't get papers to work legally."

Umm Hassane snorted. "She's young! She can sweep floors! She can mop!"

Like me, Umm Hassane had once cleaned houses for a living. Unlike me, she considered it the unassailable solution to all complaints of social injustice, from poverty to forced migration. "Let them clean houses!" she would decree, with a regal sweep of her arm, like a slightly more practical Marie Antoinette.

At the end of every walk, I would have to redraw my mental map of the neighborhood: From now on I would walk an extra block down Sidani to avoid the butcher she had insulted. And it would be a month or two before I would get up the nerve to go back to the greengrocer on Adonis.

She was especially merciless to the young students at Healthy Basket. This was a community-supported agriculture project, started by the American University of Beirut, that sold produce from small-scale organic farms in a no-frills storefront. Their food cost a little more than the imports at the grocery, but it was still cheap, tasted better, lasted much longer, and supported local farmers. (I kept quiet about this last point, figuring *fallaheen* would rank with beggars in Umm Hassane's sympathies.)

When I brought her hobbling up the stairs to Healthy Basket, the agriculture students smiled sweetly. Who was this adorable old *hajji*?

Umm Hassane looked around at the raw wood shelves, where onions and eggplants were piled unromantically in big wooden bins, and frowned. The *khadarjis* heaped their produce in rainbow-colored mounds and sprayed them with water so they glistened. They halved the finest blood orange so you could see the purple flesh within and laid it on top of the others. These people just dumped their fruit and vegetables anywhere.

"What is this place?" she demanded.

"Our food costs a little more because it's grown without chemicals," explained Eliane, one of the agriculture students. "It's healthier, and it helps local farmers make a living."

Umm Hassane's face didn't hide what she thought: This whole routine about farmers and chemicals was a scandalous ploy to put one over on dumb foreigners like me.

She picked up an apple and inspected it with rage. It was misshapen, as organic apples tend to be, with warts and dimples and a light dusting of dirt. It cost twice as much as the imported apples she bought in *dahiyeh*. She protested loudly as I paid two dollars for two pounds of apples.

My purchase was a tactical defeat for the side of honesty and thrift; so on the way out, just to show them who was boss, Umm Hassane pointed at a lavender plant in the flower bed outside the store and ordered one of the agriculture students to dig it up and give it to us. He was too stunned to disobey. He uprooted the plant and handed it to us with a nervous smile.

"They're tricking Annia, those thieves over there!" she hissed to Mohamad when we got home. *"Byidahaku alaiha,"* she fumed—they're laughing behind her back, pulling her leg.

I couldn't blame her. So many things in Lebanon were a scam. The economy was a scam; the real estate market was a scam; the political parties were nothing but pure scam. Even food was a scam: unscrupulous merchants would steam the labels off expired food, sell rotten olive oil, water down the milk. After a lifetime of mistrust, it was hard to believe that anyone would do something good for others—especially people with no *wasta*, like *fallaheen*—unless it was part of some bolder and even more sinister scam.

What annoyed her most was that these crooks didn't even bother to make up a good lie. "Without chemicals?" She rolled her eyes, held up her hands, and appealed to the heavens with wrath: "How can you grow apples without chemicals?"

She dominated our living room. She occupied the couch all day and left it mined with wads of used Kleenex when she retired at night. She commandeered the guest bathroom, took the pump-top bottle of hand soap, and crushed it in her fist to extract the soap. We would come home to find her reclining like a pasha, surrounded by relatives from Bint Jbeil, headscarved old *hajjis* and tiny old men who sat stiffly in straight-backed chairs pulled up around her as she regaled them with tales of The Operation. She got more phone calls than both of us put together. Most mornings, I'd shuffle into the living room to find her already on the phone trading condolences with some relative.

In early July, a newspaper assigned me a story on the "Playboy Plotter," the spoiled scion of a "good" Beirut family who had contacted al-Qaeda-linked groups over the Internet and expressed a desire to carry out bombings in New York City. When I called the plotter's mother, she answered right away, as if she'd been waiting for my call. I asked her why she thought her son had become an Islamic militant. *"Shu yaani?"* she cried out, bewildered. I repeated the question in Arabic, although she supposedly spoke English, but she remained mystified. Finally I figured out it wasn't the Playboy Plotter's mother at all, but an old auntie from Bint Jbeil who was already on the line, calling for Umm Hassane, when I dialed. Even our phones barely belonged to us anymore.

But food was the real battleground, and here the rhetorical question was Umm Hassane's most powerful weapon. In response to our simplest questions, she would fire a rhetorical salvo that rendered us, her assailants, impotent.

"Umm Hassane, are you hungry?"

"How can I have any appetite?"

"Umm Hassane, what do you want to eat?"

"How can I eat with all this pain?"

"Umm Hassane"—realizing that we would have to resort to specific questions if we had any hopes of an answer—"Do you want salad and potatoes?"

"If you're making some, maybe"—then, flinging up her hands in deprecation "but not if you're making it for me!"

If we asked her *"Biddik shi?"*—Do you want anything? she would answer back, despairingly, *"Shu biddi? Shu biddi akel?"*—"What do I want? What can I eat?" Mohamad called this her "not-so-subtle attempts to tell us we don't have anything to eat."

Most of the time, she would just say *"Shu baarifni?"* Literally, it means, "what do I know?" But like a teenager's *whatever,* or a wiseguy's *fuggeddaboudit,* the phrase *shu baarifni* contained a multitude of shifting meanings. In her mouth, it meant: Leave me alone; Don't leave me alone; I don't know what I want; I want you to know what I want without me having to ask, or even knowing what I want myself.

Her other favorite expression was *ma btifru maai,* "it makes no difference to me." This meant that deep, violent opinions were being suppressed through superhuman exertion on her part. All these expressions contained a depth of passive-aggressive mastery that impressed me greatly, no matter how frustrating, and I started to think Umm Hassane could make millions teaching corporate communication seminars.

In the end, most of her rhetorical tricks just meant yes. But not simply yes. They meant, Why aren't you eating? Why aren't you eating what I eat? Why aren't we all eating together, the same thing, at the same time?

The food wars came to a head one Friday, when I asked her if she wanted a cucumber-and-*labneh* sandwich. Apparently it was one thing to serve an *arous* as a snack, and quite another to offer it for lunch.

"I've been eating nothing but *labneh*," she wailed. "I ate it yesterday, I ate it this morning. *Azit nafsi*"—my soul, my appetite recoils.

"She was insulted that you offered her that," Mohamad whispered to me in the kitchen. "It's for babies."

"So what the hell *does* she want?"

Mohamad went into the living room to investigate. After the usual "What, me eat?" formalities, she presented him with a list of grievances: we had no salad, no meat, no bread. Worst of all, we lacked the most essential oil of Lebanese kitchens: Mazola. She lamented the madness of cooking with nothing but olive oil—it was not for cooking, as everyone knew, and how could we live like this?

Mohamad trotted back and forth, a reluctant ambassador, while I waited in the kitchen to find out what she wanted. Finally, after some wheedling, she consented to a *shish taouk* sandwich.

I asked him to find out if she wanted garlic, hummus, and pickles, the traditional accoutrements of such a sandwich. He got an Umm Hassane answer: "What do I need with hummus?"

"She's being insolent," he muttered, back in the kitchen, where we were both hiding from her wrath. "They're all pseudo-martyrs, my whole family."

We loved having her. We would have bought her anything she asked for—but she refused to ask. Somehow this woman, the scourge of greengrocers and agriculture students, could not say what she wanted in the privacy of our home. She was trying so hard to stay out of our way, not to be a burden, that she ended up driving us half-insane.

I was confounded. I loved to feed people, but I couldn't cook for Mohamad because most of the dishes I knew how to make relied on ingredients he wouldn't eat. And I couldn't cook for Umm Hassane because she refused to tell us what she wanted. I finally had the kitchen I'd been longing for, with a real stove and a real refrigerator and a real kitchen sink. But I had no idea what to cook.

"I have an idea," I said to Mohamad one day, as we stood in the kitchen.

What she really wanted was to be fussed over, to be coaxed and taken care of. But Umm Hassane was from my grandmother's generation: brought up to put others first, never to acknowledge their own desires, except in the context of being denied. They showed their love by cooking and complaining. For these women, the kitchen was one of the few places where they could be the undisputed queens.

I outlined a plan: I would ask Umm Hassane to teach me how to cook traditional Lebanese food, under the pretext that I needed to learn how to prepare food for Mohamad, like a dutiful wife. Instead of the fancy fusion stuff I made only for myself, she would teach me how to make Lebanese peasant food—*mlukhieh, sayyadieh, burghul wa banadura, kibbeh nayeh*. I would learn something new; she would have a mission, something to make her feel appreciated. And if it made me look like an obedient wife, that was a price I was willing to pay.

The day we planned to make *mlukhieh*, I stumbled into the kitchen late. Umm Hassane had been awake since seven a.m. rehearsing each bit of prep work. Next to the sink, a raw chicken lay spread-eagled on the counter, waiting for me with naked accusation.

"Wash her!" she commanded, hobbling into the kitchen and pointing to the chicken.

"Make coffee," I muttered, heading for the kettle. I could barely communicate in English, let alone Arabic, until I'd had my coffee.

Clearly I hadn't understood. Drawing herself to full height, Umm Hassane pointed toward the sink and repeated her orders: *"The chicken! Wash her!"*

We hadn't even started cooking, and already we were hurtling toward one of those clash-of-civilization conversations where people kept shouting

Arabic nouns over and over—*"WATER! WATER!"*—thinking I was deaf as well as simple-minded, but never explaining exactly what they wanted me to *do* with the goddamn water. Meanwhile, I would stand there, choking on basic verbs, and thinking, This is just a taste of how it must feel to be a taxi driver, a busboy, a chambermaid, any of the starter jobs immigrants get in America while they're learning English. These encounters usually deteriorated into something like this:

"Make coffee!"

"Wash chicken!"

"Coffee!"

"Chicken!"

"COFFEE!"

"CHICKEN!"

Then I remembered an old habit of my grandmother's. Whenever she was craving something—a hamburger, a cigarette, a beer—she would say: "You want a beer, don't you? Don't you want a hamburger? You want me to roll you a cigarette?"

At the time it drove me crazy. "No, Grandma, *you* want a hamburger," I would say. Why couldn't she just admit that she wanted a beer? She ran the kitchen; why couldn't she just take what she wanted? That my grandmother's life revolved around other people's hungers—that she needed to justify her desires, even to herself—was something I didn't figure out until after she was gone.

"Umm Hassane," I said. "Don't you want a cup of coffee? You like coffee, don't you?"

Thus was born our morning ritual of cake and coffee. That morning, before making *mlukhieh*, Umm Hassane and I sat out on the balcony eating chocolate cake and drinking coffee. From then on we did it every morning. We would hold blunted conversations and watch the city perform its morning rituals: pigeons wheeling in the sky, traffic jamming on the Corniche, maids beating carpets on balconies. She would stretch her legs and luxuriate in the sun. Normally, she might disapprove of such idleness; a person should be off cleaning houses. But since it was part of my cooking classes, that made it okay. Really, she was doing it for my sake.

One morning, as we sat looking at our sliver of Mediterranean water, she swung her legs down and scooted her chair closer to mine. She leaned forward, fixed me with an intense expression, and commanded:

"Bring me a baby!"

"But we have a cat," I said. "Who needs a baby?"

"A cat! What's a cat?" she said, angrily brushing aside this evasion. "Bring me a baby!"

How could I explain to her that our lives were still too unsettled, too unstable? That war correspondents don't just go gallivanting around the Middle East having babies; or that even now, as we began to tentatively settle down, we still didn't know where we wanted to be? I definitely didn't have the Arabic—or even the English, this hour of the morning—to express the array of emotions this demand evoked.

"I want a baby," I told her, all innocent shrugs, "but Mohamad doesn't."

This was another trick I had learned in Umm Hassane's school of culinary and rhetorical arts: whenever she wanted something her way, she would claim, piously, that Mohamad Ali likes it this way or Mohamad Ali wants this. But I should have known better than to try to wield the master's sword against her.

"Mohamad doesn't want one?" she growled, flicking aside his opinion with a toss of her chin. "Who cares what he says? Bring me a baby!"

PART IV

Eat, Pray, War

Eating is a small, good thing in a time like this.

—Raymond Carver, "A Small, Good Thing"

Chapter 21

Fear and Shopping

I WAS SITTING IN Arabic class, on a warm July morning, when Leena called. "Hezbollah kidnapped two Israeli soldiers this morning; I'm going to get a pedicure," she announced, as though this was the natural progression of things. "It might be a while before I get a chance to go to the beauty salon again," she explained, and that's when I began to suspect there would be more than a prisoner exchange this time.

"All right, class," said my Arabic teacher, sighing. A great beauty in her day, Hayat wore spectacles on a long golden chain and wool sweater sets. Her eyebrows were always penciled in precise arches, her chocolate brown hair reassuringly rigid. I thought she was going to send us home, but Hayat met disasters, displacement, and war like a quintessential Beiruti:

"Today I think we are going to learn some new words," she said. "Who knows the verb 'to kidnap'?"

Turning to the blackboard, she wrote the Arabic terms for kidnapping, explosion, assassination. Soon the students were shouting out vocabulary words: How do you say prisoner exchange? Negotiation? Car bomb?

A few minutes later, Hayat's phone rang and she answered. Her expression changed as she listened. *"Maal asaf,"* she said, and sighed again, "I think we should probably all go home."

I walked down Bliss Street toward home. Isolated cars and taxis were speeding toward whatever destination they believed was safe. Soldiers and armored vehicles trundled down the streets, heading for the Corniche and the airport road. Stores and schools were still open, but that first day, as the Israelis bombed southern Lebanon, most people in Beirut stayed home.

"Usually, during the civil war, people started rushing to the stores, filling their baskets, whenever they thought there would be an attack," said Hayat when I called her that afternoon. "Today the grocery stores were like normal, except less people than usual." The whole city was waiting.

The next day, Israeli warplanes bombed the Beirut airport and the fuel stores of the Jiyeh power plant. Silently, simultaneously, the entire city heard the same call to action, and all of Beirut answered the call, preparing for war with an ancient Lebanese tradition: shopping.

At Smith's the shelves were already empty. The dairy cabinet was cleaned out—no yogurt, no *labneh,* no milk. While I dithered and waited to see what would happen, my neighbors were already rampaging through the supermarket, stripping it like battle-hardened commandos—which, in a sense, they were. In wartime, shopping becomes a Darwinian exercise in amassing the most calories in the least amount of time. Beirutis were so practiced at this adrenaline-driven combat shopping that they could do it without even losing their sense of style.

I watched haplessly as a young hipster slouched through the dairy section in impeccably mussed hair and Diesel jeans, shadowed by a Sri Lankan maid in a crisp ironed uniform. With infinite boredom, he pointed at items on the shelves: a box of pasta, a jar of artichoke hearts. She retrieved these desiderata and placed them carefully in his basket. He rambled on, glancing from side to side through sleepy, half-closed eyes like the store was a nightclub and none of the girls were pretty enough for his taste. He was so cool he was barely burning any calories. I was breaking a sweat just watching him.

I wandered through the aisles picking up the random, useless products that remained: a can of creamed corn. Tricolored pasta. Vacuum-packed bacon. Dried tortellini, which Mohamad and I would eat all through the war, and forever after refer to, with a shudder of revulsion, as "the war pasta."

People bought siege food, anything that wouldn't need refrigeration—powdered milk, canned hummus, beans, cracked wheat. But they also succumbed to less rational cravings, like the yogurt, which would spoil once the electricity started going out. When I called my friend Nahlah to see what she wanted, she asked for Rice Krispies. I bought her six boxes and a chocolate cake mix for myself. And everybody lined up to buy bread.

In the Middle East, food without bread is like soup without a bowl. Most Arabic food is either made with bread, or designed to be eaten with bread, or it is bread. In lean years, bread could extend a meager serving to feed an entire family. Life revolved around bread. If a piece of bread fell to the ground, Umm Hassane would kiss it and press it to her forehead before putting it back on the counter.

Most Beirut neighborhoods have a *furn,* a communal bread oven where people gather in the mornings and early afternoon to get freshly baked *manaeesh:* crisp little pizzas topped with *zaatar,* cheese, ground beef or lamb, or spicy Armenian sausage, to name just a few incarnations. The *furn* also supplies news, gossip, conversation—communion in the most generous sense.

During the Lebanese civil war, the neighborhood bakery became even more important. When cooking gas was scarce, people reverted to the age-old practice of taking their dough to the neighborhood oven, summed up in the old proverb "Let the baker bake your dough, even if he steals half of it." Women and children went out for supplies—they were less likely to be mistaken for combatants—and the women who gathered at the neighborhood bakery became known as *niswan al furn,* "the ladies of the oven."

In my friend Barbara's East Beirut neighborhood, bakeries were neutral ground during the civil war. People would pass one shared newspaper down the line, discussing its contents. "You often had brothers in the same family in different militias, fighting each other," she said, "but when they were in the *furn,* they were neutral. There was no fighting there."

But others had darker memories. As a child, my friend Samar would stand in line for hours to buy bread, only to see fighters from Amal and other militias swagger up to the front of the line and seize the entire neighborhood's ration without even paying. "I would wait in line for bread, and then the grown-ups would come and take it, and I would cry," recalled my friend Malek (who grew up to be a professor of nutrition). Sometimes militiamen would take over an entire bakery: if they controlled the bread supply, they controlled the neighborhood.

During the war, the invisible network of obligations that we call a social contract began to break down. When the destruction reached the neighborhood bakery, it was the ultimate blow. If you had bread, you could convince yourself that you had what it represented—a stable, civilized life.

I bought five loaves of bread. It would mold in a day or two, but who doesn't feel better after smelling freshly baked bread? So many Beirutis bought bread that day that the bakers' syndicate issued a statement to the local radio stations that people should stop hoarding bread. "If you do continue to stockpile bread," the bakers warned ominously, "it will contribute to the crisis."

I had to laugh. The bakers made it sound as if an army of housewives and Sri Lankan maids had caused the war. I imagined what Umm Hassane might say: "If we stop buying bread, will Israel and Hezbollah stop bombing each other?"

After stocking up on bread, I drove to Haret Hreik with my friend Jackson, a radio reporter. Earlier that day, Israeli Brigadier General Dan Halutz had warned that unless Hezbollah stopped firing rockets at Israel, the Israeli military would start targeting Hezbollah areas, even in Beirut, and that residents of *dahiyeh* should draw their own conclusions. We wanted to ask ordinary Shiites what they thought of their brand-new war.

The streets were empty except for *shabab*, young men, whizzing past on mopeds with yellow Hezbollah flags fluttering off the backs. A few older men hurried home with hastily purchased groceries, battening down for a siege. Inside one apartment building, we saw families filing out of the elevator, mostly elderly couples fleeing the neighborhood, clutching overnight bags. All the people we talked to said that they supported "the resistance." But they looked around nervously as they said it: Hezbollah is always watching, always listening, and this is what they were expected to say. They all looked terrified.

That night the city was utterly silent. At 3:30 in the morning, it started—a humming, a shearing through the sky, coming from all directions as if it were rising from the sea. Just then, the call to prayer wavered out from the mosque. The faint recorded voice of the muezzin was drowned in the rising growl of the warplanes.

I went outside and stood on the balcony. The buildings huddled quiet all around. A flare shot up from not far away, a red shooting star, and it arced out over the silent city and toward the sea. Then came the jackhammer bursts of antiaircraft guns. Then the first bombs. I went back inside and lay awake listening until dawn drained the sky of darkness.

I woke up a few hours later when a text message bleeped into my cell phone. It was from Usama, in Baghdad. He wrote: "I hope U R OK and fine. We all here in Iraq feel worried about U." I was glad to hear from him, but his message was not reassuring.

Mohamad and I drove out to the Ghobeireh intersection, a major artery into *dahiyeh*. A massive chunk of overpass lay prolapsed in the road underneath, sliced out as if with a gigantic knife, blocking the road into *dahiyeh* and the road to the airport with one karate chop. Behind the ruined bridge, a larger-than-life-sized cement sculpture of Ayatollah Khomeini scowled out at the scene, practically untouched. He had a few scars, but whether they were from this war or the last one, I couldn't say.

At the airport, a giant plume of oily black smoke rose out of a ball of orange fire from the bombed fuel tanks. A cherry-red Ferrari parked abandoned. Billboards with vertical slats clacked and rotated with alternating ads for men's beauty salons, diamond necklaces, and electrical generators. Outside the gleaming, modern terminal, shrubbery had been pruned to spell out the airport's new name: Rafic Hariri International Airport.

Inside, the terminal was empty except for a handful of soldiers. Electric screens flashed with departure and arrival times for flights that would never happen. From a window overlooking the terminal, a gray-haired man beckoned to us to come upstairs.

In a cramped office, a skeleton crew of three Middle East Airlines employees was answering frantic calls from summer visitors trapped in Lebanon. Shehadeh Zaiter, the gray-haired manager, had kept the office open throughout the civil war. "Don't worry; we are safe," he said with pride. "During the war, we used to walk on the roads, between the bombs."

As he spoke, a missile landed just outside. The terminal shook. Then another, even closer. A soldier ran to the door of the office and shouted at us to come down to the basement. We ran down the frozen escalator, scrambling like a parody of commuters rushing to catch a flight.

Downstairs, surrounded by nervous, hungry soldiers, Zaiter took us aside. Did we think the war would last long?

We didn't know what to tell him. We said it might.

"God help us," he said quietly.

My friend Salaam, the Communist, called from Baghdad. "I am sorry to see this happening in Lebanon," he said. Then he laughed and said fiercely: "I want to see it happening in Saudi Arabia and the other Arab countries."

By now it was clear that Hezbollah had miscalculated the Israeli response when it kidnapped the two soldiers. Israel had bombed the airport and bridges, blockaded the ports, and killed dozens of people, most of them civilians. After a defiant press conference on the day of the kidnapping, Hassan Nasrallah had disappeared from sight. Rumors circulated that he had been struck by an Israeli missile. People were beginning to wonder if he was dead.

That evening, Friday, July 14, at about 8:30, Nasrallah called in a statement to Hezbollah's TV station, Al-Manar. He sounded flat and tired, but the photograph that accompanied his speech, somewhat surreally, showed his trademark apple-cheeked smile. He offered condolences to the families of the martyrs who had given their lives "in the noblest confrontation and battle that the modern age has known, or rather that all history has known." He reminded the Lebanese of the victory they had won on May 25, 2000, when Israeli troops withdrew from southern Lebanon.

Then he did something no one expected. Reminding his audience that he had promised them "surprises," he announced that they would begin momentarily. "Now, in the middle of the sea, facing Beirut, the Israeli warship that has attacked the infrastructure, people's homes, and civilians—look at it burning," he said calmly.

It was a hot night, and we had all the windows open. Manara was a mixed neighborhood, not particularly Shiite, or even exclusively Muslim, but when Nasrallah made his dramatic announcement, we could hear a susurrus of cheers and clapping from nearby apartments.

Mohamad and I ran up on to the roof. We could see an orange glow, like flares, shooting up from the sea to the sky. Out at sea, an Iranian-made C-802 missile had crashed into the warship. Down below, caravans of cars roamed through the streets honking in celebration, as though the death and destruction that had been and would surely follow were a wedding or a World Cup victory.

"This is a *war* war, this isn't a civil war," I said, a sudden vision of nation-states colliding in the air above us like the *Hindenburg*. "This isn't like Baghdad at all."

"No, it's not," said Mohamad. "That's what I've been trying to tell you."

Downstairs, Umm Hassane was unimpressed by Nasrallah's dramatic gesture.

"Why is Hezbollah doing this now? What are they thinking?" she complained. "Look at Egypt and Jordan, and all the other Arab countries—they're not attacking Israel. It's only in Lebanon that we carry the board sideways."

On Saturday morning, in the southern village of Marwaheen, the Israel Defense Forces ordered people to evacuate. When they did, the IDF fired on the convoy of fleeing villagers and killed at least sixteen.

In Beirut, people focused on details, on little tasks that seemed irrelevant but had the virtue of being something they could control. Umm Hassane stopped me just as I was about to go out reporting and urgently inquired if I was planning to mop the floor. Our entire neighborhood did laundry. Buildings flapped and rippled, suddenly festive, like the rigging of a ship. Sheets, towels, pillowcases bleached in the sun. A city of white flags. Mohamad understood the snapping white sheets in a way that I did not—as a sign that water and electricity would not last—and suddenly became bent on doing laundry. He wanted me to do it while he worked.

"Why should I do the fucking laundry?" I shouted.

"Because I have a fucking job, and you don't," he snapped.

I was working just as hard as he was: I had four stories due and had just turned down a fifth assignment. But as a freelancer I made a fraction of his salary.

"You're divorced!" I shouted.

He apologized. I apologized. We did the laundry together.

I called Hania, an animal rights activist who had helped me after I adopted Shaitan. She was going around the city feeding stray cats and dogs. "So, you're still here," she said. "I was wondering if you are one of the people who are going to leave, or if you are going to stay, being married to a Lebanese."

I went to Smith's to see if there was any milk (there wasn't). There was a young butcher at the meat counter who always told me terrible jokes in order to practice his English. He attempted one, something about a chicken wearing an egg around its neck. It didn't make a lick of sense, but I laughed anyway, because his face had the anxious look of someone trying not to burst into tears.

"Are you going to leave?" he said, as he handed me my chicken.

"No," I said. "I live here."

Back home, I stood at the kitchen sink eating a sandwich and looking out at the old black-and-white-striped lighthouse from the window over the sink. The electricity was out; I would have to cook the chicken right away, and then I would finish my stories, and then—

There was a loud metallic ping that seemed to come from all around, as if the sea were a giant metal bowl rapped with a ball-peen hammer. The windows sucked in and then bellied out, the glass as pliable as plastic wrap. Shaitan ran into the pantry and crouched underneath a shelf. The Israelis had bombed the new lighthouse, a tall silver tower not far down the Corniche. The bombing was exquisitely targeted—the tower was unharmed except at the very top, where metal hung lopsided.

It took me a few minutes to work out the obvious: the old lighthouse was just outside our kitchen and living room. If they bombed it next, no matter how precisely, the entire front of the apartment would be full of flying glass.

"Umm Hassane, we have to leave," I said. I had no idea where we would go, but we had to get out of the apartment.

"I'm not leaving," she said, flipping her chin up and settling back into the sofa with her arms folded. "I'm not going anywhere. Let them kill me, *ma btifru maai*—it's all the same to me."

* * *

Aunt Khadija's house was bombed. Aunt Nahla's house in Bint Jbeil was bombed. Batoul and Hajj Naji's house was bombed. A series of relatives showed up at our apartment, bearing suitcases and anxious expressions, and sat in the living room with Umm Hassane while they tried to figure out where to go next. Hajj Naji stayed with his cousins; Aunt Nahla stayed with her brother; Aunt Khadija's son stayed with us until he went somewhere else. It was a game, musical people, and all of Lebanon was playing it.

Every day people were streaming into Beirut, bearing ragged duffel bags of clothes and plastic sacks of bread. Drivers were charging $400 or $500 to bring people up from the south, about forty times the peacetime price. The cost of gasoline had risen, in some areas, up to 500 percent. Schools, hospitals, and the few public spaces were all packed with refugees. By the time the bombing stopped, a month later, there would be close to a million internal refugees—almost a quarter of Lebanon's population.

I went to a small public park called Sanayeh Garden with Jackson and our friend Abdulrahman, who was going around Ras Beirut buying food and medicine for refugees with his own money. Several hundred people who had fled the bombing in southern Lebanon were sleeping on the pavement and under trees. One family had camped out under a tree and hung a birdcage with a canary from its branches and set up a small gas stove. A baby waddled around the perimeter of this outdoor kitchen, gnawing on a biscuit, and a four-year-old boy shyly handed me a cookie.

We walked around and talked to the refugees for an hour. There was nobody, not a single official or representative, from the Lebanese government; no evidence of what President George W. Bush had nervously referred to earlier that day, while receiving a barrel of pickled herring from German Chancellor Angela Merkel, as Lebanon's "fragile democracy." The only people handling the refugee crisis in Sanayeh Garden were a handful of students in their teens and twenties, one of them wearing the splint and bandage of a recent nose job. Most of them were from the Syrian Social Nationalist Party, a secular group aligned with Hezbollah.

"You have militias taking care of refugees," said Abdulrahman in disgust, as we walked out of the park. *"Mish maaoul"*—unbelievable.

It was the same story all over the city. Most of the refugee centers we visited, in schools and other empty buildings, were being managed by Amal. In Tayuneh, a few blocks from Umm Hassane's apartment, there was a shopping mall under construction. Deep below the earth's surface, several thousand refugees were huddled in the underground parking lot. Hundreds of refugees packed into each level of the stone catacomb; the further down you descended, the more miserable they were, like rings of hell. The smell pressed against you and snaked inside your mouth: shit and piss and rotting food, babies throwing up and old people coughing, the sweat and recycled breath of hundreds of human beings. Enormous generators hummed and kept the flickering fluorescent lights barely alive.

To get in and out, or to move between levels, lines of people squeezed simultaneously up and down a staircase only wide enough for one. Each family had set up a temporary living room inside the painted lines marking off parking spaces. They sprawled on blankets and on straw mats, with diapers and rumpled clothes ranged around them.

Four stories below the earth, Jackson and I ended up talking to a twenty-three-year-old political science student in a pink cotton shirt, a pretty blonde with red-rimmed eyes. Her name was Rowina. "You are the third person who has come to see us," she said. The first person to descend to the refugees was from Hezbollah. The second was from Amal.

She had left her house in Haret Hreik three days earlier, after Halutz issued his warning, and ever since the warplanes bombed her apartment, she had been underground. "Sitting. Just sitting," she said, holding on to her seven-year-old sister, Fatima. "If somebody comes from outside, we ask him, 'What's the news?'"

I asked Rowina why she didn't go upstairs, why so many families stayed in the darkness. Wasn't the air much better above ground? "Yes," she replied, "but when we go upstairs, the bombings might come."

If the shopping mall was bombed, they would all be buried alive, but I did not point this out. Tensions were rising in the fluorescent half light of the parking garage. Men started shouting and pushing one another. When people are packed like rats underground for days, it doesn't take much for fighting to start. I left.

As we walked up the parking ramp, out of the reeking underground city, we ran into Hezbollah functionaries on their way down. They were wheeling five shopping carts full of groceries down the long slow curve of the ramp. The people shuffled up slowly in a patient mob, gathering silently in front of the grocery carts, waiting to be fed. As they handed out the food, the Hezbollah men intoned over loudspeakers: *"Allah Karim"*—"God is generous."

When I told Umm Hassane about the people sleeping in the park and the hundreds of families in the parking lot underground, she was furious.

"People are sleeping on the ground, and the Sayyid doesn't care," she said, referring to Nasrallah.

In a speech, Nasrallah had promised to rebuild the decimated villages and neighborhoods with the help of "friends," which was understood to be Iran. The bombed areas would be like new, he said—better than new, full of light and air.

"He said he was going to make Lebanon like it was before," she said, echoing a comment Aunt Khadija had made earlier. "Is he going to bring the dead people back to life?"

I went to visit my friend Paula. She was a friend of mine and Munir's, a sociologist with a husky laugh and intelligent eyes and crazy hair. She lived with her mother in a tiny apartment just a few blocks away from us. We sat in the kitchen chain-smoking her Davidoffs and squeezing lemons into vodka. She was supposed to be finishing her doctoral dissertation on "Women Entrepreneurs in Postwar Lebanon."

Paula's mother was sitting at an old wooden table in the kitchen, "correcting" a package of pita bread. She did this by pulling apart the two halves and laying them in the bag back to front. It's an old Lebanese housewife's trick: by exposing more of the bread's surface area to the air, you delay the inevitable invasion of mold, and thus prolong its life—a useful technique in peacetime, but even more essential during war. There was flour for now, but

Israel had bombed the roads and bridges, imposing a blockade by land, sea, and air. Who knew how long supplies would last? And so Umm Paula was correcting the bread.

In Lebanon, parents are usually known by the names of their firstborn sons, not daughters, so her real nickname was Umm Pierre. But I always called her Umm Paula, and she always laughed. Umm Paula had a square face and a sarcastic way of summing things up. She rolled when she walked, favoring one leg, like an old boxer. In 1963, she and her husband named Paula's older sister Golda, after Israeli Prime Minister Golda Meir—not the most popular person in Lebanon, considering that the two countries have been at war since 1948. When I asked Paula why, she made a fist, smacked it into her open palm, bared her teeth in a savage grin, and said, "Because they wanted her to be *tough*."

I asked Umm Paula something I'd been wondering about: What kept people going during the long, fifteen-year civil war? What sustained them? What did they *eat*?

She sat silent for a few moments. She picked up a piece of pita, peeled it apart, and laid the two halves back down again. She did it one more time. And then she spoke.

One day, said Umm Paula, a woman collected six stones. She lit a fire in the low clay oven in her yard. Kneeling in front of the oven, she set the stones on top of it. Laying the stones out in neat little rows, she sprinkled them with salt, and she began to cook.

A man passed by and stuck his head over the wall. "What are you doing—cooking stones?" he teased her, laughing.

"They're for my children," she replied. "We have nothing to eat. But I don't want them to know that. When they see the stones, they'll think I'm making them something for dinner, and they won't be hungry anymore."

Chapter 22

Mighli

T HE SKY IS sad for Lebanon," said Abu Hussein. His tired old taxi-
wheezed up Bishara al-Khoury Street, carrying Mohamad and me
into *dahiyeh* through the murky light. "The sky is crying for us."
But it wasn't rain. It wasn't the sky. The heavy gray thundercloud was part
of the city itself, suspended in midair: the pulverized remains of several hundred buildings, several thousand apartments and small businesses, and all
of their contents, blasted into a fine powder and shot up into the heavens
like confetti. The bomb clouds hung over Beirut and seemed to change the
climate itself, conjuring an eerie yellow eclipse weather that people had already started calling "the war wind."

Nine days into the conflict, Israeli warplanes had bombed 55 bridges and
dozens of roads, killing 330 people in Lebanon, most of them civilians. Anyone with a foreign passport was trying to leave the country. U.S. Marines
had returned to Lebanon for the first time in twenty-two years, to evacuate
American citizens aboard a Navy transport vessel. Nasrallah swore not to
give up Ehud Goldwasser and Eldad Regev, the two Israeli soldiers Hezbollah had kidnapped, even if "the whole universe" came to get them. Hezbollah was firing rockets into northern Israel almost every day. And almost
every day Israeli fighter jets roared over Beirut and dropped bunker-busting
bombs on Haret Hreik, the neighborhood we were driving toward, where a
photographer friend had told us that Hezbollah would be leading a "tour."

* * *

I recognized the smell right away: wet ashes, smoldering fires. Burning plastic. And something else, less definite, the collision and rearrangement of all the unnoticed organic and chemical matters that make up our everyday lives. Eight square city blocks had been bombed into a concrete goulash. A haze of cement dust blanketed the wreckage, softening sharp edges and muffling all sounds in its dreary crepuscular light. The smashed apartment buildings looked utterly abandoned.

At precisely eleven a.m., Hezbollah spokesman Hussein Naboulsi showed up. Three fighters in black jackets and dark baggy pants flanked him closely, casting glances from side to side, Kalashnikovs slung over their shoulders as casually as purses. Reporters raced to him and screamed out questions that seemed as rhetorical as anything from Umm Hassane:

"How do you justify the bombings of Israeli civilians?"

"Where is Hassan Nasrallah? Is he dead?"

"Are you using civilians as human shields?"

Naboulsi ignored all the questions. "I'm gonna speak to you; you have to follow me!" he shouted, in his peculiar falsetto monotone. "If I tell you to evacuate, you're going to evacuate! The cameramen, don't go the way you want, just follow me. You're gonna see buildings, roads, everything! We're gonna take you to the heart of Haret Hreik, where the secretariat general was . . ."

He stalked off into the wreckage, and we scrambled after him. The streets were a heaving sea of concrete. We were half-walking, half-climbing over the insides of people's lives: a red plastic rocking horse, a radiator, half a sofa. Piles and piles of CDs. Plastic chairs, pajamas, cinder blocks. A college textbook on diabetes. Naboulsi kept up a stream of increasingly frenzied patter. "This is the Israeli democracy!" he shrieked. "This is the justice in the world today! If there is a conscience in the world, wake up! Wake up! Wake up before it's too late!"

Hezbollah's packaged tour fell apart in minutes. Everyone wandered off into the maze of smashed concrete, shooting photos or writing in notebooks, and Naboulsi ended up scuttling around like a despairing third-grade teacher who had lost his field trip.

Mohamad and I wandered off on our own and ran into our friend Nadim. He was standing in the middle of a canyon that used to be a city intersection and looking up a tall apartment block. The roof had been sheared off but had not fallen, and it tilted dangerously off the side of the building like an absurdly cocked fedora. "This is so fucking unbelievable," he muttered. "I've never seen anything like this."

During peacetime, when we need metaphors, we raid the language of war. But the idiom of wartime is food: *cannon fodder, carnage, slaughterhouse.* Buildings and people are *pancaked, sandwiched, sardined.* Perhaps it is because the destruction reminds us of the knowledge we spend our lives avoiding—that we are all meat in the end. The giant disheveled ruins of apartment buildings resembled a monstrous, trashed banquet table: this building here is a club sandwich, gripped in a gigantic fist, with beds and curtains and television sets squirting out the sides like mayonnaise. That one over there is a giant wedding cake, each floor a frosted layer, the side sheared off by a blunt knife.

The Party of God had planted Haret Hreik residents among the ruins. Every so often, one of them would pop out and fulminate for the cameras. "My house is here; it was destroyed, like everyone else's," shouted a construction worker named Muhammad. He gave the stock line, which we would hear so many times before the war was through: "I will rebuild my house one, two, three, five, and ten times, God willing. Me and my wife and my kids are with Sayyid Hassan until death!"

A block or two later we ran into a cluster of Lebanese journalists we knew gathered in front of a grocery store. Patricia from *L'Orient-Le Jour* had given up trying to write in her notebook and was simply standing, stunned and aimless. Rym from *The Daily Star* was looking around, her arms folded over her chest as if she were cold. The store's metal shutters lay twisted on the sidewalk, which glittered with broken glass. Nearby, a donation box for Hezbollah's Islamic schools, charities, and hospitals stood untouched on its pole, bearing the promise in yellow Arabic script: CHARITY KEEPS AWAY CATASTROPHE.

"I used to live here," said a middle-aged *Daily Star* reporter. "It's beyond recognition."

But looking up at the splintered rooftops, we did recognize where we were. This pile of rubble was Aunt Khadija's house, where we had gone the previous Christmas to eat *mighli*.

Christmas Eve, 2005. Hanan was taking all of us—me, Mohamad, and her mother—to Aunt Khadija's to see the baby. Khadija's son Hussein had gotten married, and the young couple had just produced a daughter. Umm Hassane and I were both excited, but for different reasons, because with any luck we were going to eat *mighli*.

There is an empire that spans the Middle East, the Balkans, and Eastern Europe; an empire not of humans, or their gods, but of puddings. The inhabitants of this Pudding Belt—be they Muslims, Christians, Jews, Armenians, Turks, Greeks, Russians, Serbs, or Poles—create an endless supply of ceremonial puddings. Some are sweet, others are savory, and many are both. All these puddings have two things in common: They are all made of seeds, ancient symbols of death and rebirth—cereals, beans, nuts, or all three. And they are all made to be shared with people outside the family circle, as an offering to the gods, alms for the poor, or a dish made in thanks for a lucky event and passed out to forty neighbors—ten in each of the four directions.

These puddings belong to a deeper, more ancient tradition than any of the faiths and nations that have usurped them. Some consider them descendants of the pudding Noah made from the seeds that he took on the ark; others describe them as the foods of the Prophet's family. But the ironic and even beautiful thing is that each nationality or sect holds them equally sacred. Turkish Sunnis make *ashura* and give it to neighbors to celebrate good fortune. Polish Catholics eat *kutia* on Christmas Eve to celebrate the imminent birth of the savior. Greek Orthodox Christians make *kolyva* and share it with passersby to commemorate the dead. And Lebanese of all faiths make *mighli* to celebrate life—the birth of a child.

When a baby is born to a Lebanese family, visitors file in for weeks, like the Magi, bearing gifts and envelopes of cash. In return, the family—regardless of class, geography, and sect—serves them *mighli*, a cinnamon-scented rice pudding topped with nuts. People believe that the spices in *mighli* will help the new mother "bring the milk." But *mighli* transcends its physical function and passes into the realm of symbolism: When Leena's second cousin had a baby in New York, Leena's mother made *mighli* in far-away Beirut and served it at a family dinner, making sure to mention that it was in honor of the New York birth.

I had heard all sorts of stories about this pudding. So when I learned we were going to visit the young couple at Aunt Khadija's, I asked Umm Hassane if there would be *mighli*.

She shot me a penetrating look. "You want *mighli*?" she asked.

I could see the wheels turning inside her head: Mohamad and I had been stubborn on the baby front so far, but perhaps this interest in *mighli* betrayed a deeper hunger. If I wanted to fill my belly with *mighli*, might I not also yearn to fill it with a child of my own? And someday soon, God willing, serve *mighli* from my own hands? She threw on her long black overcoat and her best headscarf, and as we left the apartment, I saw a gleam of baby lust in her eyes.

I expected the Christmas decorations, the poinsettias wrapped in red foil, the lighted butcher shops and sweet stores, to disappear entirely once we passed the giant painting of Musa al-Sadr that guarded one of the entrances to *dahiyeh*.

But the first thing we saw once we passed the Vanished Imam was a row of giant inflatable Santas. Syrian day laborers lined the side of the road, hungry-looking men with sun-dark skin, all wearing red-and-white polyester Santa hats. The stores that sold cheap aluminum teakettles, Chinese notebooks, and plastic flowers were bursting with gigantic red Mylar bows and potted poinsettias. One store's outside wall was being stormed by a platoon of Santa commandos. Another had a six-foot mechanical Santa stationed at the entrance that roared to life periodically, swiveling his hips like a belly dancer and roaring "HO HO HO! MER-RY CHRISTMAS!" The war on Christmas, which is what American Christians were calling secular and ecumenical holiday traditions that year, hadn't made it to the Shiite heartland of *dahiyeh*.

In Aunt Khadija's living room, we sat with Hussein and his tired-looking wife, Lina, who was a schoolteacher. We chatted about the baby before turning to the national obsession—more talked about than sports or the weather, let alone religion or politics—of time off.

Earlier that year, when Hariri was assassinated, the government had immediately launched its time-tested crisis-management plan: it shut down. Come December, the prime minister decreed that everybody had to give up a few days of holiday vacation to make up for the lost workdays.

"Why should we sacrifice our holidays for the actions of the Syrians?" Aunt Khadija demanded.

"But Christmas is not our holiday," said Hussein. "What does this holiday have to do with us?"

"Christmas is a national holiday," said Aunt Khadija, severely. "It belongs to everyone."

A squall from the baby put a stop to the time-off discussion. Hussein, Lina, and Aunt Khadija all ran to the nursery. As they disappeared down the hall, Umm Hassane seized her chance.

"Should we ask about the *mighli*?" she said, leaning forward, with a glance toward the kitchen, as if this was our chance to dash in and steal some.

"No, no!" said Hanan, horrified that her mother was going to embarrass us all by asking for food.

Umm Hassane subsided, but it was only a tactical retreat. Her eyes gravitated toward the kitchen, where *mighli* awaited. She might have issued some secret old-lady signal, or perhaps a clandestine old-lady phone call had already taken place, because not long after that, Aunt Khadija came back from the kitchen with little silver bowls brimming with the pudding of fertility and life.

Mighli is as firm as flan but more solid. There are no eggs; the pudding gets its bounce from powdered rice. It is usually a warm speckled brown from the spices—cinnamon, caraway, sometimes anise, in some areas even more. Old-fashioned mothers stand over the *mighli* for an hour, stirring until it thickens. Newfangled ones make it in a "Presto," a pressure cooker, and it's ready in minutes. You put it in the refrigerator to firm, and then comes the best part. You go to your neighborhood nut seller and tell him you need "*mighli* mix." He will give you something more or less like the following: walnuts, raw peeled almonds, pine nuts, shelled pistachios, coconut shavings, and sultanas. Some people use cashews too; others put nothing but walnuts and coconut. Sprinkle the nuts on top of the *mighli*, and you're ready to bless well-wishers with your bounty. All you need is a baby.

"Or you can buy a mix," said Hussein's wife, Lina, the young and practical schoolteacher, who still exuded the weary satisfaction of a new mother. "You just pour it in boiling water, and it's ready."

Umm Hassane said nothing but fluffed herself like a chicken and radiated disapproval.

"Is it any good? " asked Hussein, shooting a cautious glance between mother, aunt, and wife.

"Yes, it's good, it's good," the young mother maintained.

Everyone raised their eyebrows and said "Hm!" in that skeptical, what-will-they-think-of-next way.

Aunt Khadija had clearly been tipped off. As we left, she detained me at the doorway, glancing first at Mohamad, and then at Umm Hassane, and pressed three giant plastic tubs of *mighli* into my hands.

I rounded the final corner, passing Aunt Khadija's flattened building, circling back to where the tour began. A bearded, black-jacketed Hezbollah gunman stood waiting against the wall. *"Yalla, yalla, "* he shouted, jerking his head to hurry us along.

"Can you believe this is Lebanon?" said Rym, walking up to our car. "Where we were sitting and smoking *argileh* two weeks ago?"

On Rym's birthday we'd sat in downtown Beirut with her friends, a mixed group of Saudis, Lebanese, Canadians, Americans, even a Polish lady she'd dug up somewhere, outside Rym's favorite restaurant, which was T.G.I. Friday's. It seemed even more distant, now, than that Christmas only seven months ago.

I shook my head: No, I can't believe this smoking wreck is the same Lebanon.

We stood next to Abu Hussein's car, afraid to stay but somehow also reluctant to leave.

Finally the bearded gunman reappeared. *"Airplane, airplane!"* he shouted in Arabic, flapping his arms like a child imitating a bird.

There weren't any warplanes overhead, but nobody wanted to risk it. Everybody ran for their cars and drove away.

Chapter 23

Cooking with Umm Hassane

I HAD *MJADARA HAMRA*. I had hummus and tabbouleh. I had *shish taouk*, juicy and orange, tucked under a blanket of warm bread soaked with tomato sauce, grilled with onions and bloody, blackened tomatoes. I had gone to our favorite neighborhood restaurant, Abu Hassan, which stayed open throughout the war, and returned with a feast. But nothing, not even the *mjadara hamra*, could tempt Umm Hassane. She frowned at the food as though it had betrayed her.

"Umm Hassane, eat something," I begged, setting the plate down on the coffee table in front of her. "You have to eat something."

"I'm not hungry," she said. "How can I have any appetite? What do I want with food?"

As the awful July continued, Umm Hassane grew more and more *mdepressa*. She stopped eating. She spent hours lying on her back on the sofa, flipping from Al-Jazeera to the Lebanese satellite channels and then back again, watching endless footage of bombing and Nasrallah's never-ending speeches. She hardly spoke. One evening, she sat straight up, glared, shook her finger, and announced: "There were going to be 1.6 million tourists to Lebanon this summer." Then she lay back down and was silent for the rest of the night. Over the past few days, as the electricity flickered in and out, the bombing thundered in the dark hours before dawn, and Nasrallah's bearded face flashed from the television screen, she had stopped eating altogether.

Umm Hassane's apartment was close to Shiyah, which ended up getting bombed, and she couldn't go home. A magazine had asked me to go to the south, but we couldn't leave Beirut because we had to take care of her, and I was beginning to get fed up. I didn't want to have a baby, to cook and clean, to keep house. I wanted to be in the south, at the front line, telling the *real* story: civilians driving up through the bombs, or trapped in their houses, under bombardment. I knew this was a purely selfish drive—to avoid the awful guilt and helplessness of war by pretending to be doing something useful—but I was a journalist, not a housewife, and it was the most useful thing I knew how to do. The last place I wanted to be was trapped in my own apartment, taking care of a cantankerous old woman who started out trying to get me pregnant and now seemed to be trying to starve herself to death.

The next day Mohamad went out reporting. "My mom's so stubborn," he complained before he left. "I told her not to sleep with the AC on, but she won't listen. Last night she got so cold she was shaking."

Later that afternoon, I was on the phone with my editor when I noticed Umm Hassane trembling. She was hunched over on the couch, her entire body shaking violently.

There was no air conditioner here in the living room. It was at least 85 degrees; she could not possibly be cold. Yet she was still shaking. I laid the back of my hand on her forehead, which burned like a hot lamp. Her face was white and drawn. She had lost a lot of weight. We hadn't noticed. We had been covering the war.

My editor was still on the line, talking about Nasrallah. I covered the phone with my hand and switched languages.

"Umm Hassane, you are too much sick," I said, in barely coherent Arabic. "You have to go to hospital."

"No, no," she said. Even her voice was trembling. "I'm fine. I don't want to go to the hospital."

She was not fine. She was too weak to sit up straight. I had to get her to the hospital right away; I had to get back to my editor, who was impossible to reach on the phone, and I had to finish my story.

At that moment the other line rang. It was Hassan calling from Paris to see if we were all right. "Hassan, you have to . . . talk to your mother," I said, struggling to keep Arabic and French in separate corners. "I believe that she is *vraiment, vraiment malade* . . . She must go to hospital. You talk to her. She must go."

She wouldn't listen to Hassan either. "*Shu baarafni*, I'm fine," she insisted. "What do I want with the hospital? They'll take money!"

I begged, I bullied, I threatened. I used words I didn't even know I knew. She wouldn't go. The war had awakened some survival instinct toward absolute refusal and immobility. "They'll take money," she kept insisting.

"Forget the fucking money!" I finally shouted at her, in English, knowing she couldn't understand.

Forget the fever; forget the war. Forget the entire Israeli military, with its Merkavas and cluster bombs and night-vision goggles. Forget Hezbollah, and its rockets and "resistance" and its black-clad commandos. If she wanted to be a martyr, I'd kill her myself.

In the five and a half hours that Mohamad sat with his mother in the emergency room, he witnessed a parade of people with symptoms of stress and shock: tightness of breath, pounding pulse, panic attacks, heart attacks. Posttraumatic stress disorder. People sick from chronic war. When the doctors got to Umm Hassane, they found she had a severe kidney infection, and they hooked her up to an IV and kept her there. If we hadn't taken her to the hospital—if we'd listened to her and left her at home—she probably would have died.

The next few weeks passed in disconnected moments, splinters of time that stand out in my memory as clear and sharp as shards of glass. I remember seeing the neighborhood kids playing in an empty lot. Before the war, all of Beirut had fluttered with polyester flags of Brazil, Iran, Germany, and other World Cup teams, and the children had been playing soccer. Now they were standing on piles of civil-war rubble, waving plastic rifles in the air, and shouting: "I'm Hezbollah! No, you're not, *I'm* Hezbollah!" I remember reading *The Satanic Verses* late at night, into the dawn, when bombs made it difficult and perhaps undesirable to sleep. The far-off explosions gently shaking the building, reminding me that people might be dying while I was safe in bed. I remember Munir calling and saying: "It's like *Waiting for Godot*, no?" Paula calling and saying "He's in denial, no? Sensitive people, they sometimes try to pretend that they are tough. It's very useful, denial. I didn't understand that until now."

I remember meeting a friend of a friend in Baromètre, an angry, bespectacled young man who said, "Your country is under attack, so you find yourself defending Hezbollah. This is a fundamentalist organization! They're against everything I stand for! But not to defend them is to say that you agree with Israel, with what Israel is doing to this country. Who else is going to defend Lebanon? Do I want the Syrian Baath Party to defeat Israel? So that it can fuck me, like it fucked me before?"

I remember sitting in a different café, interviewing the head of an anti-corruption organization, who said, "We are in a war; yet here we are, in the heart of Beirut, in a café packed with people, all very well-dressed. You might think that is very shallow, but this is what makes Lebanon different. This is what made us survive the civil war. This is the way to resist any war."

Calls from friends outside Lebanon were like echoes from a distant past. My friend Cara had once lived in Israel, just north of Kiryat Shmona, in one of the areas Hezbollah was firing rockets at. She remembered the sound of bombs falling at night. She called me almost every day. Once she called to say that her ex-brother-in-law's house had been hit by a rocket. Another time she called to see if I was okay, and I said: "I think so. I can't talk right now. I don't have any wine. I have to go get wine to cook with." The fact that I have absolutely no memory of this conversation tells me something about memory, and war, and my state of mind at that time.

I called Ali Fahs, the farmer from Souk El Tayeb, to see if he was okay. He was trapped in Jibsheet, the small southern village where he lived. The bombing was very intense there, and he hadn't left his house in fifteen days. He passed the time writing a manifesto, an open letter to Israeli Prime Minister Ehud Olmert, American President George W. Bush, and Secretary of State Condoleezza Rice. Did I want to hear it?

"Olmert, Bush, and Condi Rice, there is no difference," he read. I could hear paper rustling as he spoke. "In the name of democracy, you are killing the children and innocent people. And destroying all means of life and humanity. Instead of stopping the war, you put oil on the fire. You send funds and deliver bombs to kill more and more innocent people. Under your forged democracy, you know, and we know, the main reasons for this war is the New Middle East Plan."

For the first nine days, people in Lebanon were hoping that the United States would pressure the Israeli government to agree to a cease-fire. Then, on July 21, the Bush administration announced it was rushing a delivery of precision-guided bombs to Israel. That same day, Condoleezza Rice said that a cease-fire would be a "false promise" if it happened before Hezbollah was defeated. "I have no interest in diplomacy for the sake of returning Lebanon and Israel to the status quo ante," said Rice. "What we're seeing here, in a sense, is the growing—the birth pangs of a new Middle East, and whatever we do, we have to be certain that we're pushing forward to the new Middle East, not going back to the old one."

Describing the death of Lebanese civilians as "the birth pangs of a new Middle East" fed people's worst suspicions about the United States: that it harbored secret imperial designs on the region; that it was preparing some apocalyptic master plan; that it didn't value Lebanese lives as much as those of Israelis.

"All this war, just for that!" Ali exclaimed. "They want to make the Middle East new, to be in Israel and America's hands." There was no more talk of California or gas stations now. He finished his manifesto.

"Will you print that in your newspaper?" he asked. "Of course, you will correct my English. I didn't complete it yet, but I would like to write more. I would like to make something—I am fifteen days at home, I cannot even work."

I didn't tell him that I didn't have a newspaper, or that American editors were already bored with this little war that seemed so big to him. I asked him if he had enough food and water, if he and his family were going to be all right.

"I am a professional in food," he reminded me with dignity. "I have *labneh,* I have *laban,* I have everything. You can keep it a long time."

Of course! A siege meant nothing to a maker of *mouneh.* Until the war ended, Ali and his family would live off his *mouneh,* food meant to last through winter or war, eating away the stock he once had hoped would take them to California. He was even feeding his neighbors, who had run out of food.

"In the mountains, we have food enough for two months," he said. "We have ẓaatar, we have *burghul;* we can live for two months."

Wars are all alike, but everyone experiences them differently; part of the ugliness of war is how it intensifies those differences. You are reading my account of one war—my imperfect memories of what I saw and felt and did. Others had their own perceptions and their own realities. But everybody, even refugees who had been bombed out of their homes, said the same thing: "We don't hate the American people. Only the American government." A refugee from Haret Hreik said it to us after going back to his flattened apartment to retrieve his pet bird. A refugee from the south said it to us at the Berkeley Hotel. A talkative, roly-poly *servees* driver named Muhammad Awada said it to me while he was chain-smoking, driving across the Fouad Chehab overpass, and trying to turn around and talk to me all at the same time. "We don't hate the Americans," he kept saying. "We love America! My car, American—Toyota Corona! My cigarettes, American—Marlboro!"

I didn't explain that the car was Corolla, not Corona, or that Toyota was actually Japanese. He had enough on his mind already. In colloquial Lebanese Arabic, you "drink" cigarettes instead of smoking them; I got the feeling he might have drunk a few Coronas too, and not the Toyota kind, because he kept shouting: "I drink Marlboros! I drive Toyota! I love America!"

And then he would turn around to face me, taking his hand off the wheel to punctuate the sentence with his cigarette, causing his car to swerve across several lanes, and exclaim: "We don't hate America! We love America, we love it too much! *Why—doesn't—America—love—us?*"

After a week in the hospital, Umm Hassane came back with her complaining powers fully restored. She had disapproved of our eating habits before the war, but now they were even worse. We didn't keep much food in the house because the electricity would go out for eight, ten, twelve hours, and anything in the fridge would spoil.

I was beginning to appreciate the persistence of *mouneh*. Lebanon's history of war and famine had kept the old traditions so close to the surface that they were almost second nature. My friend Adessa was trapped in Bsharri, her ancestral village in northern Lebanon, and because they had no lemons her family had reverted to the age-old practice of flavoring their tabbouleh with *verjus,* the sour juice of unripe grapes. ("That's what kept us sane," she told me later, "that the tabbouleh tasted like tabbouleh.") The old women got their grinders out and started grinding cornmeal and flour by hand. My Arabic teacher Hayat was stuffing leftover tabbouleh into grape leaves, another old-fashioned practice that had survived because of times like these. In our house, we got by on modern-day *mouneh*—Picón cheese, ready-made hummus from Smith's (they spelled it "Homos" on the container), and cans of tuna fish.

For Umm Hassane, this haphazard eating was the final insult. Everything was falling apart: Hanan had fled to stay with friends in the mountains, everybody's houses had been destroyed, the Lebanese government was doing its best impression of a failed state. Even Nasrallah seemed lost, his beard grown into a wild gray tangle overnight. One day, as we sat down to a meal of Homos and tuna fish from Smith's, she said, "It hurts my heart to eat this food."

We interrogated her on what she meant. Did she mean it gave her heartburn? Or was she grieving that she couldn't cook? Eventually, after much cross-questioning, with Mohamad translating her cryptic pronouncements, we determined that she wanted to make *tabeekh.*

"But how can I?" she lamented.

Mohamad and I looked at each other guiltily.

"When the war is over, when we're not so busy, then we'll do some real cooking," I promised her.

A day or two later, when I had a free morning, I took Umm Hassane aside. There was a dish that only a few restaurants made—a creamy, fluffy mixture of potatoes, onions, and scrambled eggs. It was classic home cooking, the quintessential comfort food—Lebanon's moral equivalent of macaroni and cheese. Mohamad and I both loved it.

"Umm Hassane," I said. "I know you're sick, but will you please show me how to make *batata wa bayd*?"

She began by surveying my onions. Before the war, I had bought a giant wreath of small Spanish onions from Ali Fahs, dozens of them woven together by their own dried stems. They were still firm, their pearly skin striped with hints of minty green.

She held it by the tail at arm's length, like a dead cat. She tore off an onion and tried to peel it whole. It was too fresh, the skin clinging tightly to the flesh, and she threw it down in disgust.

"What are these onions?" she demanded, flaunting an accusatory palm in their direction. "Why did you buy so many?"

I took over the onion operations, cutting in half and then peeling, scoring along latitude and longitude like a vengeful god, until we had about a cup and a half of finely chopped dice.

Now for a pot. I got out my set of stainless steel pots and pans, a wedding present from a generous friend, and displayed a couple for her to choose from.

"These pots are no good," she said. "Tefal is better."

"Umm Hassane, these are very expensive pots," I told her, indignant, and pulled out the big guns: "From America!"

"From America?" she sniffed, and raised a skeptical eyebrow. That these inferior pots, with no Teflon coating, could have come from America—land of Mazola and Tylenol!—was a preposterous claim. Far more likely was that Annia got ripped off again.

"Put them in there," she says, pointing sternly to my medium-sized Tefal. She poured in corn oil, then onions, covered the pot, and turned down the flame as low as it would go.

"How long does it need?" I was writing down times and weights and measurements, poised over my notebook like a cub reporter on her first big story.

She gave me one of those *Jesus, where do they* find *you people?* looks, the kind I remember so well from my first forays into a restaurant kitchen. "Until it's ready!"

While the onions were getting themselves ready, Umm Hassane chopped the potatoes into half-inch squares with the economical knife work of a master chef. I scraped the avalanche of little squares into my big glass measuring cup.

She watched with outrage: this was too much.

"Why?" she cried out. "Why do you need to measure everything? It only needs five potatoes, two onions, and that's it!"

My Arabic was far too flimsy to convey the concept of recipe standardization, let alone the ambiguities of a world with different-sized onions and potatoes. I mumbled something about wanting to remember how to do it next time.

"Just put two onions and a few pieces of potato, and we'll be fine!" she said, with a note of pity. She dumped the potatoes in with the onions, added some salt, and covered the pot once again. "We'll cook this," she said slowly and clearly, as though explaining to a dense child, "until it's ready."

I had spent countless hours, and destroyed many a batch of potatoes, trying to figure out how to make *batata wa bayd*. I had boiled the potatoes, and then chopped them, only to see them crumble in the pan to a soggy, oily sludge. I tried frying the potatoes like short-order home fries, then adding the chopped onions afterward, and ended up with oily leathery potatoes encrusted with burnt black onions. I fried the potatoes and the onions separately, then added them together, and that wasn't right either: the flavors didn't blend. During all this experimentation, it never occurred to me that you would caramelize the onions *first,* then slow-cook the potatoes in a covered pot, or that the onions would melt into the potatoes in this lyrical way.

"I'm learning a new way to make *batata wa bayd*!" I exclaimed, delighted to finally learn the secret of this deceptively simple dish.

She frowned. I made it differently before?

"Annia doesn't usually make it this way," explained Mohamad, who had just walked into the kitchen.

"She makes it the way your brother in Spain makes it," said Umm Hassane, distressed.

"No, no, Annia makes *batata wa bayd* too, but not this way."

Umm Hassane stalked out of the kitchen and flung herself down on the sofa in theatrical despair. "If you wanted to do it that way," she cried, "then why did you ask me to make it for you?"

Mohamad realized his mistake and followed her into the living room. "No, no, we wanted to learn how to make it this way," he pleaded. "This is the right way."

"I don't know how he makes it!" she wailed, inconsolable. "They call it *tortilla*. You fry the potatoes, then you add eggs—"

"No, we want it this way," he said hastily. "When Annia makes it, she boils the potatoes, then fries everything together—"

"She *boils* the potatoes!"

Umm Hassane was aghast: this was proof that we didn't want it her way. "Well, if you wanted it that way, why did you have me do it?"

"No, we don't want it that way—we want it *your* way," he entreated.

"Well, fine. I just thought you wanted it the other way."

She stretched out full length and started whirling her prayer beads. We huddled in the kitchen and watched her warily through the door.

"Why did she want to do this complicated thing?" she demanded, addressing her suffering to the dark and silent television screen. "It would have been easier to make the *tortilla*!"

After about ten minutes, she responded to some inner culinary clock that told her exactly when the potatoes were done. She sighed, heaved herself up off the sofa, and shuffled back into the kitchen. Taking the lid off the pot, she held out a spoonful of potatoes and summoned me with the command: "Taste, taste!"

Taste! If I've got one bad habit, it's not tasting enough while I'm cooking. I'm far too prone to rely on measurements, precision directions—words on paper—over the truth of my own senses. This, too, does not fly in Umm Hassane's kitchen. She constantly forced me to sample, adjust, season: to trust my tongue instead of my words. Holding out a spoonful of the potatoes, she urged me to taste them "so we know it's ready."

They were melting, exquisite, like potato risotto, soft as macaroni and cheese. The potatoes were creamy, silky with oil and suffused with flavor from the sticky caramelized onions almost invisibly dissolved into them.

"This is better than *tortilla*!" I said.

"How do you know it's better?"

"I just tasted it!"

She softened. Just for a moment, she looked happy. Then she recovered.

"You tasted it before the eggs were in it," she grunted, and turned back to the stove.

Chapter 24

Supper of Stones

IN JUST THIRTY-THREE days, the war in Lebanon smashed the country's infrastructure, devastated its economy, and set back sixteen years of postwar reconstruction. About twelve hundred people were dead, most of them civilians, and civilians were still dying: Israel had used four million "cluster" munitions that left behind hundreds of thousands of unexploded bomblets, and as people streamed back to their homes, the cluster bomb casualties were already beginning. Hezbollah had fired nearly four thousand rockets at Israel, killing forty-three Israeli civilians, and had killed one hundred twenty Israeli soldiers during the fighting.

A few weeks after the cease-fire, Mohamad and I drove down to Bint Jbeil with Aunt Nahla. We picked her up at her brother's apartment building in Ras al-Nabaa. They were waiting for us outside when we drove up, both dressed in their finest: her in a black beaded robe, the old man in a neat little formal shirt and trousers, although he was not coming himself. He shook our hands, and we set out on the journey.

Hezbollah had lined the airport road with billboards. They were carefully color coordinated, like the banners of the independence intifada, and staggered in the manner of Burma-Shave signs. They heralded THE DIVINE VICTORY and NASR MIN ALLAH—literally, "Victory from God," but also a play on Nasrallah's name.

For the next several hours, we drove past parched tobacco fields, olive groves full of rubble, bridges cracked in half. In Ainata, a sign posted in a bombed and blackened gas station said: WE CONGRATULATE YOU FOR THE VIC-

TORY. In Tibneen, a poster proclaimed: C'EST LA VICTOIRE DU SANG ("It is the Victory of Blood"), and shortly after that we came to Bint Jbeil.

After a while you run out of ways to describe the wreckage of war. The closest thing I can think of is New Orleans under water after a hurricane, but instead of water the city is flooded with giant blocks of stone. Some passageways had been cleared, the rubble shoved to the side and piled up in great mounds. In a few of these mountains of stones, Hezbollah had planted fluttering yellow flags with its green logo, a hand thrusting up and brandishing a Kalashnikov. Yellow banners declared: THIS IS YOUR DEMOCRACY USA.

We drove to the old city, the narrow streets where Hezbollah's fighters had won its "Divine Victory." The passageway that once led to Aunt Nahla's house was gone, filled with an eight-foot-high pile of stone and rebar and wood. The entire top half of the house was sheared off. The gate was blasted open, and the stones tumbled in like a frozen wave. They reached halfway up the door.

Aunt Nahla got out of the car and walked to the edge of the pile of rubble. She seemed very small surrounded by all that stone. She looked around with an expression almost of vindication—not satisfaction, but not surprised either, as if she wanted us to think she had been expecting this all her life. Then her chin crumpled and her carefully arranged face collapsed.

"It's all gone," she said, and started to cry.

Mohamad and I climbed over the rubble and ducked into the doorway to her house. Most of the fruit trees had been crushed under the tsunami of stones. But at the back of the courtyard, hibiscus and oleander were blossoming, pink and white flowers looking out over a sea of gray. We clambered inside and tried to salvage what we could. A picture of Aunt Nahla's father, Mohamad's grandfather. A small carpet. I took a few muslin bags of her *mouneh*, carefully labeled in Arabic, which we threw out when we realized it probably wasn't safe to eat. Later we learned there could have been unexploded bombs in the rubble, but we weren't thinking about that then.

We left Aunt Nahla with her neighbors and went to visit Batoul. Her house was in ruins too, but not as thoroughly obliterated as Aunt Nahla's. The air was thick with chalky dust and a subtle but nauseating smell of decay, hopefully from rotting food. In the kitchen, the blast had picked up a jar of tomatoes and smashed it against the wall, leaving a bloodstained Rorschach splattered on the wall.

Batoul was sorting through the ruins with her daughter Zainab. She had spent the day taking anything salvageable out of the kitchen and putting it in the back bedroom, the only room with walls intact. She had gotten somebody to reattach the door so their things would not be looted. Now she was heaving trash around hopelessly, as though she didn't know what to do next, like a person puttering around in shock after a car accident. "Look at what they did to us, what Israel did to us," she wailed, sinking to the floor and collapsing onto a pile of broken concrete. "The house is destroyed. Destroyed!"

What do you say to somebody who has lost her house and most of her possessions? Hesitantly, I said hello.

She paused in the midst of her lamentations. She lifted her head as if noticing me for the first time. She looked up with eyes of Ashura, her chin trembling, thirteen hundred years of despair and dispossession staring at me through the ages.

"You've lost weight," she said, with a reproachful sniff.

Batoul spread a woven plastic mat over the chunks of plaster, concrete, and broken glass. Zainab fetched the food rations. This was what people in the south had relied on for the past month: tuna, canned hummus, bread, and bottled water distributed by international aid groups. She opened the can of hummus and glopped it into a bowl, where it retained the shape and striations from the metal can. She had no garlic, no olive oil—the jars in the kitchen had all burst from the blast of the bombs. "Hummus without olive oil!" she wailed.

We sat on the mat and scooped up handfuls of tuna and hummus with the bread. It wasn't so bad—she had found a lemon and some tomatoes—but Batoul was inconsolable. "Oh Mohamad Ali, look at what's become of us," she said as we sat and ate. "You and your mother used to come over, and we would feed you. And now we don't even have a roof over our heads!" Batoul did love to complain, like all the Bazzis, but this was literally true: the roof was blasted open to the sky.

Starving cats began to gather in the courtyard. They crept closer, craning their necks and getting ready to run—too frightened to come closer, too hungry to stay away. "This is what I used to feed these cats," said Batoul, giving them the last of the tuna. "And now we have to eat it ourselves!" It wasn't really the tuna she was upset about, but her demolished house.

A neighbor showed up, a little old man with only one tooth. He had brought a plastic bowl of grapes, nectarines, and pears. He sat on the floor a little distance away as we ate. But when he offered some tentative words of encouragement, some bromide that things would get better, Batoul turned on him.

"You got money from Hezbollah, and we got nothing!" she hissed.

After the Divine Victory, the Party of God started recording the damage and registering families for compensation. The distribution of this money would be a source of confusion and conflict for months and years to come. Israel and the Bush administration had hoped that the relentless bombing would turn the Shiite population against Hezbollah. But by destroying their homes, and for many their livelihoods, the war had made many Shiites even more dependent on the Party of God than before. They had nowhere else to turn.

The neighbor had gotten a stipend to rent an apartment until his compensation came through; but even though their house was uninhabitable, and their apartment in *dahiyeh* was utterly flattened, Batoul and Hajj Naji had not gotten any rental money. Batoul believed this was because they were not "close to" Hezbollah—in other words, they lacked *wasta*.

"I got the money because my house was destroyed," said the neighbor, shrinking away from Batoul, who was not a small woman.

"You got it because you have *wasta*," she snapped. "Look at our house? Isn't it destroyed?"

He started to say something, but she interrupted him. "Hezb *wasta*!" she shouted. "Hezb *wasta*!" she screamed again, her voice hoarse with rage, and that was how the meal ended.

A few days later, back in Beirut, I was sitting in Walimah with Munir. "I think that after this war we're going to have a lot of new believers," said Munir, gloomily lighting a cigarette. "A lot more sexual frustration."

Munir's nephew Bashar had just returned from Tyre, the southern sea-side town that was overrun with reporters and aid workers and all the other by-products of war. It was full of strange new characters now, according to Bashar—Iranian charities, Iranian money. Men with beards.

"They want to teach us how to be Shiite," he said, curling his lip. "But in the wrong way."

"What's the right way to be Shiite?"

"To love life," said Bashar. He was a young man.

Munir laughed, sounding infinitely tired, and stubbed out his cigarette. "Yes, but it can't be a one-sided relationship, you know," he said. "In order to love life, you need life to love you."

At the first Tango Night after the war, Georges and I sat over a bowl of *mlukhieh* and caught up on the past month. One of the wonderful things that happened during the war (perhaps the only good thing) was the way that Lebanon's post-civil-war generation filled the chasm left by the government's failure. Young doctors examined the refugees, prescribed medicine, and delivered babies. Young actors put on plays and theater workshops to entertain bored, frightened children. The gay rights group and the anti-corruption association fed refugees. Zico House and T-Marbouta, two of Hamra's best cafés, had converted themselves into refugee centers for the duration of the war, and ultra-chic Club Social put on a benefit concert to collect money. Georges had spent this time driving around to the schools in his neighborhood, which were full of refugees, and giving free medical exams.

"Annia, I have a question for you," he said. "During the war, I would always see these people on TV, and sometimes in the schools, saying they would sacrifice their children for Nasrallah."

The party line: *Me and my family are with Sayyid Hassan until death. I will sacrifice my sons for Hassan Nasrallah.*

"Is it true?" he said, wrinkling his smooth forehead. "Do the Shiites really feel that way?"

"Of course not," I told him.

I was a little shocked by the question. It was not my place to answer, but Mohamad was not there, and one of the reasons I loved Georges is that he bothered to question something most people believed they already knew.

After the war, I wrote a story about how Hezbollah used the ruins of *dahiyeh* as propaganda. But journalists, Israelis, and even many Lebanese were all complicit in a subtler propaganda. They were building a myth, one that bound Hassan Nasrallah and Ehud Olmert and CNN together in a convenient lie: That Middle Easterners—in this case, Lebanese Shiites—don't value their lives the way Westerners do. That they love being martyrs. That they are happy to sacrifice themselves for some apocalyptic cause. That they died because they liked it.

Dan Gillerman, the Israeli ambassador to the United Nations, used this myth to defend Israeli bombings of Lebanese civilians at Qana, including the deaths of sixteen children who, according to him, had chosen to "sleep with a missile." Lebanese PR executives would employ this myth in their sectarian postwar slogan, "I Love Life," which implied that Shiites willingly chose death over life. And Nasrallah himself used it before, during, and especially after the war, when he thundered: "They desire thrones; while we wish to be carried in coffins."

But when the television cameras went away, when the reporters put away their notebooks, and the sharp joy of survival was followed by the guilt and hatred that only bloodshed can bring—when all that was over, nobody said, "Me and my wife and children are with Sayyid Hassan until death." You did not hear "I will sacrifice my sons for Hassan Nasrallah." They said "Hummus without olive oil" or "Hezb *wasta*" or even "You've lost weight." They spoke of the practical, everyday business of food and shelter and being alive. But it didn't matter what they said in private, when the cameras were gone. Nobody heard it but themselves and their families.

Most civilians experience war not as the fighters and victims that parade across television screens, but as tired housewives peeling potatoes and wondering, all the while, at the stupidity of it. Being trapped in the house with Umm Hassane forced me to experience the awful, humiliating tedium of war without the anaesthetic of danger or the narcotic self-importance of risk—to go through it not as a witness, not as a journalist, but as a human being. That was what I had learned cooking with Umm Hassane: that *was* the real story. You have to eat the meal.

* * *

The first time I heard Umm Paula's story about the supper of stones, I thought it was the story of a mother who feeds her children's hunger on imagination and love: *"They'll think we have something to eat, and they won't be hungry anymore."* It was a story about stories—about how they can conquer hunger and hardship, turn stones into supper just as Jesus turned water into wine at Qana.

When Paula heard this interpretation, she laughed. "Well, you *can* look at it that way," she said. "It is a story, after all. We do use this phrase, a 'supper of stones.' But that's not the way we use it."

Umm Paula had said it was "an old Christian story," so I hunted for it in medieval Christian story collections. Nothing. I asked everyone I knew where it came from. Many had heard the story, and they all said it was very old; but no one knew how old. It was like trying to trace *masquf* through the murky waters of history.

Long after the war, a friend told me that the story of the stones went back to the Abbasid Empire. He said it was one of the Machiavellian tales of rulers and ruled, of eaters and eaten, that ninth-century Arabic scribes adapted from earlier story collections during the great Abbasid translation orgy in Iraq. *Kan ya ma kan*—maybe it was, maybe it wasn't. But the version he told me went like this:

In the glorious reign of the great Caliph Haroun al-Rashid, commander of the faithful, the people of Baghdad were starving to death. While the caliph was drinking wine with his courtiers, he left the caliphate to his viziers, a clever, brutal family called the Barmakids. They embezzled millions of dinars. They taxed the people without mercy. And they assured the caliph that all was well: The people loved him, Baghdad was the city of peace, the envy of creation, the navel of the world.

One day (so the story goes) the caliph decided to see for himself. He put on ordinary clothes and went walking around the great city to see what he could see. Passing by a humble house, he stuck his head over the wall and saw the woman cooking stones.

When the caliph heard her story, he realized that the Barmakids were lying to him—feeding him a story, a line: a *tabkhet bahas*, a supper of stones. And so he threw the Barmakids in jail and chopped off their heads. And everyone, as we know, lived happily and well fed from then on.

PART V

God, Nasrallah, and the Suburbs

In the so-called Age of Ignorance, before Islam, our ancestors used to form their gods from dates and eat them when in need. Who is more ignorant then, dear sir, I or those who ate their gods?

You might say: "It's better for people to eat their gods than for the gods to eat them."

But I'd respond: "Yes, but their gods were made of dates."

—Emile Habiby, *The Secret Life of Saeed, the Pessoptimist*

Chapter 25

There Are No Shiites
in This Neighborhood

T HE WAR WAS over. The rains came, and with them thunder, and
everyone who heard the first thunderstorm that fall woke up
with a shock and believed, for a moment, that the war had never
ended. In the south, the rains washed hidden cluster bomblets out of trees
and fields, a strange harvest, and brought the postwar cluster bomb fatali-
ties to twenty-six. In November, six Hezbollah-aligned ministers resigned
from the cabinet, paralyzing the government. All fall, Hassan Nasrallah
railed that Lebanese Prime Minister Fouad Siniora and what remained of his
government were American puppets. Nasrallah hinted that he was going to
follow the "Divine Victory" with something even more unforgettable.

Three and a half months after the war ended, on December 1, hundreds
of thousands of Hezbollah supporters and their allies marched into a swath
of downtown Beirut. They unloaded thousands of cloth-covered foam mattresses, just like the ones half a million refugees had slept on during the war,
and set up a tent city in their own version of the independence intifada.
Strips of barbed wire and blocks of concrete divided the demonstrators—
the have-nots, in the iconography of this new revolution—from the rest of
downtown, the haves. In parking lots where Land Rovers once ruled, farmers from Nabatieh planted green beans, tomatoes, zucchini, sunflowers, and
cucumbers. Men performed ablutions and prayed on the sidewalk outside

Buddha Bar. They chanted *"Allah, Nasrallah, wa al-dahiyeh killha"*—"God, Nasrallah, and all of *dahiyeh*," which American newspapers translated as "God, Nasrallah, and the suburbs." They demanded that Siniora resign, so that Hezbollah could form a new government in which the Party of God and its allies would hold more power. They thought that it would be a month or maybe two before the "Divine Victory" would be followed by an equally divine takeover, and they vowed to stay until this happened. Nobody knew, then, how long they would stay, or how much would happen before they would leave.

The first month was oddly festive. Throngs of veiled women and black-clad men mingled with Beirut girls wearing low-slung jeans and visible thongs in Hezbollah yellow. Men passed out orange scarves, the color of the Free Patriotic Movement, the mainly Maronite Christian party led by ex-army commander Michel Aoun. Boys wore curly clown wigs in bright orange and hoisted girls onto their shoulders to wave the Lebanese flag. A Hezbollah guy tried to score my e-mail address "for chatting." Boys gave away little green sponges to symbolize a "clean" government, and several people told me and Mohamad they wanted campaign finance disclosure laws. More than a few of the demonstrators—including people from Beirut or *dahiyeh*—told us that they had not been downtown since the civil war. "If I bought a sandwich here," said one man, pointing toward Maarad Street and Rym's beloved T.G.I. Friday's, "I'd be broke for a week."

At Christmas, Hezbollah and its allies served a feast worthy of the Abbasids: the Party of God distributed hundreds of roasted turkeys, stuffed with pistachios, raisins, and cinnamon-spiced rice, and General Aoun's movement served a forty-foot-long cake. The turkeys and cake were part of a long tradition of food as propaganda and power; of *simats* (from an old Arabic word for a meal or a cloth on which food was served), massive public banquets thrown by rulers, sultans, and caliphs to secure fealty. This food sent the same message as the groceries in the underground parking lots: *Allah Karim*. Your government may build pleasure palaces for Gulf millionaires while you scrape by on $200 a month. It may impose a regressive 10 percent value-added tax on everything except food and medicine. Its allies may send bombs to crush your houses and foul your fields and maim or kill your children. But God—and the Party thereof—will provide.

* * *

When the government failed to step down after almost two months, Hezbollah called a daylong "strike" on January 23, 2007. That morning, Mohamad and I woke up to the smell, now as familiar as an old friend, of burning metal. Najib Ardati Street curved emptily down to the Corniche. At the corner, the charcoal husk of a car smoldered forlornly, resting on its rims like a tired cow.

We went downstairs to visit our neighbor Rabih Dabbous. He was a tall, mustachioed rascal who ran a Yamaha dealership in the ground floor of our building. Militias were gathering a few blocks away, he told us: Hezbollah supporters against pro-government, with the army forming a line in between.

"If it continues," he said, heavily, "then tomorrow morning you will have civil war again. Tomorrow morning."

We walked up the street, then turned right and headed up the long block that led to the upper part of the Corniche. On the corner just outside the Abu Hassan restaurant, about a hundred men milled around. They were carrying baseball bats, lead pipes, bricks, and long planks of wood. They were all ages, but mostly young, in their teens and twenties. Some wore ski masks or bandannas over their mouths. Others wore hats or scarves in light blue, the color of the Future Movement, the Sunni political party of Saad Hariri and Prime Minister Siniora. A few had wrapped light blue ribbons around their foreheads, making them resemble some lost tribe of sectarian hippies.

We had done something stupid, but it was too late. They had seen us walking toward them, and turning around would make us look suspicious. There was nothing to do but approach them and try to forestall the inevitable question of Mohamad's last name.

"Hi!" I said, walking up to the nearest couple of young men. "Do you guys speak English? My name's Annia. I'm an *American* journalist, and this is my translator. Can I ask you a few questions?"

"Sure," said a beefy young man in a Real Madrid jersey wearing a light-blue watch cap. His name was Maher Amneh. He was thirty-two years old and had a shop in Hamra Street that sold "unisex casual sportswear." I had bought several T-shirts there. His cousin Bahi was an earnest nineteen-year-old student in a green sweatshirt and baseball cap. Bahi was majoring in management information systems, with a minor in finance, at the Lebanese American University. He hoped to graduate the following year.

They had woken up to see their neighborhood full of barricades and burning cars, and they felt that they were under attack. They had come out into the streets to fight back.

"Syria and Iran made this war in July, and we feel like we can't speak when we see the streets with barriers," said Bahi, breathlessly. "You can't have only Shiites who can have . . ."

"Can have weapons!" said Maher.

". . . and Sunnis don't have," said Bahi.

In 1989, when they signed the Taif Accord, all of Lebanon's militia leaders had agreed to give up their weapons. But Hezbollah was allowed to keep its arms as a "national resistance" against the Israeli occupation of southern Lebanon, which ended in 2000. For years, the regime in Damascus allowed Iranian arms to flow to Hezbollah through Syrian territory. After 2005, the Bush administration began pressuring Siniora's government to disarm Hezbollah. Nasrallah swore that the group would never use its weapons against other Lebanese, but many did not believe him.

"So because the Shiites have weapons," I asked Bahi, "and you don't—"

"Illegal weapons!" screamed a bystander, a middle-aged man with a face like an old shoe and wandering, dilated eyes. He was clutching a lead pipe. "Terrorists! Terrorists!"

"And they are occupying our areas," said Bahi, patiently, trying to resume. "We have to clean our area. Hezbollah belongs to suburbs and the south."

"Hassan Nasrallah is a liar!" shouted Maher. "A big liar!"

"They belong to the south and the suburbs," repeated Bahi. "They are occupying our area. So it is our duty to free it."

"How?" I asked.

"We'll go there and we'll ask peacefully to the army to free the Corniche," said Bahi. "And if they don't, we will attack them."

"Do you think that's a good idea?" I asked.

"We want to just live in peace," said Bahi. "We won't let them occupy our areas."

Our areas. "What area do you live in?" I asked.

"Here, in Beirut," said Bahi, shrugging.

Lebanon was segregated by sect, he explained. Slicing the air with his hands, he divided an imaginary city into halves, quarters: Christians in one quarter, Muslims in another, Sunnis and Shiites separated. Beirut, he said, belonged to Sunnis.

"Like here is for Sunnis, you know?" He waved his hand in a parabola around the neighborhood.

"Are you from this neighborhood?" I asked.

"Yes, yes, I live here," said Bahi.

"All the guys you see here," said the bystander, "they're from this neighborhood."

So: they were our neighbors. I did not mention this. Instead I asked them about their lives.

When the 2006 war broke out, Bahi had lost his summer job at a company that sponsored hair products. He had to skip the fall semester of college because he couldn't afford the tuition. Now he would graduate late. Iran had paid for the Shiites who lost their jobs, he told us. Who would pay for him?

"They're against everything, everything that will improve our lives," he said.

"For sure, there gonna be more fights, more injuries," said Maher, smiling amiably. "That's for sure."

Behind the two cousins, the rest of the Future *shabab* had spread out into the intersection. They were stopping cars and asking the people inside who they were and where they were going. And they were demanding to see their identification cards.

During the civil war, when a person's religion was written on his or her ID card, the card spelled the difference between life and death. The neighborhood militias stopped cars and demanded to see people's papers, just like they were doing now. If you had the wrong religion, the wrong last name, then you joined the roughly 170,000 people who were killed or disappeared during the fifteen years of the war.

"We don't want them come into our area," said Maher. "We are only searching for this. We don't want to fight them—we only want to protect our area."

"But isn't this a mixed area?" I asked him.

"No," he said, with calm certainty. "One hundred percent Sunni."

"There are no Shiites here?"

"No," he said again, patiently. "And everyone knows that."

We were standing just outside Abu Hassan—a Shiite-owned restaurant that sold *mjadara hamra* and *frakeh,* classic southern food, in the heart of what they considered a "Sunni" neighborhood. But I didn't point that out; it would have drawn attention to the fact that we ate there.

"We all know each other," explained Maher. "So if we see anyone strange, it means he doesn't belong to us."

"What would you do if you saw anyone strange?"

"We would ask him: 'What are you doing here, now, in this time?' " he said, and assumed a stern face, like a drama student stepping into the role, as he interrogated his imaginary captive. " 'So for what you are here?' Just like this. And if he didn't give us any answer, it means he comes from *them*, and he wants take a look—to count us."

In other words, he is a Shiite spy, sent to infiltrate the neighborhood and report back on their preparations.

I wondered if Mohamad had brought his Lebanese ID card or his American passport. Either way, they would know he was Shiite the instant they saw his last name. Would his American passport outweigh his religion, or would they think he was a spy? What would have happened if he had run into this checkpoint, a few blocks from our house, without me?

A black SUV drove up. One of its dark tinted windows rolled down. Inside, men with earpieces and walkie-talkies issued instructions to the guys in the street, one of whom came over and tapped Maher on the shoulder.

"We have to go," said Bahi. "We're going to open this road."

"Well," I said, smiling. I was shaking and my heart was pounding. But they couldn't see that. "Good luck!"

We walked away. They hadn't asked Mohamad's last name; hadn't discovered that there was at least one Shiite in this neighborhood.

"Oh my god," I said, as soon as we got a few dozen yards away.

Mohamad said nothing. He just looked back, over his shoulder, at our neighbors.

* * *

The street we were on led to the upper part of the Corniche. At the end of a very long block lined by apartment buildings, hotels, and restaurants, we passed into territory held by Hezbollah and Amal. Men in black lounged warily in red plastic chairs in front of the Kentucky Fried Chicken. Angry, silent men stood at intervals on the median and the sidewalk. A row of mini-vans, the kind political parties used to transport people to demonstrations, was parked along the Corniche. The carcass of another burnt car lay ashen in the middle of the street.

We walked up to a freckle-faced young man holding a long metal chain and asked him what was going on.

"We're just killing time," he said, sullen and a little fearful. He looked about sixteen or seventeen. "There's nothing happening." It was clear from his Arabic that he was from the south—he used suffixes like *-ish,* the syntax and accent we knew from Umm Hassane. We talked to a few more people; they seemed equally unsure of why they were there.

"Can we go home now?" said Mohamad.

But when we walked back across the street, we saw the situation had changed in the fifteen minutes we had stood talking. A large crowd of men in black had gathered on the corner. Some of them wore black ski masks. One held a pickaxe. Others brandished pipes. A few were collecting cinder blocks from a gutted building on the corner. Upstairs in the open-walled apartments, men perched here and there to watch the street below. The reconstruction from Beirut's last civil war supplied weapons and strategic locations for the next one.

Suddenly a rapid fusillade of shots boomed out. The echoes ricocheted off the sides of tall buildings and rattled down the street toward the sea.

"Jesus!" I shouted without thinking. (A few years earlier, it would have been "Jesus expletive Christ," but one of the lessons Mohamad drummed into me was the importance of not cursing in war zones.)

"That's the army," said Mohamad, infuriatingly calm, as he always was in situations like this. "They're shooting into the air."

Men with their heads wrapped in *kaffiehs* started running, some toward us and others away. A black-clad man with a walkie-talkie shouted at them to come back. More shots rocketed down the long narrow street.

Back the way we had come, a line of Lebanese soldiers ran across the width of the entire street. Just past them, on the other side of the line, were the Future guys we had talked to outside Abu Hassan. On our side, the black-clad Amal and Hezbollah guys surged forward. Men on both sides were shouting and throwing rocks, bricks, and cinder blocks at one another across the line of soldiers who stood in the middle holding their rifles up and ready to fire.

Suddenly more shots rang out, a barrage of them this time, much louder and much closer than before. People started running down the street, back toward the Corniche, and we ran with them, and I had the sudden feeling we would never get home again.

"We need to get away from here," I gasped.

We stood at the corner by the Corniche and watched as a shapeless melee of about a hundred men rolled our way. All of them had something in their hands: metal pipes, cinder blocks, chains, boards with nails sticking out. The chains chattered like rattlesnakes. One man swung a heavy metal chain tied into a knot at the end, a homemade Hail Mary. They were all shouting, running, kicking, hitting, throwing, melded together by some centripetal force. They gathered around a car, shouting. They beat it with pipes, lifting them high and slamming them down as though killing an animal. One of them hurt his hand and howled with rage as though the car had attacked him.

A couple of wiry, well-tanned young men with gangster fades stood at the corner next to us. They were wearing Puma tracksuits and around their necks little silver amulets of Zulfikar, the double-bitted sword of Imam Ali—a symbol of Shiites, also used by Amal as a gang sign. They surveyed the scene with feline smiles.

"This is not cool, man," I said.

"This is right down the street from our *house*," said Mohamad.

The shooting stopped. We walked back down the street, hoping to make our way home. The two sides had retreated to their respective ends of the very long block. The soldiers stood with stiff, nervous faces, their guns pointed up in the air. Broken glass, giant chunks of concrete, rocks, and pieces of wood and metal lay all around them. A couple of neighborhood kids ran out and started playing in the broken glass. They whooped with excitement.

Shouts echoed from down the street. The Future guys were coming back, marching from the direction of our apartment. They were chanting something, a slogan that grew louder as they approached: *"Airi bi Nasrallah wa al-dahiyeh killha!"*—"Fuck Nasrallah and all of *dahiyeh*!"

The new slogan summoned shouts of rage from the other side. They began approaching from the opposite direction, clanking chains and pipes, shouting their own slogan about the government's acting interior minister: "Ahmad Fatfat is a Jew!"

"Maybe we shouldn't go back this way," said Mohamad, beginning to sound distressed.

We turned and ran back toward the Corniche, again, away from our apartment. We would never get home. Men rushed past us, chanting, in the opposite direction.

"This is terrible!" I panted, as we scrambled down the street. "This is just like when you were a kid!"

"Yes!" he said, sadly. "It's like neighborhood gangs."

We stopped outside one of the small hotels on the block. A frightened-looking couple with three children were wheeling their suitcases into the lobby. They stood just inside the door, craning their necks to see down the street.

"They look terrified," said Mohamad. "As they should be."

"They picked the wrong time for a vacation in Beirut."

Later that night we realized they were probably internal refugees—Lebanese families fleeing neighborhoods where they had suddenly become the wrong sect. On Corniche al-Mazraa, where Leena lived, the clashes were even worse. The Future *shabab* there were holding up pictures of Saddam Hussein, who had been executed by Iraq's new Shiite-led government three weeks earlier.

By then we were safely home, back on Najib Ardati Street. But home was another country now, especially for Mohamad. The civil war had come and gone, a generation had grown up, and he was still just a few blocks away from the Green Line.

In 1987, after twelve years of civil war, a political scientist named Theodor Hanf conducted a study. The vast majority of the Lebanese people he surveyed wanted a democratic solution to the fighting—in other words, a negotiated peace. No victors, no vanquished.

But a stubborn 10 percent believed their militias could triumph over their opponents, expel them from the country, and rule forever after. Those 10 percent—and the blood they were willing to shed for their visions of total victory—were enough to keep the war in motion. Twenty years later, in January 2007, Lebanon stood at the edge of another civil war. Whether normal life would resume, or whether the country's long civil war would pick up where it left off, still depended on a stubborn fraction of the population.

The day after the strike, the roadblocks and burnt cars were gone. A street that was full of burning tires on Tuesday looked, on Wednesday, as if nothing had happened. Abu Hassan reopened. People drove to work, went shopping, came home, slept.

But on Thursday, January 25, at around midday, some silent but unmistakable message spread across the city. Fights flared simultaneously at several universities. Snipers at the Beirut Arab University in Tareeq al-Jadideh. Clashes at Hawai University in Hamra. Fighting near Lebanese International University in Zuqaq al-Blatt.

"The Future guys decided to clean up the neighborhoods," said Rabih, cocking his head. News updates whispered out of his Bluetooth headset. "It's going to get worse—now, you see, they'll start at AUB and LAU." These were the two big American universities that bounded Hamra.

Suddenly all the roads filled with trucks, cars, and motorcycles. Cars rammed into one another in panic. Drivers leaned out of their windows and screamed. People trapped inside lay frantically on their horns, all of them blaring at once like an insane brass band. Everyone was rushing to buy groceries, get home, and get off the streets. The air smelled like smoke. It was time to go war shopping again: time to stock up on bread, on canned soup, on pasta and lentils and rice. Time to go to our local *furn* for *manaeesh*.

Our neighborhood baker was Abu Shadi, a tree trunk of a man with a shoulder-length mane of wavy brown hair that he periodically streaked with blondish highlights. Abu Shadi had been feeding Manara *manaeesh* since 1988, and his dough was chewy, crisp, oily perfection. He was working double time, stretching the elastic rounds of bread with his enormous hands, buttering them with olive oil and *zaatar*, laying them out on long wooden paddles, and shoveling them into the roaring hot oven all at once.

Men stood in front of the *furn* and waited for *manaeesh*. Usually they would be milling around on the sidewalk, joking and talking politics and gossiping with their mouths full of bread. But this day they just listened to the radio and looked at each other uneasily. The butcher next door pulled the metal grate down over his window with a thunderous rattle. Stores up and down the block were closing their shutters and locking their doors. A couple of teenagers, about fourteen or fifteen, climbed onto a moped. One of them had a baseball bat tucked under his leather jacket.

A stooped old man in a cardigan, walking slowly up the hill, stopped and frowned at them.

"What are you doing with that stick?" he scolded.

"We don't have any sticks," the older one lied, with sullen deference.

"I see it, under your jacket!"

The younger one smiled. "We're herding sheep," he said.

The old man shrugged hopelessly and plodded on up the hill. The younger generation, who had missed the civil war, roared off to join the fun.

That night, the army imposed a curfew for the first time since 1996. Four people had been killed, and more than one hundred fifty injured. There were checkpoints like the one in our neighborhood in other parts of the city, and snipers at the university just down the street from Hanan's apartment. Snipers, checkpoints, curfews: it seemed like the seventeen years since the war had simply evaporated.

By Saturday, the city was back to the angry, paranoid stasis that passed for normal in those days. People drove to work. Restaurants and stores stayed open, but they had very few customers. People went home and stayed by the television, waiting to see what would happen.

Everyone except our friend Rym, who came over from Gemmayzeh with a car and an idea. All of Beirut was hunkering down, afraid to go outside. But downtown belonged to us, she said, just as much as it did to any of the sectarian factions fighting over Beirut's streets. She wanted to go downtown, to the one area everyone was avoiding above all others, and have lunch.

We agreed. Why not?

"What about Umm Hassane?" said Rym, as we got ready to leave. "Why don't we bring her too?"

"Umm Hassane, do you want to go out with us?"

"I just started drinking tea! Are you going to wait for me until I finish my tea?"

"We'll wait for you."

"You should have told me before I started drinking . . ."

"We'll wait for you!"

"Where are you going?"

"We're going downtown. We're going to eat."

"What do I want with food? I already ate!"

"You should come with us. You can walk around."

Walking around? "I haven't been out in a while," she said thoughtfully.

At this point, Umm Hassane did something she had probably never done before in her life: she abandoned her tea. She changed into her best black cloak, the one Mohamad called her "super *hajji*" robe, and called Hanan to brag that she was going downtown.

"Look at her, she's beaming," said Rym, as we piled into her car. Umm Hassane peered out the window of the front passenger seat. Mohamad and I rolled down the back windows and stuck our heads out like dogs. Rym was driving and laughing at the same time.

We parked by Martyrs' Square and started walking. Umm Hassane limped fiercely toward the city center, clutching Mohamad's arm. *"Shu biddi bil balad?"*—"What do I want with downtown?" she demanded loudly, with a shrug that fooled no one.

At the restaurant, we debated whether to sit inside or outside. Outside was more pleasant, but would Umm Hassane be cold? She shrugged: *"Mitil ma bidkun,"* "as you wish." Did she want to sit outside? She shrugged. *"Mitil ma bidkun."*

We sat outside, the better to enjoy the sights: the cobblestoned streets, the stray cats. There was a little old man with Tourette syndrome, a fixture of downtown Beirut. He walked around selling glossy posters of the old city center and barking at tourists. He seemed to be the only other person downtown that day. When he saw us sitting outside, he yelped with joy and ran over. We already had some of his posters, but we bought another one, a sea-blue photograph of prewar Martyrs' Square lined with palm trees and art deco movie palaces.

Umm Hassane outdid herself that day. The waitress brought menus: "Don't get me anything," she insisted. "I don't want anything; I already ate!"

The waitress brought plates and laid down table settings.

"Why is she getting me a plate? Didn't you tell her I'm not eating?"

"Keep the plate, just in case."

"I already ate!"

"Do you want tea?"

"I already drank tea!"

We ordered it anyway. She drank it instantly, although it was scalding, and complained it was too cold. Did she want more? *"Shu biddi fi?"*

We gave her some cold *meze*—hummus, stuffed grape leaves, tabbouleh. She devoured them while protesting that she wasn't hungry.

Her eyes lit up when the *batata wa bayd* arrived.

"You're eating *batata wa bayd?*" she said, drawing her head back, narrowing her eyes, and staring at it sideways.

"Yours is better, of course," I said, shoveling a big chunk of oily fried potatoes and eggs onto her plate.

She ate it.

"Taybeen, ma ishbun shi," she sniffed—"there's nothing wrong with them."

Having praised the food, she surveyed the plates littering the table and sighed.

"Why didn't we stay home?" she said with a shrug. "I would have made you *batata wa bayd!*"

Rym turned to me. "Is she always like this?" she asked in English.

Mohamad and I both laughed.

"This is nothing," I said.

"Usually," said Mohamad with pride, "she's worse."

* * *

The waitress stood over us, her hands clasped apologetically: They were shutting down early, because there were no other customers but us. Did we want anything more before the kitchen closed?

Reluctantly, we decided to go home. Then Rym had another idea.

"Umm Hassane, do you want to go see the tent city?"

Mitil ma bidkun—as you wish.

But then she added, "If you're going"—in her language the closest thing to yes.

We walked through Sahat al-Nijmeh, and Rym bought a cloud of pink cotton candy bigger than her head. The old man barked happily to see us, his only customers, again.

"Downtown is deserted," Rym kept saying. "It's *dead*!"

When we reached the blue metal barricades, we stopped, suddenly hesitant to venture across to the other side.

"Well, we're here already, let's go," said Umm Hassane, shrugging, as though we'd been dragged there against our will. She walked through the barrier, and we followed.

On the other side of the barricade, men huddled in canvas tents. Others swept up garbage. The strike had killed off the festive mood, and all that remained were hardcore Hezbollah loyalists who stared at us and then looked away. A water tank was plastered with angry slogans and cartoons of the prime minister embracing Condoleezza Rice.

Mohamad held his mother's arm as she hobbled down the street. She nodded with approval when she saw the men sweeping up garbage. "Where do they have the big gatherings?" she asked, looking from side to side.

On television she had seen tens, hundreds of thousands of people, all waving and cheering. We showed her the big pink building where people had once assembled, but there were no more happy crowds now. No more children and families dancing *dabkeh*. Just angry men sitting in tents.

I'm not sure exactly what we expected—some pride, perhaps, in the spectacle of Shiites taking over downtown. But after a minute she stopped, looked around, and frowned.

"Look at them!" she declared, at the volume of an old woman hard of hearing. "They're just sitting around!"

Hezbollah men turned and glared at us with clenched faces.

"They're not working!" she scolded, sweeping her free arm to encompass the entire city of tents.

"Your mom's going to start a civil war!" I hissed. Mohamad tried to shush her, but this only made her louder.

"They're sitting with neither work nor trade!" she crowed, using a southern expression for lazy, idle slackers. "They're getting paid to just sit around!"

Hezbollah is known for many things, but grace under criticism is not one of them. I imagined what we must look like to the Hezbollah men crouched resentfully in their tents: two unveiled women, one of them eating pink cotton candy and wearing a cherry-red jacket; one cranky old *hajji*, barely able to walk, supported by her son, who seemed to have brought her to the tent city expressly so she could parade through and tell them they were bums.

Perhaps Umm Hassane's Bint Jbeil accent and black *hijab* saved her. Perhaps it was her super *hajji* robe. More likely, they had orders not to interfere with visitors. In any case, the *shabab* contented themselves with dirty looks, and we hustled her home as quickly as we could.

The minute we walked in the door, she descended on the phone and started calling relatives. She was eager to lord it over them: she had been downtown, she had seen the tents. We retreated to the balcony to wallow in relief.

"I guess her sectarian loyalties only go so far," I said.

Mohamad laughed. "As you know, she has no compunction telling people how she feels about them," he said. "She doesn't hold back."

He looked sideways at me.

"I guess that's why I married *you*," he added. "Maybe you're not so different from her."

A week later, the military fortified the barricades that divided each side from the other. Soldiers dragged in thick gray concrete walls, wreathed in festive snarls of concertina wire. Everyone thought of the old Green Line that had once split downtown in two. The barriers were necessary to keep people from crossing over and fighting, they said, and possibly starting a civil war.

"But you know the real reason they put those barriers up, right?" I told Mohamad. "They put them up to keep your mother out of downtown."

Chapter 26

My Previous Experience in Warfare

I WAS SITTING AT my desk, next to the window, when the blast rolled up the street and smacked against the glass. The windowpane sucked in, then out, and came just short of breaking. I could hear the tinkle of glass shattering in the building next door.

By this point, June 2007, it was almost routine: A car bomb just down the block, at the Sporting swim club. Walid Eido was the fifth member of parliament to be assassinated in the past two years. We called Leena and our landlord Ralph, both of whom went to Sporting regularly, and our friends called us with an extra edge of alarm this time because it had been so close.

I called Georges back later that night. He was scheduled to leave the next day, for a four-year medical residency in Cleveland, and this valedictory car bomb did not make his departure any easier. "Annia, I can't stand this," he said. "You don't know how much it hurts to see such a thing as you are leaving. It makes it so much harder to leave."

But I did have at least some idea of how he felt. We were leaving too, and I was not happy about it. In the summer of 2007, Mohamad got two job offers: a one-year fellowship as a Middle East analyst and a position teaching journalism in New York. He accepted both. He was ready to leave Lebanon. But I was not. I was furious.

He had two jobs to go back to; I had none. I had given up a good job to go with him to Baghdad, and now, after four years of freelancing, I was finally beginning to get magazine assignments. It was more than just the jobs, though: we had friends in Beirut, people we cared about, and it didn't feel right to leave that behind. He had dragged me from one war zone to another, made me care about these infuriating people, and now, just when we were beginning to feel at home, he wanted to go back to New York and forget about the Middle East. But New York wasn't home anymore. Beirut was.

That August, we packed up our Beirut apartment and loaded all our possessions into a shipping container. We found a new home for Shaitan, because Mohamad didn't want to take her to New York, and said good-bye to all our friends. We had already said good-bye to Umm Hassane, which was hardest of all, and packed her off to stay with Hassan in France.

In New York, we unpacked a few boxes and arranged the most essential items in our new apartment. We piled the rest of the boxes in an eight-foot tower in a corner (where they would remain, unpacked, for the next two years). And then, in late fall, I came back to Beirut.

Four years earlier, when I married Mohamad and joined him in Baghdad, some well-meaning friends took my mother aside. They invoked the kitschy specter of *Not Without My Daughter*, the movie where innocent, all-American Sally Field marries an Iranian doctor. The doctor seems nice enough at first, but once they move to Iran he succumbs to some atavistic Islamic urge and makes her into a virtual prisoner and slave. This Mohamad might seem normal, the friends warned my mother. He might seem like any other American. But once he gets her over there, among his own people, the veneer of Americanness may wear off—he might, as they put it, start to "change."

My mother thought it was hilarious. She told Mohamad and me, and we all had a good laugh at the image of him reverting to some swarthy stereotype from the pages of an airport paperback. Nobody considered the possibility that the one who would change might be me.

Back in Beirut, Hezbollah was still occupying half of downtown, the government was still paralyzed, and when the president's term expired, in late November, the country's increasingly polarized factions could not agree on a replacement. By Christmas, when Mohamad came for a visit, the country had been without a head of state for a month. At this point, that seemed like a long time; later it would not. Food prices were spiraling upward, and small riots were breaking out over bread and gasoline and other staples.

Then, on February 12, 2008, the Hezbollah operative Imad Mughnieh was assassinated in Damascus. Mughnieh was one of three Hezbollah members on the Federal Bureau of Investigation's list of "Twenty-two Most Wanted Terrorists." American officials suspected Mughnieh of masterminding the 1983 bombing of the U.S. Marine barracks in Beirut, among other attacks. Everyone expected trouble.

Umm Hassane was still in France with Hassan and Annemarie. Everyone wanted her to stay and wait out the inevitable "events." Being Umm Hassane, she insisted on coming back to Beirut. I was bouncing from apartment to apartment, staying with one friend or another while looking for a furnished room that I could rent for an indeterminate period of time. Small clashes were beginning to break out, as they always did when the political parties were deadlocked. It was a way of heightening the pressure.

There was an atmosphere of fear and suspicion mixed with exhaustion. Everybody seemed permanently tired and pissed off. A taxi driver told me I was welcome in Beirut, but not my husband, because Shiites only wanted to destroy the city.

I met an old lady in Walimah. She asked me what I was doing in Lebanon. (There were plenty of Americans in Beirut, but people always seemed to be asking me that; "It's because we're all miserable here and want to leave," a Lebanese friend explained.) She seemed so sweet, so harmless, that I made the mistake of telling her my husband was Lebanese.

"*Oooh,*" she said and raised her eyebrows. She cocked her head and cooed: "And what is the family name?"

"He's Shiite," I snapped. "Since you asked."

"Oh no, I'm not . . . I didn't mean . . ." she said, trailing off and looking guiltily at the floor.

"Yes you did," I said. I felt bad, but I told myself she deserved it.

A few days later, a small but significant earthquake shook southern Lebanon. "This is all the people in Lebanon need," said Mohamad, when he called to see if I was okay. "You should come home."

But home, for me, was not New York. In the back of my mind, despite or perhaps because of everything that was happening, I was still hoping I could convince Mohamad to come back—if not now, then sometime.

A stable home in a peaceful place made me nervous. Experience had taught me that these homes could be kicked over in minutes. But if I could learn to carve out a temporary home wherever I was, even in the midst of instability, I would be safe no matter what. Home was a moveable feast; you strapped it to your back, stuffed it in a jar, dried it in the sun, dug it from the ground. Home was wherever you broke bread with people you loved. You built it out of hotel rooms or the trunk of your car or couches in your friends' living rooms. You coaxed it into existence it by reading books and cooking food and learning languages, by sharing meals and words with others. You carried it with you, folded up like a picnic blanket, and spread it out wherever you happened to be.

Mohamad called me the morning after some particularly violent street fighting. "You have to come home," he said. It was three a.m. in New York.

"What about your mom?"

"She'll be fine. She doesn't need you to take care of her this time."

I had been asking something much larger and more diffuse: Why was it so important for us to take care of her during the war but not now? Why had she stayed in Beirut and we did not? But I didn't clarify any of that.

"We're living in limbo," he said. "We can't settle down as long as you're there."

"We spent the whole time here living in limbo. Maybe I got used to it."

He sighed. "You have to come back. It's getting dangerous."

"I can't," I said. "I have to be here. It's what I'm writing about. How can I write about it if I'm not even here?"

"You know, Annia, you're dangerously close to sounding like a war junkie."

"Yeah? Like when you were in Nablus or Jalalabad? Or Baghdad right after the invasion?"

"This is more dangerous."

"Oh really? More dangerous than when you were in Islamabad, flirting with the fucking guys who killed Daniel Pearl?"

"This is worse, Annia."

"These were just clashes. They have clashes here all the time."

"This is how the civil war started. With little incidents."

I didn't say anything. It was very cold in my friend's apartment, and I had a hangover so crushing I could barely see.

"Why do you like it there so much?" he asked.

I was silent for a while. He had brought me to Beirut and then decided he hated it. I liked it for many reasons, one of which was him. It didn't make sense.

"Do you remember when we first started going out?" I said. "You used to laugh at Americans all the time. How people would get so worked up over their little emotional traumas—their parents were mean to them, they didn't get enough toys growing up, they cheated on their wife or their husband, and now they feel bad."

I used to call this his Third World Tough Guy act. But he hadn't done it for years.

"Well, maybe I feel like that now whenever I'm back in New York. Maybe I don't want to sit around in Williamsburg with our friends and trade ironic banter about the latest reality TV show. Maybe I don't want to be one of those people who think their narcissistic little problems are the only bad things going on in the world."

He was silent.

"Annia, the story's going to have to end some time or other," he said finally. "At some point you're going to have to put down your pen and accept that the war may still be going on—will almost certainly still be going on—but your story ends here."

Four days later, after three months of searching, I moved into an apartment. It was a block away from Smith's supermarket, after the end of Makdisi, the street that ran parallel to Hamra. It was bigger than I needed, but I was tired of looking, and there was no lease, so I could leave whenever I wanted. The apartment was across the street from the St. Rita Maronite Catholic Church, where Umm Paula worshipped. It had a long balcony where I could sit and watch the neighborhood dramas: pigeons mating, people filing in and out of the church, the neighborhood *shabab* hanging out in front of the bakery. The bakery served as a social club for the local Future political machine, and the *shabab* spent a lot of time washing their boss's SUV and then grooming it with a giant feather duster. Occasionally they would get into fights with one another or with *shabab* on a neighboring block, and at night they would drag chairs out of the bakery and sit in the middle of the sidewalk smoking water pipes.

A few weeks later, an old man in T-Marbouta, the Hamra café, asked me what I was doing in Beirut. He was wrinkled, gray, with a helmet of smoke-stained hair—one of the antediluvian leftists who held court drinking and chain-smoking all day in Hamra's cafés.

He watched me, frowning, as I struggled to explain why I was here in Beirut when Mohamad was in New York. It had to do with my writing, the situation, our lives. I had gone to Baghdad four years ago to be with the husband I loved. Now he was in New York—a city with parks, and sidewalks, and laws against landlords asking about your religion. And I was in a verminous, overpriced apartment that periodically had no running water, surrounded by sectarian tensions, on a vague mission that I only half believed in myself. I had my reasons, but I wasn't very good at explaining them.

When I finally petered out, the old man held up his index finger like an alcoholic oracle. With the painstaking dignity of an all-day drunk, he said:

"Don't be complicated."

I knew the old man used to be in a militia. I knew which one too, but it didn't really matter: The militias that swore to annihilate each other one day would be allies the next. It was all about strategic alliances, marriages of convenience, and the only constant was that they did whatever they had to in order to win. People would fabricate intricate lies, denying they had ever fought each other, or they would come up with complex justifications for killing people who had been their allies just months or weeks earlier. They were still doing it: General Michel Aoun had opposed Syrian rule until 2005; by 2008, he was aligned with the Syrian-backed Hezbollah. In 2004, the Druze warlord Walid Jumblatt was praising suicide bombers for killing Israeli civilians; a year later, the Bush administration and conservative pundits were touting him as a hero of the "cedar revolution." You might believe their bullshit the first couple of times you heard it, and try to follow some logic in the shifting alliances, but after a while the elaborate mental contortions of the party ideologues just made you laugh.

You couldn't live in Beirut without being complicated. But people were always telling me not to be.

"Simplicity is a virtue," a Lebanese restaurateur told me once, watching in horror as I piled one ingredient after another—*zaatar*, cheese, green onions, red pepper, sesame seeds—onto my *manoushi*.

"Yes," I said, "but it's not one of mine."

Mohamad came to visit again in April. He grumbled mightily that I was dragging him back to Lebanon, but he did get a lot of work done, and I began to believe that perhaps he was beginning to like Beirut.

One night, we went to a play called *How Nancy Wished That Everything Was an April Fool's Joke*. (Most of the plays about the civil war had complicated titles.) Onstage, four ex-fighters, three men and a woman, sat mashed against each other on a tiny couch like passengers in a crowded *servees*. They each narrated their own transformations during the civil war: They may have started off ambivalent, but then something would happen, and they would get angry—"My blood boiled over," they repeated periodically—and they would join the fight and eventually die. The secular leftist ends up joining the right-wing Christian Phalange party and dies. The Communist eventually joins Hezbollah and dies. The Sunni nationalist gets religion and joins the jihad in Afghanistan and Chechnya. (He dies a lot.) Gradually you realize that the same four people keep dying and coming back to life, only to rejoin the fighting (often with a different faction), die again, and do it all over again. Every time they came back, they would say, "From my previous experience in warfare, I knew . . ." And yet they kept on fighting.

Not long afterward, we were walking through Wadi Abu Jamil when we noticed workmen unloading hundreds of gleaming white toilets into one of the few remaining vacant lots. By early evening there were six hundred of them, all standing at attention in neatly ordered rows. A poster demanded, HAVEN'T FIFTEEN YEARS OF HIDING IN THE TOILETS BEEN ENOUGH?

The army of toilets was an installation by the Lebanese artist Nada Sehnaoui. During the civil war, people took refuge in hallways, basements, and especially bathrooms—any small, enclosed space that offered shelter from incoming fire. As a child, Mohamad had spent many sleepless nights huddled in the hallway with his parents, listening to artillery and machine-gun fire. When the fighting was particularly heavy, they would drag mattresses into the hallway and prop them against the walls.

People were tired. The rhetoric had been rising for months, but neither side had dared to do more than talk. Most Lebanese were sick of fighting. Nobody but politicians had the appetite for blood.

But then, in the early hours of Wednesday, May 7, the government issued an order outlawing Hezbollah's underground fiber-optic communications network. Since this network was part of its military infrastructure, Hezbollah accused the government of trying to disarm it on behalf of the United States and Israel. Nasrallah announced he would give a speech on Thursday at four p.m. That morning, just before noon, Mohamad went out for *foul*.

Abu Hadi, our Hamra *fawal*, was engulfed. Dozens of customers surrounded his little storefront, all of them shoving and shouting out their orders. Mohamad recognized the customer in front of him: it was one of the actors from the play, the one who had joined the jihad in Chechnya. He ordered hummus with meat, hummus *bi tahinah*, *fattet* hummus, and *msabbaha*, and by the time he was done, there was nothing left but *foul*. It took Mohamad an hour just to get two bowls of *foul*. By then he realized we should probably stock up.

We were old hands at this by now: We split up and coordinated by cell phone. I went to Healthy Basket, which was lush with the bounty of May: strawberries, tomatoes, lettuce, cilantro, zucchini. Mohamad called me from Smith's: no meat, no bottled water. No *laban* and *labneh*. Milk was running low. Bread was long gone.

The next day, the newspaper *Al-Akhbar* ran a full front-page photograph of people frantically shoving their way into a local *furn*, taken from the baker's point of view: Hands reached in from every direction, all holding crumpled little wads of bills, enough for a packet of bread. A woman's face contorted in panic as the people behind her smashed her up against the window. In the window above people's heads, almost unnoticed, a hand reached down, dangling its clump of bills: an agile shopper who decided to beat the crowd by climbing on top of the bakery stall.

At four p.m., Mohamad went to watch the speech with a friend who lived on the other side of Hamra. I was on the phone with a friend in New York, a few hours later, when I heard the crackle of gunfire. I figured it was the usual post-political-speech happy fire. Nothing unusual.

"God damn it, don't these people get tired of fireworks?" I said, so my New York friend wouldn't be alarmed.

I went to the kitchen. The back balcony faced Sadat, the street that marked the boundary of Hamra proper. This was the direction from which Mohamad would be walking. I looked out the window to see if I could locate the gunfire—not that you can "see" bullets, but visual information was always comforting.

Just then, at around seven o'clock, I heard a loud *whump*, the punch of air suddenly filling a vacuum. It was a sound I remembered from Baghdad—a rocket-propelled grenade. Men walking down Sadat Street started to run. I got off the phone. Where was Mohamad?

It was probably only ten more minutes until Mohamad got home, but it felt like hours. Hamra Street was abandoned, he said. As he ran home, he saw gunmen setting up barricades and firing RPGs. We didn't realize it until later, but he had come back just in time.

We went out on the balcony to see what was happening. At the bakery, our neighborhood *shabab* were excited. One of them disappeared into the upper floors above the bakery and reemerged wearing a black balaclava and holding a rifle. He swaggered around pretending to shoot. He held his rifle from the hip, pointing up, like a Liberian child soldier. Nobody had shown him how to hold it properly.

A couple of boys walked down the street, past the church, to the corner. One of them dragged a Dumpster into the street and then fished a couple of narrow French doors out of a pile of construction debris. He propped each French door at a delicate 45-degree angle against the side of the Dumpster.

Then he went to the Mozart Hotel across the street and commandeered several plastic planters with feathery, palmlike plants.

Mohamad and I watched in amazement. In 2006, Hezbollah had fought the Israeli military, one of the most technologically advanced armies in the world. The Party of God had Iranian-made weapons, matériel capable of disabling a Merkava tank. These guys were making barricades from French doors and potted plants.

At around eight o'clock, the streetlights blinked off all at once. The only people on the streets were teenagers on mopeds. We heard machine gun and rocket fire coming from Hamra, getting closer.

I made dinner with the pasta and vegetables we'd bought that day, peas and garlic and cherry tomatoes and basil and parsley. I was very proud of myself for thinking ahead: we might get shot, but at least we'd eat well. We went to sleep at about one in the morning to the sound of gunfire and RPGs and stun grenades. There was nothing else to do.

All night long, two tomcats staged a wailing standoff in the vacant lot under our bedroom window. There was a terrible thunderstorm that night, and the fighting seemed to stop for about three hours, but the tomcats kept going; when I woke up the next morning, at seven a.m., they were still at it. I could hear grenades too. I went back to sleep.

When I woke again, at eight, the air smelled fresh and strange, scoured clean by smoke, like the Fourth of July. I went out onto the balcony. The street was empty, all sign of Dumpsters or French doors swept away. The shooting was very heavy and very close, and I recognized the firecracker smell as cordite. I could hear shouting: *"Allahu Akbar!"*—"God is great." It was as though I had woken up in a different city.

I was still half-asleep, but some primitive sense of self-preservation told me to get off the balcony. I went back into the bedroom and shook Mohamad. "Sweetie, I think you better get up."

There was a long, narrow horizontal window high in the wall over our bed that looked out at the Mozart. We stood on the bed and looked out the window.

Across the street, there was a small leafy garden where kids usually played ball. Three Hezbollah commandos in gray-green fatigues crouched in it now, cradling Kalashnikovs in the caves of their shoulders and steadying the barrels on their knees.

More fighters were advancing slowly down the block through the gunfire. They would walk a few steps, stop, and then wait for a hand signal from the commandos in the garden, who were covering them. They held their rifles at their shoulders and swung them in tightly choreographed arcs, facing opposite directions, as they went slowly down the street in a sinister ballet. They had been very carefully trained.

"Don't go outside!" they shouted as they advanced. "Stay inside! Don't go out on your balconies!" Periodically they also shouted, *"Allahu Akbar!"*

A teenage boy with a mop of shoulder-length curly hair ran up the sidewalk toward the garden. He had taken off his shirt and shoes to show that he wasn't armed. He held his hands in the air and ran through gunfire. The commandos in the garden reached out and beckoned, shouting for him to hurry. He ducked into the thicket behind them.

One of the garden commandos swung his AK-47 around toward our building. Stupidly, I noted that it was pointing right at us.

The feeling started in the back of my neck—a great mouth picking me up with powerful teeth by the back of the neck and shaking me like a kitten. My neck told my brain to pay attention to what my eyes were observing. Very slowly, my brain took the isolated pictures my eyes had sent it and assembled them into logical sequences:

The boy surrendering; the hand signals: there were snipers in the buildings.

The commando saw the curtain flutter; he thought we were snipers: that is why his rifle was pointing this way.

"Get away from the window!" snapped Mohamad.

We dove down to the bed, then scrambled off it, away from the windows, running half-crouched back into the hallway.

The phone rang. It was our friend Ben, a radio reporter who lived further down the hill, past the garden where the gunmen had been. His back window had been shot out. He suspected there were snipers on his roof. Earlier that morning, he had looked out his window and seen a body lying on the sidewalk.

I went to the balcony and looked down the block. I couldn't see any snipers, but snipers don't want to be seen. The water tank on top of the Mozart was gushing out water. It must have been shot.

"You should come over," I said. "I think it's safer on our block." Safer was a relative term—our next-door neighbor Balsam had snipers on her roof too. But our block seemed more secure. I started filling empty bottles with tap water in case our water tank got shot out.

We looked out a little later. The gunmen were calmer, surveying the block. Then, at about nine or ten a.m., there was another blister of gunfire. We moved to the hallway and set up our computers there. The apartment had an extra sink in the hallway that led to the bedrooms. This was a common feature in older West Beirut apartments, where visitors might need to wash their hands without entering the family quarters, but it was also convenient for a situation like this, when it was dangerous to venture to the kitchen or the bathroom; I wondered, illogically, if this was the real reason for putting a sink in the hallway. We could hear intense gunfire coming from Sadat Street, just half a block away, and also from the opposite direction where Ben's apartment was.

Our friend Deb, a reporter for National Public Radio, called a little later. She was staying at a small hotel on Sadat Street called Viccini Suites. The fighting was heavy on Sadat, which led toward Hariri's palace, and everyone in the hotel had spent the night in the basement.

I looked out the window and saw two gunmen standing just outside the doorway of the Viccini. "We'll come get you," I told her. "It's safer here at our place."

It was Friday, the day observant Muslims go to the mosque for midday prayers. At noon, the muezzin started muttering the *duaa*, the invocation that signalled the beginning of Friday prayers, and the neighborhood let out a collective exhalation. Men headed down the street to the mosque. Women went to the bakery. They left empty-handed, I noticed, and I concluded that the bakers must have run out of bread.

Our street was calm, but there was still gunfire crackling up and down Sadat, and still the same two gunmen stationed outside the Viccini. I called

Deb again. She said the gunmen had come downstairs and confiscated everyone's cell phones, checked their ID cards, then gave them their cell phones back and left. "I'm coming to get you," I said.

The street seemed calm when I walked up to Sadat. I passed my landlord's brother on his way to the mosque. "Hello, Hajj Salim," I said, and nodded. But he just stared at me heavily and walked on.

I collected Deb and we walked back without incident. The gunmen had returned a second time, she told me, to apologize for taking their cell phones. "Somebody trained those guys real well," she said, shaking her head.

Ben came over, and I threw myself into feeding everybody. I made a massive tuna salad with pasta shells, shaved fennel, feta, sliced grape tomatoes, and pitted black olives. I dressed it with capers, lemon juice, olive oil, and mustard. Chopped basil and parsley. Lots of black pepper. I was being complicated again, but there was nothing else to do, and this was something useful. Food had always been a comfort, a way of reinforcing normal life. But when a normal life was impossible, through nobody's fault but my own—I could be living peacefully in New York, but I had insisted on being in Beirut—food allowed me to pretend.

I realized that I hadn't made anything for Mohamad, who refused to eat tuna. I started boiling the rest of the pasta for him. At about 2:45 p.m., just as I was about to drain it, fierce gunfire broke out so loud and so close that all four of us ran and huddled in the hallway by the sink.

Deb crouched on the floor over her cell phone, describing the battle to someone at National Public Radio. Mohamad hunched against the wall, with his computer propped on his knees, filing a story. I sat on the sink. Ben slid down to the floor. He motioned for me to get down lower, but I shook my head.

The gunfire went on and on, and I found myself wondering where all these bullets came from—hundreds every minute, like raindrops on a roof.

Suddenly I remembered Mohamad's pasta. It had been boiling for a good fifteen minutes! It would get soggy. You couldn't waste food in a situation like this.

I scuttled into the kitchen at a half-crouch, keeping my head below window level. The kitchen was a dangerous place—the big window and the glass door faced Sadat Street, where most of the gunfire was coming from.

But the certainty of soggy pasta seemed to me, at that moment, much more dire than the possibility of getting hit by a stray bullet.

"What are you *doing*?" shouted Mohamad from the hallway.

"Too late!" I shouted. I turned off the burner, dumped the pasta into the colander waiting in the sink, and rushed back into the hallway.

Deb and Ben and Mohamad looked up at me, appalled; I didn't understand why. Didn't they know that as long as I was cooking, I would be safe?

After another five minutes, the gunfire stopped, and it didn't occur to me until much later that I had been acting at all irrational.

In Hamra, the fighting was over by Friday afternoon. Later that day, we walked around the neighborhood. The streets were littered with broken glass and empty shells. At Future TV, militiamen had burned the offices and destroyed the archives, throwing the videotapes onto a smoking pyre on the sidewalk, and put up posters of Syrian President Bashar al-Assad in the offices. On Sidani, a few blocks from our house, all the food shops were open, even the Subway sandwich franchise. The gunmen stood everywhere, watching us with cool, unfriendly faces and saying nothing. On Gandhi Street, a few prostitutes walked past, dressed in pajamas, talking softly in Moroccan-accented Arabic and ignoring the gunmen completely.

Outside Abu Hassan restaurant, someone had planted a flag of the Syrian Social Nationalist Party: a swirling red swastika, rounded like the blade of a circular saw, in a white circle on a black background. Looking down Hamra, in the golden sunlight of early evening, we saw red and black flags all up and down the street. The flags stayed up throughout the crisis, which would last for about two weeks and kill at least seventy-one people.

For the next week, the streets would be ruled by gunmen, prostitutes, and the Sri Lankan, Ethiopian, and Filipina maids that Beirut housewives sent out grocery shopping when they were afraid to go themselves. The occasional civilians would scurry from one house to another and look at strangers with distrustful eyes.

The day after the fighting, the only businesses open were those that sold essentials like food or news. Knots of five or six men huddled around newspaper vendors. At Malik al-Batata (King of Potatoes), famous for *shawarma* and French fries, a small group of men had gathered to read a death notice pasted on the wall. It was for one of our neighborhood *shabab*, the teenage boys who had tried to fight off Hezbollah. He had been shot in the battle. Suddenly I remembered saying hello to Hajj Salim, yesterday outside the mosque, and the terrible look he had given me in return. There would be trouble in the neighborhood for sure.

At one p.m., we got a knock on our door. It was our friends Sean and Nizar, who lived in East Beirut. They had not been able to drive or take a taxi to Hamra; the gunmen had blocked off the neighborhood with barriers and checkpoints. But they had walked all the way from their apartment at the end of Gemmayzeh, about an hour by foot, to visit us.

"How stupid is this?" said Nizar. He strode inside and started to pace up and down. "How fucking stupid are they? This whole thing was a trap to lure Hezbollah into using their weapons against the Lebanese. And what do they do? They fall into it. How stupid are they, how fucking stupid . . . *Kis ikhta, hal balad!*"—Fuck this country!—"I'm done with it. I'm leaving this country. I'm done."

Outside our apartment, a crowd of mourners had gathered at the bakery. Some were shouting hoarsely. As we watched from our balcony, a couple of SSNP gunmen walked down Adonis Street from the direction of Smith's. They ordered the mourners to go back to their homes. People began to shout at the gunmen: "How can you do this?"

The militiamen fired into the air. The mourners dispersed, and the street was clear. Sean and Nizar decided to go back home before anything else happened.

"You know, maybe you guys should come stay with us," said Sean, as they stood by the door saying good-bye. We shook our heads: We weren't going anywhere.

The next day was the funeral for Ziad Ghalayini, the boy who had been shot, and another young man who had been killed with him. Hundreds of people stood outside on the sidewalk and in the street. The balconies were packed with women screaming and crying. The mosque muttered prayers.

A group of about twenty men ran up the street, carrying the coffins and chanting "Ziad, Ziad, *habib allah*!"—"Ziad, Ziad, the beloved of God!"—and screaming. Whenever one of them lost his grip, another would take his place. The coffins were covered in green satin cloths with yellow script. One of them had a *tarboosh* sitting on top of it, the little red fez that the Ottomans had required their subjects to wear—the symbol of a man.

They carried the caskets around the block, from building to building, rocking them gently back and forth. The women screamed and ululated, collapsing against one another, waving their arms and beating their breasts. They brought Ziad's casket into his family's apartment and left the other one in the hearse. The sobbing and shouting got louder from inside the house. Everyone in the street stood watching and listening to the screams of *"Ziad! Ziad!"* A hoarse male voice started shouting, "They should all get out! They should all get out!"

Abdelghanim, one of four friendly brothers who ran a small grocery store, came over to say hello. "Did you know him?" he asked. I told him I knew him by sight. He shook his head. "Poor kid, he was such a good kid, he was always around on the block, and he helped everyone." He expected trouble after the funeral.

The men brought the coffin down the stairs. The women waved good-bye from the balcony, weeping, clapping both hands to their foreheads, and then throwing them open wide. As the coffin came out the front door, the women ululated. They threw a shower of rose petals and rice: This funeral was the only wedding he would ever have. An old woman arranged white lilies on the hearse. Men filed out, crying, leaning on one another's shoulders.

As they carried the coffins back to the mosque for the final prayer, a Shi-ite neighbor showed up to offer condolences to the family. But the women started shoving and pushing at her. "Get out!" screamed one of the women, as they chased her away. "Go back to Nasrallah!" Mohamad and I looked at each other and decided that it was time to go back inside.

An elderly lady came up in the elevator with us. She was very upset and could not stop talking. Her sister lived in the building, she told us, and she had a daughter in America, studying at a university, and it was important to tell the Americans that not all Lebanese were like Hezbollah. She followed us out of the elevator, although she did not live on our floor, and stood in the hallway talking. It seemed rude to leave her—she was almost in shock—so we stood outside our doorway listening for a long time. "I'm very sad about Ziad," she said. "Whenever I would come visit my sister, he would always come up to me and ask for the car keys, and he would park my car. He was a very good kid."

She looked at Mohamad. Here it comes, I thought.

"What is your family name?" she asked.

"Bazzi."

"Oh," she said, lifting her eyebrows. "Bazzi. You're Shiite."

"Yes, I am."

"I'm Sunni, but my husband is Shiite. He's a doctor at AUB. He rejects everything that's happening."

She looked at him expectantly. She was going to make him say it, make him prove his loyalty to the human race.

"And you," she prompted. "What do you think of what's going on?"

"Yes, I reject it too," said Mohamad. "We all reject these things."

Abdelghanim was right: There was trouble that afternoon. In Tareeq al-Jadideh, during another funeral procession, Sunnis attacked Shiite businesses, and a Shiite shopkeeper opened fire on the crowd and killed two people. Each side blamed the other for kidnappings, forced evacuations, sectarian cleansing. "It's so dangerous," said my friend Adessa, when she called to see if we were all right. "Because how many times have you heard people from the civil war say, 'Well, *they* were going to come get *us*'?"

The rumors ricocheted around the Internet and telephones: kidnappings in Zarif, kidnappings on the Corniche. A lady at Sporting told Leena's sister-in-law that Hezbollah was kidnapping Sunnis from Zarif. Umm Hassane's neighbor told her to warn Hanan not to go home, because the Sunnis were forcibly evacuating Shiites from Tareeq al-Jadideh, where Hanan lived.

Suddenly I remembered that Munir also lived in Tareeq al-Jadideh. I had forgotten.

"Annia, you should leave," he said when I called. "This is my country, and this is the shit of my people. You don't have to tolerate it. *I* don't have to tolerate it! I was just telling Joseph: Let's leave and go to India."

In late 2006, Munir and several business partners, one of whom was a

Buddhist, had opened a gay bar and restaurant called Bardo. This was San-skrit for the place your soul goes in the afterlife while waiting to be reborn—"an enchanting place," he told me once. It fit the fantasy of India as the East, a mystical happyland of saffron-soaked enlightenment.

"*India?* Munir. Habiby. They have sectarian riots there that make this look like children playing. Hindus and Muslims, thousands of people killing each other. Setting whole trains on fire. Everyone inside burning to death."

He was silent.

Too late, I remembered that Munir had no New York to move back to. He needed his imaginary India the way I needed Tango Night—as an image of how the world could be, the kind of dream palace we all need, especially in Beirut, and it was part of what helped him not to hate.

"So they have this kind of thing in India too?" he said sadly. "The whole world has gone mad."

The retaliations began. The fighting spread outside Beirut, to battles in the Chouf Mountains between Hezbollah and its onetime ally, the Progressive Socialist Party. In the northern town of Halba, Future fighters stormed the offices of the SSNP and killed nine men inside. Three Future fighters died in the assault; their comrades videotaped the dying SSNP men with cell phones and posted the grisly videos on the Internet. Hezbollah replayed it as propaganda, pointing out that Sunnis were killing Sunnis now and warning that the footage was not for "children or the faint of heart." Umm Hassane watched the bloody video, despite the warning, and became upset. "What is this slaughter?" she said to Mohamad over the phone. "They mutilated the bodies and trampled on them. *Wallah,* the Israelis never did such a thing. What are these sights? A thing that makes the heart cry."

Hezbollah was keeping the airport closed. Sunni gunmen set up check-points on the road leading to the Syrian border and put up posters of Saddam Hussein. They checked the ID cards of anybody trying to enter or leave the country and demanded to know if they were Shiites.

I looked at the photographs of black-masked gunmen standing at the border with RPG launchers, under posters of Saddam, and suddenly under-stood Mohamad's desire to move back to New York.

"I'm sorry I made you come back here," I said.

"Well, I can't leave now," he said, and shrugged.

That afternoon, Ziad's family put up an enormous vinyl banner of their dead son, about twelve feet tall, on the outside of their building. Inside their apartment, which was directly across from ours, the windows were open into a living room lined with chairs for condolences. The chairs were full of little boys and girls around three to five years old. A woman led them in a chant:

> *Li ilaha illa Allah*
> *Al-shaheed habib Allah!*
>
> *There is no God but God*
> *The martyr is the beloved of God!*

The children pumped their tiny fists in the air, just as their older brothers and sisters had been doing for days. They shouted happily, as if it were a game, a nursery rhyme, and whoever shouted loudest would get a treat.

On Wednesday, May 14, Arab leaders flew into Lebanon to negotiate. Hezbollah removed roadblocks from one side of the airport road so the negotiators could meet with all the Lebanese political leaders. The airport was still closed, but nevertheless it felt as if a great weight had been lifted off the city. All over Hamra, people were telling each other *al-hamdillah al-salameh,* "thanks be to God for your safety." Even the religious *khadarji* smiled broadly when he saw me.

I went to Abu Hadi for *fatteh.* He ladled the steaming chickpeas into my bowl and complained happily that he was on his own—his assistant, who lived in *dahiyeh,* had not been able to make it to Hamra for days.

"Do you have customers?" asked an old man, one of his regulars, hunched over an enormous bowl of *fatteh.*

"I always have work," said Abu Hadi. "Thanks be to God."

At the cheese shop on Sidani Street, the salesman smiled. "I have to ask you something," I said, although I believed I knew the answer. "Why did you stay open that Friday, during all the shooting?"

He half-smiled, half-shrugged. He was a *ghanouj*. "Because people want cheese."

Why? Why, in the middle of a firefight, do people decide that they must have cheese?

He smiled with everything he had this time. "Because they think they will never be able to taste it again."

That night, Mohamad and I walked a friend home. The streets were still half-wild, and she didn't feel safe being out alone at night. We were walking back through Ain al-Mreiseh, along the sea, when we heard the gunfire. Such was the sectarian map that all Beirutis carry in their heads that we knew the result of the meeting as soon as we heard it: happy fire from the Amal-controlled areas meant the government must have rescinded its orders. The fighting was over for now. But the war would never end; like Mohamad said, you ended it yourself. Moving back to New York was the ending to his wars. I would have to find my own.

We walked home to the noise of gunfire, avoiding the Amal areas. We clung to the sides of buildings, under balconies, watching red blossoms of tracer fire arc through the night sky. As we approached our block, we saw a new vinyl banner stretched all the way across the street. Blood-red Arabic script declared: TREASON'S MARTYR. Underneath was a picture of Ziad standing in front of the Pigeon Rocks, the famous arched cliffs in the sea off the Corniche. He was smiling and striking a manly pose that only made him look even more like a child: hips cocked, hands in his jeans pockets, tilting his head to the side. He was wearing a white T-shirt with big black letters that said, in English, STILL VIRGIN.

"It's so sad!" Mohamad exclaimed.

That could have been you, I thought but did not say. If you had stayed in Beirut when you were ten, instead of moving to New York, that could have been you, standing in front of the Pigeon Rocks, trying to look like a warrior; it could have been me, if I had grown up here, or any one of us.

"Yes it is," I said. I took his hand, and we walked back home.

Epilogue

TWO YEARS LATER, almost to the day, I was on the phone with Umm Hassane. She was in Beirut. I was in New York.

"Umm Hassane," I said, shouting because the connection was bad and my Arabic was still wretched and she was still deaf. "I'm making *mlukhieh*. How do you make *mlukhieh* from dried leaves?"

"Why do you want to make *mlukhieh*?" she asked, rhetorically. Thousands of miles of ether snarled and hummed but I swear I could almost hear the rolling of her eyes. "You can't! It's too hard!"

Earlier that week I had gone to Sahadi's, the Arabic grocery on Atlantic Avenue, and pulled a number out of the mouth of a little machine. The store was packed with New Yorkers waiting to get at the olives and feta and hummus and *baba ghanouj*. When my turn finally arrived, I told the guy I wanted dried *mlukhieh*.

He gave me a sharp sidewise look, a skeptical who-are-you kind of look, and I braced myself for the inevitable question.

"You make *mlukhieh*?" he said.

I laughed. Not the question I had been unconsciously expecting. But I liked this one better.

"Why not?" I said, and employed my best Umm Hassane shopping behavior—a shrewd glare, a flip of the chin, a flap of the hand. A shrug of contempt, as if such a question was unnecessary between us.

"You are Arab?"

"No," I said, and smiled.

A few years ago, I might have hastened to explain that I wasn't Arab, but my husband was Lebanese, and doesn't everyone like *mlukhieh*? I might have pointed out that *mlukhieh* was African, expounded on the similarities between Egyptian *mlukhieh* and southern-style collard greens, both stewed with meat and served with onions quick-pickled in sweet vinegar. I might have offered up my Greek pedigree, or confided that an Iraqi friend had introduced me to *mlukhieh*, right here on Atlantic Avenue, back in the summer of 2001. But while these things do matter, do make us who we are, there are also times and places where we can agree to put our particular histories aside. I have learned to appreciate that.

"But you know how to make *mlukhieh*?"

"Yes."

He grinned triumphantly, as if I had just proved a point he'd put some serious money on. "Why not?" he said, and filled the bag with *mlukhieh*.

My return to the homeland did not begin well. It was late 2009, winter was coming, and everyone I knew was getting laid off. Mohamad and millions of other people were sick with swine flu. Our government was still spending hundreds of billions of dollars and uncountable lives on two wars, both of which had been grinding on for years, yet all anyone seemed to talk about was movie stars or sports. If they did talk about the war in Iraq, it was in neatly packaged, microwavable soundbites that bore no relation to Roaa, Abu Rifaat, Dr. Salama, Abdullah, or any of the other Iraqis I knew. New Yorkers were so busy fondling their smartphones they seemed to have forgotten basic skills like how to walk. Friends required me to schedule appointments weeks in advance, claiming they were "booked," as if they were hotel rooms. People seemed afraid to express strong opinions in person, yet the Internet was crawling with them. Bedbugs were back too.

I called my friend Cara. She and Mohamad had lured me back here, and I was miserable, and it was her fault.

She laughed. "Did I ever tell you what happened when I moved back here with Amiram? We were back from Israel for about a week. And then one day he came to me, and he said: 'I don't understand. Why don't the neighbors come over and drink coffee with us in the morning?' "

They do that in Lebanon too. It's called a *subhieh*, from *subuh*, morning. An Untranslatable: it could be anything from a gala charity breakfast to a group of ladies who lunch. But mostly it means an informal gathering of neighbors or friends who get together, ideally every morning, to drink coffee and talk. Something about giving a name to these gatherings elevated eating and drinking and conversing to an institution, a cousin to the *milonga*, the *tertulia,* or even Sheikh Fatih and his mother's forbidden book club. Not so much a time and place as a communion, a moment when people conspire to put the world back in its place. We don't have that here, I reflected bitterly. We have Starbucks.

"Listen, Annia," she said. "People like us are never going to feel at home anywhere. Ever. We're never going have that comfortable feeling of belonging."

War changes your mental metabolism so that a part of you is perpetually at war and uneasy with peace. This is a physical reaction as much as an intellectual one, the way living through the Great Depression made my grandparents constitutionally incapable of throwing anything away. The way I only feel at home surrounded by people on the move. The way Lebanese people are constantly honking their horns, shooting into the air, or setting off cherry bombs, because they don't feel right without noise. You will never see the egg, once you know how quickly it cracks, without imagining it shattered. A part of us secretly exults in disaster: we are proven right; things are exactly as bad as we always knew they were. That ugly part of us (and I have it in me just like anyone else) resents the people around you, the ones who seem only to see the smooth and perfect shell.

What you do with that bitterness determines what kind of person you become. You can carry it around with you, even in a peaceful place. Or you can agree to put it aside, even in a city at war.

Munir, in the middle of an uncharacteristically topical discussion of religion and politics, once reached out and picked up a wineglass.

"Look at this glass," he said, holding it up so we could admire its slender neck, its fragile bud. "It takes a lot to make it. And yet it takes very little to break it. You can break it in an instant."

It didn't seem like much at the time—a bit of drinking wisdom. But now I never drink wine without looking at the delicate curve of the glass and thinking, yes, you can break it in an instant. And yet here it is, whole and full of wine.

Months later, in the spring, I was talking on the phone with Roaa. I was still in New York. She was in Colorado. She had a husband now, and a daughter, and the three of them had traveled all the way from Baghdad to Sulay-maniya, in Iraqi Kurdistan, then to Turkey, and finally to a semi-furnished apartment in *America suburbia.*

The last time I had seen Roaa, in 2004, the sectarian violence in Iraq seemed pervasive. But it was just getting started. By 2006, the country was in the grip of a raging civil war. During this chaos, she finally fell in love. Being Roaa, she didn't do it the easy way: he was an Arab, she was a Kurd. Many families refused to accept such a match, but theirs did, and they had a beautiful baby daughter named Rania.

In 2008, Roaa's husband started getting death threats: anonymous references to "un-Islamic" behavior like drinking beer (so much for the ancient Sumerians). The threats came edged with detailed allusions to who he was, who his friends were, and where he lived. So Roaa and her husband joined the diaspora—almost three million refugees inside Iraq's borders, and 1.5 million more in cities of neighboring countries: a mass migration that will forever change the Middle East and the rest of our interconnected world. She and her husband applied to the United States refugee resettlement program, and after a series of interviews, they were accepted. Now here she was in the suburbs of Denver. She had always wanted to see the world.

We talked about cell phones and Facebook, which had helped us stay in touch, about jobs and paperwork and whether they should move to New York or try to make a go of it in Colorado, where they did not know a soul. They had no telephone or Internet yet, no car, no jobs, and very little money.

"Well," she said, and laughed, as if suddenly remembering that she had seen much worse. And then she said fiercely: "We will *make* ourselves settle down."

Things in Iraq would improve, slowly. Shahbandar Café was bombed by Islamic militants in March 2007, and rebuilt in 2009. Abu Nuwas Street was refurbished, and the *masquf* restaurants reopened. In neighborhoods where Muqtada al-Sadr's Mahdi Army had once ruled the streets, people wrote graffiti that said: WE ARE COMING WITH THE ARMY OF UMM MAHDI—the Baghdadi nickname for a *fawal*, an old woman who sells *foul* on the street. (Mocking political leaders with legumes was not a new phenomenon: In 2003, Abu Rifaat had showed me a graffito that said NO HAKIM, NO CHALABI, I JUST WANT BEER AND LABLABI—comparing both religious and secular politicians, unfavorably, to beer and chickpea soup.)

Salaam the Communist had to leave his neighborhood for three years, while Sunni insurgents tried to turn it into an Islamic mini-state. He returned in 2009 and was astounded to see liquor stores: whisky bottles lined up, right there in the windows, a thing that would have earned the shopkeeper an execution just a year earlier. He called a friend and said: "Now I feel safe, because I see liquor stores." But then a series of bombings would rip through markets and cafés and ice cream shops, the war would reassert itself, and the cautious tide of civilization would retreat once more. *Youm aasl, youm basl*—day of honey, day of onions.

In Beirut, the gunmen disappeared as quickly as they had appeared. Hezbollah dismantled its tents from downtown, there was a parliamentary election, and a new government that included all the factions. Yet you could still smell the hate simmering just below the surface. The political parties kept it on a low flame, but they could bring it back up to a boil whenever they wanted. *You can break it in an instant.*

But no matter how powerful the aftertaste of hate, you don't remember it as vividly as you do the other things. When I thought of Baghdad, I thought of the way people there treasured books; their sense of humor, of history, the way someone would always bring up the Epic of Gilgamesh. The old-fashioned cafés. The smell of *masquf*. The way everyone was constantly breaking into poetry, or relating the same stories they had been telling since before the Abbasids. When I thought of Beirut, I did not remember the gunmen, or our neighbors checking identity cards, or the Hezbollah men hunkered in tents like Ibn Khaldun's Bedouin hordes. I remembered the smell of lamb being grilled by the neighbors on Sundays, mixed with the fragrance of roasting coffee and cardamom from the shop downstairs. The screech of roosters echoing off concrete, the cry of Kaaaaaa-*eek!* from the old man selling *kaak*. I imagined the moment during Ramadan, just before *iftar*, when the streets were suddenly empty, the neighborhood perfectly silent and still, as all of Hamra held its breath and waited for the *muezzin*'s voice to break the fast. I remembered watching the fortuneteller predict the next year's events on New Year's Eve on Lebanese TV, followed by a young woman forecasting the weather in a black leather bustier. I pictured the *fattoush* at Baromètre, a pyramid of red and green, and it occurred to me that if I walked into Baromètre at that very moment I would probably see someone I knew.

I did not miss the bombs. But I did miss my friends, and the way we would all call each other after a bombing to make sure everyone was all right. I missed the way Umm Adnan or Abu Ibrahim recited recipes when I bought *khubaizeh* or wild fennel; the bored teenaged cashier at my local supermarket in New York was perfectly nice, but she did not do that when I bought a plastic bag of prewashed spinach.

There was no point to staying in Baghdad or even Beirut. No point to being there simply because our friends could not or would not leave—no use, as Mohamad would point out, to staying in a war zone out of loyalty to friends who have no choice but to remain. But there is something to be said for memory, and for raising what small flag you can, even a tattered one, against forgetting.

Whenever I missed Beirut or Baghdad, I would head to a farmers' market. I would find something familiar, or something unfamiliar, and I would make something out of it. I would call friends (the ones who weren't "booked") and invite them to dinner.

Food alone cannot make peace. It is part of war, like everything else. We can break bread with our neighbors one day and kill them the next. Food is just an excuse—an opportunity to get to know your neighbors. When you share it with others, it becomes something more.

I spread the dried green *mlukhieh* out on the table. I picked through the leaves, throwing away the brown ones and snapping off the stems. It looked and smelled like tea. I made it exactly the way Umm Hassane had instructed, and it was terrible.

"Umm Hassane," I shouted, the next time we called her. "The *mlukhieh.* How do you cook it when it's dried?"

"You boil it!"

"Yes, but do you boil the leaves separately first, before you put in the chicken?"

"Of course!" (Her standard response for any step she has forgotten to tell you about.)

"For how long?"

"Until it's done!"

She seized any opportunity to point out the impossibility of making *tabeekh* in America. The butchers in America would not be able to grind the meat finely enough. The tomatoes would not taste right. The *mlukhieh* was not really *mlukhieh*. This was her way of saying that she missed us, and of trying to bring us back to Beirut. But when we called to tell her we were coming for a visit, she snorted, as if she'd believe it when she saw us.

Cara was right: we will never find that feeling of belonging. I will not find it in a store, or a city, or even a farmer's market, because it is not something you find but something you make. I will plant a garden, read a book. I will have coffee with my neighbors. I will cook dinner with my friends. I will not wait to make an appointment. I will call Georges in Cleveland or Roaa in Denver or Adessa in Beirut. I will call my mother and ask what she is eating. I will buy a sandwich and eat it on the street, remembering to marvel at the fact that the sidewalks here are for people, not cars, like in Beirut.

When I walk down the streets of New York, there will be moments when I happen to make eye contact with a guy just as he is wrapping his mouth around a hot dog or a burrito or a falafel, and he will look up with a sudden, almost doglike look of shame, because his mouth is full and he is eating in public, and that is an American's standard response to being caught communing with our food. And without thinking, I will start to say *sahtain*. I will think, for the millionth time, that it's a crime we don't have such a word in English, that we do eat in public here, but we do not really celebrate it quite like they do around the Mediterranean. So I will say it anyway, even though the guy will probably think I'm crazy: *Sahtain!* Eat, for God's sake!

Acknowledgments

THE HARDEST PART of acknowledging others is how they refuse to behave. Translators become friends (and vice versa). Sources metamorphose into mentors. A manuscript reader is also a sharer of culinary secrets. I tried to organize them for the sake of space, but many of the people I thank below transcend categories.

Some of those who were most helpful to me cannot be thanked by name, for their safety and that of their loved ones. They know who they are and how much I owe them.

When I showed up in Baghdad and Beirut as a freelancer new to war zone reporting, fellow journalists were generous with sources, satellite phones, accumulated wisdom, alcohol, and grilled meat. They included Chris Albritton, Jackson Allers, Anne Barnard, Nick Blanford, Kate Brooks, Andrew Lee Butters, Thanassis Cambanis, Charlie Crain, Babak Dehghanpisheh, Yochi Dreazen, Farnaz Fassihi, Kim Ghattas, Ben Gilbert, Christine Hauser, Betsy Hiel, Warzer Jaff, Larry Kaplow, Ashraf Khalil, Ibrahim Khayat, Rita Leistner, Joe Logan, Matt McAllester, Challiss McDonough, Andrew Mills, Diana Moukalled, Evan Osnos, Scott Peterson, Jim Rupert, Moises Saman, Kate Seelye, Anthony Shadid, Tina Susman, Letta Tayler, and Liz Sly.

In Baghdad, Betsy Pisik gave me a crash course on conflict reporting ("No one wants to read about sanitation," she told me, "but *everyone* wants to read about babies"). Hazem Al-Amin and Maher Abi Samra supplied *arak* and occasional Arabic-to-French translation. Rebecca BouChebel brought the spirit of Beirut to war-torn Baghdad; Manal Omar and Hassan Fattah made it possible to laugh when there was every reason to cry. And the Institute for War & Peace Reporting created an island of civility, hospitality, and journalistic ethics in Baghdad, thanks to the remarkable people we met there, including Michael Howard, Salaam Jihad, Steve Negus, Hiwa

Osman, Usama Redha, Maggy Zanger, and Hiwa's immortal Thanksgiving turkey tandoori.

Amir Nayef Toma, the Virgil of Baghdad, showed me the beauty in the ordinary and extraordinary life of his city. He is a modern-day al-Jahiz and a true citizen of the world. Reem Kubba and her husband, Sadiq, regaled us with poetry in their beautiful home; Oday and Usama Rasheed, Ziad Turky, Basim al-Hajar, Basim Hamed, Faris Harram, and Nassire Ghadire talked about B.B. King, the songs of al-Qubanshi, *The Exorcist*, *Three Kings*, the Iraqi poet al-Jawahiri, and The Doors.

Alan King's deep compassion for the people of Iraq, and his dedication to learning all he could about their history and religion, was an example to me. I thank him also for introducing us to Sheikh Hussein Ali al-Shaalan, from whom we learned so much, and Adnan al-Janabi, who inspired me to seek out books by Hanna Batatu, Ali al-Wardi, and Ibn Khaldun.

Special thanks to Dr. Salama al-Khafaji, Sheikh Fatih Kashif al-Ghitta, and Dr. Amal Kashif al-Ghitta. I hope it is clear from this book how much their friendship means to me. *Beitkum aamra, sufrah aamra.*

All of the superb editors I worked with at *The Christian Science Monitor* and *The New Republic* deserve my gratitude. But I owe a special debt to those crucial first editors—Josh Benson, Jeremy Kahn, and Jim Norton—who read and responded to pitches from an unknown freelancer in Iraq. Without them, I would never have had the good fortune of working with Franklin Foer, Richard Just, Joshua Kurlantzick, Adam Kushner, Kate Marsh, Amelia Newcomb, Clay Risen, and David Clark Scott. Adam Shatz and Roane Carey at *The Nation* pushed me to produce the kind of writing I didn't think I could do. James Oseland, Georgia Freedman, and Dana Bowen at *Saveur* made food writing seem smart, down-to-earth, and ruthlessly cosmopolitan.

As a journalist, I had the privilege of talking to some of the most brilliant scholars, activists, and political analysts in the world. I owe an intellectual debt to Charles Adwan, Khalil Gebara, Timur Goksel, Nadim Houry, Samir Kassir, Isam al-Khafaji, Chibli Mallat, Jamil Mroue, Amal Saad-Ghorayeb, Paul Salem, Nadim Shehadi, Lokman Slim, Fawwaz Traboulsi, and Mai Yamani, who all shared their deep understanding of Middle Eastern history, politics, religions, culture, and civil society. Ahmad ElHusseini and Fouad Ajami dazzled me with their knowledge of Shiite history, politics, and theology over the course of a seven-hour lunch, one of Ahmad's always unforgettable meals. Entifadh Qanbar revealed the secret sectarian life of Iraqi food. Rami Khouri and the Issam Fares Institute unlocked the doors to the American University of Beirut's library by making me an affiliate scholar.

Lizzie Collingham, Martin Jones, Nawal Nasrallah, and Dani Noble shared food scholarship and insights into the culinary history of the Middle East. Faleh Jabar and Sami Zubaida allowed me to bask in their generous, wide-ranging intellects and their memories of old Baghdad. Shadi Hamadeh of the Food Heritage Foundation introduced me to Aunty Salwa, the SNOB theory, and Wardeh's orange-blossom lemonade. Rami Zurayk talked to me about food and farming and power, words that should always be put together.

Barbara Abdeni Massaad wrote the book (literally) on *manoushi*, as well as on *mouneh*. Her intrepid reporting informs this book, which her passion and endless curiosity inspired me to finish. Malek Batal and Beth Hunter also made an incalculable contribution to this book. Malek taught me culinary stories, proverbs, history, and how to scrub out my cast-iron skillet with coffee grounds. Beth shared her economic research and her cynical sense of humor. As if that wasn't enough, they introduced me to Wassim Kays and Maha Nasrallah, who fed us pumpkin *kibbeh* and watermelon one perfect afternoon in Batloun.

To everyone who shared recipes and cooking secrets, much gratitude. Nelly Chemaly, Muna al-Dorr (better known as Umm Ali), Ali Fahs, Kamal Mouzawak, and everybody at Souk El Tayeb dispensed recipes and other forms of wisdom. Adessa Tawk showed up at my house with apples, tomatoes, cucumbers, spinach, olive oil, *mouneh*, and family recipes. Georges Naassan, his mother, and Katia ("Monique") Medawar recited recipes over red wine at Bardo and Walimat; and Samar Awada taught me the secret to real tabbouleh. Bassam Badran (aka "The Foul King") and Rawda Mroueh of Matbakh al-Beiti gave recipes from their restaurants. Siad Darwish, Ali Shamkhi, and all the other Iraqis I cooked with in Beirut (I can't name them, but they know who they are) taught me the joy of Iraqi cooking. Eliane BouChebel, Wardeh Loghmaji, Leena Saidi, Malek Batal (again!) and Umm Nabil divulged *mlukhieh* secrets. And special thanks to Aunt Khadija, Aunt Nahla, and, as always, Umm Hassane.

"It is normally supposed that something always gets lost in translation," Salman Rushdie once wrote; "I cling, obstinately, to the notion that something can also be gained." Rayane Alamuddin, Bassam Moussa, Usama Redha, Leena Saidi, and one or two I cannot name opened up a world of connotations, double meanings, verbs and proverbs, poetry, and puns. I think they know how fortunate I was to have them as translators and friends. Hayat Shibl taught me how to say "thank you" four different ways; and Samar Awada, sometime tutor and always friend, taught me not to be afraid of written Arabic.

Sirene Harb and Bassem Mroue told us stories, jokes, and history over *fattoush* at Abu Hassan and Baromètre. Paula Khoury fed me vodka, cigarettes, and books. Rhonda Roumani showed me around Damascus; Tania Mehanna always made us happy to come back to Lebanon; and Rym Ghazal, among other things, found a home for our beloved Shaitan. Jiro Ose and Julia Zajkowski got me the quietest apartment in Beirut; Ralph Schray and Riad Hanbali proved that landlords can also be gentlemen; and Rabih Dabbous rescued me from the *Bukhala* of Ras Beirut.

Bilal El Amine, Maha Issa, and Abdulrahman Zahzah of T-Marbouta, who turned their café into a refugee center, reminded me that the root of the word restaurant is *restore*. Maren Milligan shanghaied me to Baromètre and was my research guru. Romola Sanyal made the best butter chicken I've ever had. Munir Abdallah beat me at Scrabble, made magic with cardamom, and created Tango Night, where I met Adessa Tawk and Georges Naassan, whose friendship runs through every page of this book.

While finishing this book, I stayed at the very best writers' colonies: my friends' apartments. In New York, visiting Pamela Roberts was like getting locked in the library overnight (my secret goal in life). Victor Araman, the most glamorous college professor I know, played musical apartments with us. And we treasured our peaceful weeks in Les Payne's gracious brownstone, and above Barbara and Gary Primosch's backyard garden.

In Beirut, I got to watch Imma Vitelli read everything she could before heading off to a new assignment and leaving her apartment to me. Nahlah Ayed, a fearless reporter and a true friend, proved that you can be the hardest-working woman in television and still make a mean *maqlubeh*. And if I have a tribe, Nizar Ghanem and Sean Carothers Lee are part of it. I slept on their couch, raided their refrigerator and their bookshelves, and took advantage of their knowledge of everything worth knowing.

And then there is Cara Hoffman, who lent me the courage to call myself a writer. I learned more about writing from staying with Cara for ten days than I did in the previous ten years; I would never have finished this book without that white-knuckle trip to the Upstate Writers' Gulag. Eli Ben-Yaacov and Glenn Hoffman kept us human with exquisite dinners; Hunter S. Thompson, Iggy Pop, and Seneca Drums gin helped us finish the job.

Maren Milligan, Georges Naassan, Christa Salamandra, and Robin Shulman all read the manuscript and gave invaluable comments. Suhail Shadoud spent hours correcting my Arabic and suggesting transliterations, both of which he did with the eloquence of a poet and the precision of a dentist. And I was fortunate to find Jennifer Block, a stellar investigative reporter, for a fact-checker. She saved me from making a fool of myself on too many occasions to mention. Any mistakes were inserted by me once her back was turned.

This book could not have happened without our New York friends and mentors. William Serrin inspired me to pursue a master's degree in journalism at New York University, where Dick Blood taught me how to count the bullet holes and how to eat the meal. Brooke Kroeger inspired me to believe I could be a foreign correspondent, and then an author, and never let me stay satisfied with work that was just good enough. Jimmy Breslin and Ronnie Eldridge married us off; Frankie Edozien, Bob Roberts, and Hilary Russ kept America safe while we were gone; Rukhsana Siddiqui's annual visits to New York were reason enough to come back. Robin Shulman and Ethan Miller helped me imagine this book over long-distance phone calls from Beirut. Indrani Sen, Tracie McMillan, and Kim Severson made me see food writing as an essential form of journalism. Alyssa Katz, Robert Neuwirth, Azadeh Moaveni, and Jennifer Washburn gave indispensable advice on agents and proposals and contracts. Once the machinery was in motion, Mary Anne Weaver advised me to always go up the hill; Deborah Amos, Laurie Garrett, Tim Phelps, Scott Malcomson, Suketu Mehta, Dan Morrison, Fariba Nawa, Basharat Peer, and Helen Winternitz all helped me believe that books do, one day, actually get finished.

I owe special thanks to Flip Brophy at Sterling Lord Literistic. She encouraged my early attempts at book conception, and later introduced me to my agent and dear friend, Rebecca Friedman. Rebecca understood what I was trying to write even before I did; her literary skills and insight turned a half-baked idea about food and war into a proposal and then a book. She brings books into existence through sheer intelligence and faith.

Dominick Anfuso and Martha Levin at Free Press believed in *Day of Honey* from the beginning. Wylie O'Sullivan, my quiet, supportive, yet formidable editor, guided me through the psychological warfare of memoir writing with an almost biblical patience. Her perceptive editing shaped a manuscript into a story, and I was lucky indeed to work with her. Mara Lurie eased the words onto paper with the unflappable skill of a short-order cook. Ellen Sasahara designed the text that makes the book a visual feast. Nicole Kalian handled publicity, and Eric Fuentecilla designed the cover, so it's thanks to them that you're reading this at all. To Sydney Tanigawa and everyone else who endured me: many, many thanks and endless baklava.

Finally, family. Hassan, Hassane, and Ahmad Bazzi welcomed me into theirs, and Hanan Bazzi made me feel at home in Beirut. Umm Hassane and Abu Hassane need no introduction, but to them I would like to say one last thank you. My mother, Janina Ciezadlo, didn't blink an eye when I told her I was moving to the Middle East; she played it cool the whole time I was in Beirut and Baghdad, but I know how hard it is to have a loved one in a war zone. Her unwavering emotional and intellectual support have sustained me throughout my life. I only wish my grandparents, John and Constance Ciezadlo, were still around to hold this book in their hands and say, with that skeptical, wondering tone: *Will you look at that!*

And at long last, Mohamad. One of the worst things about writing a book is how it takes you away from the people you love—an especially frustrating irony when you are writing about how much you love them. Mohamad endured this for three years, during which he kept me going with his usual combination of strength, intelligence, dry wit, and sheer classiness. This book is dedicated to him.

Author's Note

THE STORY OF the Caliph and the Byzantine ambassador on pages 96–97 draws from the accounts of the eleventh-century historian al-Khatib al-Baghdadi, beautifully translated and annotated by Jacob Lassner in *The Topography of Baghdad in the Early Middle Ages*. The lines from Abu Nuwas's poem about the neighborhood bar, on page 95, are adapted from a translation by the Princeton Online Poetry Project. I've paraphrased them into contemporary speech; I like to think Abu Nuwas would approve.

And finally, in order to protect their safety and preserve their privacy, I have changed the names of some of the people in this book.

Recipes

Fattoush

Levantine Bread Salad

Serves 4 to 6

*I*n the Middle East, people of all religions consider it a sin to waste bread. The necessity of using up day-old flatbread has created a universe of foods—including traditional Arabic dishes like *fatteh* (see *Fattet Hummus*, page 338), *fattoush,* and the bread soups of the Arabian peninsula—that transforms leftovers into something magnificent.

Ingredients

Dressing (makes about 1 cup)

2 garlic cloves (about 2 teaspoons mashed)
¼ teaspoon coarse sea salt
Juice of 1 lemon (about 3 tablespoons)
1 teaspoon pomegranate molasses*
⅔ cup extra virgin olive oil

Salad

6 cups chopped romaine (about 12 ounces)
½ cup roughly chopped mint leaves
½ cup roughly chopped parsley leaves
1 cup sliced scallions (about 2 ounces)
2 cups purslane leaves (about 2 ounces), thick stems removed **
2 Persian cucumbers (about 4 ounces), halved lengthwise and sliced into half-moons (about 1 cup)
1 pound juicy tomatoes (about 4), chopped (about 2 cups)
2 radishes, quartered lengthwise and sliced into quarter-moons
1 large or 2 medium (six-inch) Arabic pitas, preferably day-old
Extra virgin olive oil
1 teaspoon sumac, or more to taste
Freshly ground black pepper

---

* I like the Cortas brand. Look for it in the "ethnic food" section of your supermarket, in Arabic or Greek groceries, or online.

** Hard to find but worth seeking out for its oily, lemony crunch. You can find purslane in farmers' markets, in ethnic groceries (often under the Spanish name "verdolaga"), or in your own backyard, where it may be growing as a weed. You can also substitute watercress, mâche, lamb's quarters, sorrel, pea shoots, or whatever wild edible greens grow in your area.

Equipment
Mortar and pestle
Large salad bowl

1. Mash the garlic and salt together to make a paste. Squeeze the lemon juice over the garlic, stir in the pomegranate molasses, and let it macerate while you assemble the salad.

2. Combine the romaine, mint, parsley, scallions, purslane, cucumbers, and radishes in a large bowl. (Make-ahead moment: you can prepare the salad up to this point and refrigerate until serving.)

3. Preheat the oven to 300°F. Peel the two surfaces of the pitas apart, then spray or brush them lightly on all sides with olive oil. Toast until crisp and golden brown, about 5 minutes (watch closely, they burn fast). Take them out immediately. When they are cool enough to handle, break them into bite-sized pieces.

4. Add the tomatoes and bread chips to the salad just before serving. Whisk ⅓ cup olive oil into the dressing and pour it over the salad. Dust with sumac and ground pepper. Wash your hands thoroughly, then toss the salad by hand, making sure that every leaf and vegetable is coated with dressing. Taste and adjust for salt and sumac. Serve immediately.

VARIATIONS

Consider this recipe a template: *fattoush* is a chance to save, improvise, and reinvent. You can make it with any leftover bread instead of pita. Some like it chunky; others prefer the salad finely chopped. Different palates prefer more or less sumac. Some people add fresh herbs (try tarragon or summer savory), and a brave or reckless few add foreign objects like raw cauliflower. (I recommend feta cheese, sliced bell peppers, avocado, and *ʒaatar*.) And so on.

I love garlic, but some people prefer *fattoush* without it. If you like garlic but want a less assertive salad dressing, split a clove of garlic in half lengthwise. If there is a green shoot, remove it. For a whisper of flavor, rub the inside of your salad bowl with the cut halves; for a little more, put them into your salad dressing and let them infuse it (but remember to remove them before serving).

Some people fry the bread in olive oil instead of toasting it. Cut it into bite-sized squares or triangles of roughly the same size (kitchen shears are good for this). Heat ½ inch canola or pure olive oil (not extra virgin) in a skillet. When it shimmers, fry the pieces in small batches, turning them gently, until uniformly crisp and golden brown. Drain on paper towels or a brown grocery bag.

Batata wa Bayd Mfarakeh
Crumbled Potatoes and Eggs
Serves 4 generously

S low cooking is the essence of this dish. Some cooks deep-fry the potatoes, but I prefer Umm Hassane's method, which makes for a consistency more like home fries. The standard recipe is just eggs, onions, and potatoes. But this simple base lends itself remarkably well to improvisation: try adding chopped bell peppers and/or garlic to the onions; add smoked salmon, cream, or your favorite cheese with the eggs (I like feta, goat cheese, or cheddar). It's also good with cumin, black mustard seeds, and a pinch of curry powder.

Ingredients

10 ounces onions (about 2 medium-large), diced (about 2 cups)
2 tablespoons canola or olive oil
3 pounds russet or Idaho potatoes (about 4 medium-large),
    peeled and cut into ½-inch cubes (about 4 cups)
1 tablespoon sea salt, plus more for salting potatoes and to taste
Optional: 2 tablespoons chopped fresh herbs such as oregano,
    rosemary, and/or thyme
8 eggs

Equipment

Medium-sized pot or Dutch oven with a lid

1. Sauté the onions in the oil in a heavy or nonstick pot over medium heat. Stir frequently and do not let them burn. Once the onions begin to soften, after 2 to 3 minutes, cover the pot and turn the heat down to medium-low. Check the onions and stir every 10 minutes or so to keep them from sticking and burning. Do not let them brown at this point; you want them to caramelize very slowly. When they start expelling a lot of liquid and are turning translucent, turn the heat down as low as possible.

2. While the onions are cooking, sprinkle the potato cubes generously with salt, toss, and let them sit for about 5 minutes. Rinse very well under cold water.

3. After about 30 minutes, the onions should be starting to turn dark gold.

Increase the heat to medium and remove the lid to evaporate as much of the liquid as possible. Add the tablespoon of salt and potatoes and mix. If you're using fresh herbs, add them now.

4. Turn the heat to very low and cover. Sweat the potatoes until they are soft—usually 10 to 15 minutes—stirring gently and tasting every so often. If you like them crispy, turn the heat up, add a bit more oil, and let them crisp for a few minutes between stirs. The potatoes are done when they just begin to disintegrate around the edges and you can pierce them easily with a fork. Taste and adjust the seasoning.

5. Crack the eggs directly into the pot. Stir until they just begin separating into creamy curds. Take the pot off the heat and keep stirring until the eggs are done (they will continue to cook for a minute or two in the pot). Taste and adjust the seasoning with salt, pepper, or whatever else you like.

Umm Hassane strongly recommends that you serve *batata wa bayd* with salad. It also goes remarkably well with salted sliced tomatoes drizzled with olive oil.

VARIATION

For a less creamy, more distinct version, deep-fry the potatoes while the onions are caramelizing. Pour 2 inches canola or any other neutral, high smoke-point oil in a pot or deep skillet and heat to 300°F. Fry the potato cubes in small batches—don't crowd the pan—until light golden brown. Take them out with a slotted spoon and drain them on paper towels or brown grocery bags. Add to the caramelized onions and crack in the eggs as directed above.

Shawrabet Shayrieh
Noodle Soup

Serves 4 to 6

*T*his soup is a Bazzi family favorite. I figured it for a recent invention, a soupy adaptation of the classic spaghetti and meatballs. Then I discovered that the practice of cooking meatballs and fine noodles in soup goes all the way back to medieval Baghdad (and probably further). Arab colonizers introduced noodles to the Italians, who perfected the art of making *pasta secca;* Moorish conquerors brought the tiny, filbert-sized meatballs called *al-bunduqieh* to the Spanish, who called them *albóndigas;* and the Spanish completed the recipe by sailing to the New World and bringing the tomato to the Mediterranean. This recipe combines pasta, meatballs, and tomato sauce in a soup of old and new, tradition and innovation, Europe and Asia and the New World.

Ingredients

2 tablespoons pure (not extra virgin) olive oil
1⅓ cups angel hair or fideos pasta, crushed into roughly ¾-inch pieces
8 ounces *Kafta* (recipe follows), formed into small meatballs
2 meaty cloves garlic, crushed (about 2 teaspoons)
One 28-ounce jar tomato sauce or puréed tomatoes (or 2 pounds fresh toma-
    toes, grated on a box grater, and 1 tablespoon tomato paste)
Salt and freshly ground black pepper to taste

Optional

2 tablespoons finely chopped sundried tomatoes
Splash of red wine (about ¼ cup)
1 tablespoon chopped fresh oregano or 1 teaspoon dried
2 tablespoons chopped basil or 2 teaspoons dried

Equipment

Large, heavy-bottomed soup pot
Plate or bowl for setting aside noodles
Spatula for sautéing noodles and meatballs

1. Heat the olive oil in a large soup pot over medium-high heat until it shimmers but does not smoke. Add the noodles and sauté, stirring constantly, until they smell toasted and turn uniformly golden brown, about 2 minutes. Remove the noodles, leaving as much of the oil as possible in the pot, and set aside.

2. Sauté the meatballs in the remaining oil, shaking gently, until they are evenly browned, about 3 minutes. If they stick, increase the heat slightly and wait for them to release; do not try to pry them loose. Add the crushed garlic (and sundried tomatoes if using) and sauté for another minute or so.

3. When the garlic begins to release its fragrance, deglaze the pan with to-mato sauce (or red wine, or the reserved onion juice you may have if you made your own *kafta*). Simmer for about 30 seconds, then add the reserved noodles and all the other ingredients except basil. Salt to taste. (The oregano may taste a little bitter at first.)

4. Simmer for 10 to 15 minutes. If you're using basil, stir it in just before turning off the heat and let it wilt for a minute or two. Taste it again and adjust for salt and herbs. Add water if needed. Serve.

VARIATION

If you're in a hurry, you can make *shawrabet shayrieh* in about 15 minutes using premade ingredients—canned tomato sauce, frozen meatballs, and precrushed noodles. Or you can make everything by hand, from scratch, and enlist family and friends to help. It's a favorite among kids of all ages.

Kafta

Makes about 48 tiny meatballs, 24 big

I usually make a double or quadruple batch of these meatballs and freeze the remainder.

Ingredients

½ medium onion

2 tablespoons finely chopped parsley

2 tablespoons chopped sundried tomatoes

8 ounces beef or lamb, finely ground*

2 tablespoons Aleppo pepper

¼ teaspoon allspice

¼ teaspoon fine salt

¼ teaspoon freshly ground black pepper

⅛ teaspoon cumin

⅛ teaspoon coriander

⅛ teaspoon cinnamon

---

* I strongly suggest one not buy already ground meat. This is easy in Lebanon, where the butcher will grind the meat in front of you and add whatever you want. In America, where we're not always lucky enough to have butchers, there's a cheap, simple alternative—buy a good cut of meat and grind it yourself in a food processor. Here's how it works:

1. Buy whatever cut of meat you prefer (I recommend beef chuck or lamb shoulder). Cut out any gristle or bits of bone. You can keep a little fat if you like, or you can keep your meatballs lean and mean—this is the beauty of grinding your own meat.

2. Chop the meat into small enough chunks for your food processor to digest. Pulse it a few times in the bowl of the processor, just enough so it sticks together. Grind it a little more finely if you want a denser, fine-grained meatball, or leave it chunky if that's how you like it.

Equipment

Grater

Food processor if you're grinding
your own meat

Small sieve or tea strainer

Mixing bowl

1. Finely grate the onion half and let drain in a small sieve or tea strainer. Save the juice for the soup. Chop the parsley and sundried tomatoes very finely (if there's any extra, save it for the soup).

2. Mash all the ingredients together with a couple of forks or by hand. Don't overmix—you don't want the meat packed too tightly.

3. Tear off a teaspoon or a tablespoon of meat at a time (depending on what size meatballs you like). Roll it very lightly between your palms until it just forms a ball. Repeat for a total of 24 to 48 times.

That's it. You're done. Just be sure to thoroughly clean your food processor and anything else that touched the raw meat.

Abu Hadi's Foul Mdamas

Buried Fava Beans

Serves 4

Every city, country, and region has its own way of serving *foul*. In Egypt they serve it with butter, among other things; in Aleppo, with the hot red pepper the city is famous for; and in Damascus there is a kind of *foul* topped with yogurt called "lactating *foul*." I like mine with melted feta cheese, hot peppers, and a fried egg.

Ingredients

1 cup dried fava beans*

3 cups water for soaking, plus more
for cooking

¼ teaspoon baking soda

⅔ cup dried chickpeas

2 cups water for soaking, plus
more for cooking

¼ teaspoon baking soda

(Ingredients continued)

---

* The single most important secret to good *foul* is good beans. The fava beans should be tiny, about the size of dried black beans, and a light warm brown in color. (The red-skinned ones are old; you can cook them, but they take longer and don't taste as good.) The chickpeas should be the smallest ones you can find.

1 teaspoon coarsely ground sea salt
1 tablespoon mashed garlic (about 3 cloves)
3 tablespoons lemon juice (about 1 lemon)
½ cup extra virgin olive oil, divided
½ teaspoon cumin
¼ teaspoon paprika
Bread, chopped tomatoes, scallions, raw green hot peppers,
 and olives for serving

Equipment

2 covered glass or ceramic bowls for soaking dried beans
2 medium cooking pots
Pestle
Large serving bowl

COOKING THE BEANS

1. Soak the beans in separate containers for 7 to 12 hours or overnight. (Unless it's very cold, soak them covered in the refrigerator.)

2. Pour out the soaking water and rinse the beans well. Put each kind of bean in its own cooking pot with ¼ teaspoon baking soda. Add just enough water to barely cover—you should be able to see tiny bumps on the surface of the water.

3. Bring each pot of beans to a vigorous boil and keep it there for 10 minutes. Don't stir the beans or skim off the scum. Add just enough water to keep the beans barely covered. After 10 minutes, drain the water from the fava beans and replace with 3 cups cold water. Turn the heat down to medium-low on both pots. Simmer gently until the beans are done—anywhere from 90 minutes to two and a half hours, depending on the bean—adding just enough water as needed. The beans will finish at different times, so keep tasting them and watching them closely.

4. The chickpeas are done when the insides are soft, the skins are beginning to come off, and some of the beans have begun to split in half. When the chickpeas are finished, put the pot in the sink under cold running water. Tilt the pot and let the foam run off. Once the beans are cold enough to handle, reach in and grab two handfuls. Very gently rub them against each other, just enough so the skins rub off but the beans stay intact. Keep rinsing off the skins with cold water. Once you've removed most of the skins, rinse one more time, just to get out all the baking soda. (Make-ahead moment: Once the beans are cooked and peeled, you can store them in the refrigerator for a day or two until you're ready to make *foul*. Or you can freeze them for up to 3 months.) Add ½ inch water to

the chickpeas and simmer over low heat—just enough to keep them warm but not enough to make them disintegrate. Keep the level of water at about ½ inch.

5. The fava beans are done when they are soft inside and most of the skins have begun to split open. When they are finished, drain them very gently, being careful not to disturb them too much. Add ½ inch water and simmer as for the chickpeas.

MAKING THE *FOUL*

1. Smash the salt and garlic into a paste in a large serving bowl with a pestle. Pour in half the lemon juice and let it sit for about five minutes. (The lemon juice will "cook" the garlic; the longer it sits, the mellower the flavor.)

2. When you're ready to serve the *foul,* ladle all of the fava beans and half of the chickpeas, along with some of their cooking liquid, into the bowl with the garlic. Gently mash some of the beans with the pestle as you mix them into the garlic. Drizzle in about half the olive oil. Add more chickpea liquid if it seems dry—I like mine soupy, garlicky, and well mashed, about the consistency of a good Tex-Mex chili. Taste and adjust for olive oil and salt.

3. When you're satisfied with the taste, make a depression in the middle of the foul and ladle in the rest of the chickpeas. Drizzle the rest of the olive oil over, then the rest of the lemon juice. Dust with cumin and paprika. Serve with optional sides and whatever else you desire.

VARIATION

Making beans from scratch is worth the time and effort (especially if you make a double batch and freeze the extra). But if you just don't have the time, you can make this recipe with two 14- or 15-ounce cans. Look for fava beans and chickpeas together, but if you can't find them, use one can of each.

Rinse the beans thoroughly under running water. Warm them in a pot (or pots if you're using separate chickpeas and favas), then go straight to Making the *Foul*. Reduce the salt to ¼ teaspoon (canned beans already have a lot) and start with 2 cloves garlic, 2 tablespoons lemon juice, and ⅓ cup olive oil. Adjust the salt, spices, and other flavorings to suit your taste.

Abu Hadi's Fattet Hummus

Chickpea *Fatteh*

Serves 2 generously

The key to this deceptively simple dish is getting all the elements ready as quickly as possible. Abu Hadi's version of this popular Levantine dish is a little different from the typical Beirut one, reflecting his Damascus upbringing. I have taken some liberties with his recipe, such as heating the cumin and paprika in the butter, and adding olive oil. I'm sure Abu Hadi would forgive me; he likes to experiment with new flavors.

Ingredients

1¾ cups cooked chickpeas or one 15-ounce can*
2 cloves garlic (about 2 teaspoons mashed)
1 teaspoon coarse sea salt
2 teaspoons lemon juice (about ¼ lemon)
1½ tablespoons tahini
2½ cups whole milk yogurt
1 large or 2 medium (six-inch) day-old pitas, two halves separated

1 tablespoon butter
1 tablespoon olive oil
2 tablespoons pine nuts
¼ teaspoon paprika
½ teaspoon cumin
½ teaspoon dried mint

Equipment

Small cooking pot
Pestle
2 small bowls

1 or 2 serving bowls
   (I recommend glass)
Small skillet

1. Rinse the chickpeas and rub them very lightly between your hands to remove as many of the skins as possible. Warm them in a small cooking pot with ¼ inch water over very low heat. Add more water if necessary.

2. In a small bowl, mash the garlic and salt together with a pestle until they make a smooth paste. Add the lemon juice and stir until you have a loose slurry. Set aside.

3. Take half of the lemon-garlic mixture and put it in a second bowl. Add the tahini and mix until smooth. Add the yogurt and whisk until fully combined. Set aside.

---

* Approximately ⅔ cup dried. For cooking method, see the recipe for *foul mdamas*, page 335.

4. Toast or fry the pita halves until just golden brown (for a step-by-step explanation, see the recipe for *fattoush,* page 329). When they are cool enough to handle, break them into bite-sized pieces—roughly ½-inch squares or triangles. Set aside half of them. Layer the other half on the bottom of a serving bowl.

5. Pour the chickpeas with their cooking liquid into the bowl with the remaining lemon-garlic slurry. Mix them until coated thoroughly, mashing about half the beans with the pestle. Dump them in your serving bowl on top of the toasted bread. Top with the yogurt mixture.

6. Melt the butter in a small skillet over medium heat with the olive oil. Add the pine nuts and toast, shaking the pan so they cook evenly, until golden brown. Add the paprika and cumin and stir gently to coat. Dump the nuts on top of the yogurt and top with the remaining toasted bread. Garnish with dried mint, and if desired, dust with more cumin and paprika.

Umm Hassane's Yakhnet Kusa
Zucchini Stew

Serves 6 to 8

This is my favorite *yakhne,* or vegetable stew—perhaps because it was my first—but they're all exquisite. Once you have the basic formula, you can vary it by substituting two pounds of whatever vegetables are in season. I love the ones with roasted cauliflower or thick green beans cut in bite-sized chunks. Mohamad likes one with peas and carrots. Invent your own.

Ingredients

4 tablespoons olive oil, divided, plus more if needed
1 pound beef chuck or lamb shoulder, cut into rough 1-inch cubes
18 cups water, divided
3 small or 2 medium-large onions, peeled and cut into quarters
6 cloves garlic, peeled
1 bay leaf
2 cloves

8 peppercorns
1 allspice berry
1 tablespoon sea salt, plus more to taste
2 pounds small zucchini
6 tablespoons *Taqlieh* (recipe follows, 341)
Freshly ground black pepper
3 to 4 lemons

Equipment

2 medium-large Dutch ovens or stockpots
Medium-sized mortar and pestle, or food processer
Colander or wire-mesh strainer
Rubber scraper

1. Heat 2 tablespoons of the olive oil in a Dutch oven or stockpot over medium-high heat. Add the meat and sear on all sides until well browned and fragrant, about 5 minutes. (It will stick to the bottom of the pot at first; do not try to pry it up. After a few minutes, it should release on its own. If it doesn't, increase the heat.)

2. Add 6 cups of the water, turn the heat up to high, and bring to a rolling boil. Turn the heat down a little to medium-high and let it boil until the scum stops rising, about 5 minutes. Pour off the water from this initial boil and discard. (For an explanation of this unusual technique, see the *freekeh* recipe, page 341.) Rinse the scum off the meat in a strainer or colander.

3. Wipe out the pot and add 12 cups cold water. Add the meat, onions, garlic, bay leaf, cloves, peppercorns, allspice, and 1 tablespoon salt. Bring to a boil again, then turn the heat down to very low. Cover and simmer until the meat is soft, about 2½ hours.

4. While the meat simmers, cut the zucchini into ½-inch rounds and make the *taqlieh*. When the meat is done, strain the stock through a colander into a second pot. Save the meat and onions. Pick out the spices and bay leaf and discard.

5. Wipe out the first pot. Add 2 tablespoons olive oil and heat over medium-high heat until hot but not smoking. Add the *taqlieh* and sauté for about 2 minutes, stirring constantly and scraping the sides and bottom constantly so it doesn't stick or burn.

6. When the *taqlieh* releases its fragrance but before it becomes dry enough to stick to the pan, dump in the zucchini. Don't stop stirring. Sauté for 2 to 3 minutes, shaking the pan occasionally to coat each piece of zucchini with *taqlieh*. Add more olive oil if necessary. Do not let it brown.

7. When the zucchini starts to look tired and a little translucent, dump the stock and meat back in and turn the heat down to medium-low. Simmer, covered, until the zucchini is soft but not mushy, 25 to 45 minutes depending on size of the zucchini. Taste it periodically, sticking a fork in the zucchini to test for desired firmness. Add salt to taste.

8. Serve with salt, pepper, and lots of fresh lemon juice to taste. Umm Hassane would only ever serve this dish over rice, but I like it with bread, bulgur wheat, or even simply as a soup.

Taqlieh

Cilantro-Garlic Paste

Makes about 6 tablespoons

Ingredients
1 head garlic, peeled and smashed (about 3 tablespoons mashed)
1 teaspoon coarse sea salt
1 bunch cilantro, thick stems removed, roughly chopped (about 1½ cups)

Pound the garlic and salt in a mortar with a pestle into a paste. Add the cilantro and mash them together until you get a chunky, fragrant pesto.

Taqlieh freezes beautifully. I usually make a double recipe, scrape the extra into small containers, and pour over enough olive oil to cover (this seals in the flavor). In a good freezer, it can keep for up to 6 months.

Freekeh Dajaj

Roasted Cracked Green Wheat with Chicken

Serves 6 to 8

I find cooking *freekeh* to be a lot like cooking risotto. During the first stage, you don't really have to stand over it stirring constantly and adding tiny amounts of stock (although you certainly can if you want to). But toward the end, if you want to strike a perfect osmotic balance between liquid and grain, you probably should. You want the grains to gradually swell as they absorb the liquid. At the same time, they should expel enough gluten to bind the remaining stock into a creamy sauce. Umm Hassane's technique of giving it a rest midway helps the grains absorb liquid and flavor. Sometimes the most important ingredient is time.

There are two main ways of making *freekeh* with chicken: the usual way, where you keep the chicken and the grain separate; and the country-style way Umm Hassane makes it, a rich meld of meat and grain. I've given you Umm Hassane's version.

One final note: *freekeh*'s nutty, roasted flavor beautifully complements gamy meats, making it ideal for soaking up post-Thanksgiving turkey meat, gravy, and stock.

Ingredients

2 cups *freekeh**
1 tablespoon butter and/or olive oil
1 carrot, diced
1 small onion, diced
1 stalk celery, diced
4 cups Chicken Stock, plus more as needed (recipe follows)
1 tablespoon salt (preferably kosher or sea salt), plus more to taste
1½ teaspoons cinnamon
¼ teaspoon freshly ground black pepper
¼ teaspoon ground allspice
⅛ teaspoon ground nutmeg
Pinch ground cloves
2 cups cooked chicken meat (about half the meat from the Chicken Stock; recipe follows)

Equipment

Mixing bowl or a rice-washing bowl (available at Asian grocery stores)
Big wire-mesh strainer (optional, but makes life easier)
Big stockpot or Dutch oven

1. Soak the *freekeh* in cold water in a mixing bowl for 15 minutes. Rinse it in the sink under running water. Grab handfuls of grain and rub them between your palms, alternately rubbing and squeezing, for about 5 minutes. Some chaff should rise up to the surface as you rub the husks off the grains. (I've found everything from stones to lentils to bits of rope in my *freekeh*.) Tip the bowl to let the water and chaff run off the top. Pour off as much of the water as you can. If you have a big wire-mesh strainer, dump the *freekeh* in it and rinse under running water.

2. Heat the butter and/or oil in a big stockpot or Dutch oven over medium heat. Add the vegetables (I like to add the carrots first and let them caramelize a

---

* When Arab home cooks make *freekeh*, they almost always use roasted green wheat that has been parboiled and cracked—*not* the roasted whole green wheat berries often labeled as "freekeh" in the U.S. This recipe requires the cracked kind. The best place to get it is a Middle Eastern grocery store, but you can also order it online (look for *freek, farik, frik, frick, fareek, freekeh, fareekeh*, and any other spellings you can think of).

little, releasing a sugary sweet-potato smell, before adding the onions and celery). Sauté for a few minutes until they begin to release their fragrance and some of their water.

3. When the onion begins to soften, add the *freekeh* and sauté until it begins to give off its nutty aroma, about 3 minutes. Before it gets a chance to burn, add 4 cups stock and the salt and turn the heat up to medium-high. Bring to a boil. As soon as it boils, turn the heat down to low and add the spices. Cover and simmer for about 30 minutes, checking and stirring frequently. It's usually pretty soupy at this point, but add more liquid if you need to.

4. Remove from the heat. At this point, the *freekeh* probably won't have absorbed all the liquid—the individual grains will still be al dente, and the whole thing will be a gluey, watery, unappetizing mess. Let it sit and cool and absorb the stock for about 15 minutes while you do something else, such as sauté nuts for the Brown Butter Nut Topping (optional, but highly recommended; recipe follows). After 15 minutes, add the chicken meat to the pot.

5. If the stock has all been absorbed by this point (unlikely), add more ¼ cup at a time. This is where we enter risotto territory.

6. Bring the *freekeh* over medium-high heat to a boil. Lower the heat to medium-low and simmer for 30 minutes, stirring frequently and adding stock as needed. Keep tasting the grains to see how hard they are. When they are chewy and fluffy, no longer al dente, they're done. Taste and adjust for salt and spices.

Umm Hassane serves her *freekeh* just like this, and I love it this way. But if you want to impress people with a fancy presentation, see the instructions for the Brown Butter Nut Topping, below.

Brown Butter Nut Topping

Ingredients

1 tablespoon butter

1½ cups chopped nuts (I use equal parts pine nuts, pistachios, and blanched slivered almonds)

⅓ cup currants

½ teaspoon ground cinnamon (plus more for serving)

¼ teaspoon ground allspice

¼ teaspoon ground black pepper

⅛ teaspoon ground ginger

Pinch of ground nutmeg

Pinch of ground clove

½ teaspoon sea salt

Olive oil for oiling the bowl

Equipment
Small skillet

1. Heat the butter over a medium-high flame until it begins to foam. Toast the nuts in the butter, stirring constantly. When they are turning golden brown all over, and the butter is browning, add the currants, spices, and salt. Stir just long enough for the currants to plump and the spices to become fragrant, then remove from heat. When it cools, taste and adjust for salt and spices.

2. For an elegant presentation, oil a round bowl for each serving and layer a few tablespoons of nut topping in the bottom. Layer some chicken meat over the nuts, then top with cooked *freekeh* and pack it in all the way to the top. Place a serving plate over the bowl, face downward. Holding plate and bowl firmly together, invert them so the bowl is sitting on top of the plate. Gently pivot the bowl to release the food inside. Remove the bowl (you may need to slide a knife just under the edge and lever it up). Dust with additional cinnamon. Serve to universal acclaim.

Chicken Stock

Makes about 8 cups

I'm sold on the ancient Mesopotamian technique, still widely used in Iraq, of parboiling the meat and discarding the water from the initial boil when making stock. I've found it makes a clearer stock with a cleaner, more resonant flavor.

Ingredients
One 4-pound chicken, cut into quarters
4 quarts cold water, divided
4 large sprigs parsley (including stems)
2 sprigs fresh thyme
1 bay leaf
3 medium onions or 3 medium leeks (white and light green parts only),
    chopped
2 medium carrots, halved lengthwise and then cut into 1-inch segments
1 stalk celery or ¼ bulb fennel, diced
6 medium cloves garlic, peeled
1 teaspoon coarse sea salt
8 peppercorns
3 cloves

Equipment
Large stockpot, at least 6 quarts
Big strainer or colander
Butcher's twine
Second pot for collecting stock
Large slotted spoon or tongs
Fine strainer

1. Put the chicken in a large stockpot, add 2 quarts cold water (or enough to cover), and bring to a rolling boil. Turn the heat down and simmer until the scum stops rising, about 5 minutes. Pour off the water from this initial boil and discard. Rinse the chicken in a strainer or colander.

2. Wipe out the pot and add 2 quarts cold water. Tie the parsley and thyme together with a bit of twine. Add the chicken, herbs, vegetables, garlic, salt, peppercorns, and cloves and simmer very gently (you should only see one bubble at a time breaking the surface) for about half an hour.

3. Once the chicken begins to fall off the bone, scoop out the pieces with tongs or a big slotted spoon and let it cool it in a clean strainer or colander set over a pot. When it is cool enough to handle, pull the meat off the bones and set it aside. Discard the bones and skin (or, if you prefer a richer stock, return them to the pot and continue to simmer for up to five hours).

4. Strain the stock through a fine strainer or a colander lined with cheesecloth. Discard the solids. The stock will keep for 2 to 3 days in the refrigerator (boil for 2 minutes before using). Or freeze it, leaving a layer of fat on top to seal the flavor.

Umm Hassane's Mjadara Hamra

Red Mjadara

Serves 8 to 10

I've taken a few liberties with this recipe. Umm Hassane would never add spices because in her village this dish gets its flavor solely from caramelized onions. The trick is to bring the onions just to the point of burning without actually burning them. You will be stirring continuously (at first occasionally, then almost nonstop) for about half an hour. But because cooking times will vary according to the water content, freshness, and size of the onions, I recommend you watch them very closely and trust your senses—smell, sound, and sight—more than your clock. Your kitchen will smell like heaven when you're done.

Ingredients

2½ cups small brown lentils
2 cups coarse (#3) bulgur wheat*
2 tablespoons salt, divided, plus more
  to taste
8 cups water, plus more as needed
2 cups cold water
½ cup pure olive oil (not extra virgin)
½ cup canola oil
2¼ pounds onions (about 5 large),
  finely diced (5 to 6 cups)

1 teaspoon ground coriander
1 teaspoon cumin
1 teaspoon freshly ground white
  or black pepper
1 teaspoon Aleppo pepper
¼ teaspoon allspice
¼ teaspoon cinnamon

Equipment

Medium cooking pot
Large, heavy-bottomed pot or Dutch oven

COOKING THE LENTILS

Rinse the lentils and bulgur separately and drain. Put the lentils in a medium cooking pot with 1 tablespoon of salt and eight cups of water. Bring to a boil and skim off the scum. Cover the pot and turn the heat down to low. Simmer the lentils very slowly, about 40 minutes. Stir the lentils occasionally, adding more water if needed.

COOKING THE ONIONS

1. Get 2 cups cold water ready to throw over the onions when they're done (once they get going you won't have time). Heat the olive and canola oils in a large pot or Dutch oven over medium-high heat. When the oil starts to heave and shimmer, throw in a little of the onion; if it sizzles dramatically, the oil is ready. Add the onions and cook for about 5 minutes, stirring occasionally.

2. At this point the onions should be expelling a lot of liquid, almost boiling in the mix of oil and onion juice. They will still smell sharp and a little raw

---

* Most of the bulgur wheat available in supermarkets is the pale gold kind. The dark brown bulgur (usually imported from Lebanon or Syria) has a higher nutritional value and a heartier taste that suits this dish better. You can find it at Middle Eastern grocery stores or online.

from the sulfur evaporating. Turn the heat up and stir them enough to keep from sticking.

3. After 10 to 15 minutes, the onions should have expelled most of their liquid. When they begin to caramelize, developing little flecks of reddish brown at the edges, lower the heat slightly and keep stirring. This is a good time to check your lentils. They should be simmering very quietly, gently swelling up with the heat. If they're bubbling at all, turn the heat down and add more water if needed.

4. By now the onions should be golden brown all over and darker brown around the edges. Start stirring them more frequently—you can ignore the lentils for now—and turn the heat up under the onions. Once they start turning reddish brown and crispy, almost burning, make sure your 2 cups of water is handy. Do not stop stirring. The next few minutes will be crucial. If the phone rings, don't answer.

5. At a certain point, usually about 35 to 40 minutes after you put them on, the onions will begin to change very rapidly. They will puff up like Rice Krispies and start turning dark reddish brown, almost maroon. They will start to give off a bacony, almost-burnt aroma that distinguishes *mjadara hamra*. As soon as that happens, immediately throw the cold water over them, take them off the heat, and keep stirring. They will continue to sizzle furiously for about 30 seconds. Keep stirring until they settle down.

COOKING THE *MJADARA*

1. Check the lentils. By now they should have soaked up most of the water. If they are soft and some of them are beginning to burst, they're ready.

2. Move the onions back over high heat. When they are boiling vigorously, throw in the lentils, spices, and enough water to cover by about 1 inch. Bring back to a boil and continue to boil for about 10 minutes.

3. Test the lentils. They should be really soft now, almost crumbling. Taste for salt and adjust. Add the bulgur and turn the heat down to medium-low. It should be grumbling softly, making a comfortable growling noise as the bulgur absorbs the liquid. Let it cook for 10 minutes.

4. Taste the bulgur for doneness. It should be soft and chewy, almost fluffy, without a hint of bite. Adjust for salt again, cover the pot tightly, and let it sit in a warm place—over very low heat, with a flame tamer, or in a warm oven (some people wrap it in a towel)—for at least 1 hour before serving. Serve with something acidic: pickles, lemons, tomatoes, tabbouleh. I love it with lemony *fattoush* and whole-wheat pita bread.

VARIATION

If you just can't get enough of caramelized onions, add this optional garnish:

2 large onions, sliced into ⅛-inch rings
¼ cup olive and/or canola oil

Fry the sliced onions in the oil over medium-high heat until they are reddish brown and crispy. Top the *mjadara* with them.

Kibbeh Nayeh
Raw Kibbeh

Serves 4 to 6

Rule number one: don't make this unless you trust your meat. Rule number two: don't buy already ground meat unless you really, really trust your butcher. The safest method is to grind it yourself (see the *kafta* recipe, page 334, for instructions). Rule number three: do not ever let this dish sit, not even in the refrigerator. It must be eaten immediately.

Umm Hassane, who does not trust the butchers in America, first maintained they wouldn't grind the meat finely enough for *kibbeh*. "How are you going to make *kibbeh nayeh* in America?" she told me once. "You can't!" But then she discovered we could grind our own meat at home, in a food processor, and since then I haven't done it any other way.

Ingredients

1 cup fine (#1) bulgur wheat, preferably the dark brown kind
½ cup roughly chopped onion
¼ cup roughly chopped parsley leaves
¼ cup roughly chopped mint leaves
2 teaspoons *Kamuneh* (recipe follows)
1 teaspoon sea salt

1 teaspoon grated lemon or orange zest
8 ounces lean lamb shoulder or beef chuck, trimmed of fat and muscle, roughly chopped
Ice water
¼ cup blanched walnuts, pine nuts, cashews, or nuts of your choice

To Serve

5 or 6 sprigs mint
Raw hot green peppers
Several small onions, peeled and quartered
½ cup extra virgin olive oil, plus more to taste
Arabic flatbread

Equipment

Fine-mesh strainer
Small mixing bowl
Food processor
Medium mixing bowl

1. Rinse the bulgur wheat thoroughly, getting rid of any chaff. Drain it in a fine-mesh strainer and put it in a small mixing bowl. Add water gradually, mixing it with your hands, rubbing the grains to soften them, until they feel moist but not waterlogged. Soak for 1 hour.

2. Grind the onion, parsley, mint, spices, salt, lemon or orange zest, and ¼ cup of the bulgur in a food processor until you have a grainy, fragrant paste. Remove and set aside.

3. Wipe out the food processor, add the meat, and grind until it's smooth and almost buttery. (Depending on your processor, you may have to finely chop it first.) Massage the meat into the bulgur mixture with your hands, bit by bit, kneading with the same kind of motion you would use for bread dough. Add splashes of ice water periodically (some people do this part in the food processor with crushed ice, but Umm Hassane disapproves). You want a consistency that's firm and solid but also smooth, like wet clay.

4. When you've achieved the desired smoothness, form the *kibbeh* into a patty and score it with a fork. Press the nuts into the top, making pretty patterns if you feel inspired, and garnish with sprigs of mint, hot green peppers, and chunks of raw onion. Pour the olive oil over it liberally until it's swimming in a little pool of oil. Serve with flatbread to alternate with bites of mint and raw onion, and add more oil when it begins to dry out. Eat immediately. (If you have any left over—I never do—you can form it into tiny meatballs, freeze it, and use in *shawrabet shayrieh*.)

In the mountains of Lebanon, where people still make their own wine and *arak*, *kibbeh nayeh* is washed down with a shot of the fiery anisette liqueur. If you don't have any *arak*, try Turkish raki, Greek ouzo, or Italian sambuca. It's also good with a strong red wine, something spicy and not too sweet.

Kamuneh

Cumin Mix

Makes almost 3 tablespoons

"Kamuneh" is a diminutive of *kamun,* cumin. It's one of those Levantine spice mixes with as many variations as Lebanon has warring sects. In certain Beirut neighborhoods, old women sell *kamuneh* on the street, by the pound, with hot peppers on the side so you can adjust the heat. Hanan gets hers from a local baker, who puts in rose petals; Aunt Nahla's is elegantly simple, mostly cumin seeds and hot red peppers; and Adessa's family recipe is even simpler—cumin, allspice, black pepper, and white pepper. I buy mine from a Lebanese women's collective called Earth & Company, which adds ten spices, and Ali Fahs makes his with no less than thirteen ingredients. Everyone believes his or her version is the best. They are all correct.

Ingredients
1 tablespoon ground cumin
1 teaspoon freshly ground black pepper
1 teaspoon freshly ground white pepper
1 teaspoon allspice
1 teaspoon Aleppo pepper

Optional (but recommended):
¼ teaspoon ground cinnamon
¼ teaspoon ground coriander
¼ teaspoon dried culinary rose petals
¼ teaspoon dried marjoram
¼ teaspoon dried oregano
⅛ teaspoon ground cloves

In a small bowl, mix spices. Add optional ingredients as desired, crumbling the petals and dried leaves. Store in a cool dry place.

VARIATIONS

TOMATO *KIBBEH*

This is a classic peasant dish for people who can't afford meat or for villagers observing the traditional mourning custom of giving up meat after the death of a relative or neighbor.

1. Substitute 2 cups chopped ripe tomatoes for the meat. (You can peel and seed them if you want, but I usually don't bother.) Salt the tomatoes lightly and let them sit for a few minutes. Drain off the juice and set aside. Use the juice to moisten your bulgur instead of water.

2. Mix the bulgur, spices, onions, and herbs as for *kibbeh nayeh*. Mash the tomatoes in a mortar and pestle, adding olive oil very slowly, while massaging in the bulgur bit by bit. You want the olive oil to emulsify with the remaining tomato juice, making a velvety suspension much like traditional Spanish gazpacho. Keep adding, tasting the whole time, moistening with the reserve tomato juice, until you have a mixture about the consistency of a loose tapenade. Serve as a side dish or *meze*.

POTATO *KIBBEH*

Substitute 2 cups boiled or baked floury potatoes, mashed, for the meat. Only use the first 5 spices (cumin, black pepper, white pepper, allspice, Aleppo pepper) in the *Kamuneh* and do not include the parsley, mint, or nuts. Increase the lemon zest to 2 teaspoons and add the juice of ½ lemon. You may also want to increase the salt, olive oil, and Aleppo pepper.

RAW FISH *KIBBEH*

Same as *kibbeh nayeh,* but substitute sushi-grade raw fish for the meat. Only use the first 5 spices (cumin, black pepper, white pepper, allspice, Aleppo pepper) in the *Kamuneh*. Instead of 1 teaspoon lemon zest, add the juice and grated zest of 1 whole lemon. Experiment with other spices and garnishes—this is especially good with lemongrass and grated fresh ginger.

Umm Hassane's Mlukhieh

Jew's Mallow

Serves 6 to 8

This is not your standard Beirut *mlukhieh* (puréed leaves, meat cooked separately, served with onions and vinegar). This is a fiery, down-home, southern-style *mlukhieh*, garlicky and pungent, with whole leaves and chicken simmered together and drenched in lemon juice.

Ingredients
4 ounces dried *mlukhieh* leaves*
4 cups water
4 cups Chicken Stock (page 344)
⅔ cup *Taqlieh* (page 341)
2 tablespoons olive oil
1 onion, diced
3 large Swiss chard leaves
3 tablespoons lemon juice (about 1 lemon)
1 head garlic (8 to 10 cloves), peeled
6 chiles de arbol
1 tablespoon sea salt, plus more to taste
2 cups cooked chicken meat from Chicken Stock
    (page 344)
Quartered lemons for serving

Optional (but highly recommended) for serving:
Aleppo pepper
Cooked rice

Equipment
2 large stockpots or Dutch ovens
Strainer

---

*Mlukhieh is available at Middle Eastern grocery stores and online as *mlukhieh, melokhiya, melokhia, malikiya,* or a variety of other spellings; you may also find it as Jew's mallow, jute, and sometimes nalta jute or tossa jute. It is known in the Philippines as *saluyot.*

RECONSTITUTING DRIED *MLUKHIEH*

1. Spread the leaves out on a clean surface and pick through them. Snap off stems and discard brownish leaves and any foreign objects you find.

2. Bring to a boil 4 cups water. Put the leaves in a stockpot or Dutch oven and pour the water over them. Cover and let soak until cool, at least 1 hour.

3. Rinse the leaves thoroughly under cold running water until it runs clear. Drain and return to the pot. Add the chicken stock and bring to a boil. Turn the heat down and simmer until the leaves are tender, about 2 hours (this will vary according to size and age). You may have to add more stock or water.

COOKING THE *MLUKHIEH*

1. Prepare the *taqlieh*. Heat the 2 tablespoons canola or olive oil in a second large pot over medium-low heat. Add the onion and sauté slowly, without burning, until it is brown and fragrant, about 30 minutes.

2. Turn up the heat under the caramelized onions. Add the *taqlieh* and chopped Swiss chard leaves and sauté until it is fragrant and sizzling, scraping frequently with a spatula to make sure it does not burn. When the *taqlieh* starts to get dry and stick stubbornly to the bottom (about 2 minutes), deglaze the pan with the lemon juice. Add the *mlukhieh* leaves with their liquid, the garlic, chiles, and salt. Turn the heat down to low and simmer until the leaves are very tender, about 1 hour. Add the chicken meat and simmer for another 15 minutes.

3. Like all stews, this will improve if you refrigerate it for an hour or two, or preferably overnight, before serving. Reheat gently and squeeze lemon juice over extravagantly. For heat lovers, sprinkle with Aleppo pepper. It is usually served over rice.

COOKING FRESH OR FROZEN *MLUKHIEH*

Use 1 pound fresh or frozen leaves. Omit the Swiss chard leaves (they're used with dried *mlukhieh* to give it a fresh green color). Skip the first three steps and go straight to "Cooking the *Mlukhieh*." After sautéing the *taqlieh*, add the lemon juice, then the garlic, chiles, and fresh leaves, turning them with the spatula to coat with the garlic and cilantro. Once they are well coated, add the 4 cups chicken stock and bring to a boil. Turn the heat down to very low and simmer until the leaves are tender, about 1 hour. Serve as directed above.

VARIATION

Mlukhieh can be hard to find here in the U.S. If you want to try this recipe but can't find *mlukhieh*, try the simpler spinach *yakhne*.

Yakhnet Sbanegh

Spinach Stew

Serves 6 to 8

Ingredients

3 pounds fresh spinach, stemmed
2 tablespoons olive oil
⅔ cup *Taqlieh* (page 341)
6 chiles de arbol
4 cups Chicken Stock (page 344)
1 teaspoon salt, plus more to taste
2 cups cooked chicken meat from Chicken Stock
   (page 344)
Lemon halves for serving

Optional

Rice for serving

1. If you're using fresh-picked spinach, rinse it at least five times, until every trace of grit or dirt is gone from the bottom of your washing bowl. Chop it roughly.

2. Heat the olive oil in a deep skillet or Dutch oven over medium heat. Add the *taqlieh* and sauté until fragrant and sizzling, scraping with your spatula to make sure it does not burn. When it starts to dry and stick to the bottom (about 2 minutes), add the chiles and then the spinach a handful at a time. Turn the spinach with a spatula, coating it with the garlic and cilantro, until it wilts and turns bright green, 4 to 5 minutes.

3. Add the chicken stock, 1 teaspoon salt, and meat. Simmer gently, just long enough to let the flavors mingle, about 5 more minutes. Taste and adjust for salt. Refrigerate for an hour or two, or overnight, before serving. To serve, reheat gently and squeeze lemon juice generously over. In the Middle East, it is usually served over rice (and occasionally over crushed day-old bread and topped with yogurt as a *fatteh*).

֍

Ali Shamkhi's Tebsi Baitinjan
Eggplant Casserole
Serves 6 to 8

This is my favorite Iraqi *marga,* or stew, an art form that deserves a book of its own. Some people make it with oblong patties of ground spiced meat (like the *kafta,* page 334); others make it with strips of meat, as I have here; and many make it without meat at all. For Roaa's vegetarian version, simply omit the meat and adjust the spices down a little.

Ingredients
1 pound eggplants
1 pound potatoes, peeled and cut into ¾-inch rounds
1 large onion, cut into ¾-inch rounds
1 green bell pepper, stemmed, seeded, and quartered
1 red bell pepper, stemmed, seeded, and quartered
2 large ripe beefsteak tomatoes (about 1 pound), cored and cut into
    1-inch rounds
Canola or other neutral, high smoke-point oil for frying
1 pound beef top round, cut against the grain into 8 inch-thick strips
1 large clove garlic, cut into eighths
⅔ cup tomato paste
2 ripe tomatoes, puréed or grated (optional, but gives the sauce
    a fresh flavor)

1 cup water, plus more as needed
1 tablespoon coarse sea salt, plus more for salting eggplants and to taste
1 teaspoon Iraqi *Bharaat* (recipe follows), plus more to taste

Equipment
Bowl and plate for soaking salted eggplant
Large pot or Dutch oven for frying
Slotted spoon or tongs
Bowl for beef
Deep skillet or medium pot
Large, deep ovenproof cooking pot, casserole, or Dutch oven
    (at least 6 quarts) with cover

1. Peel and cut the eggplants into ¾-inch rounds. Place in a bowl and sprinkle with salt. Fill the bowl with cold water and cover with an inverted plate to keep the eggplants from floating (you may need to weigh down the plate with something heavy—a bowl filled with water works well). Let it soak while you slice the rest of your vegetables. Rinse thoroughly and pat dry.

2. Pour 2 inches oil into a large pot for frying and heat over high heat until it reaches 360° F. Fry the eggplant and potatoes in small batches, turning, until just golden, about 2 minutes. Remove with tongs or a slotted spoon and drain on paper towels or brown grocery bags. Repeat with the onion (90 seconds); the green pepper (1 minute); the red pepper (1 minute); and 1 of the sliced tomatoes (15 seconds). Fry the beef until just browned, about 30 seconds, and remove to a bowl to catch the juices.

3. Transfer 3 tablespoons of the oil to a deep skillet or saucepan and heat over medium-high heat. Add the garlic and sauté until fragrant, about 1 minute. Add the tomato paste and cook, stirring, until browned, about 30 seconds. Add 1 cup water, the tablespoon of salt, 1 teaspoon of the spices, the puréed tomatoes, and reserved meat juices. Turn the heat down and simmer gently.

4. Preheat the oven to 350°F. Layer the remaining raw tomato on the bottom of a large, deep cooking pot. Alternately layer the beef and vegetables all the way to the top, sprinkling a pinch of the remaining spice mix over each layer. Taste for salt as you go.

5. Pour the tomato sauce over the top and let it sink in. If needed, pour in enough water to reach just below the top layer. Slide a spatula around the edges of the pot to distribute the sauce to the bottom. Press down gently on the top with a spatula or wooden spoon. Bring to a simmer on the stovetop, then cover and bake for 1 hour. Let it rest for 30 minutes before serving. Serve over rice if desired.

Iraqi Bharaat
Iraqi Spices
Makes about 2 tablespoons

Ingredients
1 ½ teaspoons black peppercorns
2 white or green cardamom pods
2 whole allspice berries
2 whole cloves
½ teaspoon cumin seeds
½ teaspoon coriander seeds
1 chile de arbol, seeds and stem removed
¾ teaspoon dried rose petals
¼ teaspoon grated nutmeg
¼ teaspoon ground cinnamon
⅛ teaspoon ground ginger
⅛ teaspoon ground turmeric

Equipment
Heavy skillet
Spice grinder or mortar and pestle

Heat a dry skillet over medium heat. Add the peppercorns, cardamom, allspice, and cloves and toast until fragrant, about 2 minutes. Add the cumin and coriander seeds and cook, shaking the skillet, until just toasted, about 2 minutes (trust your nose—take the spices off the heat if you smell them beginning to burn). Transfer to a plate to cool. Grind to a powder with the chile and rose petals. Stir in the ground spices.

Lebanese Mighli

Serves 8 (small servings)

This recipe is adapted from two spectacular cooks—Georges Naassan's mother, who shared her recipe with me at Tango Night, and Rawda Mroue of Côte de Veau (a.k.a. Beiti, which means "my house"), a tiny hole-in-the-wall that offers some of the best home cooking in Beirut.

Ingredients

Pudding

2 cups sugar
1 cup rice powder, sifted
8 cups cold water
2 tablespoons ground cinnamon
2 tablespoons ground caraway seeds
2 tablespoons ground anise or fennel seeds

Topping

¼ cup walnut halves
¼ cup slivered or blanched almonds
¼ cup pine nuts
¼ cup pistachios (shelled and unsalted)
½ cup coconut flakes

Equipment

Medium cooking pot
Wire whisk
Eight small ramekins

MAKING THE PUDDING

1. Mix the sugar, rice powder, and water in a medium pot. Bring to a boil, whisking constantly. Let it cool.

2. Add the spices and simmer, whisking often, until it thickens, about 1 hour. Pour into 8 small ramekins and chill, covered, overnight.

3. Mix the nuts and coconut flakes together (you can lightly toast the coconut flakes if you like). Divide into 8 portions (roughly 2 tablespoons each), and top the puddings with them.

Glossary

*D*ay of Honey introduces non-Arabic readers to some of the words I got to know and (in most cases) love. Many of these words are colloquial Arabic, which varies widely from the written language. For that reason, I almost always spell words phonetically, instead of trying to literally represent Arabic letters, some of which have no equivalents in the Roman alphabet. When balancing consistency or faithful transliteration with readability in English, I have always chosen the latter. And for the sake of comprehension, I have translated idiomatic Arabic expressions into their closest English equivalents.

ain Spring, fountainhead, or eye (among other meanings).

ajnabi (male)/ ***ajnabieh*** (female)/ ***ajanib*** (plural) Foreign, alien; foreigner(s).

akil Food (from the root *akala*, "to eat").

Allah Arabic word for God (literally, "the god") dating back to before Islam. Used by Muslims, Christians, Jews, Baha'is, and other Abrahamic religions.

arak A clear alcoholic beverage flavored with anise and sometimes other ingredients. Usually distilled from grapes in Lebanon and dates in Iraq. Traditionally served with *meze,* especially those made with raw meat.

arous 1. A bride. 2. A sandwich of Arabic flatbread wrapped around *labneh* and cucumber, *zaatar,* cheese, or other fillings.

balad 1. Country, city, community. 2. Downtown (colloquial).

banadura Tomato or tomatoes. From the Italian *pomodoro.*

Bedouin English word, derived from Arabic, for members or descendants of nomadic Middle Eastern and North African desert tribes.

boub al-kusa Southern Lebanese dialect for the insides of hollowed-out zucchini. From *lub,* heart or core.

dahiyeh 1. Suburb or outskirts. 2. In Beirut, a shorthand for "the Misery Belt," a constellation of municipalities just south of the city limits, now mostly inhabited by Shiites.

dajaj Chicken.

daymeh Always (also pronounced "dayman"). Used in expressions like "*daymeh, inshallah*" (always, God willing).

diwan Among other meanings, a reception room for entertaining guests or holding audiences with the public (colloquial).

Druze A heterodox sect of Islam found mostly in the Levant. Originated as a mystical offshoot of Ismaili Shiism, a branch of Shiite Islam.

duaa 1. The act of appealing to or invoking God in a variety of situations. 2. The invocation itself.

fallaheen Peasant farmers or sharecroppers.

faqir (male)/*faqirah*(female)/*fuqara* (plural) 1. Poor, or the poor. 2. Down-to-earth, not a snob (colloquial).

fawal A maker of *foul*.

fatayer Baked pockets of bread dough stuffed with meat, cheese, or vegetables.

fattoush Levantine salad made with crumbled Arabic flatbread (from *fatta*, to crumble or break down into small pieces).

fatteh A variety of layered bread dishes made with crumbled Arabic flatbread; a base of meat or vegetables; and usually topped with garlic-infused yogurt.

fattet hummus *Fatteh* made with chickpeas.

fesenjoon An Iranian dish of meat (usually poultry) stewed in ground walnuts and pomegranate sauce. Also common in southern Iraq and southern Lebanon.

foul 1. Fava beans, usually dried. 2. Common shorthand for *foul mdamas*.

foul akhdar 1. Fresh fava beans (literally, "green fava beans"). 2. The dish of whole fresh fava beans braised with onions, garlic, and cilantro.

foul mdamas The dish of dried fava beans stewed until soft and mashed with garlic, lemon juice, olive oil, spices, and sometimes chickpeas or other ingredients (literally, "buried fava beans").

freekeh (also *freek, farik, farikeh,* etc.) 1. Fire-roasted green wheat, usually cracked for easier storage and preparation. 2. The dish of roasted green wheat cooked with meat, broth, and spices.

frakeh A dish of raw meat mixed with bulgur wheat and spices, common in southern Lebanon. From the same root (*faraka*, "to rub") as *freekeh*.

furn 1. An oven, especially a baking oven. 2. A neighborhood bakery (colloquial).

ghanouj (male)/*ghanoujah* (female) A teasing, flirtatious person.

hadarah Civilization, especially settled civilization; the opposite of nomadism. Often connotes modernity and urban life.

hajj The pilgrimage to Mecca, one of the five pillars of Islam, that all Muslims are required to undertake once in their lifetime.

Hajj (male)/*Hajji* (male or female)/*Hajjieh* (female) Honorary titles given to Muslims who have made the hajj (and often used to address old people, even if they did not perform the hajj, as a sign of respect). In Iraq, a man who has made the Hajj is a *Hajji*, while a woman is a *Hajjieh;* in Lebanon, the more commonly used titles are *Hajj* (for a man) and *Hajji* (for a woman).

halal Anything permissible, especially under Islam (often used for food).

hamudh 1. Anything sour or acidic. 2. Lemons or lemon juice (colloquial).

haraam Anything forbidden, especially under Islam.

hijab 1. A veil, screen, curtain, or other things used to hide, protect, or shutter. 2. The clothing, often a headscarf, used to conceal a woman's hair, neck, and body.

hindbeh 1. Chicory, dandelions, and other wild bitter greens. 2. The dish of bitter greens sauteed with olive oil, garlic, and caramelized onions.

hummus 1. Chickpeas. 2. Universal shorthand for *hummus bi tahinah*, the dish of ground chickpeas with tahini, garlic, and lemon juice.

iftar Literally, "breaking the fast"; the dinner that breaks the daylight fast throughout the month of Ramadan.

inshallah God willing (literally "*in shaa Allah,*" "if desired by God").

jabalieh Literally, "from the mountain" or "of the mountain." Often used to describe mountain fruits, vegetables, or dishes.

jajik A salad of yogurt, cucumber, garlic, and chopped herbs (usually mint). A slightly different version shows up in medieval Iraqi cookbooks.

jazar Carrot (colloquial).

jizr 1. Root or stem. 2. Three- or four-letter root of most Arabic words.

kafta Ground meat mixed with spices, onions, and herbs, and shaped into balls, patties, tubes, kebabs, or other forms.

kafta bi saynieh In Lebanon, large *kafta* balls or patties baked on a tray with vegetables (usually tomatoes, potatoes, and tomato paste).

kamouneh 1. The cumin-based mixture of spices added to *kibbeh nayeh;* a diminutive of *kamoun* (cumin). Also called *tahwheeshet kamouneh*. 2. In southern Lebanon, a mixture of bulgur wheat, spices, and mashed vegetables that can be eaten on its own or added to raw meat to make *kibbeh nayeh*.

kan ya ma kan Translators and linguists give this phrase different origins and meanings. Some translate it as "*kan yama kan,*" which means something like "once upon a time" or "a long, long time ago." Others render it as "*kan ya makan,*" which is more like "there was a place." Some link it to the old classical phrase "*kan fi makan fi qadim al-ʒaman,*" which is something like: "There was a place once upon a time." Still others translate it as "*kan ya ma kan,*" or "there was and there wasn't."

katab al-kitaab An Islamic marriage contract. (Literally, "writing the book" or "writing the contract.")

khadarji A greengrocer.

khubaizeh *Malva sylvestris,* a thick-leaved green mallow that grows wild in the Levant. Named for the way its round leaves resemble *khubʒ Arabi,* Arabic flatbread.

kibbeh A Levantine dish of grain (in Lebanon, usually bulgur wheat) often mixed with very finely ground meat. Can be made into balls stuffed with ground meat, pine nuts, and spices (*kibbeh qras*); layered with ground meat on a tray (*kibbeh bi saynieh*); or served raw (*kibbeh nayeh*), among other forms. The Iraqi version is called *kubba* and may be made with farina or ground rice.

kubbet hamudh Iraqi *kubba* served in a tart, lemony vegetable soup.

kunya Last name; also a nickname, usually derived from the name of a firstborn child or from a personal characteristic.

labneh Strained yogurt.

lahmajin Pizza-like bread topped with ground meat, spices, and herbs and baked in a hot oven. (From *lahme bi ajin*, meat with dough.)

maal asaf Literally, "with sorrow." Colloquially used to mean "I'm sorry" or "Alas."

makdous Baby eggplant stuffed with walnuts, garlic, and hot peppers and preserved in olive oil.

manoushi (sing.)/**manaeesh** (plural) Pizza-like Levantine bread baked with a variety of toppings, the most common of which is a mixture of olive oil and *ʒaatar*. (Literally, "the painted," or "the engraved," after the toppings on the bread.)

maqlubeh A casserole of vegetables, meat, and rice. Ingredients vary by region, but it is almost always served upside down (literally, "the inverted").

marga 1. Broth. 2. In Iraqi Arabic, any one of a variety of stews made with meat, vegetables, fruit, or all three. (Also "*marag.*")

mashawi/mashweeyat Grilled meats, in Levantine and Iraqi dialect, respectively.

masquf Iraqi grilled fish; literally, "the ceilinged," from *saqf*, ceiling.

mdepress (male)/**mdepressa** (female) Colloquial Arabic conjugation of the English word *depressed*.

Metawali A derogatory term for Shiites, dating back to Ottoman times, and often used among Lebanese Shiites as a form of bonding.

meze A galaxy of small dishes, both hot and cold, similar to tapas. Usually served at the beginning of a meal, in large groups, or in restaurants and bars.

mfarakeh Literally, "the rubbed" (from the same root as *freekeh*). In Lebanon, often refers to vegetables diced small and sautéed with eggs.

mhalabieh A pudding usually made of milk, sugar, and cornstarch, and flavored with rosewater, pistachio, and cardamom. Literally, "the milkified."

mjadara An ancient dish of lentils and grain (literally, "the pockmarked," for the lentils embedded in grain). Also called "the favorite of Esau," reflecting the belief that it was the Biblical "mess of pottage" for which Esau sold his birthright to his brother Jacob.

mjadara hamra An old-fashioned village-style *mjadara*, especially common in southern Lebanon, made with bulgur wheat and onions caramelized a deep rich red (literally, "red *mjadara*").

mlukhieh 1. *Colchorus olitorius*, the jute plant known in English as Jew's Mallow and in the Philippines as *saluyot*. 2. The stew made from *mlukhieh* leaves and meat (usually chicken or lamb, but in coastal regions occasionally shrimp or seafood).

mtabal Arabic term, common in Lebanon, for the roasted eggplant dish also known as *baba ghanouj*. (Literally, "the spiced.")

mutah Literally, pleasure; shorthand for *zawaj mutah*, or "pleasure marriage," a form of temporary marriage mainly practiced by Shiites.

nafis Soul, psyche, appetite, identity, animation, desire (among other meanings).

peshmerga Kurdish for guerrilla fighters; literally, "those who face death."

qarnabeet Cauliflower.

qifa nabki Literally, "halt, and let us weep." A phrase made famous by the pre-Islamic poet Imru al-Kays. Often used to gently mock nostalgia or sentimentalizing, especially for that which may never have existed.

sahtain Literally, "double health." Used like "to your health" or "bon appétit" to congratulate someone who is eating, about to eat, or has just finished eating.

sayadieh Fish served with spiced rice and tahini sauce.

Sayyid 1. A direct male descendant of the Prophet Muhammad. 2. A Shiite cleric.

servees In Lebanon, a shared taxi. From the French pronunciation of "service."

shajar 1. Zucchini, in Iraqi dialect. 2. A tree, in Lebanese dialect.

shariah Islamic law.

shawrabet shayrieh Noodle soup.

shish taouk Turkish term, widely used in the Levant, for chicken kebab.

shu baarifni Literally, "What do I know?" Often used to mean "Don't ask me!" or "How the hell should I know?"

souq (also souk) A market or bazaar, especially a street market.

suhoor The predawn meal eaten by Muslims before performing dawn prayers and commencing the daylong fast during Ramadan.

sujuk A small spicy dry sausage, believed to be Armenian in origin, found from Central Asia to Eastern Europe.

tabbouleh Levantine salad of chopped parsley, tomatoes, mint, green onions, and bulgur wheat.

tabeekh Meals traditionally cooked at home in a *tabkha*, usually a pot. Literally, "cooking."

tanoor A cylindrical oven with an open top, often used in the Middle East for making bread. Virtually identical to the ancient Mesopotamian *tinuru*, the Iranian *tanura*, and the South Asian *tandoor*.

tashreeb An old Bedouin soup, beloved by the Prophet Muhammad, made of crumbled bread topped with meat and broth. Also called *thareed*.

yakhne Slow-cooked vegetable stews, with or without meat, found from the Eastern Mediterranean to South Asia.

yaprakis Turkish term for stuffed grape leaves (from *yaprak*, leaf).

walimah Banquet or feast. Often used for weddings or other celebrations that can last for days.

wasta 1. An intermediary or channel for exerting influence on someone's behalf.

zaatar 1. Catchall term for a variety of Mediterranean herbs, from *origanum syria-cum* (Syrian oregano, often mistranslated as "thyme") to *satureja hortensis* (summer savory). 2. The green-brown powder made from salt, sumac, sesame seeds, and the dried leaves of various herbs known as *zaatar* (and other ingredients depending on region).

Select Bibliography

FOR THIS SELECT and highly subjective bibliography, I have deliberately neglected the bestsellers—the Thomas Friedmans and Robert Fisks—in favor of less well-known but equally important books by writers like Sami Zubaida, Zuhair al-Jezairy, Fawwaz Traboulsi, and Hanan al-Shaykh. Likewise, those familiar with Middle Eastern food will already know Claudia Roden and Paula Wolfert; here are lesser-known cookbooks by Sonia Uvezian, Nawal Nasrallah, Malek Batal, and Barbara Abdeni Massaad. *Sahtain*.

FICTION AND PERSONAL NARRATIVE

Abinader, Elmaz. *Children of the Roojme: A Family's Journey from Lebanon*. University of Wisconsin Press, 1997.

Awwad, Tawfiq Yusuf. *Death in Beirut* (Published in Arabic as *Tawaheen Beirut* or "Millstone Beirut"). Three Continents Press, 1984.

Fassihi, Farnaz. *Waiting for an Ordinary Day: The Unraveling of Life in Iraq*. Public Affairs, 2008.

Hage, Rawi. *De Niro's Game*. Harper Perennial, 2008.

Jezairy, Zuhair al-. *The Devil You Don't Know: Going Back to Iraq*. Saqi, 2009.

Kadi, Joanna, ed. *Food for Our Grandmothers: Writing by Arab-American and Arab-Canadian Feminists*. South End Press, 1994.

King, Alan. *Twice Armed: An American Soldier's Battle for Hearts and Minds in Iraq*. Zenith Press, 2006.

Maalouf, Amin. *The Rock of Tanios*. Abacus, 1995.

Makdisi, Jean Said. *Beirut Fragments: A War Memoir*. Persea, 1999.

Samman, Ghada. *Beirut '75*. University of Arkansas Press, 1995.

Shaykh, Hanan al-. *Beirut Blues*. Anchor, 1996.

———. *The Locust and the Bird: My Mother's Story*. Pantheon Books, 2009.

Stark, Freya. *Baghdad Sketches*. Marlboro Press, 1996.

Yahia, Mona. *When the Grey Beetles Took Over Baghdad*. Peter Halban, 2000.

HISTORY AND NONFICTION

A Community of Many Worlds: Arab Americans in New York City. The Museum of the City of New York/Syracuse University Press, 2002.

Aburish, Saïd K. *Saddam Hussein: The Politics of Revenge*. Bloomsbury, 2000.

————. *The St. George Hotel Bar*. Bloomsbury, 1989.

Ajami, Fouad. *The Vanished Imam: Musa Al Sadr and the Shia of Lebanon*. Cornell University Press, 1992.

Badre, Leila. "Post-war Beirut City Centre: A Large Open-Air Museum." Study Series 9, International Committee for Museums and Collections of Archaeology and History, 2001.

Batutu, Hanna. *The Old Social Classes and the Revolutionary Movements of Iraq: A Study of Iraq's Old Landed and Commercial Classes and of its Communists, Ba'thists, and Free Officers*. Saqi, 2004.

Blanford, Nicholas. *Killing Mr. Lebanon: The Assassination of Rafik Hariri and Its Impact on the Middle East*. I.B. Tauris, 2006.

Bou Akar, Hiba. *Displacement, Politics, and Governance: Access to Low-Income Housing in a Beirut Suburb* (bachelor in architecture). American University of Beirut, 2000.

Bowen, Jr., Stuart W. *Hard Lessons: The Iraq Reconstruction Experience* (Draft Document). Office of the Special Inspector General for Iraq Reconstruction, February 2, 2009.

Cockburn, Andrew and Patrick. *Out of the Ashes*. HarperCollins, 1999.

Damrosch, David. *The Buried Book: The Loss and Rediscovery of the Great Epic of Gilgamesh*. Henry Holt, 2006.

Eisenstadt, Lt. Col Michael, "Iraq: Tribal Engagement Lessons Learned," *Military Review*, September–October 2006.

Goitein, Shlomo. *Studies in Islamic History and Institutions*. Leiden, Netherlands: E.J. Brill, 1966.

Ibn Khaldun, Abdurahman. *The Muqaddimah: An Introduction to History*. N. J. Dawood, ed., Franz Rosenthal, trans. Princeton University Press, 2004.

Irwin, Robert. *Night and Horses and the Desert: An Anthology of Classical Arabic Literature*. Anchor Books, 2002.

Jabar, Faleh A. *The Shi'ite Movement in Iraq*. Saqi, 2003.

Jahiz, Abu 'Uthman "Amr ibn Bahr al-. Jim Colville, trans. *Avarice and the Avaricious* (kitab al-bukhala'). Kegan Paul International, 1999.

————. R. B. Serjeant, trans. *The Book of Misers: A Translation of al-Bukhala*. Garnet Publishing Limited, 1997.

Johnson, Michael. *All Honourable Men: The Social Origins of War in Lebanon*. I.B. Tauris (in association with the Centre of Lebanese Studies), 2001.

Karsh, Efraim, and Rory Miller, "Freya Stark in America: Orientalism, Antisemitism and Political Propaganda," *Journal of Contemporary History* vol. 39, no. 3 (July 2004).

Kassir, Samir. *Histoire de Beyrouth*. Librairie Arthème Fayard, 2003.

Kennedy, Philip F. "Dangling Locks and Babel Eyes: A Biographical Sketch of Abu Nuwas." From *Abu Nuwas: A Genius of Poetry*. Makers of the Muslim World Series. Oneworld Publications, 2007.

Khalaf, Samir. *Heart of Beirut: Reclaiming the Bourj*. Saqi, 2006.

Khalil, Samir al- (aka Kanan Makiya). *The Monument: Art, Vulgarity and Responsibility in Iraq*. Andre Deutsch, 1991.

Khater, Akram Fouad. *Inventing Home: Emigration, Gender, and the Middle Class in Lebanon, 1870–1920*. University of California Press, 2001.

Kovacs, Maureen Gallery, trans. *The Epic of Gilgamesh*. Stanford University Press, 1989.

Lapidus, Ira M. *A History of Islamic Societies*. Cambridge University Press, 1988.

Lassner, Jacob. *The Topography of Baghdad in the Early Middle Ages: Text and Studies*. Wayne State University Press, 1970.

Mas'udi, Ali al-. Paul Lunde and Caroline Stone, trans., ed. *The Meadows of Gold: The Abbasids*. Kegan Paul International, 1989.

Mitchell, Stephen. *Gilgamesh: A New English Version*. Free Press, 2004.

Salibi, Kamal. *A House of Many Mansions: The History of Lebanon Reconsidered*. University of California Press, 1990.

Sandars, N. K., trans. *The Epic of Gilgamesh*. Penguin Books, 1972.

Thomas, Bertram. *Alarms and Excursions in Arabia*. Bobbs-Merrill Company, 1931.

Thompson, Elizabeth. *Colonial Citizens: Republican Rights, Paternal Privilege, and Gender in French Syria and Lebanon*. Columbia University Press, 2000.

Tripp, Charles. *A History of Iraq*, Second Edition. Cambridge University Press, 2000.

The Travels of Pedro Teixeira, 1609. London: The Hakluyt Society, MDCCCCII.

FOOD

Appadurai, Arjun. "How to Make a National Cuisine: Cookbooks in Contemporary India." *Comparative Studies in Society and History*, vol. 30, no. 1 (January 1988), pp. 3–24, Cambridge University Press.

Baghdadi, Muhammad al-. Charles Perry, trans. *A Baghdad Cookery Book*. Prospect Books, 2005.

Batal, Malek, ed. *The Healthy Kitchen: Recipes from Rural Lebanon*. American University of Beirut Press, 2008.

Bottéro, Jean "The Culinary Tablets at Yale," *Journal of the American Oriental Society*, vol. 107, no. 1 (January—March 1987), pp. 11–19.

———. "The Most Ancient Recipes of All," from *Patterns of Everyday Life*. David Waines, ed. *The Formation of the Classical Islamic World*, vol. 10. Ashgate Publishing, Ltd., 2002.

———. *The Oldest Cuisine in the World: Cooking in Mesopotamia*. University of Chicago Press, 2004.

Collingham, Lizzie. *Curry: A Tale of Cooks and Conquerors*. Oxford University Press USA, 2006.

Ellison, Rosemary. "Methods of Food Preparation in Mesopotamia (c. 3000–600 BC)." *Journal of the Economic and Social History of the Orient*, vol. 27, no. 1 (1984), pp. 89–98.

Flandrin, Jean-Louis, and Massimo Montanari, eds. *Food: A Culinary History*, English edition by Albert Sonnenfeld (Penguin Books: 2000/First published by Columbia University Press, 1999).

Goody, Jack. *Food and Love: A Cultural History of East and West*. Verso, 1998.

Hattox, Ralph S. *Coffee and Coffeehouses: The Origins of a Social Beverage in the Medieval Near East*. University of Washington Press, 1985.

Homan, Michael M. "Beer and Its Drinkers: An Ancient near Eastern Love Story." *Near Eastern Archaeology*, vol. 67, no. 2 (June 2004), pp. 84–95.

Jones, Martin. *Feast: Why Humans Share Food*. Oxford University Press, 2007.

Karim, Kay. *Iraqi Family Cookbook: From Mosul to America*. Iraqi Family Cookbook, LLC, 2006.

Kurlansky, Mark. *Salt: A World History*. Walker and Co., 2002.

Limet, Henri. "The Cuisine of Ancient Sumer." *The Biblical Archaeologist*, vol. 50, no. 3 (September 1987).

Manning, Richard. *Against the Grain: How Agriculture has Hijacked Civilization*. North Point Press, 2005.

Mardam-Bey, Farouk. *Ziryab: Authentic Arab Cuisine*. Ici La Press, 2002.

Massaad, Barbara Abdeni. *Man'oushe: Inside the Street Corner Lebanese Bakery*. Alarm Editions, 2005.

————. *Mouneh: Preserving Foods for the Lebanese Pantry*. Self-published, 2010.

Mintz, Sidney W. *Sweetness and Power: The Place of Sugar in Modern History*. Penguin Books, 1985.

Nasrallah, Nawal. *Delights from the Garden of Eden: A Cookbook and History of the Iraqi Cuisine*. 1stbooks, 2003, 2004.

Potts, Daniel. "On Salt and Salt Gathering in Ancient Mesopotamia." *Journal of the Economic and Social History of the Orient*, vol. 27, no. 3 (1984), pp. 225–271.

Symons, Michael. *A History of Cooks and Cooking*. Illinois University Press, 2004.

Uvezian, Sonia. *Recipes and Remembrances from an Eastern Mediterranean Kitchen*. The Siamanto Press, 1999.

van Gelder, Geert Jan. *God's Banquet: Food in Classical Arabic Literature*. Diane Publishing Co, 2000.

Waines, David. "Cereals, Bread and Society: An Essay on the Staff of Life in Medieval Iraq." *Journal of the Economic and Social History of the Orient*, vol. 30, no. 3 (1987), pp. 255–285.

Wright, Clifford. *A Mediterranean Feast: The Story of the Birth of the Celebrated Cuisines of the Mediterranean, from the Merchants of Venice to the Barbary Corsairs, with More Than 500 Recipes*. William Morrow and Company, 1999.

Yazbeck, Chérine. *The Rural Taste of Lebanon: A Food Heritage Trail*. Self-published, 2009.

Zubaida, Sami, and Richard Tapper, eds. *A Taste of Thyme: Culinary Cultures of the Middle East*. Tauris Parke Paperbacks, 2000.

Zurayk, Rami, and Sami Abdul Rahman. *From 'Akkar to 'Amel: Lebanon's Slow Food Trail*. Slow Food Beirut, 2008.

FOOD WEBSITES

Accad, Joumana. "Taste of Beirut: Lebanese Food Recipes for Home Cooking," http://www.tasteofbeirut.com.

Karam Khayat, Marie, and Margaret Clark Keatinge. "Food from the Arab World, 1959," http://almashriq.hiof.no/general/600/640/641/khayat/

Massaad, Barbara Abdeni. "My Culinary Journey Through Lebanon." http://myculinaryjourneythroughlebanon.blogspot.com/

Riverbend, Herb. "Is Something Burning?" http://iraqrecipes.blogspot.com/

Somekh, Rachel. "Recipes by Rachel: The Jewish-Iraqi Cooking of Rachel Somekh." http://www.recipesbyrachel.com.

Index

About the Author

Annia Ciezadlo was a special correspondent for *The Christian Science Monitor* in Baghdad and *The New Republic* in Beirut. She has written about culture, politics, and the Middle East for *The Nation, Saveur, The Washington Post, The New York Times, The New York Observer,* and Lebanon's *Daily Star*. Her article about cooking with Iraqi refugees in Beirut was included in *Best Food Writing 2009*. She lives with her husband in New York.